A SOCIAL HISTORY OF HOUSING
1815–1970

JOHN BURNETT

Illustrated by Christopher Powell

First published in Great Britain in 1978 by
David & Charles Ltd
Brunel House, Newton Abbot, Devon

First published as a University Paperback in 1980 by
Methuen & Co. Ltd
11 New Fetter Lane, London EC4P 4EE

Printed in Great Britain at
The University Press, Cambridge

**British Library Cataloguing in
Publication Data**

Burnett, John
  A social history of housing, 1815-1970.—
(University paperbacks).
  1. Housing—England—History
  I. Title II. Series
  301.5'4'0942   HD7334.A3

ISBN 0-416-73720-X

CONTENTS

LIST OF ILLUSTRATIONS

PLATES

FIGURES

PREFACE

The social history of housing, like that of man's other basic needs, food and clothing, has for long remained a neglected study. This statement may seem surprising in view of the large number of books on building and architecture which any visit to a public library will reveal, but the fact is that almost all these treat of the development of architectural style and are therefore confined to that small minority of houses which were professionally designed for comparatively wealthy clients. At the other end of the social scale, works on vernacular building have traced the history of types of rural dwellings in pre-industrial times. Neither approach has examined the development of mass housing occupied by the working classes and the lower levels of the middle classes in the nineteenth and twentieth centuries and provided predominantly by speculative builders and local authorities.

In the last twenty years or so, some aspects of housing history have begun to receive serious academic attention. A number of economic historians have researched into building cycles and their relation to changes in demand and investment; the developing area of urban history has produced some important studies of town and suburban growth in which housing provision is viewed as part of a wider process; again, studies of the intervention of the state and local authorities into housing policy have produced much quantitative data on housing need and provision. Yet, in these considerations of the number, location and provision of houses, the history of the house itself has been strangely neglected. The aims of this book, therefore, are to describe the types of accommodation, both existing and new, which were available to the majority of people in the period between about 1815 and 1970, to measure and evaluate changes in housing quality over time and to seek an explanation of the determinants of built form. It is not an economic history of housing, nor of the social policy of housing, and still less of architectural style, though it necessarily touches on all of these. It should also be said that the area of investigation is England only—not Wales, Scotland or Ireland, all of which had distinct housing experiences.

ACKNOWLEDGEMENTS

Anyone familiar with these studies will recognize that I owe a large debt, I hope suitably acknowledged in the text, to a number of scholars who have surveyed and excavated parts of the landscape over which I have journeyed. Especially, I wish to record my admiration of, and obligation to, the work of Professor H. J. Dyos, Professor J. N. Tarn, Dr S. D. Chapman, Dr E. W. Cooney, Dr W. V. Hole, Dr A. R. Sutcliffe and their numerous collaborators. Their detailed researches into particular towns and particular housing types have provided much of the original data on which I have drawn in trying to construct a general history of housing conditions over a century and a half. Some of them may think that until more investigation into local variations has been carried out, such an attempt is premature, but I believe that enough evidence now exists to warrant some useful generalization. Future studies will continue to modify and, perhaps, re-draw the picture.

I also wish to thank particularly a number of friends and colleagues who have read and commented on my drafts—Anthony D. King and Robert A. Hall of Brunel University, Christopher Powell of the Welsh School of Architecture, and Robert Thorne. I have benefited greatly from their guidance and knowledge, though sometimes exigencies of space prevented my taking full advantage of their suggestions. They are, of course, in no way responsible for any errors or omissions. Christopher Powell also drew many of the illustrations in the text and supplied and annotated the plates, with the exception of those relating to middle-class housing in Chapters 4 and 7, which were generously provided by Robert Thorne. Finally, my sincere thanks are due to Valerie Radford, who not only typed but checked my manuscript and thereby prevented many mistakes.

PART I: 1815–1850

1

PEOPLE AND HOUSES

To believe that a housing problem in England dates only from the nineteenth century would be no more defensible than to argue that there were no poor, hungry or badly clothed people before that time. Any historian of medieval times, or of the Tudor or Georgian periods, knows that inadequate and insanitary living conditions were always the lot of a sizeable proportion of working people, whether in town or country. Slums were not new in the nineteenth century, any more than damp floors, rotting walls, leaking roofs and open sewers. But, in a real sense, the modern housing problem was a creation of the nineteenth century—both because new demographic trends multiplied and exacerbated the inherited problems, and because new social trends gradually raised housing expectations and produced a climate of opinion in which, for diverse reasons, housing evils came to be regarded as unacceptable. The nineteenth century therefore witnessed both an acceleration of the housing problem and the origins of policies aimed at its solution.

Any discussion of housing has two main aspects—quantitative and qualitative. People need shelter, but they also need shelter which is adapted to geography, climate and place of work, and which provides certain standards of construction, space, hygiene and comfort in which the business of home-making can go forward effectively. Houses are physical structures, homes are social, economic and cultural institutions. But the most urgent housing problem of the first half of the nineteenth century was that, because of a phenomenally rapid growth of population, the stock of accommodation had to be utilized and expanded at a rate which constantly fell short of need, and which produced many ill-effects on the comfort and health of the inhabitants.

In 1750 England had still exhibited many of the economic and social characteristics of a pre-industrial society—a primary dependence on agriculture, low levels of national income and economic growth, a lack of specialization and of regional integration.[1] Above all she had exhibited a rate of population growth so slow as to convince many contemporaries that numbers were static, if not actually declining. Exactly what those numbers were no one can be certain, for there was no official census of population before 1801, but a number of estimates agree in crediting England and Wales in 1750 with no more than between 6 and $6\frac{1}{2}$ million people.[2] But, so far as we can tell, this stability was suddenly interrupted in the middle of the century, probably in the decade of the 1740s, and from that time numbers began to grow at a rate which was first modest, soon rapid, and ultimately explosive. By 1801 the population of England and Wales had already risen by some 50 per cent to 8,893,000, and between 1801 and 1851 it almost exactly doubled to reach 17,928,000:[3]

Year	England and Wales	Percentage increase in decade
1801	8,893,000	—
1811	10,164,000	14·0
1821	12,000,000	18·1
1831	13,897,000	15·8
1841	15,914,000	14·3
1851	17,928,000	12·7

The explanation of this phenomenal increase has puzzled both contemporaries and subsequent historians, and the debate continues. Briefly, the answer must lie in the relative movements of birth and death rates, since a third general possibility—large-scale immigration—can be confidently discounted. The traditional explanation, broadly held until the 1950s, was an increase in life expectancy due to a substantial fall in the death rate and, more particularly, in child mortality. This was credited to improved standards of living and diet, the growth of medical knowledge and practice, improved hygiene and the reduction of specific diseases. But modern demographers have thrown serious doubt on the evidence for all of these with one possible exception—the conquest of smallpox by inoculation—and have argued for an increase in birth rate, due primarily to increasing economic opportunities for labour, both in the countryside and in the multiplying industrial towns. A fall in the average age of marriage during the eighteenth century, perhaps by five or six years, would have increased the child-bearing span at its most fertile period and resulted in better chances of survival for the progeny.[4]

Whatever its sources may have been, a population which trebled within a hundred years, and doubled within half that time, would have imposed an unprecedented need for accommodation on a building industry which was ill-equipped by experience, organization and technology to meet it. But the new population had certain characteristics which heightened and concentrated that need in new ways. Although the initial upsurge of numbers in the 1740s may be attributable primarily to a fall in the death rate stemming from the reduction of certain epidemic diseases, the factor which accelerated it to new and sustained heights was probably an increase in births. By the 1780s, population was increasing by 10 per cent per decade, by the 1790s by 11 per cent, and by the 1810s by 18 per cent—the peak point of growth. During this period, from 1780 to 1820, the English birth rate is estimated to have stood at around 36–8 per thousand (almost exactly double that of the present day). It seems more than likely that the expanding employment opportunities afforded by the industrial revolution and, for some at least, the chances of substantially higher earnings than agriculture had offered, were encouraging earlier marriage and earlier families than in the past. This implies that the average age of this new population was very low, that more young people were marrying, that more children were entering the world and that as child mortality began to lessen they were surviving longer to form more new families in their turn. In 1841, 45 per cent of the population were under twenty years of age, less than 7 per cent over sixty.

Since most people live in family groups, these are more significant than individuals or total numbers in the context of housing. The Census statistics from 1801 onwards provide data on the numbers of families, from which it is possible to calculate the average number of persons in each:[5]

Year	No of families	Percentage increase in decade	Average no of persons per family
1801	1,897,000	—	4·69
1811	2,142,000	13·0	4·74
1821	2,493,000	16·4	4·81
1831	2,912,000	16·8	4·77
1841	—	—	—
1851	3,712,000	—	4·83
1861	4,492,000	21·0	4·47

On this evidence, average family size varied relatively little during the first half of the century, the fastest rate of family formation, and the largest fall in average size, occurring in the decade 1851–61.

At first glance the figures seem to suggest an average family of two adults and three children in the period under review, but first glances here may be deceptive. We know all too little about the family structure of nineteenth-century England, still less about variations in that structure between different social classes. The 'average' family of 4·7 or 4·8 persons includes families which were childless—a significant proportion in Victorian times, accounting for 8 per cent of all marriages in the 1870s compared with 18 per cent which had ten or more live births and 43 per cent which had between five and nine—and families in which the children had already left home. In rural communities this typically occurred at around the ages of twelve or thirteen, as boys left home for farm work or apprenticeship and girls went into domestic service, so relieving pressure on overcrowded cottage bedrooms. In towns the age of leaving home was almost certainly later, since more work was available near at hand, and there were fewer opportunities for boarding-out, at least for boys. Engels, describing home life in Manchester in 1844, writes critically of the independence of young factory-workers who leave home at fifteen to take lodgings elsewhere, which suggests that this was regarded as precocious emancipation.[6] But Lancashire, with its possibilities of relatively high earnings for young adults in the cotton industry, was a special case: in the towns, children commonly stayed at home until marriage and, not uncommonly, where house accommodation was scarce, for some time after marriage.

The answer to the puzzle of seemingly low average family sizes in the early nineteenth century may well be the same as that which Peter Laslett found for pre-industrial English society—that 'a very high proportion of people actually lived in large families although the average size was small'.[7] Certainly, there is abundant contemporary evidence of families of six, eight and even ten and more children, and, given the still high rate of infant mortality until late in the century, one can only marvel at the number of pregnancies and conceptions involved in producing so many survivors. We must suppose a far greater variety of family size than we are familiar with today, more barren marriages and, equally, more very fertile ones, as yet beyond the reach of effective contraception. Knowledge of such methods was more widely diffused in town than in country, and the heavier urban infant mortality rates also helped to keep family size down. One of the few studies of the subject suggests that in Nottingham in 1851 only 18·4 per cent of working-class families had four or more surviving children.[8] For our purpose, the important point is that the 'fit' between family sizes of wide variety and houses of a much more standard size could not be a very close one: some houses would be grossly overcrowded, at least at some stages of the family cycle, while others would be under-occupied.

THE GROWTH OF TOWNS

The problem of accommodating this growing population would have been difficult enough if its growth had been regular over time and space, but this was far from so. We have already seen how the pace of growth varied from one decade to another, though it was always upwards. Equally important, the new population was much more mobile than its ancestors had been, moving, wandering, migrating in patterns which at first seemed random, but which soon began to display two main directional characteristics— towards the north and towards the towns.

Although the early censuses are not too helpful for this purpose, in 1801 probably around 80 per cent of the population of England and Wales was still 'rural' and only some 20 per cent 'urban', defined as living in towns having more than 5,000 inhabitants. What was to happen now, under the impetus of industrialization, was a decisive shift in the balance of the economy from farming to manufacturing, and a parallel shift in the balance of population from country to town. The rapid growth of towns, and particularly of the industrial towns of the Midlands and North, was the most dramatic, immediate and visible social transformation of the industrial revolution, which was to have profound effects on almost every aspect of life. Within only half a century, by 1851, the decisive tilt had taken place, and more than half the English people were already town-dwellers: by then, 54 per cent of people were living in 'urban' areas as against 46 per cent in 'rural'.[9] Even more significant, it was the large towns and cities and the 'conurbations' of the future which grew most rapidly of all. By 1851 there were already ten urban areas with populations of more than 100,000 each, accounting for no less than 24·8 per cent of the total population. A further 141 towns between 20,000 and 100,000 population made up only another 12·8 per cent. Already the age of great cities was at hand. People, once thinly and relatively evenly scattered over the countryside of England, were beginning to be concentrated, to be drawn as if by powerful magnets into the towns. London, always a great metropolis, had the strongest attractive powers of all—in 1801 it had contained 9·7 per cent of the whole population, and by 1861 14·0 per cent—but it was in the 'new' industrial towns like Manchester, Leeds and Birmingham, Bradford, Sheffield and Nottingham, that the numbers piled up in unprecedented, terrifying proportions.

Who were the new town-dwellers? It is important to try to discover the answer, for their origins, and the habits, attitudes and values which they brought with them, would have helped to shape the character of life in the new environment. The answer is simple in form though complex in process. The new town inhabitants were partly the results of natural increase of existing inhabitants but, more importantly, they were immigrants from the countryside. That the increase cannot have been mainly 'natural' is obvious, for the towns grew far more rapidly than the population as a whole, and what evidence there is on a dim subject suggests that urban-dwellers were rather less fertile than countrymen (and women). To quote only one example, between 1841 and 1851 English towns grew by 25·9 per cent, the total population by 12·7 per cent. In the 1851 Census, the sixty-two largest towns of the country contained 3,336,000 persons over the age of twenty, of whom only 1,337,000 had been born in that place; the others had moved in during their lifetimes, some, no doubt, from other large towns, but the majority from the little market towns, the villages, hamlets and fields of England, Wales, Scotland and Ireland.

The processes of this vast rural migration have recently become somewhat clearer. Earlier investigators tended to argue that as a result of technical and tenurial changes in agriculture accompanying the industrial revolution—the enclosure of common land, the growth of large estates, new methods of cultivation, rotation, drainage and farm management—large numbers of small peasant proprietors had their economic position undermined and were 'driven' off the land to 'flock' (they always 'flocked') into the towns. Whole families, it was supposed, migrated from predominantly agricultural counties like Dorset and Wiltshire to the industrial areas of the Black Country, Lancashire, and the West Riding of Yorkshire. Recent researchers have, however, disputed that the agricultural changes of the period reduced employment opportunities on the land, though they may have changed the status of the occupier; in some respects, enclosures and more intensive farming methods actually increased the demand for labour. Again, long-distance migration has been questioned at a time when overland travel was both difficult and expensive, and the cheapest way of getting from London to Manchester was by canal, a journey taking five days and costing 14s per person, about twice the weekly wage of the labourer.[10]

On the whole, it seems likely that more people were attracted into the towns than were pushed into them. Some, undoubtedly, came unwillingly and fearfully, the victims of a particular land redistribution which had prejudiced them or of a drastic decline in earnings from domestic industry as spinning and weaving moved from home to factory. Some who came with eager anticipation found life in the new world just as poor and hard as the one they had left, and without the compensations of friends, community and familiar things. But most of those who came were drawn by positive attractions—the hope of new skills and better-paid work, wider social and sexual relationships, opportunities for children, even the possibility of rising in the economic and social scale into the ranks of the employing classes. That only a few were able to make that transition once the early, heady days of the industrial revolution were over did not destroy the hopes of the many. Towns offered change, excitement, new kinds of work and new kinds of pleasure, above all, perhaps, a measure of freedom and independence to people whose lives had been rigidly structured in a traditional, unchanging society.

Those who came were usually young, single men and women, or newly-marrieds, rather than extended families or the old, sick or infirm. Probably they were not drawn from the most highly-skilled farm workers or village craftsmen, for whom the old life could still offer reasonable rewards; equally, they were probably not the poorest, the unemployables, the shiftless, the paupers immobilized by the need to claim relief from their native parishes. Like immigrants at any time, they included the respectable, hard-working and ambitious as well as the sly, the unvirtuous and the seekers after easy money. Careful researches have shown that, in general, they did not travel long distances—perhaps an average of no more than thirty or forty miles, a distance that could be comfortably tramped. There were 'currents of migration setting in the direction of the great centres of commerce and industry',[11] mainly from the adjacent agricultural counties. As the inhabitants of an area immediately surrounding a town moved into it, gaps were left in the rural population to be filled by migrants from further afield: the pattern therefore resembled a series of concentric circles, with the great towns at the hubs. Ultimately, even the most remote corners of the kingdom were touched by the ripples of these waves, though it was not until the decade after 1851 that some of the English rural counties first began to show an absolute, as opposed to a relative, decline in numbers.

By contrast, the absolute decline of the Irish population was already well advanced in the decade before 1851. Migration to England from that hapless country had always been tempting and relatively easy, the sea passage from Dublin to Liverpool costing no more than 2s 6d, and brought down by fierce competition in the 1820s to as little as 4d or 5d. The failure in 1845–7 of the potato crop, the staple diet of Ireland, turned a steady stream of migrants into a torrent. Between 1841 and 1851 the population of Ireland fell from 8,175,000 to 6,552,000, the result partly of death by disease and starvation, partly of migration to England, America and the colonies: in the single peak year of emigration, 1851, it fell by a quarter of a million. In the areas where they settled—for the Irish preferred to live in communities of their own people—they soon formed sizeable proportions of the population—in Liverpool in 1851 one-fifth of the whole, in Manchester one-seventh. Unlike the majority of English migrants to the towns, these were men, women and children in extreme poverty and desperation, described as 'bringing pestilence on their backs, famine in their stomachs', and not uncommonly dying in the streets on arrival. The survivors were glad enough to take whatever work, wages and accommodation they could find, in sub-divided houses, tenements, single rooms and even cellars. In the places where they settled—Lancashire predominantly, but also in parts of Yorkshire, South Wales and London—the Irish exacerbated the already difficult problems of the towns, for they introduced, through no fault of their own, standards of living, comfort and cleanliness lower than most English workers had experienced. To its own problems of dirt, disease, over-crowding and squalor, the industrial town now had to add a new dimension.

The growth of towns in the first half of the nineteenth century has been summarized thus: 'many more towns of substantial size, a steady increase in the size of what might be regarded as typical, and the emergence of a few towns of enormous size, so that a small number of places contained a high proportion of the total population of the country'.[12] How rapidly some expanded can be seen from the following table (figures shown in thousands):[13]

	1801	*1831*	*1851*
Birmingham	71	144	233
Bradford	13	44	104
Derby	11	24	41
Huddersfield	7	19	31
Leeds	53	123	172
Liverpool	82	202	376
Manchester	75	182	303
Nottingham	29	50	57
Oldham	12	32	53
Portsmouth	33	50	72
Sheffield	46	92	135
Wolverhampton	13	25	50

Yet even such an enumeration tends to conceal the phenomenally rapid growth of certain places within a remarkably short period—of Manchester, which grew by 40·4 per cent in the decade 1811–21, or Liverpool which increased by 43·6 per cent between 1821 and 1831, or Leeds by 47·2 per cent in the same period. It also disguises the fact that it was not only the industrial town that grew with such rapidity. Towns of a different sort—the spas like Bath and Cheltenham and the coastal towns such as Brighton and Scarborough—were attractive as leisure resorts to the expanding middle classes and, hence, to those who were needed to supply and service their pleasures. The eleven seaside resorts listed in the Census of 1851 had grown by no less than 214 per cent since 1801, a rate quite as rapid as many of the new centres of industry and commerce.

The processes of town growth were local and individual, and do not easily fit into any pattern. A simple but useful classification was adopted by the Health of Towns Committee of 1840—the metropolis, manufacturing towns, seaport towns, great watering places, and 'county and other inland towns not the seat of any particular manufacture'; though far from comprehensive, this immediately indicates the variety of English urban development. An even more basic classification—into 'old' and 'new'—may also be useful, because for housing purposes the expansion of an existing town offered fewer opportunities for planning the development than did the creation of a virtually new settlement. In general, English towns were not planned. They grew by expansion outwards—determined by a variety of topographical, tenurial, technical, economic and social considerations—and by in-filling within the existing boundaries, but not, to any very great extent outside London, by building upwards. Usually, remaining pockets of spare land were first built on, the open sides of courts were completed, rear gardens were acquired and additional rows of houses in-filled behind the earlier ones: then the town began to move outwards, as long terraces sprawled across the countryside, their direction often determined by the siting of factories, mines or other opportunities of employment. Nearness to places of work was the outstanding reason for the cluster-ing and overcrowding of the industrial town, for before the development of urban transport systems, men, and for that matter, women and children, needed to live very near to work-places if they were to get and keep jobs. Especially was this true for unskilled and casual labourers for whom work was often only available if they were first on the spot.

So it often happened that the centres of cities, where once the prosperous commercial and professional classes had lived in substantial houses, now came to be the poorest quarters, the houses sub-divided and overcrowded to become 'rookeries' (the future 'slums') as the former occupants departed to the more salubrious air of new suburbs. Outside the centres, working-class housing throughout the Midlands and North was typically in terraces, often back-to-back, or forming courts, in either case economizing on land to the greatest possible extent, and achieving the highest possible densities to the acre. In one cul-de-sac in Leeds, Boot and Shoe Yard, in 1842, thirty-four houses were found regularly to contain 340 people, and up to twice as many at particular times when itinerant labourers came into the town: at the time of the cholera epidemic seventy-five cartloads of manure, which had been allowed to accumulate for years, were removed from the area. 'This property is said to pay the best annual interest of any cottage property in the borough.'[14]

It was in the nature of such developments that they were unplanned—save, that is, by considerations of immediate profit. So far as there was any general thought on the matter it was that needs would be served by demand, that as employers built factories according to economic requirements, pop-ulation would move into the district and speculative builders, motivated by the same economic law, would provide appropriate accommodation. To plan development would have required a common will to do so, a legal control over land and building, and an administrative machinery to enforce it, all of which were lacking. What instances there are of consciously-designed urban growth in the first half of the century came about for particular and exceptional reasons. Where a single landowner owned the whole or the bulk of land in an expanding town he could, if so minded, lay down regulations for the width and direction of streets, the construction of houses, drainage, water supplies and other matters. Something approaching this happened in the cotton town of Ashton-under-Lyne, where the Earl of Stamford made conditions about 'good, firm and substan-tial' building when granting leases. In Huddersfield the local landowner, Sir John Ramsden, enforced wide streets and 'good, straight houses', and at Glossop, in Derbyshire, the Duke of Norfolk laid out the town land in a regular form, regulating 'the streets, avenues, passages, drains, sewers and other conveniences'.

Other opportunities for planning arose where a new industry—a factory, textile mill, coal-pit or iron-works—was set down in a sparsely-populated

rural area and the employer had the obligation of providing housing for his
workforce. The 'company' town or village was no rare phenomenon, its
origins reaching back to the establishments of Arkwright at Cromford
(1771), Strutt at Belper (1776) and Gregg at Styal (1784), and the line
stretching forward through Ashworth, Akroyd and Salt to Cadbury and
Lever at the end of the nineteenth century. Again, the construction of the
railway towns like Swindon, Crewe and Wolverton afforded further
opportunities for employers to plan a coherent development with proper
attention to site layout, landscape and amenities besides well-constructed
houses. Some of these were model communities, demonstrating that
industrial life did not need to be harsh, graceless and brutalizing: some were
no better than the barracks which speculative builders were running up
elsewhere, and the first estate built by the Great Western Railway Company
at Swindon was the most closely built-up district of the town. Occasionally,
'planning' could be disastrous, as in part of Canning Town where houses
were built on Plaistow Marshes, below the level of Thames high water, and
where in one street the only drain passed into a well which was the source of
drinking water.[15]

Much more thought was given by builders and contractors to the planning of urban areas for the more prosperous classes, in both old and new
towns, and especially in the spreading suburbs. Town improvement
schemes for the wealthier parts of London had been well-known in the
eighteenth century, but the largest scheme of all, designed and executed by
John Nash between 1815 and 1830, went beyond the purely private by
involving Crown and Parliamentary approval. It included the laying out of
Regent's Park and the Terraces, the construction of Regent Street, Carlton
House Terrace and Gardens, Pall Mall East and Trafalgar Square, larger
plans still remaining uncompleted. Of the speculative builders of middle-
and upper-class London housing, much the most successful and imaginative
was Thomas Cubitt, who moved on from Highbury and Islington in the
mid-20s to build a large part of the Duke of Bedford's estate including
Gordon Street and Square, Endsleigh Street and Woburn Place. Later he
was responsible for Belgrave Square, Lowndes Square and Eaton Place and
Square, the most fashionable parts of Victorian London, laid out with great
attention to visual harmony, spaciousness and the use of trees. Outside
London, the best examples of middle-class planning were to be found in the
seaside resorts and spas, modelled to some extent on eighteenth-century
Bath, but catering also for the permanent residence of retired businessmen,
manufacturers and colonial servants. Southport, Bournemouth, Tunbridge
Wells, Torquay and Scarborough were all substantially new towns of the
first half of the century, owing much to the original planning of a few large
local landowners until later developments were taken over by improvement
commissioners, local boards of health and corporations.

Such places, interesting and curious as they were, were exceptional in the history of English urban development, and had no general influence upon it: they were the refuges of the relatively rich, deliberately set well apart from the centres of industry and having no structural contacts with them. For the merchant, manufacturer and professional man who needed to be within daily reach of the city centre, the alternative was a house in the suburbs, on the fringe of a town distant from the smoke and smell of industry and the noise and dirt of humanity. Victorian social observers were often surprised at what seemed a recent phenomenon, and some expressed concern at the segregation of the classes which inevitably accompanied suburban development, yet the origins of the suburb were certainly pre-Victorian, and probably pre-nineteenth century.[16] As we have seen, the English town grew by gradual accretion of new areas on its fringes which eventually became absorbed as integral parts of the town, and migration of the wealthier classes outwards from the crowded city centres had for long been part of this process. In London there might be strong social reasons for the wealthy to remain close to the centre—at least for part of the year—but in the new towns of industrial England there were not. In fact, it seems unlikely that rich and poor had ever lived as immediate neighbours even in the medieval town, and eighteenth-century towns had certainly had their fashionable and disreputable districts. But as people, traffic, dirt and disease multiplied in the nineteenth century, the once-fashionable ceased to be desirable: large houses were abandoned for sub-letting and tenementing, and those who could afford to keep a horse and carriage moved out to new suburban villas where the air was cleaner and the neighbours politer.

In time, some of these new areas were overtaken by the same forces, and the movement further out had to continue. Its limits were determined geographically—until the 1840s the distance that a man who did not need to be in his counting-house at a precise time could ride or drive to work, and, after that, could travel by the new railways. The great age of suburban development was, therefore, post-1850, and its patterns were largely determined by the directions of the iron ways. Yet, it has been estimated that by 1855 some 20,000 people were commuting daily by bus into London, about 15,000 by steamboat and 6,000 by rail,[17] almost all, it may be assumed, middle-class. The artisan suburb was just beginning, though it took the development of trams and workmen's fares in the 1880s to make it a significant feature of town development. An interesting proposal in 1845 by a London architect, Moffatt, to house 350,000 people in garden villages within ten miles of London, at an estimated cost of £10 million, was wildly premature and came to nothing.

THE PROVISION OF HOUSES

There are no annual statistics of house-building in the nineteenth century except for a few particular towns of which Liverpool, exceptional for its Irish immigration, has the longest record. The national censuses, taken every ten years from 1801 onwards, did count the numbers of houses, however, and so provide a 'frozen' portrait of people to houses at ten-yearly intervals. Expressed simply, the position in England and Wales was as follows:[18]

Census year	Total population	Total no of inhabited houses	Average no of persons/house
1801	8,893,000	1,576,000	5·67
1811	10,164,000	1,798,000	5·68
1821	12,000,000	2,088,000	5·76
1831	13,897,000	2,482,000	5·62
1841	15,914,000	2,944,000	5·44
1851	17,928,000	3,278,000	5·46

The results are surprising for at least two reasons—first, for the general consistency, and even slight improvement in the 1840s, of the number of persons per house, and second because they apparently fail to reflect the overwhelming opinion of many contemporaries that much working-class housing was grossly overcrowded, and that the extent of this was increasing rather than diminishing. In themselves, of course, the figures neither prove nor disprove this, since they are straight national averages taking no account of regional, income, class or other variables. It is important to remember that industrialization in the first half of the century was widening social and economic differences within and across the classes—was enriching and enlarging the middle classes as a proportion of the whole population, and also creating wider differences of income and status within the working classes. Many skilled workers, and even semi-skilled but relatively highly-paid factory workers, must have been improving their housing conditions in the period, moving, for instance, from one or two rooms to a three- or four-roomed artisan's cottage. 'In this event,' Professor Flinn has commented, 'the constancy of the national density over the whole period must, as a result, have increased crowding of those in the lower income groups.'[19] This would be reinforced by middle-class occupation of larger houses, a tendency which grew markedly in the period with the accumulation of the 'paraphernalia of gentility' and the swelling armies of domestic servants to be accommodated: although still numerically a small class—perhaps 15 per cent of the total population by 1851—their occupancy rate was quite disproportionate to their size.

Regrettably, the censuses did not count rooms—still less, room sizes—but we should be grateful that they did, at least, count 'empties'. (The above-quoted figures refer to houses actually occupied.) These are shown in the following table:[20]

Census year	Number of uninhabited houses	Percentage of uninhabited to inhabited houses
1801	57,476	3·65
1811	51,000	2·84
1821	69,707	3·34
1831	119,915	4·83
1841	173,247	5·88
1851	153,494	4·68

These 'uninhabited' rates are substantially lower than for the second half of the century, and in no way surprising in a period of high mobility when existing houses were often in the 'wrong' places. More important for our purpose is the 'fit' of houses to families, and, as the following figures show, this worsened during the first half of the century in the sense that an increasing number of families became surplus to the available houses:

Census year	No of families	No of inhabited houses	No of surplus families
1801	1,896,723	1,575,923	320,800
1811	2,142,147	1,797,504	344,643
1821	2,493,423	2,088,156	405,267
1831	2,911,874	2,481,544	430,330
1841	—	2,943,945	—
1851	3,712,290	3,278,039	434,251

To express this in terms of individuals, in 1801, 1,500,000 people were 'surplus' to the inhabited house accommodation, in 1851, 1,900,000, though, since total population had doubled in the period, this represented a considerably reduced proportion.

Beyond this, the census figures do not take us, and recent researches have not added greatly to our knowledge of housing provision in the period. We need to know more about provision between the census years and about the rates of building nationally and regionally, but in the absence of official records of houses themselves, attention has been turned to the materials of building—bricks, timber, slate and glass—many of which bore duty at different periods and were, therefore, nationally recorded. This technique was initiated by H. A. Shannon, who constructed an index of the output of bricks between 1785 and 1849.[21] Although this is valuable as an indication of variations in building activity generally, it cannot be taken as a guide specifically to house-building, since bricks were also used in the construction of public buildings, factories, railways and so on, where cycles of activity may have been quite different. A more recent study by B. Weber is based solely on records of residential construction from particular towns, and is therefore potentially more useful for our purpose, but it begins only in 1838 and, until after mid-century, rests on only one, untypical, town—Liverpool.[22]

What these calculations do make clear is that building activity moved, not in step with the increasing population or social need, but in waves or cycles determined in part by external economic considerations. House-building was subject to two types of economic fluctuation—short-term, averaging between five and ten years, and based on the business cycle, and long-term, of twenty or more years' duration and of wider amplitude: the latter was much more evident from the 1860s onwards, the short-term more significant for the first half of the century. Thus, although the period from 1801 to 1841 saw the fastest rate of house-building of the century, within this time there were peaks and troughs of wide disparity—peaks in 1819, 1825, 1836, 1847, troughs in 1821, 1832 and 1842.

Using the census information on houses under construction, it is clear that the rate of house-building grew steadily during the early decades of the century, the percentage increase of houses in 1801–11 being 13·5; in 1811–21, 16·8; in 1821–31, 20·6 (the fastest in the century); and in 1831–41, 19·8. By 1841–51 it had fallen drastically to 10·1, and it did not exceed 15 at any later time in the century.[23] These are, of course, national statistics, and local studies have shown that particular towns and areas did not necessarily follow the national trends. Thus, although there was a profound slump in house-building generally in the 1840s, Liverpool experienced strong activity between 1844 and 1846, which was due partly to the heavy Irish immigration at that time, but perhaps more importantly to the fact that the city corporation was preparing to introduce the first building by-laws in 1846, and speculative builders, anticipating tighter controls, were rushing to run up houses.[24] Again, house-building increased in Middlesex in the 1840s, probably following demographic and migration patterns in a rapidly-growing area.

It is not suggested that speculative builders—small-scale, un-revolutionized and unsophisticated as the great majority of them were—either knew of or still less understood, the theory of the business cycle. They were motivated not by the demonstrated needs of society, by social, aesthetic or philanthropic considerations, but by their calculations or guesses as to the likely profit to be made from building a house which could be let at a certain weekly rent. Such guesses could often be wrong, because builders were peculiarly subject to fluctuations in the cost of materials, nearly always bought on credit, and because the actual construction of houses, which was by nature a lengthy and somewhat incalculable process, could mean completions appearing on the market at inappropriate times. It seems that building activity did not correspond precisely with the trade cycle, builders preferring to start in the earliest phase of recovery from a trough, when interest rates were still low and material costs had not yet begun to rise. Land costs often remained fairly high in the period of depression, but this does not seem to have been so decisive as the other factors. Wise builders, then, decided to build ahead of demand, so as to put completed houses on the market at the peak of the cycle when high prices or rents could be charged: by then, they would have slackened their rate of building because credit, materials and wages would all now be expensive, and because new starts would now be completed in unfavourable down-swing or trough periods. These were nice calculations, which could spell the difference between riches and bankruptcy, notoriously high in the industry. In such conditions the surprising thing is that demand and supply kept as closely in step as they did, at least until the 1840s. Cairncross and Weber concluded that 'demand was dominated by demographic changes', though a decline of effective demand in that decade due to reduced wages and increasing unemployment must also have been influential.

Extending such considerations, it has been tempting to try to discover the fundamental regulator of building activity in the movement of interest rates. It is obviously true that building requires large capital outlays and that at different times it must be in competition for that capital with other demands—industrial or commercial expansion, transport, public services and so on. H. Barnes has argued that the rate of building was higher in the years 1801–41 than in the next half-century because in this earlier period building and agriculture were still major industries, employing the largest numbers of people and able to attract adequate investment, whereas subsequently the development of industry, the new railways, and profitable spheres for investment overseas, tended to deprive building of the necessary resources.

> In times of great trading, commercial and industrial activity, building will slacken owing to the engrossing and profitable character of other occupations. It is roughly true to say that money is not made on building, it is spent on it. Whether it be on domestic building or otherwise, it is surplus that is spent, after the living expenses of the individual and the working expenses of the industry are discharged . . .[25]

The assertion that 'money is not made on building' is open to challenge, but the general argument that building has to compete for its capital is readily acceptable. The decline of house-building activity in the 1840s at the boom period of railway construction is also an attractive hypothesis: in 1845 alone £700 million was raised for railway speculation, and by 1850, 6,000 miles of line had already been built at an average cost of £56,000 a mile. On the other hand, when money was cheap to borrow and alternative investments not so attractive, building was favoured—as between 1801 and 1841 when the yield of consols fell from 5·3 to 3·2 per cent and the wholesale prices of many commodities also fell after the peaks of the Napoleonic War years.

Beyond a simple statement that building activity could be stimulated or discouraged by general movements of prices and interest rates, it is, perhaps, wise not to venture. The theory that economic growth in Britain and the United States were inversely related to each other, engagingly summarized by Professor Phelps Brown in the dictum that 'Whether a house is built in Oldham depends on and is decided by whether a house goes up in Oklahoma',[26] has been disputed by other authorities.[27] The evidence seems to suggest that building was, for the most part, internally determined, that it was a highly imperfect (in the economists' sense) industry, and that population growth and migration patterns at the local level were usually more powerful determinants than material and labour costs and minor variations in rents. Ultimately, the decision whether to build or not was taken at the local level by a man in a small way of business, with his own network of credit facilities, materials suppliers and labour. His calculations, such as they were, rested on his expectations of the price at which the completed house would be sold or rented, based on his knowledge of the area and his guesses about future demand. To the structure and organization of this 'industry'—'trade' was the contemporary and more appropriate description—we now turn.

THE BUILDING INDUSTRY

After agriculture, building was the largest employer of labour in the first half of the century. Because of the great variety of crafts which went to make it up—masons, bricklayers, carpenters, joiners, painters, glaziers, plumbers, paviours, slaters and tilers—it is impossible to be precise about numbers, especially for the earlier years, but a reasonable estimate for 1831 would be 350–400,000. For 1851 we have a precise statistic, 463,491. The figures include skilled men, always a high proportion of the trades concerned, apprentices and labourers, who were important in all those departments where fetching and carrying was to be done.

The industry was characterized by a large number of small firms, and, with some exceptions to be noted shortly, was largely unchanged in methods and organization since the later Middle Ages.[28] According to Sir John Clapham, the term 'builder', meaning an entrepreneur who organized building operations, and not merely one particular craft's part in them, came into use in the later half of the eighteenth century, and was applied mainly to bricklayers and carpenters who had graduated from craftsmen to contractors, designing and estimating for buildings and employing their own workforce.[29] That such activities involved a high risk was clearly evident to a contemporary, Campbell, in 1747: 'Building Projects of their own . . . often ruin them. It is no new thing in London for these Master Builders to build themselves out of their own Houses, and fix themselves in Jail with their own Materials.' But however dubious the origins of some may have been, by 1831 'builders' were a respectable and defined category, the census of that year listing 871 for London, but much smaller numbers for the agricultural counties—7 in Berkshire, 9 in Bedfordshire, 12 in Buckinghamshire, 147 for the whole of Wales: It is clear that the distribution of the occupation corresponded closely with the urban areas.

Although building underwent no 'industrial revolution' comparable with what was occurring in the textile and iron industries, important changes in organization were taking place which enabled it to respond with some success to the new demands. In a study of the origins of the Victorian master builders,[30] Dr Cooney has categorized four types of firm to which the term was applied:

Type 1   Master craftsmen, eg carpenters, bricklayers, who worked only in their own trades and employed small numbers of journeymen.

Type 2   Master craftsmen, responsible for constructing entire buildings, directly employing labour only in their own trades and contracting with other master craftsmen for the rest of the work.

Type 3   A builder, not himself a craftsman but an architect or merchant (eg timber), erecting complete buildings on the basis of contracts with the various master craftsmen.

Type 4   A master builder, erecting complete buildings by employing a substantial and permanent workforce covering all the principal building crafts.

It has often been supposed that the first true master builder (Type 4) was Thomas Cubitt (1788–1855) of London, who is accredited with developing a new kind of organization between 1815 and 1820, and of being the prototype of all the subsequent large-scale building contractors. In fact, it was probably Alexander Copland who should be so regarded. Copland was a builder who engaged in large-scale construction of barracks for the government during the Napoleonic Wars, and who was paid no less than £1,300,000 for work done between 1792 and 1806. His method was to have a comprehensive organization in which he directly employed all labour—up to 700 men at some times—bought all materials, provided workshops and sawpits and opened up brickworks. There appear to have been about half a dozen other contractors at this time, organized on similar lines, and dependent on the exceptional wartime demand, but in the years after 1815 large-scale organization was encouraged by the growth of urban demand and, particularly, by the great activity in public building—churches, docks, bridges, warehouses, the Houses of Parliament, the National Gallery, the Royal Exchange, and so on. Thomas Cubitt, though not the originator of large contractor-building, was undoubtedly the man who took most advantage of the new opportunities. Beginning as a master carpenter in Holborn in 1809, by 1815 he was typical of the 'Type 2' builders, constructing whole buildings but sub-contracting for work outside his own craft. Shortly after this, however, he set up his own workshops, brought together a large body of workers covering all the principal building trades, established proper supervision by skilled foremen, and provided continuous employment for his workforce. By 1820 he was moving into large-scale speculation in estate development and house-building, which was to culminate in the construction of much of Belgravia and Pimlico: in 1828 he had about 1,000 men in employment.

Yet Cubitt's 'revolution' in organization, if such it can be called, had not more than a handful of imitators, even in London, until much later in the century. Firms of a small size and craft basis continued to predominate, 'Type 2' remaining the typical unit of organization, especially among the speculative builders who were responsible for the great majority of working-class and middle-class housing in the provinces. At the census of 1851, nine London firms were reported as employing more than 200 men and fifty-seven 50 or more, and outside the capital 10 was considered a large firm. Although it is possible to identify three categories of builders by the 1830s—'contractors' working on large public buildings, 'master builders' specializing in shops and business premises, and 'speculative builders' (the term was already in use)—it was mainly the last who concentrated on the building of smaller houses. Almost always they were self-promoted craftsmen, most commonly either bricklayers or carpenters. Their method of organization was to buy or rent the land—perhaps for a whole future street, but, more likely, for a small row of terraced cottages—to execute their own part of the work, which might be foundations and walls only, having secured materials on credit, then to raise a mortgage on the half-built house with which to pay subsequent workers sub-contracted to them, and finally to sell the finished house at a profit, usually to a landlord looking for a safe investment.

Clearly, there were numerous risks in these transactions, and the rate of failure in the trade was notoriously high, especially in years of financial crisis such as 1816 and 1826. Equally clearly, it was tempting for such men to maximise profits by skimping in whatever ways were possible. The traditional method of the small employer—to 'sweat' his men by paying sub-standard wages—was often not open in a trade where labour was generally well-organized for the time. The alternative was to provide sub-standard work—cheap materials, dubious construction methods, inadequate or non-existent paving and draining, and minimal internal fittings. Such was the 'jerry-builder', the man supposedly without conscience who built in the cheapest and flimsiest manner down to the lowest possible limits of saleability and had no thought for the durability of the structure or the comfort of its occupants. The use of the word, a corruption of the nautical as in 'jerry-mast' and 'jerry-rig' to mean something temporary, inferior, used in an emergency, was apparently first applied to building in Liverpool about 1830, a town which, as we have seen, was experiencing a rapid influx of immigrants and extreme pressure on existing accommodation.[31] Many of the houses built at this time were undoubtedly flimsy structures, with walls only half brick ($4\frac{1}{2}$in) thick, and some were blown down in a great storm in 1822. Contemporary evidence suggests that they were regarded as of a lower and unacceptable standard than normal, a grand jury referring to 'the slight and dangerous mode of erecting dwelling houses now practised in this town and neighbourhood'.

The jerry-builder has been rightly reviled in contemporary literature and in historians' accounts of the industrial revolution, but Professor Ashton has pointed to some of the circumstances which help to explain his emergence and survival. House-building, artificially held back during the French wars, had to spurt forward after 1815 to meet an enormous and growing demand, and at a time of greatly increased costs. Most of the Liverpool 'slop houses' were run up by very small builders, many of them Welsh quarrymen backed by lawyers who had land to dispose of on lease. They bought shoddy materials on three-monthly credit and for cheapness employed apprentices rather than skilled men.[32] Credit was needed at every turn, and while the usury laws prohibited interest rates of more than 5 per cent, and the government itself was offering nearly as much for (and during some of the war years more than) this, credit for building had been virtually unobtainable. The gradual fall of interest rates in the 1820s allowed the trade to expand, but the costs of building materials had greatly increased since 1788 while wholesale prices generally stood only about 20 per cent above that level: lead had risen by 58 per cent, deal by 60 per cent and bricks and wainscotting had doubled.[33] In part, these high prices were due to the duties on bricks, timber, tiles, stone and slate, which, Joseph Hume estimated in 1850, were responsible for £20 of the cost of a £60 cottage. The window tax, levied until 1851, and the rising level of local rates also contributed to the problem in that landlords sought to recoup them in the rents charged. Builders of all kinds, but perhaps especially the speculative builders who built for the working class, were seriously handicapped both by credit difficulties and by costs, a large part of which arose from indirect taxation.

Major economies in labour were generally not possible in an industry which depended on craft-work and was scarcely touched by mechanization in the period. The crafts were traditional, conservative, relatively well-organized and powerful, certainly among the smaller firms, and in the periods of brisk building activity. 'Slop-masters' might take on larger proportions of unskilled men and apprentices and might disregard the established 'working rules'. At the other end of the scale, a very large firm

like Cubitt's might sometimes act tyrannically, as in 1834, when they tried
to prevent any beer except that brewed by Combe, Delafield and Co being
brought into their yards. But between the extremes, the majority of skilled
men seem to have maintained, and probably improved, their economic and
working conditions. Wage-rates (computed for a ten-hour day) for
carpenters, bricklayers and masons rose steadily from 3s a day in 1788 to 5s
a day in the years 1826–47.[34] A weekly wage in the region of 30s—if it
could be sustained against the vicissitudes of bad weather, short-time and
unemployment—put such men, if not among the labour 'aristocrats', at
least among the 'respectable' skilled workers. Building labour was, except
in the years of depression, in strong demand, and was unionized at an early
date, the Carpenters and Joiners founding a general union in 1827 and the
Bricklayers in 1829. Although the ambitious Operative Builders' Union fell
in the general collapse of trade unions in 1834, individual societies like the
Operative Stone Masons survived throughout the thirties and forties with
reduced membership. In general, it seems that building workers were men
of some spirit, intelligence and independence, not easily oppressed by their
employers in normal times.

Of the other prime costs of building, land was as yet a less important
factor. In general, the speculative builder built on leasehold land, and his
product 'reached the ultimate consumer, often enough, only through a
maze of intermediate leases and subleases between the ground landlord and
the tenant'.[35] This was especially the case in London, whereas in the
provinces plots of freehold land were more commonly available, both in surviving corners within old parts of towns and in new areas of suburban
development. In some towns, it is true, local geographical and tenurial
factors limited the quantity of land available for building, and added to the
gross overcrowding of accommodation. This, it has been argued, was the
case in Nottingham, where open space on three sides of the town could not
be used owing to the refusal of the aristocratic owners to sell or of the town
burgesses to give up their ancient common rights:[36] the result was extreme
overcrowding in 8,000 back-to-back houses until enclosure of the commons,
partly for building land and partly for recreational use, was carried through
in 1845. Again, topography helped to determine the availability of suitable
building land in many parts of the country, not least in the West Riding of
Yorkshire where the new woollen towns naturally tended to straggle along
the valley bottoms rather than climb into the hills. The general point here is
that property values affected the density of building, and that where
speculation in land was active in forcing prices up, building tended to
respond by being either high, or overcrowded, or both. Where land values
were high, as in the dock town of Liverpool (the cheapest land in the 1860s
costing 16s a yard freehold, or 1s a yard yearly ground rent), tenement
blocks on four or five floors were common, whereas on the cheaper land of
Leeds (2s 6d to 5s a yard freehold) the less economical back-to-backs were

usual. When such cottages were built in Liverpool, with minimal dimensions of a 12ft frontage and 13½ft depth, the land could cost from £28 to £56, compared with building costs of £80 to £110.[37]

The speculative builder's activities were, therefore, constrained by the availability of land on the market at any particular time, and by the suitability of such land from the point of view of constructional costs and ultimate demand. Where outright purchase of the land seemed to represent the best bargain, the builder bought. Often, and especially in London, he preferred to take it on a short (up to ninety-nine years) building lease, since although a slightly higher rate of interest normally had to be paid on capital borrowed on leasehold estates, it gave the small builder the great advantage of avoiding a heavy capital outlay. Owners also often preferred to retain the freehold interest in building land as an investment which would fructify over time, and, on the expiration of the lease, would give the opportunity of rack-renting the improved property at perhaps five or ten times the equivalent of the original ground rent. Professor Dyos, in his careful study of the development of a south London suburb, Camberwell, has shown that this was the usual practice here, where in 1837 half of the land had still been pasture, a quarter arable and market-garden, and the remainder previously built-up. At that time there were 173 freeholders, sixty-one of whom owned less than an acre and 7 of whom owned more than a hundred.[38]

In such conditions there could be no plan or coherent development, even within the relatively small area of one suburb, and what homogeneity of type and style Camberwell came to display was largely fortuitous. The speculative builders who were entirely responsible for its development were mainly craftsmen become entrepreneurs, but sometimes suppliers of building materials who had been led into the business to recover bad debts, and sometimes purveyors of capital, like building societies, who became builders in order to complete half-built properties on which they had had to foreclose. At the peak of building activity in Camberwell, in 1878–80, 416 different firms or individual builders were at work on 5,670 houses, more than half of them building no more than six houses in the three years. In an earlier phase of activity, 1850–2, 90 per cent of firms built twelve houses or less each, and very few of the firms in existence then were still at work thirty years later. The great majority had local addresses, or came from districts immediately adjacent to Camberwell. A very few of the new streets were developed by one or two builders alone, but, in general, Dyos found that 'the building of Camberwell's streets was the unconcerted effort of many builders', and only two of the larger firms, each responsible for several hundred houses, so concentrated their activities on particular estates that they could be said to have had a dominating influence on the general character of the district. One of these two, Edward Yates, became by the 1880s the largest builder in south London, but his early methods of financing were probably typical of any speculative builder of the period. The land for Dragon Road, where he ultimately built forty-six two-storeyed houses in terraces down each side, was leased for seventy years from a local landowner by a series of leases each covering two, three or four houses; the ground rent varied from £1 9s 6d to £4 a year, depending on size of plot. The total capital, about £7,000, was raised by mortgages for fourteen years from building societies and solicitors, probably at the prevailing rate of interest of 5 per cent, and the completed houses, the prime cost of which was about £190 each, were let at an average annual rent of £26. Professor Dyos has estimated that the margin of profit on gross outlay may have been no more than a half of one per cent.[39]

In later ventures Yates wisely sold his houses rather than letting them himself, the practice followed by the great majority of smaller builders. Most lived on almost hand-to-mouth existence, without the long-term financial commitments that Yates entered into, the usual practice being to raise a mortgage on one floor of a house in order to finance the next stage, and on completion to assign the lease at a premium which would dispose of the mortgage and cover the builder's capital costs and profit. But in respect of his financial sources, Yates was probably quite typical. Building societies were, at this period, a major source of finance for new building: so, too, were solicitors in private practice, seeking solid investments for clients' money, and not uncommonly seeking out known credit-worthy builders to offer advances. Major financial institutions were wary of lending to a trade with a notoriously high rate of bankruptcy, and since many of their own investments were in existing property had no interest in encouraging too much new building which might over-stock the market and depress rents. Small speculative builders, it seems, relied mainly on local networks of private sources of finance, built up over the years on the basis of personal knowledge and trust. This was especially true of the tiny firms outside London, essentially jobbing builders who might or might not build a house or two a year between repair work, and in order to hold a small labour force together. Such men were unlikely to be welcomed by banks, building societies or insurance companies: their credit came in many cases from the landlord himself, who would sometimes even supply bricks and other materials, or internally from the trade in the form of short-term loans from other builders or informal partnerships which divided the profit on completion.[40]

The contribution which the architectural profession made to the activities of speculative builders in this period was small, and to the builder of working-class housing, minimal. Professor J. N. Tarn has written that 'Until Norman Shaw designed the middle-class suburb of Bedford Park in 1876, no architect found a place in the history of nineteenth-century architecture who also played any significant part in the development of the housing movement'.[41] In general, it is true, architects of the first half of the century were not so concerned with the building itself as with what Ruskin described as 'that art which impresses . . . on [the building's] form certain characters, venerable or beautiful, but otherwise unnecessary'.[42] Their art was directed much more towards public buildings, churches and town and country mansions than towards the problem of housing the multitude, to which it was too readily assumed that architectural solutions did not apply. So, when Gilbert Scott was called in by Sir Edward Akroyd to design his working-class suburb in Halifax, his plans were described as 'not adapted to modern requirements', and had to be radically altered. Architects were certainly involved in some of the larger middle-class housing developments in London, as we shall see later, though not, it seems, in the building of a suburb like Camberwell and still less in the general provision of working-class housing in the industrial towns. Occasional instances of the employment of architects for designing workmen's cottages may certainly be found, as in Halifax where some unusual five-storey blocks, consisting of two-storey 'through' houses built on top of three-storey 'back-to-earth' houses have been traced to a local architect, W. A. D. Horsfall: the reason here may well have been the difficulty of the site, a steeply sloping hillside.[43] But generally where architecture had any influence on ordinary housing, it was not on the spatial plan but on the mere decoration, the 'better' sorts of houses imitating 'as pompously as they could the architectural grandeur of the mansions owned by the large incomes'. The crude fact was, of course, that the design of an artisan's cottage could not normally bear the cost of a plan which would ultimately have to be reflected in the price or rent. Where architects did involve themselves at all in this kind of work was through some of the philanthropic or semi-philanthropic housing societies which began to build tenement blocks and cottage flats from the 1840s onwards on a scale which could offer professional interest and challenge. The outstanding example was Henry Roberts, architect to Shaftesbury's Society for Improving the Condition of the Labouring Classes, founded in 1844, but even Roberts was by this time virtually retired and engaging in the Society's work largely from charitable motives. Truly professional architects, like Henry Darbishire of the Peabody Trust and Frederick Chancellor of the Metropolitan Association, only emerged in the 1860s and 1870s, and it is significant that even then one of London's largest housing agencies, Sidney Waterlow's Improved Industrial Dwellings Company, could boast that the expense of an architect was quite unnecessary.

Speculative builders generally worked from experience and empirical knowledge, planning their buildings with reference to the site possibilities and the prevailing house-forms of the locality. At the upper end of the housing scale, there is some evidence that architects' working drawings were available to builders of suburban villas, while at the other end, the erection of a standard 'back-to-back' could probably dispense with both plan and specifications. For the inexperienced builder there was, in any case, a mass of instructional literature which provided simple plans, designs, bills of quantities and details of estimating and pricing for, as one author said, 'a builder who has no leisure to travel and copy widely'.[44] One of the earliest and most influential of these was J. C. Loudon's *Encyclopaedia of Cottage, Farm and Villa Architecture* of 1833, although in general this type of literature seems to have enjoyed its greatest popularity during and after the 1850s.

No revolutionary technical innovations affected the building of houses during these years. Houses continued to be built of the same materials that had long been available, and by the same methods that had been used for centuries. Major changes in methods of building construction would probably have received little support from an industry which was so small-scale, traditional and conservative in outlook, yet its receptivity to change was hardly put to the test. Where new constructional materials or techniques were developed in the period their use was in civil engineering or large-scale constructional work rather than in house-building. This was the case, for instance, with cast-iron, used so dramatically as the frame for the Crystal Palace in 1851 and for the roof of the Houses of Parliament, but practically confined to similar structures and a few large factories and offices. Potentially even more important, Portland cement was only coming into use for difficult engineering projects like Marc Isambard Brunel's tunnel under the Thames and for the foundations of large buildings. 'Hydraulic' (water-resistant) cement had been first discovered in 1798, but it was the stronger 'Portland' cement, patented in 1824, which ultimately stimulated interest in the structural possibilities of concrete blocks and reinforced concrete in the second half of the century.[45]

Where technical progress did have effects was in extending the use of certain existing building materials, either by new methods of manufacture or by new methods of distribution. The most important to be so affected were bricks and glass. A surveyor of the twentieth-century townscape could easily be forgiven for supposing that the traditional English building material was brick, but this is not so; suitable brick-earth deposits were not widely diffused, fuel for firing bricks was scarce in many areas, and transport of the finished product over any great distance was difficult and costly. The result was that no one building material predominated, and that, except in the construction of large, expensive houses where aesthetic considerations could prevail over economic, English houses before the nineteenth century had been built of a wide variety of locally-available materials. These included stone (either 'dressed' or 'rough' and supplemented with turves, furze or any mixture of available materials), timber (for building a frame, filled in with clay, wattle and daub, lath and plaster, or weather-boarding), and, in areas where neither of these was easily available, like East Anglia, clunch and flint.[46] English brick-making, which had died with the Romans, was probably reintroduced in the fifteenth century, but only developed importantly from the seventeenth century onwards, when the gradual supersession of frame building by load-bearing brickwork was made possible by the use of coal instead of timber for the firing of bricks.[47]

The widespread use of brick also depended on the availability of cheap bulk transport, both for the movement of coal and for the distribution of the finished product, and it was the development of water navigation in the eighteenth century and of railways in the nineteenth which fulfilled these needs. The actual processes of brick manufacture in the period before 1850 owed very little to technological change, the great expansion of output from 841 million in 1815–19 to 1,794 million in 1845–9 being almost entirely due to more intensive use of traditional methods of manufacture. The brick-making industry in the period was characterized by a large number of firms of small size, and even in 1870, by which time some growth in scale had occurred, there were still 1,770 works employing on average only thirteen men each. 'Getting' the clay remained a matter of pick and shovel, and bricks were almost entirely hand-made by being pressed into moulds. Attempts in the eighteenth century to mechanize the process had come to nothing, and the first successful machine was the 'plug-mill' for grinding the clay in the 1830s; it was followed in 1838 by a machine which extruded plastic clay and cut it into batches of a dozen bricks by an arrangement of wires. A satisfactory machine for making pressed bricks was designed by Oates about 1856, and from then on both processes were extensively used, hand-made bricks gradually declining to a small, specialized market. The pressed-brick system was potentially of great importance, for it made possible the use of harder clays, shales and marls occurring among the carboniferous limestone deposits of the industrial North Midlands and North of England. It therefore greatly extended the regional availability of brick in the later half of the century, and, combined with improved transport, made it the normal building material of the English town. The important technical developments were, however, post-1850, when the removal of the excise duty on bricks in that year had the effect of encouraging experimentation.

The supersession of a variety of vernacular building materials by brick gave to English domestic architecture a uniformity and monotony of appearance which traditionalists found it easy to condemn, a uniformity which was reinforced by the gradual adoption of Westmorland and Welsh slate as the principal roofing material for houses. It should, however, be remembered that the new materials, properly used, were more durable, sanitary, cold- and damp-resistant than most of those they replaced, and that they brought what in the eighteenth century had been fashionable and exclusive building materials into the ambit of working-class housing. Nowhere was this more true than in the case of glass, which before the nineteenth century had been an expensive luxury, owing partly to the high costs of production and partly to the excise duty on glass and the tax on windows. The excise duty which, claimed a critic, raised the price of glass to three times its untaxed cost, was repealed in 1845. The tax on windows was halved in 1823, the tax-free number was raised from six to seven in 1824, and the tax finally abolished in 1851. Glass production was undoubtedly stimulated by these fiscal changes, and by the general building boom of the period, moving closely in line with the cycles of activity in 1822–5, the mid-30s and the mid-40s.[48] More and bigger windows were also a major concern of the sanitary reformers, who argued that lack of sunlight and ventilation were among the chief causes of the high incidence of disease. Yet the mass production of cheap window-glass in the nineteenth century would not have been possible without both technical changes in manufacture and organizational changes in the producing firms. Previous methods of manufacture, which had produced cylinder glass, crown glass and plate glass, were revolutionized in the second quarter of the century and a small-scale craft industry quickly became concentrated in a few large firms. First, in the 1830s, the Chance Brothers introduced improved continental methods of making cylinder glass by the old device of persuading French craftsmen to bring their skills to England: in 1838 they patented a revolutionary device for polishing the thin sheets to produce an unblemished glass which was used for the Crystal Palace in 1851. Then, in 1847, Hartleys introduced a new method of casting thin plate glass which could be fluted and patterned by being passed through rollers. Being stronger than cylinder glass, it was particularly useful for the roofing of factories, railway stations and other large areas. By mid-century cheap window-glass was at last available to meet the bulk demand of the booming housing market. Crown glass, which had suffered both from its high price and from the fact that it could only be produced in small sizes, was now quickly replaced by the new products, which suited and, in part, helped to determine, the Victorian taste for large-paned windows; the many small glass-works which had made it easily fell victim to the concentration of the industry in three large firms—Chances, Hartleys and Pilkingtons.

The glass industry affords the best example in the period of cost-reducing product innovations which greatly expanded the use of a socially desirable building material. Nowhere else in the building industry did invention have nearly so significant an effect. The houses of early industrial England were built by the same methods, and of the same materials, as for generations past, though some, notably brick and slate, became much more widely diffused as a result of developments in transport. Similarly, organizational changes of the kind pioneered by Cubitt had, as yet, no effect on the provision of houses for the mass of people. So far as the building industry can be said to have responded to the challenge of a population explosion, it was merely by the employment of larger numbers of work-people and the use of greater quantities of materials in old ways. These ways were not, in themselves, necessarily bad, inadequate or inefficient. Much would depend on the structural form in which they were employed—the kind of house, that is, that was built. On what criteria did that depend; what determined the shape and size of houses, and of rooms; how were rooms in fact used; what were the requirements of a 'decent' working-class house or of a 'desirable' middle-class one; what, in short, shaped the form and design of houses? To these questions we turn in the succeeding chapters.

2

THE COTTAGE HOMES OF ENGLAND

> Ye gentle souls who dream of rural ease,
> Whom the smooth stream and smoother sonnet please,
> Go! If the peaceful cot your praises share,
> Go look within, and ask if peace be there;
> If peace be his—that drooping, weary sire,
> Or theirs, that offspring round their feeble fire;
> Or hers, that matron pale, whose trembling hand
> Turns on the wretched hearth th' expiring brand!
>
> George Crabbe, *The Village* (1783)

To many Victorians, as to many of their successors, the life of the countryman seemed to offer all that was best in English society—simple and well-understood human relationships, a life attuned to the peace and beauty of nature and a pattern of work and leisure dictated by the seasons rather than by the relentless throb of machinery. For the early generations of town-dwellers, adjusting with difficulty and sometimes with bitter resentment to the new conditions of urban life and work, it was, perhaps, inevitable that they should look back to a 'golden age' when their peasant ancestors had been happy and prosperous, independent and honoured; but which existed only in their nostalgic imaginations. And if the worker was unable to articulate such opinions for himself, William Cobbett and others were ever-ready to remind him of that vanished Arcady which the engrossing farmers and the city stockjobbers had destroyed by their greed and avarice. Yet the image, because it was essentially a literary, poetic one, was at least as much 'middle-class' as 'working-class.' For many successful manufacturers and businessmen a house in the country, or, at least, in the suburbs, represented an escape from the competitive pressures and accumulative instincts of the age of industry, and, at the same time, an approach to the life-style of the landed gentry with whom the Victorian middle classes had a strangely ambivalent love–hate relationship. Throughout the nineteenth century few English people, of any social class, came to terms with the idea of permanent residence in the city. The Englishman's 'natural' home was in the country, and the most 'natural' of all Englishmen was the small yeoman farmer, neither very rich nor very poor, but proud, sturdy and independent, the master of his own destiny and of all he surveyed.

Close to the heart of this romantic myth stood the country cottage, solidly built of local materials, preferably thatched, and with mullioned casements affording glimpses of a comfortable interior in which a cheerful fire reflected the patina of ancient furniture and well-scrubbed floors. It was, as Richard Heath rightly observed, the one form of human habitation that was always in harmony with the scenery around it.

> In Yorkshire and in Wales their aspect is bleak as the moor or mountain side; in Cumberland and in Devonshire they are alike built of stone; but in the north their architecture is in keeping with the stern face nature presents among the Cumbrian hills, while in the south, covered with ivy and hidden amongst gardens and orchards, each little cot appears a poem in itself. This harmony is partly due to the fact that the same soil which produces the natural scenery produces the material of which the cottages are built. In the north, wood is scarce, stone plentiful: hence the stone villages of Lancashire and Yorkshire. In the pottery districts and the midland counties clay is abundant: here, therefore, brick cottages are the rule. In Westmorland the red sandstone is used, in Kent the ragstone, in Lincolnshire the Ancaster stone, in Cornwall granite, in Essex and Herts flints from the chalk hills, in Hampshire mud mixed with pebbles, in Norfolk and Suffolk lumps of clay mixed with straw.[1]

But at this point romance begins to dissolve into reality. 'Picturesque and harmonious from the artist's point of view,' Heath continued, 'these cottages are in most other respects a scandal to England.' Just as the agricultural labourer was among the worst-fed of all fully-employed workers in the nineteenth century,[2] he was almost certainly the worst-housed, and to write of the ramshackle, insanitary and overcrowded 'Cottage Homes of England', as did Mrs Hemans, 'smiling o'er the silvery brook, and round the hamlet fanes',[3] was at best unconscious satire, and at worst blatant hypocrisy. Different images sprang to the mind of Cobbett, who, for all his prejudices, was a sharp and accurate observer of the country scene. At Cricklade, Wiltshire,

> The labourers seem miserably poor. Their dwellings are little better than pig-beds, and their looks indicate that their food is not nearly equal to that of a pig. Their wretched hovels are stuck upon little bits of ground on the road side, where the space has been wider than the road demanded. In many places they have not two rods [60 square yards] to a hovel. It seems as if they had been swept off the fields by a hurricane, and had dropped and found shelter under the banks on the road side![4]

And in Leicestershire,

Look at the miserable sheds in which the labourers reside! Look at these hovels, made of mud and of straw; bits of glass, or of old, off-cast windows, without frames or hinges frequently, but merely stuck in the mud wall. Enter them, and look at the bits of chairs or stools; the wretched boards tacked together to serve for a table; the floor of pebble, broken brick, or of the bare ground; look at the thing called a bed; and survey the rags on the backs of the wretched inhabitants; and then wonder if you can that the gaols and dungeons and treadmills increase, and that a standing army and barracks are become the favourite establishments of England![5]

To describe the labourer's cottage of 1815, or, for that matter, of any date, is to describe an inheritance.[6] Cottages were built to last, whoever the builder might be—landowner ensuring for himself and his successors a settled supply of labour, speculator seeking a lasting investment for his capital, even the labourer himself running up a shack on the edge of the common or waste. Any building involved initial costs, yet in the nature of things it could not yield high initial returns; its value lay in its future, and it would be the height of improvidence to build a cottage which would not survive more than one generation. The tragedy was that so many survived all too well, and that cottages which had been inadequate in terms of size and sanitation when built in the seventeenth and eighteenth centuries were still in use by the greatly expanded families of the nineteenth century.[7]

Because much of the stock was inherited, the quality of cottage accommodation which came down to the early nineteenth century was almost infinitely varied. Nearly all of it was vernacular and local, uninfluenced by architectural form or by the mass-produced materials which were beginning to characterize building in the industrial towns. Not all was bad. Some of it reflected native craftsmanship of a high order, a proper attention to foundations and finish, a sympathetic use of materials and a design which combined utility with some grace. But most of the cottages of England were not the products of such purposive concern. They had not been planned with any regard to need or use beyond minimal protection from the elements: no architect, designer or sanitary engineer had been engaged in their construction nor, in many cases, even a professional builder. Craftsmen might have been employed for particular parts of the work—the joinery, the thatching, the plastering if any—but the basic construction of a cottage was a matter of local custom and folk-learning which almost any man might be expected to possess.

Much information about the actual state of cottages at the beginning of the century may be gathered from the numerous County Reports which were presented to the Board of Agriculture between 1794 and 1815. Sir John Clapham summarized this evidence by writing that 'broadly, the houses of Britain grew worse the farther one went northward and northwestward, reaching the lowest average level in Scotland and Wales'.[8] As a generalization this may be useful, but there were good and bad patches in every county of England, and it is the immense local variety rather than any pattern which is remarkable. South of the Thames the brick cottage was common, or, from an earlier period, the half-timbered; the likelihood was that it had only one living-room and one 'hay-loft' bedroom approached by a ladder. Yet even so close to London as Surrey and Hampshire were still to be found in the 1820s turf huts of squatters on the edges of the wastes, and plenty of Dorset cottages had been reported in 1794 as having mud walls made from road-sweepings. 'Mud' generally meant wattle and daub ('dab' or 'deb'), though to Cobbett it apparently meant 'cob', that is, earth or chalk mixed with straw. Accommodation of an entirely different kind was found in the far north around Alnwick in Northumberland. Here there was a sparse population, with few villages from which to draw labour, and the great new capitalist farmers had responded by building a species of tenemented accommodation for their labourers. Cobbett viewed this with indignant horror in 1833:

> Here we get among the mischief. Here the farms are enormous. Here the thrashing machines are turned by STEAM ENGINES: here the labourers live in a sort of barracks, that is to say, long sheds with stone walls, and covered with what are called pantiles. They have neither gardens, nor privies, nor back doors . . . There are no villages, no scattered cottages; no upstairs; one little window and one doorway to each dwelling in the shed or barrack.[9]

Each section was about 17ft by 15ft; there was no ceiling and no floor except the earth, but in this one room the labourer, his wife and family had to live, cook, eat and sleep.

Some of the most primitive of all housing was undoubtedly to be found here in the far north. As late as 1850 James Caird reported that in some parts of Northumberland the labourer's cow and pig were still lodged under the dwelling-house roof, 'the cow house being divided only by a slight partition wall from the single apartment which serves . . . for all the inmates'.[10] In other parts of Northumberland cottages were equally deplorable, 'composed of upright timbers fixed in the ground, the interstices wattled and plastered with mud. The roofs, some thatched and others covered with turf; one little piece of glass to admit the beams of day; and a hearthstone in the ground, for the peat or turf fire'. Along the Tyne were better houses of stone and clay, and some modern ones of stone and lime with tiled roofs; like many northern cottages, they were single-storey and had only one room 16ft by 15ft, but seem to have been solidly constructed. Cumberland cottages were, predictably, of stone, the older ones thatched and the more recent slated; though simple, they usually had two rooms—the 'kitchen' in which the family lived, cooked, and ate, and the 'parlour' where they slept and sometimes kept their milk, butter and cheese.[11]

North Lancashire, too, had its roomy and well-built cottages of stone and slate, or brick and tile in the west, while Yorkshire and Derbyshire also had a generally good record with cottages of stone or brick, like the farmhouses, and with stone or tile roofs.[12] Perhaps among the best in the whole of England were those of the East Riding, with two lower rooms and two bedrooms, though they were in very short supply and the good effects of four separate rooms tended to be negatived by overcrowding. But after this the picture darkens again. The 'mud' cottage still predominated throughout the Midland counties, though commercially-made brick was beginning to take over. East Anglia generally had a bad reputation, while in Kent there were many cottages of clay, having chimneys of poles daubed inside and out of the same material.[13]

Despite Clapham's strictures on the far North, perhaps the worst of all accommodation—like the lowest wages and the poorest diet—was to be found in the West, in Devon, Somerset, Dorset and Wiltshire. Except where there was local stone or chalk, cob and thatch predominated, and even walls made of earth or of clay and straw which were occasionally washed away during unusually heavy storms.

In summary, it may be said that the 'typical' English cottage of 1815 was built of stone or of brick where these occurred locally, otherwise of half-timber, of clay or of mud; thatch or tiles were the common roofing materials, stone slabs or slates where these were easily available. Usually, it had only one ground-floor room, with perhaps a small 'out-shot' for scullery, larder or store-room; two small bedrooms above were probably the average, but very many had only one, and three would be quite exceptional. The floor might be of earth, lime, brick, cobble-stones or paving-stones. The upper rooms would usually be without ceilings, open to the roof. Windows would be few and small, and often not made to open, while piped water and privies would be virtually unknown in 1815. The chief defects of such structures were that they were often dark, damp and insanitary, difficult to warm in winter or to ventilate in summer, inconvenient for cooking and cleaning and, above all, grossly overcrowded for the often large families who had to eat, cook, sleep and sometimes work at domestic industries in them. Yet, bad as they were by any civilized standard, the greatest complaint was that there were simply not enough of them.[14]

The fundamental cause of the problem was that cottage accommodation had not expanded to meet the demands of a rapidly growing population, and, in some areas, had absolutely contracted. This was, in turn, due to a variety of demographic, economic, administrative and tenurial factors which profoundly affected English farming and landholding during the period under review. As we saw in Chapter 1, the population of England and Wales doubled between 1801 and 1851 from 8·9 million to 17·9 million, and although the new industrial towns grew faster than the country districts, the rate of increase in the latter was still very rapid. Table 1 indicates the growth in numbers between 1801 and 1851 in some predominantly agricultural counties where industrialization had had relatively little effect. Rural depopulation, which was to have profound effects on the English countryside and on English occupational and social structure in the latter half of the century, was not yet evident in 1851. No agricultural county showed an absolute decrease of population during the previous half-century; many showed a 50 per cent increase, some a rate of growth almost as fast as that of the population as a whole.

TABLE 1

Population of selected English counties, 1801–1851 (in thousands)*

	1801	1851
Berkshire	111	170
Cambridgeshire	89	185
Devonshire	340	567
Dorset	114	184
Herefordshire	88	115
Lincolnshire	209	407
Norfolk	273	443
Oxfordshire	112	170
Somerset	274	444
Suffolk	214	337
Wiltshire	184	254
Yorkshire (North Riding)	158	213

* Table adapted from B. R. Mitchell and Phyllis Deane (eds), *Abstract of British Historical Statistics* (1962), Table 7, p 20.

Those who might have responded to the pressure of increasing numbers by building additional accommodation were mainly of two kinds—land-owners employing farm labour themselves or indirectly doing so by the lease of land to farmers, and speculative builders putting up cottages for rent at a profit. A third possibility—the labourer who built his own simple cottage—was statistically insignificant, and became even less so as common and waste land disappeared with the spread of enclosures. Stories, perhaps apocryphal, survived to the late eighteenth century of squatters throwing up a shack in a matter of hours, and Sir Frederic Eden wrote in 1797 that 'poor people have, more than once, availed themselves of a long night to rear a hovel on the road-side',[15] but he went on to say that even when a labourer possessed the small sum of money needed to build a cottage, he could seldom now obtain the consent of the lord of the manor to build on the common. 'I know several parishes in which the greatest difficulty the poor labour under is the impossibility of procuring habitations.'

A major problem, as Eden recognized, was that speculative builders were rarely interested in building in country parishes. The market was, almost by definition, an uneconomic one, for the rural labourer, whose earnings in the period averaged 8s to 10s a week (ranging, in 1824, from 4s 6d a week in some southern counties to 12s in Lancashire and 15s in Cumberland),[16] could rarely afford a rent of more than about 1s 6d a week. On this basis, a modest cottage costing around £60 to build would not even repay capital cost in fifteen years, to say nothing of interest or repairs, even if it were constantly occupied by regularly-paying tenants. In the pauperized parishes of southern and western England, where many labourers were under-employed, casually employed, or existed only by Speenhamland 'doles' in aid of their wages, regular payment of rent was unlikely. In any event, many speculative builders had much more remunerative outlets for their activities in market towns, industrial villages and the spreading manufacturing towns.

The need, if it was to be met at all, would have to be met principally by landowners who were willing, for humanitarian, paternalistic or other reasons, to build labourers' cottages which would almost certainly not provide a return on capital commensurate with other possible investments. A few, it is true, had a remarkable and distinguished record in this respect, which will be considered shortly: the majority did not. During the prosperous years of the Napoleonic Wars, when farmers obtained unprecedented prices for their grain, much might have been done. Manor and farm houses were enlarged and embellished, but little attention was paid to cottages except for necessary repairs. In the post-war depression after 1815, when prices and profits slumped, the most obvious economies lay in reducing wages and building costs. But the wealth of the war years had bred new tastes and habits in the farmhouses of England and, in particular, the old practice of boarding farm servants with the farmer's family was found increasingly objectionable for social as well as economic reasons. Now that the farmer produced for the market, the less his household consumed the more he had to sell, and beginning in the last decade of the eighteenth century, labourers were increasingly put on 'board wages' and forced to live out. Inevitably, this increased the pressure on accommodation in existing cottages and villages. In this respect, the root cause of the rural housing problem was not so much, as Edward Smith believed, 'habitual national indifference'[17] as the habitual local indifference of landowners and farmers who recognized the need to house their cattle and horses adequately, but not their labourers.

In some parts of the country, especially unfortunate, the problem was not merely that cottage accommodation had failed to keep pace with the growth of numbers, but that it had actually contracted. This had happened for two main reasons. Since at least the eighteenth century the trend in landownership had been towards consolidation of holdings into great estates and large farms, appropriate for the new techniques of intensive agriculture. The process was accompanied, and furthered, by enclosures, which increased markedly after about 1760 and became rapid after the General Enclosure Act of 1801. In the redrawing of the parish map which came with enclosure, cottages which did not fit into the new plan might well be demolished. David Davies could complain in 1795 that 'Formerly, many of the lower sort of people occupied tenements of their own, with parcels of land about them, or they rented such of others . . . But since those small parcels of ground have been swallowed up in the contiguous farms and enclosures, and the cottages themselves have been pulled down, the families which used to occupy them are crowded together in decayed farmhouses with hardly ground enough about them for a cabbage garden.'[18] Even Arthur Young, the staunch advocate of enclosure, had to admit that in one parish 'Three small farmhouses have each been divided into three tenements . . . forty-five souls will now be found to occupy the dwellings which were before inhabited by fifteen'.[19]

Demolition of cottages was also sometimes encouraged by the operation of the Poor Law and the Settlement Acts. After 1795 the burden of increasing poor rates bore particularly heavily on great landlords who owned all the property in 'closed' parishes, and were assessed appropriately in order to support the local poor. An obvious economy was to demolish any cottage accommodation surplus to the labour needs of the estate in order to prevent settlement of 'immigrants' who might become a chargeable liability. An even less defensible extension of the same logic was virtually to depopulate an entire parish by the destruction of accommodation, and to draw labour from a neighbouring 'open' parish (that is, one in which there were many small proprietors) into which it was forced to migrate. The classic instance of this was at Castle Acre in Norfolk where the landowners in adjacent 'closed' parishes, 'persons of birth, education and station', had deliberately allowed cottages to become derelict, so forcing labourers into the already overcrowded and insanitary village of Castle Acre, 'the coop of all the scrapings in the country'; from here they now employed labour only as they needed it, and mainly in the form of 'gangs' of women and children.[20]

Such abuses of the Old Poor Law were well known to the framers of the Amendment Act of 1834.

[The owner of land] may, indeed, be interested in introducing them [poor law abuses] into the neighbouring parishes if he can manage, by pulling down cottages or other expedients, to keep down the number of persons having settlements in his own parish. Several instances have been mentioned to us of parishes nearly depopulated, in which almost all the labour is performed by persons settled in the neighbouring villages or towns, drawing from them, as allowance, the greater part of their subsistence, receiving from their employer not more than half wages, even in summer, and much less than half in winter, and discharged whenever their services are not wanted.[21]

Yet the abuse was far from being cured by the Poor Law Amendment Act. It was now made impossible to acquire a right to relief anywhere but in the place of birth, and since the parish was left as the rating unit the same incentive remained to discourage unwanted settlements. In 1846 a new Act charged the place of abode with the duty of relief, removal being impossible after five years' residence. In 1865, finally, the Union Chargeability Act transferred the burden of the poor rate from the parish to the Union, and at last removed the economic advantage of pulling down cottages; it did nothing, however, to encourage the building of new ones.

The discussion of the merits and demerits of 'closed' and 'open' parishes, which came to a head in the 1830s and 1840s, was central to the wider question of labourers' rents and tenures. Stated simply, the labourer might either be a freehold owner or a tenant of his cottage—in by far the majority of cases the latter. Ownership might have been acquired, exceptionally, by purchase of the freehold, and it was certainly not unknown for old-established families who had lived in the same parish for several generations to save up the necessary capital for outright purchase. This had been the case with the Arch family, when Joseph Arch's grandfather, 'a famous hedger and ditcher in his day', had gradually accumulated £30 to buy his cottage. Significantly, he and his wife had both been in the service of the Earl of Warwick, and had built up their inheritance while 'living-in' at the lodge, Warwick Park.[22] The alternative route to ownership was by self-construction on a piece of land granted by the lord of the manor or on the edge of a common waste or roadside with, at least, the acquiescence of the local proprietor. As we have seen, opportunities of this kind rapidly diminished as commons were enclosed and landowners became increasingly suspicious of squatters who might thereby acquire a settlement and become chargeable to the rates. Some cottages of this kind certainly survived from an earlier period into the nineteenth century, but it is unlikely their number increased significantly, except, perhaps, in a few late-enclosed counties.

The great majority of farm workers occupied their cottages as tenants of other owners. In the villages, many were owned by small builders and tradesmen who were able to command an economic rent because of the pressure on accommodation in 'open' parishes. On the land, cottages generally 'went with the farms'—that is, were included in the tenancy of the farmer, who then sub-let them to his own labourers or to others who applied for them.[23] In this case, the farmer might charge a rent which was merely nominal, or which covered his outgoings for rates and repairs, or which was the maximum his labourers could afford in relation to the wage he paid them. Exceptionally, he might charge no rent at all, or remit it on a selective basis as a means of retaining his most valued hands. Thus Mr Burgess, farmer of Tarrant Launceston in Dorset, reported with evident pride to the Poor Law Commissioners in 1843:

> I pay my labourers 8s a week, and taking task-work in, they get 11s a week on the average. A great many have no house-rent to pay, which is a saving of £2 or £3 a year to them; they all get fuel carriage-free . . . I let my labourers have from 20 to 40 perches of potato ground, according to their families . . . But they can't continue to have these wages if wheat keeps at its present price.[24]

This, by the standards of the day, was a generous employer and landlord. Where a farmer 'gave' a free cottage with the job he usually adjusted the wage accordingly, so that the labourer was little or no better off in real terms than when paying rent. But whether he paid rent or not, his position as an occupier was subject to the same fundamental disability, that he had no security of tenure and could be turned out and rendered homeless at a week's notice if he became redundant or if he merely offended his employer. For this reason, advocates of agrarian reform since the late eighteenth century had recommended that cottages and allotments should be let directly to labourers by the chief landlord, and not sub-let to them by farmers who took advantage of the situation to make additional profit. This would mean not only lower rents to the labourer, but greater security of tenure since his home would not be at the mercy of his immediate employer. Nathaniel Kent believed that landlords should provide specially capable labourers with larger cottages and three acres for cow-pasture, and that by so encouraging gradations among labourers, the broken bridge between the lower orders and the middle classes would be restored.[25]

How heavy the burden of rent was to families whose economic hold on life was always precarious can be assessed by reference to actual budgets which have survived from the period. In general, it can be said that rent was the next largest item of expenditure after food, but unlike food, clothing and other things, it was a fixed and regular incident which could not be varied in the light of circumstances. Thus, Sir Frederic Eden could rightly remark in 1797:

> It cannot be denied that the article of expenditure of a poor working family which, though not the heaviest in amount is, in effect, their heaviest disbursement, is their rent. It is an article of expense that has all the inconveniencies of a direct tax, and is often called for at the moment when it is most inconvenient to pay it.[26]

Eden collected details of the budgets of fifty-two agricultural labourers' families from many parts of England. Only five are listed as paying no rent, and, presumably, having 'free' cottages which went with their work. If Eden's households were anything like representative this suggests that only about 10 per cent of all cottages were rent-free at this period. In general, rents increased with family size, the obvious inference being that a family of seven or eight persons would need a cottage with two bedrooms rather than one, or, preferably, with three where such could be found. The budgets also disclose some important differences in rent between different parts of the country. In Bedfordshire the average was £1 15s 0d a year, in Cumberland £2 6s 0d, in Lincolnshire £1 10s 0d, in Norfolk £2 17s 0d, in Suffolk £2 10s 0d. On this evidence, rents did not precisely follow the usual 'north–south' distinction, Norfolk and Suffolk being the 'high-rent' counties, though not the 'high-wage' ones. But local differences were probably more important than regional ones, at this time at any rate. Within the single village of Hinksworth in Hertfordshire, cottages ranged from £1 5s 0d to £7 5s 0d a year, the latter being occupied by a family of eight where several children worked and the annual income was the exceptionally high £47. In general, in 1796, about £2 a year was the average cottage rent: less than 30s was a cheap one, and more than £3 a dear one.[27]

Between the 1790s and the 1850s the movement of cottage rents was undoubtedly upwards, though again, the degree of local variation makes precise quantification impossible. When Arthur Young carried out his surveys in the 1770s the average rent was 34s a year, or 8d a week; by the time of James Caird's investigation of 1850–1 it was 74s 6d a year, or 1s 5d a week.[28] Caird therefore recorded a rise of 112 per cent since 1770 as against a rise in wages of 34 per cent (66 per cent in the north, 14 per cent in the south), and although wheat had fallen in price, meat, butter and other foods had risen sharply.[29] Much of the rise in house-rent had occurred during the rapid inflation of the war years, as a witness before the 1824 Committee on Labourers' Wages made clear.

> The rent of cottages is so high that it is one of the chief causes of the agricultural labourers being in a worse state than they ever were; before the war, the average rent of cottages, with good gardens, was 30s a year; it is now in our neighbourhood commonly as high as five, seven, or even ten pounds per annum; and where cottages are in the hands of farmers, they always prohibit the labourers from keeping a pig, and claim the produce of the apple trees and of the vine which usually covers the house.[30]

This witness ascribed the rise to four main causes—the increase of population, the growth of the practice of 'boarding-out' labourers, the destruction of cottages, and early marriage which many contemporaries believed was induced by the Speenhamland system of poor relief.[31] He might have gone on to point out that the very common practice of parishes paying the rents of poor families was almost certainly a major cause of their inflation, since landlords could be reasonably confident that if they fixed rents too high for the labourer to afford, the parish would indemnify. In this way, property-owners who were assessed to the poor rate made sure that a proportion of what they paid came back to them in the shape of increased rents virtually guaranteed by the parish: without such an assurance, rents would have had to be adjusted, downwards, in relation to wages. Low wages and high rents were both consequences of the interference with market forces which the critics of the Old Poor Law were loud to condemn. The Commissioners of 1834 found the practice in many parts of the country 'nearly universal'. To quote only one instance, from Suffolk (a 'high-rent' county):

> The payment of rent . . . is unquestionably a very frequent way of giving relief . . . It is, in general, difficult to ascertain the length to which this practice is carried, as in the entry of the charge in the parish books it is

usually described as relief 'in distress' without specifying the purpose for which it is granted. There is no kind of property which gives a higher rent or of which the rent is better paid than that of houses occupied by the lower orders. When the landlord once adopts rigorous measures to enforce his demands, the parish takes good care that the payment shall afterwards be regularly made, under the plea of avoiding the expense which would be incurred if a whole family were thrown on it for support by being deprived of their goods.[32]

Rents in the 1840s still exhibited the same great variations that they had displayed fifty years earlier. Though, as we have seen, the average had probably doubled, some low rents of £1 15s 0d a year could still be found in Wiltshire, though £3–£4 a year was more general for three rooms. In Yorkshire rents ranged even more widely, from £1 a year for a one- or two-roomed shack to £7 10s 0d for a house with two living-rooms and three bedrooms, though £4–£5 was the typical amount paid.[33] Yet there was no evidence of any general improvement in the quality of cottage accommodation—on the contrary, the Reports of the 1840s reveal a state of decay, overcrowding and insanitariness which could scarcely be equalled by the worst slums of the industrial towns.

Much of this evidence came to light in the famous *Report on the Sanitary Condition of the Labouring Population* of 1842, for which Edwin Chadwick, Secretary of the Poor Law Commissioners, acted as editor and collator of the mass of material which poured in. In that it had been initially prompted by a violent outbreak of fever in Spitalfields in the winter of 1837, the enquiry was principally concerned with the health of town inhabitants, and the relationship between disease, poverty, bad housing and other environmental factors, but it also revealed much as to the sanitary state of the countryside and the effects of generations of neglect of rural housing.

Of the general picture of dirt, squalor, overcrowding and disease a few examples only must suffice. Near Tiverton, Devon, where malaria had recently broken out, many of the cottages were built directly on marshy ground, without flooring, or against the side of a damp hill; the sewers were all open, in some cases running immediately in front of the houses, 'and some of the houses were surrounded by wide, open drains full of all the animal and vegetable refuse'; roofs were of thatch, often rotten and saturated with wet.[34] Cottages in the Cerne Union, where typhus had occurred, were described as 'mere mud hovels . . . the mud floors of many are much below the level of the road, and in wet seasons are little better than so much clay'. In one family of six persons, two had the fever, one a boy of eleven years; the only 'bedroom' was a partly-boarded loft reached by a step-ladder, and the sick-bed was so near the edge of the space that in a fit of delirium the boy had jumped out of bed and fallen to his death below. In the neighbouring county of Somerset conditions were, if anything, worse. Here, 5,417 persons had died of fever in the previous year, many of them

from an area between Bristol and Bridgwater known as the South Marsh.
The cottages were situated close to stagnant dykes, and generally consisted
of only one room to a family; 'a pig-stye ... is frequently attached to the
dwelling, and in the heat of summer produces a stench quite intolerable'.
But so scarce was accommodation here that old poor-houses had been converted into a kind of barracks, one family to a room: 'here, filth and poverty
go hand-in-hand without any restriction and under no control ... the floors
are seldom or never scrubbed ... the walls never get white-limed ... the
windows are kept air-tight by the stuffing of some old garments'. At Todd-
ington, Bedfordshire, another fever spot, 'very few of the cottages were furnished with privies that could be used, and contiguous to almost every front
door, a dung-heap was raised on which every species of filth was
accumulated. Scarcely any cottage was provided with a pantry, and I found
the provisions generally kept in the bedrooms'. Again the medical officer of
the Epping Union stated that 'many of the cottages are neither wind nor
water-tight. It has often fallen to my lot to be called on to attend a labour
where the wet has been running down the walls, and light to be distinguished through the roof, and this in the winter season, with no fire-place
in the room.' Yet, as in the 1790s, the worst of all conditions were probably
still to be found in the border cottages of Northumberland and Durham.
The Vicar of Norham reported that they were

> built of rubble and unhewn stone, loosely cemented, and from age or from
> badness of the materials, the walls look as if they would scarcely hold
> together. The chinks gape in to ... admit blasts of wind ... the rafters are
> evidently rotten ... and the thatch yawning to admit the wind and wet ...
> window-frame there is none. There is neither oven, nor copper, nor grate, nor
> shelf, nor furniture of any kind ...

Conditions such as these, reproduced substantially throughout the
countryside and towns of Britain, were alarming enough to lead to the first
general attempt at sanitary reform in the Public Health Act of 1848. But it
would be wrong to conclude that these examples of gross sanitary neglect
represented the 'typical' living conditions of the rural working classes in the
1840s. Looking in detail at one county, Norfolk, Edward Twisleton, an
Assistant Poor Law Commissioner, discovered in 1840 that a very few
people still lived in the one-roomed hut, but the majority inhabited a two-
roomed house, perhaps with a lean-to 'back-house' serving as a scullery. In
a number of cases, a wash-house and bake-house stood apart, and served
two or three cottages. The greatest evil was the necessity of sharing a single
bedroom by a large family, who often endeavoured to ensure some privacy
by erecting an old curtain or a screen of garments across what was already
a small and stuffy room. But the 'yearly men' with responsible positions on
the farms could expect to live better than this—a three- or even four-
roomed cottage in which their wives added to scrupulous cleanliness 'a

degree of taste which was manifested by the table coverlet, the chairback net and the chimney ornament'. On some of the great Norfolk estates, like that at Holkham, a few 'model' four-roomed cottages had been built, giving exceptionally good accommodation, and furnished in an equally 'model' style:

> On the brick floors of the principal room there may be five or six strong wooden chairs, two or even three tables, a chest of drawers, and sometimes a clock. In the chimney-piece there may be bright brass candlesticks and neat pieces of crockery. On the walls pictures are not uncommon . . . the majority relate to religious subjects, such as the History of Joseph, of David, or of Christ. . . . Besides these, we may notice portraits very unlike the originals, among them Her Majesty and Prince Albert.[35]

These were the homes of the fortunate few, the men, like Joseph Arch and his ancestors, who had unusual skill as hedgers and ditchers or as ploughmen or carters, dairymen or shepherds, whom no good farmer could afford to have ill-housed and discontented. The poorest accommodation was occupied by the day-labourers—unfortunately, the majority of farm workers—and those increasing numbers for whom there was only irregular or casual work and who depended on the labour of their wives and children. The *Report on the Employment of Women and Children in Agriculture* of 1843 echoed and amplified the findings of Chadwick the year before. We read of twenty-nine human beings under one small roof, of the sleeping space of eleven adults confined to a single bedroom 10ft square, of tattered shawls constituting the sole partition between the sexes, of women delivered of children on the bare boards of crowded bedrooms, of holes in roofs, windows stuffed with rotten rags, and a score of other horrors. In the rural parts of Selby in Yorkshire, living-rooms were only 8–10ft square. Again, some of the very worst conditions were in Wiltshire, Dorset and Devon, where, Alfred Austin reported, 'the want of sufficient accommodation seems universal'.[36]

Such descriptions may occasionally be quantified with more precise statistics. In 1864 an enquiry was made into rural housing which referred back to conditions in 1851 and can, therefore, be taken as a reliable guide to the situation in mid-century. 821 parishes were surveyed in detail, scattered all over England: in them 69,225 cottages housed 305,567 persons, or 4·4 per cottage. Less than 5 per cent had more than two bedrooms, 40 per cent had only one; single-bedroom cottages averaged 4 persons per bedroom, the two-bedroom type 2.5 persons. But the statistics need to be seen in relation to size of rooms. The average amount of bedroom air space available per person throughout the sample was 156cu ft, compared with the legal minimum of 250cu ft allowed in common lodging-houses at the time. On this basis, a bedroom 10ft by 10ft with a 7ft ceiling accommodated on average four or five people.[37] Many 'bedrooms' must have been mere cubby-holes.

It was this aspect of overcrowding, and, especially, the overcrowding of bedrooms, which most excited the sanitary and moral concern of contemporary reformers. As Edward Smith put it:

> A man may carry his rheumatism, acquired from the sweating walls and 'heaving' floor of his ruinous dwelling, to a good old age; the peasant, gaining immunity from his open-air existence, may escape the noxious results of stagnant drains, and even of impure water; but it is his sleeping accommodation which produces the most insidious (and often fatal) results upon his health. Overcrowding has probably killed more than all other evil conditions whatever.[38]

As we have seen, the construction and room sizes of many cottages made overcrowding inevitable, and Chadwick's Report of 1842 was strongly of the opinion that 'from many districts . . . overcrowding has increased' due partly to larger family size and partly to the increasing sub-division of accommodation to separate families and lodgers. Much of this evidence, Chadwick believed, had only recently come to light with the formation of the Poor Law Unions after 1834, the previous censuses being defective in their counts of accommodation.

What such overcrowding meant in personal terms was documented the next year. At Stourpain, a village near Blandford, Dorset, a two-roomed cottage was occupied by a family of eleven. The single bedroom, 10ft square, contained three beds, one occupied by four sons aged 17, 15, 14, and 10, one by three girls aged 20 (twins) and 7, and the third by the mother, father, and two young children: there was no partition or curtain and only a single small window 15in square.[39] Mr Spooner, surgeon of Blandford, had recently treated three typhus patients, a woman and her two children, who were all lying in the same bed in an outhouse which contained a well and a large tub of pig-food: 'the floor was earthen, with no ceiling but the thatch of the roof'. At Milton Abbas each pair of houses contained on average 36 persons, or 9 to every two rooms, but this was as nothing compared to conditions at Studley where Mr Phelps, agent of the Marquis of Lansdowne who was responsible for taking the 1841 census, discovered 29 people in one cottage—'married men and women and young people of nearly all ages'. Ten children to one bed was reported from Kent, and as Mr Hart of Reigate, Surrey, put it, 'The great difficulty is to say at what age brothers and sisters do not sleep together in the same apartment, but generally until they leave home, be that at ever so late a period; many cottages have but one room, and the whole family sleep in one bed'.

Whether it was the physical or the moral effects of such overcrowding which most alarmed Victorian philanthropists is uncertain, but it was probably the latter. Their greatest anxiety was reserved for the mixing of sexes in a single bedroom which, if the contemporary accounts are to be believed, was productive of almost every kind of vice, licentiousness and bestiality. So, the Honourable and Reverend Sidney Godolphin Osborne, Rector of Bryanston, near Blandford:

> I do not choose to put on paper the disgusting scenes that I have known to occur from this promiscuous crowding of the sexes together. Seeing, however, to what the mind of the young female is exposed from her very childhood, I have long ceased to wonder at the otherwise seeming precocious licentiousness of conversation which may be heard in every field where many of the young are at work together.

In a very few cases, it was reported in 1843, two neighbours would arrange that all the men should sleep in one cottage, and all the females in another, but this was very rare. Mr Spooner, surgeon of Blandford, reported:

> The consequences of the want of proper accommodation for sleeping in the cottages are seen in the early licentiousness of the rural districts— licentiousness which has not always respected the family relationship. It appeared to me that generally the accommodation for sleeping is such as necessarily to create an early and illicit familiarity between the sexes, for universally in the villages where the cottages are the most crowded there are the greatest number of illegitimate children, and also the greatest depravity of manners generally.

So, too, the agent to the Marquis of Lansdowne spoke of the high incidence of bastardy in the very crowded village of Studley where cottages were rented at £3–£4 a year, but contrasted this with the high moral tone of the neighbouring village of Foxton where the Marquis let model cottages at half this price, and insisted that only one family should occupy a cottage: 'the labourers are a very different kind of people to those at Studley'. Many cases of immorality naturally came to the attention of the clergy. The Rev T. Harvey of Cowden, Kent, knew of cases of incest, 'but such instances have always been held in abhorrence by the labouring classes, lightly as they may view seduction, or even infidelity in a wife'. The Rector of Brede put the matter more delicately:

> I regret to state that too many young women are in a situation previous to their marriage which indicates anything but that sense of modesty which it would be desirable to find. I am thankful to say that there is no common prostitution in the parish.

Sexual licence was a major, though not the only moral, consequence of overcrowding. Cottages, it was often said, were such squalid and cheerless homes that husbands and young men escaped as often as circumstances would allow to the village inn or beer-shop where, for a time, they could forget the dirt, the discomfort and the crying of children. In this way, early intemperance was often the result of inadequate housing, and young men grew up to become drunken and irresponsible fathers. Equally, it was claimed, girls who were brought up in such homes, and who often had to engage in field-labour from the age of nine or ten, received no training in domestic skills and became slatternly, shiftless housewives on marriage. So the cycle of wretchedness was completed and perpetuated, and the quality of family life constantly deteriorated. Children who grew up in poor and overcrowded homes early learnt the language and ways of vice: when poverty drove them out to work at an early age these habits were confirmed. Men lost all ambition save the satisfaction of carnal lusts, and women who did not become sluts gradually sank into an endless round of pinching drudgery.

For those who had the strength of will and the intelligence not to succumb, the alternative was to leave, to migrate to the town or emigrate abroad, and the 'flight from the land' which became so marked a phenomenon in the period after 1850 had its roots in the domestic discomfort of the first half of the century. A contributor to the *Agricultural Gazette* in 1853 wrote:

> Home has no attractions for the young labourer. When he goes there, tired and chilly, he is in the way amidst domestic discomforts; the cottage is small, the children are troublesome, the fire is diminished, the solitary candle is lighted late and extinguished early . . . He naturally, then, goes to the public-house, where a cheerful fire and jovial society are found, and becomes a loose character . . . [40]

Part of the domestic discomfort which many labourers suffered—part, perhaps, of the explanation of their alleged intemperance and immorality—was the inadequacy of cooking arrangements under which the housewife laboured. Before enclosures, wood for firing could generally be picked up from commons and wastes and hedgerows, but by the early nineteenth century the sources of free fuel had disappeared in many parts of the country, and coal now had to be bought at a price, which, in the south of England, included the costs of long carriage. Already in 1797 Frederic Eden was suggesting recipes for 'artificial fire' and 'fire-balls' which included sawdust and chopped straw as well as coal; 'for the poorer sort, cow-dung mingled with sawdust and small coal' was recommended.[41] An expenditure on fuel of 1s to 1s 6d a week in the winter months was commonly reported in the 1840s, except in those cases where the labourer was allowed to cut free turf or the farmer undertook to pay the costs of carriage. Probably, as Count Rumford and others believed, much fuel was wasted on open hearths and in ill-designed chimneys, but few cottages were fitted with enclosed, cast-iron ranges, or 'kitcheners', which would heat water on one side of the fire and cook on the other, until after the middle of the century. The result was that for reasons of cost and convenience, the dietary pattern was adapted to one that required little cooking, but with serious losses to the nutritional value and palatability of the labourer's food.[42]

The whole nature of the labourer's environment—his home, his habits, his diet and his work—had debilitating effects on his health and physique. Contrary to the romantic belief that rude health engendered by an open-air life would bring him to a ripe old age, the labourer's chances of survival were notably less than those of other classes in the countryside. As Chadwick's Report showed, the average expectation of life in the rural districts of Wiltshire in 1840 was:[43]

Gentlemen and persons engaged in professions, and their families	50 years
Farmers and their families	48 years
Agricultural labourers and their families	33 years

Much of this mortality was due to the early deaths of children in over-crowded and insanitary cottages where, as we have seen, epidemic diseases like typhus and cholera could spread unchecked, but even in adult life confined and unventilated rooms made the labourer a prey to tuberculosis and respiratory complaints which often proved fatal.

Such facts were known empirically, if unproved statistically, long before the 1840s, and since the late eighteenth century a few landlords—usually, though not always, of great estates—had interested themselves in the provision of 'model' cottages for their labourers. The impulse was largely philanthropic, and it is no coincidence that the pioneer of improvement was John Howard who, in the 1760s, had reconstructed all the cottages on his estate at Cardington in Bedfordshire.[44] But the obstacles were formidable, and Howard's example was not contagious. In many areas a clean sweep was precluded by the property rights of individual owners or speculative builders, tenants themselves were often resistant to improvement, and above all, indifferent and absentee landlords whose primary concern was to draw rents from their estates could not be interested in schemes of cottage-building which were, more often than not, economically unprofitable. One of the main tasks of the reformers was to stress the moral responsibility of proprietors, and to seek to persuade them that there were tangible benefits in having a well-housed peasantry in terms of labour efficiency, nearness to work, and reduction of disease and of poor-rates.

Cottage improvement came to be strongly urged in the closing decades of the century by individuals like Nathaniel Kent, David Davies and Frederic Morton Eden, and in the Agricultural Surveys issued by the Board of Agriculture during the years of war. In 1800, for the first time, the Board offered prizes for the best plans of 'model' cottages, a device which was to be repeated with tedious regularity throughout the nineteenth century. Three years earlier, in 1797, the Society for Bettering the Condition of the Poor, of which the founders included Sir Thomas Bernard, William Wilberforce, the Thorntons and the Barclays, had declared its principal aim, 'to carry domestic comfort into the recesses of every cottage', and actively interested itself in cottage improvement and the provision of gardens and allotments. A closely similar clause was included in the objects of the Royal Agricultural Society, founded in 1838, and the Society's *Journal*, particularly in the 1840s and 1850s, devoted numerous articles to the subject of rural housing, requirements, costs and plans. The sanitary revelations of the 1840s added yet another spur to interest, and in the following years several semi-philanthropic cottage improvement societies were founded with the object of demonstrating that good rural housing could be supplied at a price which would give a modest return on capital. The best-known of these was the Windsor Royal Society, established in 1852 under the auspices of the Prince Consort who had been instrumental in exhibiting model cottages in Hyde Park the previous year. This Society paid an average dividend on capital of $4\frac{1}{2}$ per cent through the 1850s, the Hertford Society about 4 per cent, the Redhill and Reigate Society 5 per cent and the Hastings Cottage Improvement Society, founded in 1857, 6 per cent by its third year.[45]

The model cottage movement generally had as its object the building of sanitary accommodation which would provide, by the standards of the day, adequate space for living, cooking and sleeping, with separation, at the least, of parents and children and, if possible, of the sexes. There should also be sufficient storage space for food and tools, and, externally, a privy and pigsty preferably surrounded by a good-sized garden. The challenge of meeting these requirements at a modest cost attracted the interest of some leading architects, especially when the opportunity was presented of designing a group of cottages or even a whole model village. Thus, many cottages at Blaise, near Bristol, were designed by John Nash, the architect of old Regent Street, in 1809, the village of Nuneham Courtenay was rebuilt by William Mason, and both Sir John Soane and John Wood, the architect of Bath, published plans for labourers' cottages in the 1790s.[46] Many of the designs of the period were in the romantic, 'Picturesque' style, which viewed cottages as part of an idealized rural landscape and sometimes paid scant attention to the comfort of their occupants, as Christopher Holdenby pointed out in 1913:

> Only too often are the inhabitants made to suffer from the artistic sloping roofs and tiny windows. When one has no choice of bedrooms, gables and eaves are often a picturesque cruelty by every inch of height and light and air of which they deprive human beings.[47]

The comment was justifiable, yet even those cottages which suffered from the worst excesses of Gothicism were almost certainly healthier and more convenient than the generality of rural accommodation.

The model cottage movement was relatively unimportant as a contribution to the rural housing problem, but more so as an indication of ideals to which reformers aspired throughout the rest of the century. Designs ranged from simple, strictly utilitarian forms to elaborate 'Gothic' lodges which were more suitable for gentlemen's shooting-boxes than for the daily needs of labourers' families. Among the most modest were those of Nathaniel Kent, who believed:

> All that is requisite is a warm, comfortable, plain room for the poor inhabitants to eat their morsel in, an oven to bake their bread, a little receptacle for their small beer and provisions, and two wholesome lodging apartments, one for the man and his wife and another for his children. It would, perhaps, be more decent if the boys and girls could be separated, but this would make the building too expensive ...

The cottages were to be built either of brick or wood; the living-room was 12½ft square, the pantry 6ft by 4½ft, the cellar 7½ft by 6ft, and the two bedrooms 12½ft by 11ft and 12½ft by 7½ft. The cost would be £66 in brick, £58 in wood, and the suggested rent 5 per cent, about £3 a year.

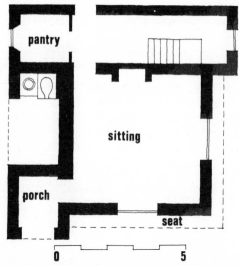

1 'Model' cottage plan. Ground floor of Diamond Cottage, Blaise; sitting room is c 15ft 6in (4·7m) square. Drawing by C. G. Powell based on information in *Nine Lithographic views of the cottages comprising Blaise Hamlet* published by T. Bedford in 1826

With small variations—the addition of a porch for shelter and the storage of tools, a third bedroom for large families, and an external privy—this remained typical of the models of the late eighteenth century, and, indeed, of the first half of the nineteenth. Some very simple designs by Thomas Postans in 1830 suggested a single-storey dwelling with a living-room 14ft by 13ft, two bedrooms 10ft by 9ft and two small store-rooms or pantries. Built of clay and straw walls and pole and thatch roofs, they would cost £35 a pair and yield a rent of £3–£4 a year each. Room sizes and requirements had apparently altered little, though it is noticeable that by

COTTAGES BUILT BY THE EARL OF LEICESTER.
AT HOLKHAM. IN NORFOLK.

The Rent for them (including Garden Ground) is 3£ 3s a year.

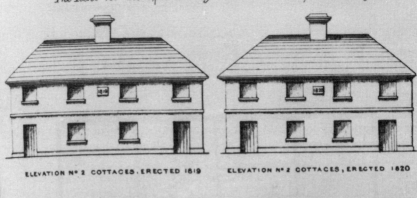

ELEVATION N° 2 COTTAGES. ERECTED 1819   ELEVATION N° 2 COTTAGES, ERECTED 1820

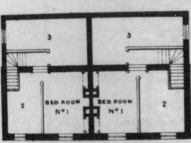

CHAMBER PLAN N° 2 COTTAGES, 1819.   CHAMBER PLAN N° 2 COTTAGES, 1820.

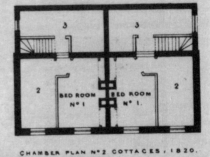

PLAN OF OFFICES N° 2 COTTAGES, 1819.   PLAN OF OFFICES N° 2 COTTAGES, 1820.

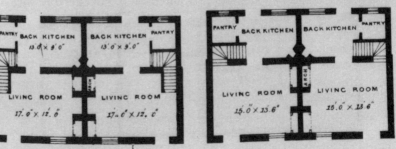

CROUND PLAN N° 2 COTTAGES, 1819.   CROUND PLAN N° 2 COTTAGES, 1820.

mid-century more attention was being paid to the need for adequate drainage, ventilation, water supply and sanitation. In particular, more care was given to the construction of floors and their height above ground level, the height of bedroom ceilings, the need to provide a privy and to separate the pigsty from the main house.

The effect of the campaign for labourers' gardens and allotments, which had been growing strongly since the 1830s, is also noticeable in the recommendations as to plot size, the usual suggestion being for a half-acre garden. Building costs (excluding land) in the 1840s had risen to around £40–£60 for two rooms and £60–£100 for four rooms, with yearly repairs averaging around 10s to £1 and generally reckoned at 1 per cent[48], but there was a very wide range with costs generally lowest in the North and highest in East Anglia and the South. At the very end of the period, in 1849, J. Young McVicar produced designs which set a new standard and approached more nearly to what would now be regarded as minimal requirements: a porch, living-room 14ft by 13ft, separate access to a scullery (kitchen) 9½ft by 9ft fitted with sink and boiler, a pantry 8ft by 6ft, a cupboard under the stairs and three bedrooms 14ft by 10ft, 9½ft by 9ft, and 9ft by 8ft; outside there was a coalhouse, privy and dustbin.[49]

Model cottages were, by almost universal opinion, successful in their objects of improving the sanitary and moral condition of the agricultural labourer.[50] There were a few critics who implied that the labourer was not worthy of them, and who pointed with scorn to their occasional misuse, much in the way that opponents of council housing in the 1920s raised the 'coal-in-the-bath' bogey. Russell M. Garnier voiced a typical complaint:

> Often enough I have bitterly experienced that the extra room provided, after much difficulty, is only regarded in the light of a potato store, or of lodger accommodation. The family still pigs together in the remaining sleeping space, on the plea that numbers supply that warmth which the expense of a coal fire denies.[51]

Or, as one disillusioned landowner put it: 'If you built a palace, and furnished it to match, you would scarcely induce the people to leave these places into which you would hardly put a pig to live.'[52]

But these were untypical views. Most contemporaries believed, with Chadwick, that improved cottages and the provision of cottage gardens or allotments produced moral regeneration, decreased pauperism, disease and drunkenness and increased contentment. In such surroundings the labourer would give up the beer-shop to cultivate his vegetables, the woman would

---

2   Estate cottage plan. Built at Holkham, Norfolk, by Earl of Leicester, 1820. The annual rent for a three-bedroom cottage in 1842, was £3 3s. Living room 15ft × 13ft 6in (4·6 × 4·1m). From *Report . . . from Poor Law Commissioners . . . into Sanitary Condition of Labouring Population of GB* published in 1842 by W. Clowes for HMSO

become a proud and capable housewife, and the children, observing the benefits of hard work, sobriety and thrift, would grow up to become industrious and honourable supports to their parents in old age. Private philanthropy, it was widely believed, could not be better applied than in the provision of improved dwellings.

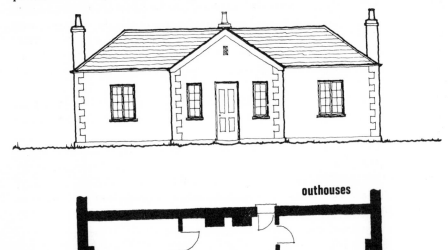

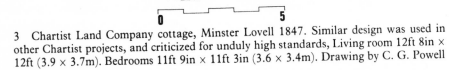

3   Chartist Land Company cottage, Minster Lovell 1847. Similar design was used in other Chartist projects, and criticized for unduly high standards, Living room 12ft 8in × 12ft (3.9 × 3.7m). Bedrooms 11ft 9in × 11ft 3in (3.6 × 3.4m). Drawing by C. G. Powell

A list of landowners who made significant contributions to model housing on their estates would include the Earl of Winchelsea in Essex, the Marquess of Buckingham at Gosfield, Joseph French at East Horndon and the Rev Mr Scott at Oakley, in Suffolk the Earl of Stradbroke and the Rev Mr Benyon, in Norfolk, at Holkham, the Earl of Leicester, in Cambridgeshire, the Duke of Rutland and Lord Dacre, in Northumberland, the Duke of Northumberland and Earl Grey, in the West Riding, Lord Wenlock, in Nottinghamshire, the Duke of Newcastle and, in Staffordshire Lord Dartmouth, to name only a few. It is noticeable that improved cottages frequently went with improved estates—that landowners who were interested in the new techniques of 'high farming', who rebuilt or renovated their mansions, laid out ornamental parks and home farms, were also often concerned to improve cottages, both because rows of derelict shacks were visually unpleasing, and because they recognized the responsibilities of stewardship. Moreover, such men were able to afford to subsidize uneconomic housing, commonly to the extent of 5 per cent a year.

However, although individual philanthropy of this kind was impressive at the local level, it was of little importance as a contribution to the national problem. The counties which had benefited most from such activities by mid-century were probably Bedford, Norfolk, Suffolk, Lincoln and Stafford, but even here there were notoriously black spots of open parishes where good example had not penetrated. Despite all the publicity and official encouragement which it received, cottage improvement remained exceptional, if not eccentric, and its products stood out as isolated oases in the general desert of neglect. As yet, no legislation had seriously invaded the sacred rights of property; economic and financial considerations alike militated against interference. Above all, perhaps, the labourer himself, imprisoned by his own poverty and ignorance, had not yet reached the point at which private discontent turns to public protest. Only in the decade of the 1840s was the 'problem' of rural housing coming to be identified, described and analyzed by the social investigators, and it would be many years yet before solutions could be proposed and decisions adopted.

3

THE HOUSING OF THE URBAN WORKING CLASSES

A proper assessment of the housing experience of the English town worker during the first half of the nineteenth century is a daunting and perhaps, as yet, impossible task. Although detailed local studies in recent years are beginning to assemble invaluable evidence, adequate data on a national scale are still not in existence. Town workers as a class had nothing like the relative homogeneity of farm labourers, and their housing conditions were infinitely more varied. Given the contrasts in standards of living between, say, a handloom weaver, a miner and an engineer, and the variations in regional building forms between a London tenement, a Nottingham back-to-back and a Durham miner's terrace, the difficulty is to know what the 'norm' was, or, indeed, whether the concept of a norm is useful where abnormality was so typical.

Nor can the historian of housing derive much help, for this period, from the parliamentary papers, official reports and enquiries which illuminated so many aspects of Victorian social life. Chadwick and his co-workers were concerned to identify, investigate and ameliorate the dirt, disease and squalor which the rapid growth of towns had magnified to intolerable levels; they were interested in houses only tangentially—as places where overcrowding transmitted disease, or where the lack of water or sanitation discouraged cleanliness and modesty. The public health reports are not, then, a major source of information on working-class housing, and where they did treat of the subject as such they tended to select the worst examples in their laudable attempts to shock public conscience into activity.

Architectural historians have also tended to avoid the subject of working-class housing, for the obvious reason that it was not 'architecture'. Their interest has focused mainly on the attempts of philanthropic bodies at the very end of the period to accommodate the working classes in 'associated dwellings' or tenement blocks, since these were sufficiently large either to be designed by architects or, at least, to offer scope for architectural form, construction and detail.[1] For the rest, architectural historians have tended to content themselves with easy, usually pessimistic, generalizations which

imply a deterioration from previously higher standards. Thus, a distinguished scholar of middle-class domestic style and taste has written of
working-class housing during the industrial revolution:

> The slave quarters of the Roman villa-house, the wattle-and-daub huts of
> Saxon serfs and medieval villeins, were better than [these] dank, brick boxes,
> designed and built by greed. Only the very cheapest materials were used.
> Bricks, far inferior in quality to those normally employed, were set in the
> poorest mortar . . . The new, excessively cheap bricks that were made in mil-
> lions, could compete in price with weather-boarding, so no more pleasant
> wooden houses were built after the beginning of the [nineteenth] century.[2]

The fact that brick had been regarded as the fashionable, luxury building
material no further back than the seventeenth century, and that from
almost every constructional point of view its properties were superior to
those of timber, is ignored. The serious and systematic study of nineteenth-
century vernacular building by architectural historians has only just begun,
but so far the limited results do not lend support to the theory of increasing
deterioration.[3]

With so much uncertainty and variety in the data, contemporary
observers and subsequent historians have had little difficulty in finding
examples which support their particular contentions. In the continuing
debate over the effects of industrialization on the standard of life of the
worker, housing has almost always been used as evidence for the
'pessimistic' argument, and even some observers who normally find
themselves among the 'optimists' have felt obliged to admit that in this
respect there were no immediate gains to the urban working class. The
original picture, copied scores of times subsequently, was first drawn by Dr
James Phillips Kay in his classic study of the Manchester cotton workers in
1832:

> The houses, in such situations, are uncleanly, ill-provided with furniture; an
> air of discomfort, if not of squalid and loathsome wretchedness pervades
> them; they are often dilapidated, badly drained, damp: and the habits of their
> tenants are gross—they are ill-fed, ill-clothed and uneconomical—at once
> spendthrifts and destitute—denying themselves the comforts of life in order
> that they may wallow in the unrestrained licence of animal appetite.[4]

Much of the evidence he drew on related to the poorest parts of the town
where Irish immigration was already having detrimental effects. But
already, in Peter Gaskell's *Manufacturing Population of England* (1833)
the particular has become the general:

> The houses of great numbers of the labouring community in the manufactur-
> ing districts present many of the traces of savage life. Filthy, unfurnished,
> deprived of all the accessories to decency or comfort, they are indeed but too

truly an index of the vicious and depraved lives of their inmates. What little furniture is found in them is of the rudest and most common sort, and very often in fragments—one or two rush-bottomed chairs, a deal table, a few stools, broken earthenware such as dishes, tea-cups, etc., etc., one or more tin kettles and cans, a few knives and forks . . . a bedstead or not, as the case may happen to be, blankets and sheets in the strict meaning of the words unknown—their place often being made up of sacking, a heap of flocks, or a bundle of straw . . . and all these cooped in a single room which serves as a place for domestic and household occupations.[5]

The 'extinction of decent pride' of which Gaskell wrote was an important and regrettable characteristic of a section of the urban working classes, especially of some of those who were forced to live, for one reason or another, in cellars, overcrowded tenements and insanitary 'rookeries'. Every town had its courts and yards and its half-criminal tenement quarters, and they rightly attracted the attention of the reformers, but the historian must try to avoid confusing the worst (or, for that matter, the best) with the average, and must be cautious about generalization. Frederick Engels, who was not normally given to over-optimism about the standard of life of the worker, observed with an accuracy unusual among his contemporaries: 'houses of three or four rooms and a kitchen form throughout England, some parts of London excepted, the general dwellings of the working class'.[6] William Cobbett, whose hatred of industrialization was second to no man's, noted in his *Rural Rides* that the Durham miners were well-housed: 'Their work is terrible, to be sure . . . but at any rate they live well, their houses are good and their furniture good'.[7] Again, homes of the skilled Coventry weavers are described in the *Handloom Weavers' Report* of 1840 as 'good, comfortable dwellings; some of them very well furnished; many have nice clocks, and beds, and drawers; some ornamented with prints: and some have comfortable parlours'.[8] And although the same *Report* reveals that the houses of the Yorkshire handloom weavers, a class now suffering the effects of factory competition, 'bore vestiges of better days', they still had 'all the marks of frugal housewifery—cleanliness, good order and regularity'.[9]

The starting point in the controversy must be numbers, and we have previously seen that while the whole population of England and Wales doubled during the first half of the century, the proportion of town-dwellers within that total rose from a third to well over a half. Urban population growth was, in fact, far out-pacing the total growth rate, rapid as that was: (Table 2). But the geography of urbanization reveals major differences in the rates of town growth, the fastest being in London and the Home Counties, the industrialized North-West, the West Riding of Yorkshire, the North-East and the East and West Midlands. Those areas where the industrial revolution first took root, like Manchester and the Lancashire cotton towns, had their fastest rates of growth early in the century: others, associated with the

'London going out of town – or – the march of bricks and mortar'. Runaway urban growth as seen by George Cruikshank, 1829. The countryside retreats before the onslaught of terraces (*British Museum*)

Brickmaking by hand in 1821; plentiful labour but costly transport (*Radio Times Hulton Picture Library*)

Influential 'model' hamlet. Diamond Cottage, John Nash, 1809. Plan shown as text illustration 1, page 49. Taken from O'Neil, Harding and Ashmead *Nine Lithographic Views of the Cottages Comprising Blaise Hamlet* published by T. Bedford, Bristol, 1826 (*City of Bristol Museum & Art Gallery*)

Rural decay: labourer's cottage near Blandford, 1846. The picturesque setting distracts attention from the decrepit roof (*Illustrated London News*)

Rural interior: Blandford
labourer's cottage, 1846.
Although not the poorest type,
deep cracks in walls and ceiling
indicate advanced deterioration
(*Illustrated London News*)

Tightly grouped dwellings in a
Bristol court in Albert Square,
not long before clearance c1936.
Date of building is uncertain
but window details suggest a
time early in the period, or
before; cellars are visible.
External walls are part brick
and part stone (*Environmental
Health Department, City of
Bristol*)

Inside and outside Manchester cellar dwellings in the 1840s. Not all streets were as well paved as this. Curved railings outside, and fairly generous ceiling height within, suggest that this example had perhaps slipped down the social scale since it was first built. Compare with Liverpool cellars in text illustration 4. From *Pictorial Times* c1847, reproduced in *Lancashire: The First Industrial Society* published by Helmshore Local History Society 1969

Goulstone's Buildings, a Bermondsey court standing condemned in 1914. This is a more ordered and less enclosed space than many courts: a unified development, not one which accumulated haphazardly (*Greater London Council*)

rather later developments of metal industries in the Midlands, grew fastest in the middle decades of the century. Thus, by the 1850s Manchester and Liverpool had almost ceased to grow, whereas Birmingham increased in the decade 1841–51 by 22·3 per cent, Sheffield by 22·4 per cent and Wolverhampton by 21·8 per cent.[10] In the period with which this chapter is concerned the housing problem tended to be concentrated in those towns which had either experienced the first impact of industrialization—like Manchester and the surrounding cotton towns—or, like London and Liverpool, were seaport magnets which attracted constant waves of migrants. In Manchester/Salford, which grew by 47 per cent between 1821 and 1831 alone, in West Bromwich which grew by 60 per cent and in Bradford which grew by no less than 78 per cent in the same period, over-crowding and a deterioration in housing standards were almost inevitable consequences of the explosive and unpredicted expansion of numbers. To that extent, the housing problem was a local, or regional, one, that affected different towns at different times in different degrees, defying national explanations and remedies.

TABLE 2

Growth Rates of Population in England and Wales, 1801–1851 *

	Total growth rate (per cent)	Urban growth rate (per cent)
1801–11	14·0	23·7
1811–21	18·1	29·1 (fastest)
1821–31	15·8	28·0
1831–41	14·3	25·0
1841–51	12·6	25·9

* Table based on C. M. Law's 'The Growth of Urban Population in England and Wales, 1801–1911', *Transactions of the British Institute of Geographers*, Vol XLI (1967), pp 125f.

By 1851 seven English towns had topped 100,000—Liverpool 395,000, Manchester 338,000, Birmingham 265,000, Leeds 172,000, Bristol 137,000, Sheffield 135,000, Bradford 104,000.[11] London, with 2,363,000 inhabitants in the inner (the old LCC) area, was so far ahead of the rest as to be of a different order, the greatest city in the western world and still growing by 20 per cent per decade in the middle of the century. Most of this increase came as a result of migration to the capital—perhaps a third from the Home Counties, a quarter from southern counties and East Anglia, the rest from further afield, from Ireland, Scotland and overseas.[12] In this respect, London was more cosmopolitan than any other English city, but all shared the same experience of large proportions of new arrivals, many of them first-generation town-dwellers, often coming from regions or countries of very different economic, social and cultural characteristics. In his study of the growth of South London, H. J. Dyos concluded that the 'cumulative effect [of migration] was to create urban communities in which not more than half their members had been born within South London at all',[13] though elsewhere he adds the important rider that the worst areas of London slums were not mainly migrant, but recruited largely from second-generation Londoners; non-Londoners tended to settle in the suburbs wherever possible, whereas Bethnal Green, 'one of the most extensive congeries of slums in the metropolis', was 88 per cent London-born in the 1880s.[14] Slum-dwellers generally were nomadic, constantly on the move within the vortex of a whirlpool, but not long-distance migrants.

From these general considerations of urban growth we turn to an examination of the quality hierarchy of accommodation that was available to the working classes.

CELLAR-DWELLINGS

It is debatable what constitutes the lowest level in this hierarchy, for within each category good and bad examples existed, but to the contemporary mind the cellar-dwelling seemed to represent the lowest general category of accommodation that was available for human, or sub-human, existence. Almost always, cellar-dwellings are described as dark, damp and airless, the abodes of the most feckless, improvident and intemperate sections of the population, and the sources of much of the dirt and disease which sullied the industrial towns. Very often they are equated with the period of rapid Irish immigration from the 1820s to the 1840s, with the implication that cellars had not been used for habitation by the English worker until his standard of living was forced down by alien influence. Undoubtedly, housing and sanitary horrors abounded in some of the cellars, and rightly attracted the reformers' indignation. One of the classic, much-quoted, accounts is by Peter Gaskell in his description of Manchester of 1833:

> Most of these houses have cellars beneath them, occupied—if it is possible to find a lower class—by a still lower class than those living above them. From some recent enquiries on the subject, it would appear that upwards of 20,000 individuals live in cellars in Manchester alone. These are generally Irish families—handloom weavers, bricklayers' labourers, etc., etc., whose children are beggars or match-sellers in conjunction with their mothers . . . These cells are the very picture of loathsomeness—placed upon the soil, though partly flagged, without drains, subjected to being occasionally overflowed, seldom cleaned—every return of their inmates bringing with it a further succession of filth—they speedily become disgusting receptacles of every species of vermin that can infest the human body . . . The Irish cottier has brought with him his disgusting domestic companion, the pig: for whenever he can scrape together a sufficient sum for the purchase of one of these animals, it becomes an inmate of his cellar.[15]

A similar report from Leeds in 1842 by a surgeon, Robert Baker, describes Irish cellar-dwellings which he had visited:

> I have been in one of these damp cellars, without the slightest drainage, every drop of wet and every morsel of dirt and filth having to be carried up into the street; two corded frames for beds, overlaid with sacks for five persons; scarcely anything in the room else to sit on, but a stool or a few bricks; the floor, in many places absolutely wet; a pig in the corner also; and in a street where filth of all kinds had accumulated for years.[16]

In one cellar in 'Little Ireland', Manchester, described by Engels in 1844, 'the water constantly wells up through a hole stopped with clay, the cellar lying below the river level, so that the occupant, a handloom weaver, had to bale out the water from his dwelling every morning, and pour it into the street'.[17]

For many reporters, like Chadwick and his co-workers, the chief evil of cellars was the sanitary one—that deficient ventilation, the near-impossibility of keeping damp floors and walls clean and warm, and the gross inconvenience, often avoided, of disposing of refuse made cellars the breeding-grounds of disease, especially of epidemic diseases such as typhus. Thus, the report of one of the medical officers of Liverpool:

> In the year 1836–7 I attended a family of 13, twelve of whom had typhus fever, without a bed in the cellar, without straw or timber shavings—frequent substitutes. They lay on the floor, and so crowded that I could scarcely pass between them ... yet amidst the greatest destitution and want of domestic comfort I have never heard, during the course of twelve years' practice, a complaint of inconvenient accommodation.[18]

Dr Duncan also reported on Liverpool cellars that they were sometimes so wet that the inhabitants had to take the door off its hinges and lay it on the floor supported by bricks, that sometimes the 'fluid matter of the court privies' oozes into them, and that in one, a well four feet deep into which such fluid drained was discovered below the bed where the family slept.[19] In this city, where Dr Duncan estimated the number of cellar-dwellers at 40,000 one in twenty-five of the population were annually attacked by fever, and the average age at death of 'labourers, mechanics and servants' was fifteen years compared with thirty-five years for 'gentry and professional persons'.[20]

Much of the evidence of the appalling condition of some cellar-dwellings dates from the period of sanitary enquiry and concern in the 1830s and 1840s, but cellar occupation was not new to that time or peculiar to the Irish. Wherever pressure on available accommodation was intense, and wherever there existed poor or destitute people who could not afford the rent of something better, cellars had been used for human occupation since at least the eighteenth century, and possibly much further back in time. In 1797, before the great wave of Irish immigrants to the town, Liverpool cellars already accommodated 9,500 people, one in eight of the population of 77,000;[21] it seems that here, unlike the Lancashire cotton towns, cellars were specifically built, from the first, for residential purposes, and were successfully defended against an attempt of 1802 to close them on the ground that, having a separate entrance and being detached from the rest of the house, they were more healthy from a sanitary point of view than rooms in a tenemented house which all communicated by a common staircase.[22] In Leeds cellars were certainly in use by the third quarter of the eighteenth century, but rapid building subsequently took place in the outer wards of the township, and population densities in the old centre declined.[23] Again, J. Aikin, reporting on Manchester in 1795, noted that in some parts of the town cellars were so damp as to be unfit for habitation,[24] implying that cellar-habitation was otherwise normal.

In fact, as has previously been suggested, there were bad cellars and not-so-bad cellars. At the best, they were basements like those used as domestic quarters in most middle-class houses. Approached by steps from an area fronting the street, these had a front door and a window only partly below street level, admitting a fair amount of light and ventilation. Cellars of this type usually had two rooms, one behind the other, with a fireplace in the front room which was used for living and cooking. Ceilings inevitably tended to be low—not more than 6ft in the Stockport area[25]—but the room sizes normally corresponded with those above—usually 15ft square in Leeds, with some smaller ones 14ft by 13ft,[26] but less generous in Liverpool at between 10ft and 12ft square.[27] Here, where cellar conditions were probably at their worst, the floors were typically 4–6ft below street level, many of them unflagged and provided only with brick 'stepping-stones' to keep feet clear of the wet. At worst, a cellar might have no proper window at all, merely a grating or high sky-light, and where the houses were built on rising ground the back cellar, if there was one, could be totally underground, without natural light or ventilation. 'In such places', wrote Dr J. Ferriar of Manchester in 1805, 'where a candle is required, even at noon-day, to examine a patient, I have seen the sick without bedsteads, lying on rags; they can seldom afford straw.'[28]

As always, the difficulty is to know what was the normal, what the exceptional. Liverpool cellars in the 1840s usually accommodated between 3 and 4 persons (the highest ratio was in Pitt Street ward, with 4·6 persons) implying that single-family occupation was the general rule, but given the fact that many appear to have been used by the aged poor, widows and spinsters, some at least must have contained larger families. In some there was undoubtedly gross and grievous overcrowding, especially in those reported cases where cellars were used as schools for 40–60 children, or as common lodging-houses for up to 30 Irish immigrants. A rent of 1s to 1s 6d a week seems to have been general throughout the industrial towns, the maximum around 2s for a larger, two-roomed basement. They were not always tenanted by the poorest, one in Chorlton-upon-Medlock being let at this price to a handloom weaver's family of seven whose joint weekly income was no less than £2 7s 0d. Here, the unpaved back cellar was occupied by the loom and was also used as a sleeping room.[29]

Cellar-dwellings were by no means universal, even in industrial towns. They were particularly characteristic of older industrial areas, and of the older parts of such towns. The newer cotton towns like Bury and Ashton-under-Lyne had very few. Nottingham, with many housing evils of other kinds, had only between 100 and 200 in 1831.[30] Birmingham had none, and Leeds comparatively few, with 555 in 1840 out of a total of 17,839 dwellings, accommodating about 3 per cent of the population. The highest proportions were in Manchester and Liverpool, which had early experienced the effects of overcrowding and of immigration. The statistics cannot be precise since it must sometimes have been in the interests of landlords or sub-letting tenants not to disclose, and it would probably be right to assume that the official counts erred on the low side. For Manchester the lowest estimate for 1840 gives as few as 3,571 cellar inhabitants;[31] the Select Committee on the Health of Towns (1840) reported 'nearly 15,000, being 12 per cent of the working population'; Peter Gaskell in 1833 cited 'some recent enquiries' which indicated that 'upwards of 20,000 individuals live in cellars in Manchester alone';[32] while Engels, after correctly pointing out that the official estimates referred to the town proper, continued: 'the cellar dwellings in the suburbs are at least as numerous, so that the number of persons living in cellars in Manchester—using its name in the broader sense—is not less than forty to fifty thousand'.[33] The weight of evidence is in favour of 15–20,000 cellar inhabitants of the central borough. The estimates for Liverpool are somewhat closer, the lowest being 24,072 for 1842 at an average of 3·29 persons per cellar,[34] and another for the same time being 38,000 out of a population of 175,000, or 22 per cent;[35] some even higher estimates are unauthenticated. Whatever the precise numbers, it is clear that, especially in Liverpool and Manchester, large proportions of the population regularly lived in semi-subterranean 'homes', which at best were unsatisfactory from a sanitary point of view and, at worst, were disgusting and offensive insults to humanity.

LODGING-HOUSES

It is arguable whether even worse conditions did not prevail in some of the 'common lodging-houses' which were to be found in all sizeable towns, but especially in those like London, Manchester and Liverpool where there were large numbers of migratory or transient workers. The problem was that while a single man 'on tramp' might not take too much harm from one or two nights' lodging in such places, they also sometimes accommodated whole families who could not find anything better for a week, a month or even a quarter. Intended primarily as very temporary shelter of a minimal kind, all too often they became permanent homes for the near-destitute and near-criminal classes and almost indistinguishable from a normal tene-mented house except by their gross overcrowding and promiscuity. Because, at their worst, such places represented an affront to decency and morality, and an invitation to disease, crime and prostitution, common lodging-houses early pricked the Victorian conscience and were the first category of working-class accommodation to come under legislative control.

Here again, there were bad and not so bad—or appalling and not quite so appalling—examples, though the generality seems to have been very bad indeed. Some examples may be cited. In Manchester, according to Dr Kay,

> The establishments thus designated are fertile sources of disease and demoralization. They are frequently able to accommodate from twenty to thirty or more lodgers who, reckless of the morrow, resort thither for the shelter of the night—men who find safety in a constant change of abode, or are too uncertain in their pursuits to remain beneath the same roof for a longer period. Here, without distinction of age or sex, careless of all decency, they are crowded in small and wretched apartments; the same bed receiving a succession of tenants until too offensive even for their unfastidious senses.[36]

An enquiry by the Churchwardens in 1832 revealed 267 such houses, which on an optimistic guess of only 20 lodgers a night would suggest over 5,000 occupants; given the very temporary duration of most tenancies, the number of occupiers during a year would, of course, be far greater. Peter Gaskell continues the description of Manchester lodging-houses:

> The extraordinary sights presented by these lodging-houses during the night are deplorable in the extreme ... Five, six seven beds—according to the capacity of the rooms—are arranged on the floor—there being, in the generality of cases, no bedsteads or any substitutes for them; they are covered with clothing of the most scanty and filthy description. They are occupied indiscriminately by persons of both sexes, strangers perhaps to each other, except a few of the regular occupants. Young men and young women; men, wives and their children—all lying in a noisome atmosphere, swarming with vermin, and often intoxicated. But a veil must be drawn over the atrocities which are committed: suffice it to say that villainy, debauchery and licentiousness are here portrayed in their darkest character.[37]

From many industrial towns came similar reports. After an outbreak of typhus fever in Leeds in 1851 had been traced to some users of lodging-houses, it was discovered that within a half-circle of a radius of a quarter of a mile from the parish church there were 222 lodging-houses accommodat-ing 2,500 people. They averaged $2\frac{1}{2}$ persons to a bed, and $4\frac{1}{2}$ to a room; only 40 houses were even moderately clean, and 6 were cellar-dwellings in a filthy condition.[38] It was some of these houses, situated in narrow alleys running out of the Kirkgate, which had been described by a Children's Employment Commissioner a few years earlier as 'mere dens, with no sort of comfort save a good fire . . . Several of the smaller brothels were visited, but they were mostly empty, the inmates being at the beer-shops or about the streets. They presented a far more cleanly aspect than the lodging-houses.'[39] Here, at least, brothels and lodging-houses were apparently separated, but in many cases they were described as almost synonymous. In Birmingham, as reported by Chadwick, lodging-houses could be divided into three types—mendicants' houses, houses where the Irish resorted, and houses in which prostitutes live or frequent; there were also some Italian lodging-houses used by street-musicians 'with their stock of musical instruments, monkeys and other small animals . . . as well as one which is frequented only by the Flemish or German broom-girls'. And in Durham the medical officer reported, 'I have known 40 persons half-clothed, lodged in one of those wretched dwellings, three or four lying in one bed upon straw, and only a single counterpane to cover them, which is never changed. Excrementitious matter was allowed to accumulate and lie about the rooms in all directions, the stench being most revolting.'[40]

London, with its vast migrant population, had the largest number of all with accommodation, Henry Mayhew estimated, for 10,000 in the 'low lodging-houses' and for another 70,000 in the somewhat more respectable sorts. The difficulty, discovered by those who tried to administer the Lodging Houses Act of 1851, was how to define (and therefore control) accommodation which ranged from filthy, overcrowded thieves' dens and 'twopenny brothels' at the bottom to reasonably comfortable boarding-houses for artisans, commercial travellers, clerks and students at the top. Philanthropy took the direction of trying to provide 'model' lodging-houses for the respectable and industrious, who could thereby be separated from the corrupting influences of the rest. Because of the scarcity of accommodation in London, unmarried mechanics were sometimes sleeping six, eight and even ten to a room, and respectable married men with families were also obliged to live, cook, eat and sleep in one small room. It was for this reason that the Society for Improving the Condition of the Labouring Classes included in its first building scheme of 1845 in Clerkenwell, east of Gray's Inn Road, model lodging-houses of from one to three rooms, and followed this widely-acclaimed venture by building a five-storey model lodging block in George Street, St Giles, at the heart of the most notorious slum area in central London. Here was provided accommodation for 104 'inmates' in large dormitories partly partitioned to give some privacy to a small bed-space; there was a communal living-room, kitchen, wash-house and water-closets on each floor. For such amenities, the rent of 2s 3d a week was modest, though more than the 2d or 3d a night paid in the private lodging-houses, and for family accommodation much higher rents had to be charged by the model societies—5s a week in St Pancras for a living-room, kitchen and bedroom. It is not surprising that another, in Compton Street, Soho, had 'unfortunately not been well filled'.[41]

The model societies, of which more later, had never intended to provide sufficient lodging accommodation for the population as a whole, still less to solve the much larger housing problems which were beginning to be identified in the 1840s. They saw their role as exemplary—to demonstrate that healthy accommodation of some specific types could be built and let at a price which would yield a modest return, usually fixed at 5 per cent, on capital. Even with the resources of organized philanthropy behind them, they were by no means always successful even in this limited objective, though their early concern with the social and sanitary evils of the common lodging-house did help to direct public attention to the problem and to bring about some amelioration in the following decade. Some local authorities, London and Liverpool included, had already taken powers to control the worst abuses before the first general Common Lodging Houses Acts, pioneered by Lord Shaftesbury, reached the statute-book in 1851–3. Although many still escaped the inexactitudes of the law, in theory lodging-houses were now required to be registered and inspected: minimum standards of space, cleanliness and ventilation were laid down, basement bedrooms forbidden and unmarrieds of the opposite sex separated.[42]

TENEMENT HOUSES

The line between the lodging-house and the tenemented house is shaky and indefinable. In theory, lodging-houses were intended for short-stay migrants and tenements for longer-term tenancy by the week, month or quarter, but in practice such a distinction often broke down. Tenement-ing—the subdivision of existing houses into separately-occupied floors or single rooms—was the most obvious response of owners and tenants to increased pressure on accommodation, and by nature was usually informal and unrecorded. One of the few attempts to investigate the duration of working-class tenancies was made by the Statistical Society for the parishes of St Margaret and St John, Westminster, in 1840, where it was shown that of 5,366 houses no less than 1,834 had been occupied for periods of one to six months only,[43] but even this does not take account of sub-letting. In all large towns, the poorer working classes whose employment was ill-paid, casual or interrupted by unemployment, or who devoted an undue propor-tion of those earnings to self-indulgence, occupied not houses, but rooms or a room in houses.

Although this was true of all towns, it was especially the case in inner areas of rapidly-growing towns, which often provided the kind of houses most suitable for subdivision and strategically placed in relation to employ-ment opportunities. The origins of the slums—what contemporaries in the mid-nineteenth century usually referred to as 'rookeries'—were to be found here, in St Giles, Saffron Hill, Ratcliffe Highway, Jacob's Island, Berwick Street (St James's) and Pye Street (Westminster) in London, in Oxford Road, Little Ireland, Parliament Street, and 'Gibraltar' in Manchester, in Boot-and-Shoe Yard in Leeds, in the 'shambles' behind Long Row in Nottingham, and in the heavily-tenemented districts in Durham, Newcastle and Barnard Castle. Some, like those of the North-East, had been originally designed as flats in tenement blocks, intended from the first for multioccupation. Some were new houses built as single-family accommodation, but too large and highly-rented to attract family tenants. George Godwin drew attention in 1859 to the 'vast numbers' of new houses rising up in London 'built with a view to their occupation by single families which, even from the time they are finished, are let as tenements to two or three', finding them especially common in an area to the west of Caledonian Road.[44]

But, in general, tenements were to be found in existing, and often old, houses which had once accommodated families of substance, if not affluence, but which had now sunk to rooming-houses of an infinite variety of respectability and disreputableness. They were part of the process of town decay in which, from the late eighteenth century onwards, the better-off classes had begun to desert the noise, dirt and smell of overcrowded city centres for the peace and social homogeneity of the suburbs, leaving behind a vacuum that was quickly filled to overflowing by waves of fresh migrants. In a literal sense, much tenement housing was residual—what had been left over and abandoned after the needs of the more prosperous had been satisfied in newer, more salubrious, districts. The consequence was that 'streets of houses originally erected for the "merchant princes" are now in ruins . . . now the abodes of the improvident, the vagrant, the vicious and the unfortunate'.[45]

The origins and processes of rookery-formation were admirably and graphically first described by Thomas Beames in 1850.[46] There was an analogy, he believed, between 'these pauper colonies and the nests of the birds from whom they take their name; the houses, for the most part, high and narrow, the largest possible number crowded together in a given space—common necessity their bond of union'.

There were, Beames believed, rookeries which had been so almost from the first—like Agar Town which had been occupied by a 'squalid population, originally a band of settlers who seem . . . to have squatted there'. There were whole districts of new houses which were 'mere lath and plaster', so badly built and lacking in amenities that almost immediately they became dilapidated slums. But, like Rawlinson, Beames believed that many rookery houses were old, the former homes of the prosperous.

In the dingiest streets of the metropolis are found houses, the rooms of which are lofty, the walls panelled, the ceilings beautifully ornamented, (although the gilding . . . is worn off), the chimney-pieces models for the sculptor. The names of the courts remind you of decayed glory—Villiers, Dorset, Buckingham, Norfolk, telling of the stately edifices which once stood where you bow beneath the impure atmosphere of a thickly-peopled court . . . The most aristocratic parishes, as they are termed, have a background of wretchedness, and are too often so many screens for misery.

He next proceeded to describe in detail the conditions of life in some half-dozen London rookeries. In St Giles, lying just off New Oxford Street, there were many Irish 'who annually seem to come in and go out with the flies and the fruit', while the native residents of the area were mainly labourers who had come to London to seek work—costermongers, dog-breakers, hawkers of sprats, herrings, cheap prints and toys, street-sweepers, thieves, tramps and vagrants. In one room, only 6ft by 5ft, eight people slept; in one house the average number of persons to a room was twelve, in another seventeen. In many rooms there was no furniture beyond a single bedstead for a family, and in some only straw or shavings spread out for a bed.

It was gross overcrowding of this kind, and the dangers to health and morality which accompanied it, that most concerned contemporaries. Although national statistics of housing density could apparently demonstrate constancy, and even slight improvement, over the first half of the century, the detailed investigation of particular areas, streets and houses occupied by the poorer working classes showed, as Chadwick constantly affirmed, increasing overcrowding and deterioration of living conditions. The twenty-seven houses (averaging five rooms) in Church Lane, Westminster, had housed 655 people in 1841, but 1,095 people in 1847, an increase in density from 24 to 40 persons per house in six years. Part of the explanation here was 'improvements' in the area, which had demolished some old property to widen streets and had thereby concentrated the population into the remaining ones—a phenomenon to be repeated throughout the century in the cause of commercial development and railway construction.

The subdivided house was especially subject to such deficiencies as a lack of water supplies, an adequate number of privies, and proper arrangements for sanitation, sewerage and removal of refuse, and all too often it lacked any supervision from absentee landlords who saw little need to maintain or repair property which never wanted for tenants. One privy to 380 inhabitants, 'placed in a narrow passage, whence its effluvia infest the adjacent houses', did not deter the poor from living in Parliament Street, Manchester, nor did the filth from gas-works, bone-works, tanneries, tripe and catgut factories render uninhabitable the 'crazy labyrinth of pauper dwellings' known as 'Gibraltar'[47]: of 6,951 houses in Manchester, as reported by Dr Kay in 1832, 960 were in need of repair, 1,435 were damp and 2,221 required privies.

Tenement houses of this kind, scarcely distinguishable in the hierarchy of quality from cellars and lodging-houses, were a direct consequence of housing maldistribution, of pressure for accommodation exerted in localized areas where the only possible response was subdivision. It was always cheaper and quicker to subdivide than to build, especially in central areas which were usually already heavily built up and where land prices were forced up by commercial competition. A substantial part of the new urban population—the part which had to be very near its work and could not afford the rent of a whole house—was therefore absorbed first by overcrowding. At the other end of the earnings scale, some highly-skilled workers were undoubtedly improving their standards of accommodation and comfort in the period, occupying some of the 60,000 new houses in 200 miles of new streets which, Mayhew reported, were built in London between 1839 and 1851, or the respectable artisan suburbs and villages which were now developing at a suitable distance from the crowded cores of midland and northern industrial towns. But 'filtering up' of those below did not happen on any significant scale, mainly because of the nature of their employment and their low and irregular earnings: the poor could not exercise any real choice, and, like flotsam, they constantly eddied back and forth but ended up in the same places. Shaftesbury estimated later in the century that there were between 60,000 and 70,000 migrant Londoners who never stayed longer than three months in one place, but simply 'deposit their filth and go'. James Pennethorne said in 1840 that the worst slums were not inhabited by workers—'I should think they get their living as they can . . .'[48]

Room density seems to have gone with occupation, and crowded living conditions were related to the general structure of the labour market. Relevant statistics for the first half of the century are lacking, but it would not be unjustified to argue from a survey of 1887 when it was found that in the poor parish of St George's nearly half the working men and their families occupied single rooms or less (one-third were out of work and a quarter earned less than 19s a week), compared with the respectable parish of Battersea where two-thirds of families occupied three or more rooms and earned more than 25s a week.[49] The big jump—the first step towards social distancing and the 'respectability gap'—was the transition from one room to two, for two rooms implied a separation between living and sleeping, and the further possibility of separating parents from children, or adult males from adult females. Two rooms were the irreducible minimum of respectability, the difference between a home and a mere shelter: with two rooms one could begin to take pride, to cook and clean, furnish and decorate, comfort and cherish the family.

Many, perhaps most, of London's working class had no more than this. Rent was necessarily second in priority to food, and when half or two-thirds of all income went to this alone, a rent of 2s 6d to 4s a week for two rooms was all that most labourers and semi-skilled workers could afford. Beyond

this, one progressed to a whole floor of three or four rooms which, Mayhew
reported in mid-century, would cost 5s to 7s a week; he had known a skilled
carpenter to rent a whole house at £70 a year, but only by sub-letting most
of it into apartments.[50] In London, rooms were the norm of working-class
housing, but in the provinces as a whole there was no one norm, only for a
particular town or for a particular part of a town. In Chadwick's report of
1842 some of the worst overcrowding—and, therefore, the most tenement-
ing—was in Manchester, Liverpool, Ashton-under-Lyne and Pendleton in
the north-west, and in Durham, Gateshead and Barnard Castle in the
north-east. In Liverpool many working-class houses had a single 'day-room'
with two bedrooms above, which were often separately let; in Durham 'the
great bulk of the working-classes inhabit . . . tenements, and they seldom
occupy more than two rooms, many only one'; in Barnard Castle about
four-fifths of the weavers and half the rest of the labouring poor lived in
rooms in large, tenemented houses, each accommodating fifty or sixty
persons, with one privy for five or six houses; in Gateshead the 'indigent
class' were accommodated in small, ill-ventilated rooms each containing a
family, and often lodgers, totalling seven to nine persons. In such towns
tenement living for the poor was normal and inescapable. So, too, in Leeds,
where 'not one half of the working-classes . . . occupy . . . above two rooms,
one for living in and one for sleeping in, called "the lodging room" '.[51] But
elsewhere most men in regular work expected to occupy not rooms, but a
house, and regarded anything less as a descent into destitution.

Life in divided houses was not necessarily squalid, though it was almost
certainly lacking in amenities like water and sanitation, and was always
exposed to the vagaries of near neighbours with whom facilities had to be
shared. Common complaints were about the state of shared territories such
as staircases, landings and privies, noisy, dirty and drunken neighbours, the
neglect of repairs by absentee landlords, the behaviour of children and
animals. But inside her own domain a 'respectable' housewife could sometimes preserve astonishingly high standards against all the temptations to
sloth and fecklessness. Henry Mayhew, in describing the homes of three
London costermongers, all of whom lived in tenemented houses, found
much to praise in one, inhabited by an old woman and her son and
daughter. They lived in a large, airy first-floor room ('The "drawing-room"
as she told me, laughing at her own joke'), well lighted by a clean window,
the coke fire burning bright and warm and a savoury-smelling dinner of
stew about to be served. The mantel-piece was adorned with a row of bright
tumblers, wine-glasses and Staffordshire pottery figures: the walls were
decorated in four different papers, there was a long dresser against one wall
containing clean blue plates and dishes, a stained chest of drawers and a
silver gilt Dutch clock 'which might be relied on with the greatest safety'.[52]
Here were provident people, teetotallers all, with a regular trade which
allowed for domestic planning and even gave a small margin for occasional

luxuries. In the other two cases there were varying degrees of poverty, dirt and squalor, the bed on the floor, the inevitable broken window-panes covered with brown paper or stuffed with balls of rags.

From the tenant's point of view the economy of overcrowding lay in the fact that for a very small sum, usually from 1s 6d a week upwards, he could buy a room providing minimal shelter and a base for work: from the owner's viewpoint, a tenemented house was an admirable investment. According to Thomas Cubitt, most belonged to 'a little, shop-keeping class of persons who have saved a little money in business . . . I think very few persons of great capital have anything to do with [poor people's houses] at all';[53] and James Hole calculated that 'the poor wretches who lodge in the miserable dens of St Giles pay rents averaging £6 [a year] per thousand cubic feet—as much as is paid for the most aristocratic mansions in London'.[54] His point was that those with irregular earnings, or with improvident habits, often paid as much for one room as a respectable working man paid for a cottage, and that the chief beneficiary was the landlord. But in London, Beames believed, many rookeries and their tenements were the hereditary property of country magnates who maintained upon the proceeds their 'costly establishments of hounds and horses', while others belonged to corporate bodies, to public charities, deans and chapters, and endowed schools. The real criminal, in his view, was the 'middle-man'—'the broker, the crimp, the tallyman'—who interceded and broke the relationship between lessor and lessee, engrossing the bulk of the profit to himself. 'The houses are let out, and under-let again and again, so that there are several links between the owner and the occupier—the latter perhaps not knowing the name of the former.'[55]

A rent of 1s 6d to 2s a week represented the minimum that would buy a single room of the poorest description in London in mid-century; 2s 6d a week was more normal in central areas. The writers on domestic economy seem to have accepted that this was the most that could be spared out of the budget of an unskilled or semi-skilled worker, one in 1824 suggesting 2s 3d out of a wage of £1 1s 0d (the wage at which Sir Robert Peel found plenty of recruits for the Metropolitan Police). In 1841 Bosanquet allocated 2s 6d out of an unskilled wage of 15s a week, but where the family size rose to husband, wife and five children he calculated that 4s a week would have to go to rent, and that the wage would need to be 30s; even at this level 'the wages . . . are wholly expended, leaving $10\frac{1}{2}$d for clothes, beer, medicine, tools and other accidents and contingencies'. These were 'ideal' budgets, allocating every penny in a rational, economical way, but they indicate the gulf between a family of two children and one of four or five—the difference between one room and two, and between a rent of 2s 6d and one of 4s–5s. The actual budgets collected by Le Play in 1855 make it clear that for a London working man to rent a whole house was exceptional. Only a working cutler, whose budget is £1 16s 9d a week, does so, occupying a small house in Whitefriars Street for 7s 9d a week: it is described as damp and sunless, but has water laid on in the cellar and 'latrines', and the furniture, which includes a carpet put down on Sundays, is valued at £26 10s 0d.[56] Here we are in a different world from the labourer at 15s to 20s a week.

BACK-TO-BACKS

The types of working-class accommodation so far described—cellars, lodging-houses and tenements—were not specifically designed as such: they were strictly residual, left over and adapted from their original use as family dwellings for better-off classes, and because never intended for multi-occupation, necessarily lacking in the requisite amenities. In this respect the next house-type upwards in the quality hierarchy—the back-to-back—should have had distinct advantages in that it was intended from the first for occupation by a single working-class family. Some, it is true, possessed a third storey intended as a workroom, some had a cellar which was sometimes separately let, and many accommodated the occasional lodger—but essentially the back-to-back of 'one down and one up' or 'two down and two up' was the speculative builder's answer to the mass demand for urban working-class housing which was economical of land and materials, easy and quick to build, and yet would provide an identifiable house with minimal amenities such as a cooking-range or fireplace in the kitchen, possibly one in the bedroom, some storage provision and shared water and privy. As a house-type it was not necessarily inferior or undesired. Commonly it had more space than a farm labourer's cottage, was built of more sanitary materials, usually brick and slate, had a boarded upper storey reached by staircase rather than ladder,[57] a flued chimney, windows that opened, and so on. Compared with older tenement houses, room sizes tended to be smaller, but a back-to-back did have the great advantage of its own front door and comparative privacy within the house. And although condemned almost unanimously by the sanitary reformers, there is some evidence of working-class preference for the back-to-back on the grounds that while it provided a structurally separate dwelling, it had the advantages of warmth and community neighbourliness.[58] Its long survival in some northern industrial towns and cities—it was still being built in Leeds in 1937—suggests that there were cultural as well as economic reasons for its persistence.

The classic description of the back-to-back was given in Chadwick's report of 1842:

An immense number of small houses occupied by the poorer classes in the suburbs of Manchester are of the most superficial character; they are built by the members of building clubs, and other individuals, and new cottages are erected with a rapidity that astonishes persons who are unacquainted with

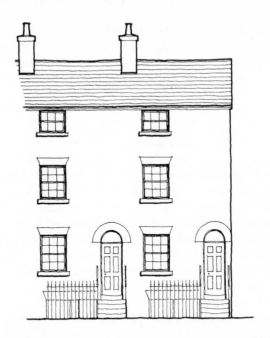

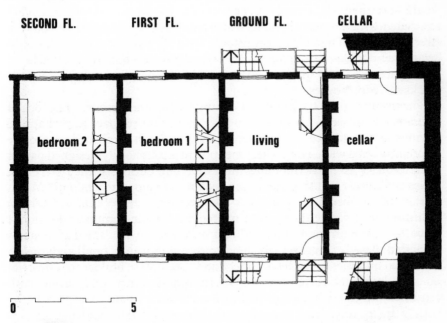

bedroom 2　　　bedroom 1　　　living　　　cellar

0 ⌐⌐⌐⌐ 5

4　Classic back-to-backs of 1843. Duke's Terrace, Liverpool, had back-to-back houses on three floors built over single room cellar dwellings. Room size 12ft 6in × 10ft 9in (3·8 × 3·3m). Drawing by C. G. Powell based on information supplied by J. Hunter of Liverpool their flimsy structure. They have certainly avoided the objectionable mode of forming underground dwellings, but have run into the opposite extreme, having neither cellar nor foundation. The walls are only half brick thick, or what the bricklayers call 'brick noggin', and the whole of the materials are slight and unfit for the purpose ... They are built back to back; without ventilation or drainage; and, like a honeycomb, every particle of space is occupied. Double rows of these houses form courts, with, perhaps, a pump at one end and a privy at the other, common to the occupants of about twenty houses.[59]

It makes clear the essential features—that they were built in double rows, each house having only a front wall, containing door and windows, which was not a party wall, but being joined to other houses at the back and sides: there was therefore no back door, and no windows or ventilation except on the front face. This determined the plan of the house, which could normally only be one room deep as there was no effective way of lighting an inner room, although some examples have been found of a back room using 'borrowed light' from an unglazed aperture from the front room. 'One down and one (or two very small) up' was, therefore, the simplest use of the available space, with variations of a cellar and an additional attic storey. A 'two up and two down' implied a double-fronted house with rooms either side of the door, or, rarely, at the end of a terrace, a through house which would not then be a back-to-back at all. In layout, it was normally associated with a 'court' plan, in which the 'back' house faced not on to a street, but on to a narrow court, usually 10–15ft wide, across which would lie another double row of houses. Privies and pumps would be situated here, having access, as did all the court houses, from narrow passages between blocks of front houses.

The origins of the back-to-back are uncharted and obscure. The idea of building one house to back on to another in a confined space is, perhaps, so obvious as not to need a discoverer, and no doubt happened in a quite unpremeditated way. The earliest mention of a consciously-designed pair of back-to-backs is in Bermondsey in 1706, but curiously they were not artisans' houses, and the type never became common in London.[60] M. W. Barley, the historian of vernacular architecture, believes that it would be unhistorical to blame the speculative builder for the dominant position it came to occupy in many midland and northern towns: 'the design stems from that of earlier cottages which had only one entrance, [and] underneath the visual qualities given by architect and speculative builder to industrial housing lay solid social traditions'. In the sixteenth and seventeenth centuries the English cottage had evolved from a single room to a house with a living-room and perhaps a scullery downstairs and one or two bedrooms above. This separation of living (including cooking and eating) from sleeping came to be desired and normal in the eighteenth and nineteenth centuries south of the Border, though not north of it, and the back-to-back was merely a rather crude attempt to give expression to this ideal for a mass market at low cost. Rural labourers' cottages without back doors ('blind-backs') were common enough. So also in some Pennine valley towns were 'back-to-earth' houses, built against steeply sloping hillsides, and sometimes used as a 'foundation' for 'through' houses or 'back-to-backs' above. The 'back-to-earth' was an interesting transitional type, which in the hierarchy of housing quality should probably rank between the cellar-dwelling and the true back-to-back.[61]

In this sense, the back-to-back did not represent a deterioration of previous standards so much as an improvement in the slow continuum of vernacular housing. House for house, it was almost certainly better than its rural predecessor, and better than the former accommodation of the urban working class. The outstanding disadvantage of the back-to-back lay in its inadequacy of amenities and in the fact that its external environment was degraded by the close proximity of so many houses, and, consequently, so much humanity, densely crowded together 'in narrow courts and confined streets [where] the means of occasional exercise and recreation in the fresh air are every day lessened as ... buildings spread themselves on every side'.[62]

The court system was, in fact, almost inseparable from the back-to-back, although in origin it too was an inheritance from pre-industrial times. The use of land behind existing buildings—yards, gardens, orchards and so on—for more houses was an obvious use of a scarce resource: such houses could conveniently be grouped round small, closed courts, having access to the existing streets by alleys or passages. What was new in the early nineteenth century was the imposition of a formal, rectilinear plan on this informal structure, and the conscious designing of acres of back-to-back housing which fitted so easily into a court pattern. Between the two extremes—the small, isolated court of six or eight houses built behind a row of shops and the fully-developed estate of hundreds of back-to-backs built on new urban land—there was, of course, a line of evolution. First, isolated courts behind existing buildings were often linked by alleys to make an intercommunicating system, so forming a warren of passage-ways through a densely built-up internal area. From this, it was sometimes possible to elongate the original square courts, so that something like an irregular secondary street system emerged, though constantly broken and changing direction to accommodate existing buildings. The final stage of the process was the opening-up of one or both ends of the courts to give better access from the streets, and to meet, in part, the objections of sanitary reformers that narrow, enclosed courts were a danger to health by not admitting free access of air.

In a back-to-back development planned on vacant ground the rectilinear grid plan could be imposed from the first, with adaptations necessitated by changes in ownership and field or plot shapes, and here it was also possible to insert occasional 'through' houses into the terrace in order to better ventilate the courts. However justifiable environmentally, the mixing of tenants of markedly different income levels was not widely acceptable, and by the 1860s, when building by-laws were beginning to be effective in many towns, the idea was generally abandoned in favour of tighter controls over the width of courts, sanitary arrangements and so on. By this stage, the back-to-back estate had become an area solely of single-class housing, and earlier industrial and commercial uses had become separated, except for the occasional corner shop or public house. Minor, but significant, architectural differences between 'street-side' and 'court-side' houses continued, however, symbolizing nice social distinctions: street-side houses frequently had decorated door and window arches and lintels, string-courses and plinths, while court-side houses were usually devoid of any embellishment.

The back-to-back was essentially an urban, industrial type, and though they probably occurred sporadically in London (there is a reference to what seem to be back-to-backs in Alfred and Beckwith Rows, Bethnal Green, by Dr Southwood Smith in 1838), their existence south of Birmingham was exceptional. Bristol had very few, the through terrace being the normal type from as early as the 1830s. But in the Midlands, the West Riding and South Lancashire towns they were in regular use from the late eighteenth century onwards, and in some they became the almost universal type. Nottingham probably had a higher proportion than any other large town—between 7,000 and 8,000 out of the total of 11,000 houses in the 1840s, consisting of two, and sometimes three, rooms on successive storeys, each about 11ft square, and with a small closet under the stairs for coal and food.[63] Leeds, by 1886, had 49,000, constituting 71 per cent of all houses, built at between seventy and eighty to the acre; Sheffield had 38,000 by 1865, and there were great numbers in Birmingham, Manchester, Liverpool, Bradford, Huddersfield, Batley, Keighley, Dewsbury, Halifax, Todmorden, Pudsey and Chester-le-Street.[64] The predominance of the West Riding is noticeable, especially in the later half of the century, by which time many towns elsewhere had banned further back-to-back building by by-laws—Manchester in 1844, Nottingham nominally in 1845 but effectively in 1874, Bradford in 1860, Liverpool in 1861.

There are no very obvious reasons for this concentration in certain areas. Although, as Beresford has pointed out, it was commonest and persisted longest in the wool textile towns, it had no functional role in the industrial process there,[65] though in Nottingham, Hinckley and other Midland hosiery towns a third storey was often used to accommodate knitting frames. In Leeds, where so many were built, land was not dearer than elsewhere where none were built, and within Leeds itself they were put up equally on dear and cheap land. Nor was their construction determined by building materials, since although most were of brick, Pennine stone was also used. The reasons for their apparently random distribution are almost certainly local. In Leeds they fitted neatly into the size of existing fields and the pattern of landownership, in Nottingham they were an obvious solution to the problem of a town which could not expand its area because of the existence of common rights on several sides—but we need to know much more about the circumstances of particular towns before generalizations can be hazarded.

It was, despite its extreme monotony on a large scale, a surprisingly adaptable building form. At its smallest and meanest it provided merely one small room on top of another, the typical ground floor area in Sheffield being 150sq ft, giving rooms of about 12ft square. In Nottingham, as we have seen, they were often only 11ft square, but sometimes with a third storey used as a workshop, or as both workshop and second bedroom; in Leeds they tended to be slightly larger with an overall plot size of 15 by 15ft, and consisting of a cellar, a living-room (known as the 'house') and an attic chamber. In Liverpool, too, there was usually a cellar, a kitchen 10–12ft square, and two small bedrooms above. In Birmingham, some back-to-backs designed for a superior artisan class had cellar, ground-floor kitchen, a chamber floor and an attic above. Beyond this, the back-to-back could only expand laterally, with a room either side of the front door and corresponding rooms above, but this was a rare and expensive form, using almost double the conventional 12–14ft frontage. Other variations were sometimes determined by topography, as in steep West Riding valleys where four-storey terraces at two levels, the lower one being 'back-to-earth', were sometimes used.

Internally, the back-to-back provided minimal privacy, minimal separation of domestic activities, facilities for cooking by an open fire or, increasingly by mid-century, by a small iron range containing oven and water-boiler, rooms which could be heated and, to some degree, ventilated (despite the constant criticism of contemporary sanitary reformers of 'no through ventilation', single-aspect rooms are not in themselves unhealthy), and a home on which a 'respectable' housewife could lavish considerable care and pride—cooking, cleaning and polishing, whitening doorsteps and window-sills, and so on. Its outstanding defects were its lack of proper amenities—almost certainly no piped water-supply to each house, except in Nottingham and one or two other favoured towns, its shared and often neglected privy at some distance from the house, the lack of adequate services for refuse removal from unpaved courts and alleys and, even where communal wash-houses were provided, the absence of open ground to hang out washing to dry, necessitating the use of lines across the dirty streets. The way in which such houses were used has been described for Sheffield, a town with a generally comfortable working class and better-than-average housing:

> The cellar was not normally inhabited. The daily activities of the family were
> concentrated in the living-room, which served as kitchen, scullery, dining-

room, living-room, as wash-room and bathroom, and on wet days the clothes were hung up in it to dry. The room was usually paved with flags, its fireplace was filled with an oven for baking, with a side boiler for hot water, and there was also a dished slopstone with a lead pipe into the sewer or the street channel. The cooking was done on 'grindle-cokes' (worn down grindstones) placed in front of the fire.

In the chamber, a room with a boarded floor and fireplace, slept husband and wife and the younger children. The attic at the top was a low room, no more than seven feet high and often with sloping ceilings, and had only a low window. It formed the sleeping apartment of the older children and, if necessary, the lodger.[66]

It was a logical, virtually inescapable, use of restricted space, but Hole records that some families inhabiting rather better houses, evidently with social pretensions, lived in the cellar, and reserved the ground-floor room as a parlour which was 'scarcely ever used, except perhaps on Sunday'.

The rent of the most modest two-roomed back-to-back in mid-century was from 2s 6d a week upwards. A larger, four-roomed house, such as might be occupied by a textile factory worker with several children, cost 3s 6d a week in Manchester, taking rather more than one-eighth of the earnings of around 25s, and, if coals at 1s 6d a week are added, one-fifth.[67] In Leeds, a great many did not exceed 3s a week since at this level rate-relief was claimable by the landlord and there was a natural inducement to keep rents down to this, though some larger Leeds back-to-backs were rated at as much as £20 a year in 1866. Building costs in Liverpool for the smallest type with cellar were about £80, plus land at £1 per square yard adding from £25 upwards. Normanby's abortive Bill of 1841, which would, *inter alia*, have outlawed the building of back-to-backs, was opposed by a Liverpool witness on the ground that it would raise the cost of the cheapest house from £96 to £119, and that of a third-class house, generally occupied by skilled artisans, from £141 to £179: such increases would have to be reflected in the rents charged. The Town Clerk of Leeds also opposed the clauses, arguing that it would drive the working classes into lodgings.[68] Here was the real rub, and the rock on which attempts to ban the back-to-back foundered for many years in some towns. The working classes could not—would not, some said—pay more than 3s–4s for the rent of a house, on the principle that though they might be able to afford more in good times, they would certainly not be able to do so in bad. Equally, if costs rose, more houses would become untenanted, and house-building would not then attract investors' capital. Higher standards might be socially desirable, but were economically impracticable.

'THROUGH' TERRACED HOUSES

For most town workers in the first half of the century the quality hierarchy ended here. For a few, and, by the middle decades, a growing number of skilled artisans, it extended to a higher level—that of the 'through' terraced house, with two ground-floor rooms and with light and access at both front and back: it followed that there would also be some small area of private space—garden or yard—at the rear of the house with entrance from a continuous alley running behind the terrace. In London, Bristol, parts of the Potteries and elsewhere the simple through terrace had long been the typical building form, and was never replaced by the back-to-back. Unlike the back-to-back, it was no new form, being a direct descendant of the Georgian town terrace and of even earlier groups of rural cottages. As a building type it was more spacious and flexible than the back-to-back, giving two living-rooms and two bedrooms above, with the extra possibilities of attic and cellar, and the additional advantage from a sanitary point of view of an individual privy at the bottom of the yard or, more often, groups of two or four privies shared by a number of houses. It was, in fact, the increasing preoccupation with privies—at this time usually 'dry' closets which depended on the regular removal of 'night soil' neutralized by earth or ashes—that largely determined the grid-iron street and back alley layout of terraces, giving convenient access to the 'night-soil men'. Only when waterborne sewage systems brought the WC into the house could alternative layouts be devised.

Internally, the terraced house could provide substantially more space, privacy and segregation of functions. Two living-rooms allowed for a separation between the domestic chores of cooking and washing in one, and eating and living in the other, encouraged in the artisan class by the fact that wives did not normally work outside the home, and could devote more care and time to domestic duties. For the socially pretentious, the front room often became the 'parlour', transformed from its original use as the principal sleeping-room to a 'state' room, containing the best furniture and used only occasionally for entertaining and ritual purposes. In this case, the parlour was not the focus of family life, but the ideal, which proclaimed to the world through its lace-curtained window and revealed objects the cult of respectability. Upstairs, the two or three bedrooms allowed a more or less proper separation of the sexes, a family with several adolescent children making a third bedroom almost obligatory and an attic room a valuable asset.

The through terrace was a much more flexible form than the back-to-back, and lent itself to a process of natural evolution. The house frontage continued to be narrow, since this minimized external walls and maximized party walls for economy, and this determined the plan of one room behind the other as opposed to two rooms fronting the street, but it was still possible to extend the depth of the house into the rear yard by the addition of a scullery annexe. The need to avoid blocking light to the rear room was solved by keeping its window to one side, and building the annexe only partially across the rear wall. The annexe could then be lighted by a window on the side or end. Single-storey annexes of this kind, provided with a sink and boiler which allowed a separation between washing and preparation functions and the cooking and eating functions of the kitchen, were becoming common in upper working-class and lower middle-class districts by mid-century. From this, it was only a short step to further elaboration—the incorporation of the yard WC into the annexe and the addition of a second storey over it to provide a third, small bedroom. The ultimate stage of development, reached only after mid-century, was to widen the frontage by three or four feet to provide a narrow hall and separated staircase, and to deepen the house still further by providing a kitchen, wash-house and WC all within the annexe. This then gave two living-rooms as well as the kitchen, and up to four bedrooms, each with independent access.

The terraced house in a respectable part of town or in one of the new inner suburbs, involving a weekly rent of 5s–7s 6d, and more in London, represented the upper limit of working-class housing in mid-century. At this level it was possible to accommodate a family in seemly decency, to enjoy the comfort of one or two rooms from which the dirtier, smellier household tasks had been banished, to entertain friends and visitors in a parlour which announced not only respectability but some degree of refinement—in short, to pattern a home life along the lines which the early Victorian middle classes were busily creating for themselves. In the hands of a competent builder, the house itself could even reflect some taste and discernment in internal fittings such as doors, fireplaces and joinery, but, more especially, in its external street façade, where the Georgian traditions of symmetry, restraint and simple but effective detail had not yet been wholly destroyed. Considerable attention was often given to well-proportioned sash windows (rarely bay-windows before 1850), to door-mouldings, lintels, string-courses, iron-work and other decorative features which were still generally executed in broadly 'classical' rather than 'Gothic' forms.

WORKSHOP HOUSES

The precise point at which class distinctions in terms of housing can be drawn for this period is uncertain, and, again, almost certainly local. Terraces continued to be fashionable for the wealthy in London long after they had lost class elsewhere, for example. But the next stage upwards in the quality hierarchy—the semi-detached house—seems to have been uniquely middle-class at this time and unattainable by urban manual workers unless they had made the transition to some kind of commercial or professional occupation. Two further types of working-class housing do need mention, however, both of which lay outside the normal domestic accommodation. In many parts of the country where domestic industry was carried on, especially in the domestic textile areas of the Midlands and North, houses survived from the pre-factory age, and continued to be built at least until the middle of the century, which combined the functions of home and workshop. The handloom-weavers of Yorkshire and Lancashire, the hosiery-knitters of Nottinghamshire, Derbyshire and Leicestershire, the silk and

5   Workshops over dwellings. Four small back-to-back houses with loomshop over, Halifax Road, Rochdale. Internal dwelling size 18ft 8in × 16ft 6in (5·7 × 5·0m). Many buildings of this sort had external stairs to upper floor workshops. Most, like this pleasing stone-built example, were readily identified by their numerous large windows. Drawing by C. G. Powell

ribbon-weavers of Coventry, Macclesfield and Spitalfields, the nail-makers of Birmingham and district, shoe-makers, glove-makers, straw-plaiters and other local craft-workers scattered throughout the country used their homes as workrooms as had their ancestors for generations before, and where the nature of that work required special machinery or working conditions these could have important effects on the form of the structure.

R. W. Brunskill has shown that the effects of domestic industry on the home passed through two stages—first, the modification of the living-room to accommodate machinery such as handlooms or knitting frames, second, the provision of a separate room for a workplace, either as a ground-floor annexe or as an additional storey. Such modifications might be made to existing cottages, or might be incorporated into new houses built in blocks or in short terraces.[69] As these hand trades were gradually superseded by factories, the houses reverted to purely domestic use and only became noticeable by the survival of such features as the unusually wide third-floor windows of Nottinghamshire hosiers' houses. The requirements for domestic textile workers were good daylight, derived from windows extending as far along the wall as structural stability would allow, and often on both long sides of the room, unobstructed space for working, storage accommodation such as a loft in the attic room above the machinery, controlled ventilation where the work demanded a smoke- or dust-free atmosphere, and access for raw material sometimes provided by a 'taking-in hole' and hoist. Where outside workers were employed, or where the working accommodation was separately let, there might be separate access by an external stairway, and in some cases the weaving-lofts of several adjoining houses were allowed to run together to form a long, continuous workshop.

Houses used for domestic industry span the quality hierarchy from top to bottom. Given a reasonable separation of working from living in a large or purpose-built house, and given a prosperous state of trade with good and regular earnings, the quality of life of a domestic worker could in nearly every respect be more comfortable than that of a factory worker. Samuel Bamford, visiting the home of a flannel weaver near Rochdale in 1844, found a house about 24ft by 21ft in area, containing a living-room with good oak furniture—chests of drawers, couch chairs, pictures and needlework—a kitchen, a parlour (still used here as a bedroom), a cellar and two chambers above, the larger of which was also the workroom containing a couple of looms, a warping-mill, jennies and other implements besides 'a good bed in an old-fashioned black oaken bedstead'. Despite the admixture, everything in the house was bright, neat and thoroughly clean.[70] But in the large towns and industrial villages, especially where the industry was now in decay in the face of factory competition, conditions were far otherwise.

In Nottingham in the 1840s, where upwards of 40,000 worked at hosiery, lace and bobbin net, the government commissioners commented that 'in comparison with these wretched places, factories are Elysiums'.[71] Cases were reported where fifteen to twenty children were crowded into a low garret 12ft square, working fifteen hours a day for a pittance: when the girls reached womanhood and married, they were 'as uneducated for wives and mothers as if they had been brought up in the Sandwich Islands'. In Lancashire towns the majority of cotton handloom weavers worked in cellars 'sufficiently lighted to enable them to throw the shuttle, but cheerless because seldom visited by the sun. The reason cellars are chosen is that cotton requires to be woven damp ... I have seen them working in cellars dug out of an undrained swamp ... and water therefore running down the bare walls . . .'[72] In Spitalfields, the district inhabited by the silk weavers was described as one of 'ruinous buildings, streets without sewers, overflowing privies and cesspools and open ditches filled with a black putrifying mass of corruption . . . There are streets and alleys from which typhus fever is never absent the year round'. Here, often in single rooms, lived and worked the silk weavers whose fabric was so delicate that cracks in the window-frames were carefully pasted over to avoid exposure to the atmosphere. And in the Birmingham nail-making trade a government commissioner reported in 1840, 'I never saw one abode of a working family which had the least appearance of comfort or of wholesomeness, while the immense majority were of the most wretched and sty-like description'.[73] Whatever the effects of domestic industry on home life may have been in the past, there can be little doubt that by the first half of the nineteenth century they were disadvantageous for all but a favoured few, and that the ultimate separation of work from home was a condition precedent to the development of a decent home life for the vast majority of industrial workers.[74]

EMPLOYER HOUSING

A second type of working-class accommodation which also defies categorization because it could be either very good or very bad was that provided by factory or mine employers for their workforce. Since the late eighteenth century, employers had been faced with the problem of attracting labour to new factory sites located outside existing towns and therefore requiring the provision of accommodation, and, in some of the larger establishments, employing several thousand workers, whole communities were developed with shops, schools, churches, libraries and recreational facilities, which form an important chapter in the history of town planning.[75] We are concerned here only with the housing aspects of such schemes, which although of varying quality, were generally of a higher standard than that provided by speculative builders, partly because good housing was designed to attract and retain an industrious, moral labour force, and partly because, unlike most privately-owned property, it was not necessarily expected to show a normal rate of return on capital. In this respect, employer housing often had a philanthropic aspect, favoured by 'model' employers who, without accepting Robert Owen's political philosophy, recognized that the provision of a decent environment for their workers was both a social obligation and an economic advantage.

At worst, some employers provided low-quality housing for which they charged average or higher-than-average rents, exploiting a monopoly position in the same way as their truck-shops did. This was particularly the case in remote coal-mining villages where, according to John Simon, the settlements were 'foul, priviless, ill-watered, unscavenged, overcrowded lairs' and the interiors of the houses filthy and unfurnished. Here, short leases, often for only twenty-one years, and exorbitant ground rents charged by the landowners, appear to have discouraged coal-owners from providing anything more than minimal shelter.[76] But in the textile areas of the Midlands and North, factory-owners seem generally to have been disposed to provide above-average housing, unless it is that only the better examples are now known. The records of Burr's Mill, near Bury, from 1800 to 1803, show that nineteen of the twenty-five families employed there lived in the firm's houses. They paid only 1s 3d a week for a two-roomed cottage in a row of back-to-backs, but had the advantage of nearby allotments rented at 2s 6d the year. Much better accommodation was provided for his 300 workpeople by Thomas Ashton at Hyde, where the cottages had sitting-room (parlour?), kitchen, scullery and either two or three bedrooms and a walled yard outside.[77] At a meeting of the British Association in 1837, Mr Ashton disclaimed any benevolent intention by stating that 'for every shilling of money he had laid out in providing comfortable and respectable dwellings for his workpeople, and furnishing them with conveniences, he received a very liberal interest'. At Turton, near Bolton, Henry Ashworth gradually enlarged and improved his cottages after an outbreak of 'malignant fever' among the workpeople had disclosed the filthy and overcrowded state of their dwellings: he ultimately found the best size to be a living-room 15ft by 9ft, a back kitchen of the same size, and three bedrooms. 'These houses were sought after with the greatest avidity, and families allowed to remove to them as an especial favour; the increased rent of 1s to 1s 6d per week was a small consideration . . . where the income was from 24s to 50s or 60s per week, as is frequently the case with families employed in manufactories.'[78] The Ashworth cottages come out very near the top of the quality hierarchy. Each house had its private, walled backyard with a separate lavatory (Ashworth condemned back-to-backs); kitchens were fitted with water-boiler and an oven by the fireplace, and there was piped water to the 'slop-stone' from 1835 onwards. When Lord Ashley visited them in 1844 he found mahogany chests full of good clothing, beds with a proper complement of blankets, sheets and quilts, and many bedrooms with bed- and window-curtains and strips of carpet. The return on the cottage property was 5·2 per cent, less than that on the factories.[79]

By the decade of the 1840s, employer housing and community experiments—more often planned than realized—were becoming almost a fashionable pastime of the enlightened. Idealized schemes for commuter satellites of London and for model towns like Victoria proposed by James Silk Buckingham were mirrored on a smaller and more mundane scale by the railway towns such as Wolverton, Swindon and Crewe built by the companies alongside their junctions and engine works. Most of these were only fully developed after the middle of the century, but Wolverton in Buckinghamshire became an engineering centre for the London and Birmingham Railway in 1838 and by 1849 had a population of 1,400. A contemporary description reads:

> It is a little red-brick town composed of 242 little red-brick houses—all running either this way or that way at right-angles—three or four tall red-brick engine chimneys, a number of very large red-brick workshops, six red houses for officers—one red beer-shop, two red public-houses, and, we are glad to add, a substantial red schoolroom and a neat stone church ... in short, the round cast-iron plate over the door of every house, bearing the letters L.N.W.R., is the generic symbol of the town.[80]

The houses were plain two-storey terraces with annexes and rear access from a back lane, but end-of-terrace three-storey houses gave some architectural pretensions to the composition.

Crewe, developed by the Grand Junction line during the 1840s, was a much larger and more ambitious undertaking with a proper categorization of housing for different social grades:

> First, the villa-style lodges for superior officers; next, a kind of ornamental Gothic constitutes the houses of the next in authority; the engineers domiciled in detached mansions, with accommodation for four families, with gardens and separate entrances, and, last, the labourer delights in neat cottages of four apartments, the entrances within ancient porches.[81]

Each house had gas, and a backyard privy emptied by the Company, and the town had a good range of social and educational amenities. House elevations were a good deal more pretentious than at Wolverton.

Swindon grew up as a by-product of Brunel's London to Bristol line after 1842, and within ten years 243 cottages had been built to designs reputedly of Sir Matthew Digby Wyatt. They were small, in stone terraces running in straight east–west lines, but the streets were wide, the houses had small front gardens, and although the backs were cramped and badly organized with the inevitable alley access, some care was given to the visual effect of the front elevations. Its drainage system and water supply were hardly those of a model community, however, as a serious outbreak of typhus fever in 1853 was to show.

PHILANTHROPIC HOUSING

Such developments, limited and misguided as some of them were, were potentially of great significance as attempts to plan the urban environment instead of leaving its growth solely to the play of market forces. Quantitatively, they supplied homes for, at most, a few thousand workers, but, more importantly, they provided examples of what could be achieved in terms both of housing standards and of environmental quality by the exercise of conscious thought and imagination. The same comments apply to the more specifically philanthropic attempts of the 1840s to remedy the

problems of squalor and overcrowding in London. They began in 1841 with
the foundation by the Rector of Spitalfields of the Metropolitan Association
for Improving the Dwellings of the Industrious Classes which, although it
aimed at building on some scale by attracting commercial investment,
deliberately limited its profits to 5 per cent per annum, its declared object
being to provide 'the labouring man with an increase of the comforts and
conveniences of life, with full compensation to the capitalist'. Significantly,
the capitalist was not greatly interested, for in the next four years only
£20,000 was raised. The Association eventually commenced building in
1847 in Old St Pancras Road with a block of family dwellings—21 two-
roomed and 70 three-roomed tenements, built on the principle of the
enclosed staircase system. An even larger scheme in Spicer Street,
Spitalfields, of tenements for 40 families and a model lodging-house for 300
men was completed in 1850. Soon after this, however, the Association
seems to have experienced financial difficulties. Its high building standards
resulted in sets of rooms in Old St Pancras Road costing £160, and by 1853
its annual dividend was down to an unattractive 1½ per cent. The solution
which it had attempted—high-density blocks in central areas of London,
providing self-contained flats of two and three rooms with associated
sculleries and lavatories—was so costly that it was available only to the
artisan class who, as transport facilities improved in the later nineteenth
century, could afford to live in the healthier suburbs anyway. Densities of
1,100 to the acre, however 'sanitary', were socially unacceptable to a class
whose ambition was a semi-detached suburban villa.

The Society for Improving the Condition of the Labouring Classes,
established in 1844 by a committee which had as leading members Lord
Ashley and Dr Southwood Smith, had broadly similar intentions though a
somewhat different emphasis. The Society, which took over the earlier
Labourers' Friend Society, never intended to build on a large scale but to
demonstrate 'a planned dwelling or cottages' which would combine
'comfort with economy' as model examples for commercial builders to
imitate. The Queen was patron of the Society and the Prince Consort took
an active interest, presiding at the annual general meetings. Building began
in 1845 at Bagnigge Wells, Pentonville, off Grays Inn Road, with a double
row of two-storey houses to accommodate 23 families, 9 in three-roomed
flats and 14 in minimal two-roomed apartments; there was also a lodging-
house containing 30 rooms for widows and other single women. Attention
was paid to the recommendations of the recent Health of Towns Commission, 'particularly with respect to drainage, ventilation and an ample supply
of water';[82] several had the luxury of indoor privies—a 'necessity' indeed
since few had any backyard. After some conversions of existing lodging-
houses, the Society turned to its most ambitious scheme—a multi-storey
tenement block for families in Streatham Street, Bloomsbury, in 1849.
Behind a restrained post-Georgian five-storey façade, a novel idea of access

to the individual flats by wrought-iron balconies was employed, the avowed intent being to preserve 'the domestic privacy and independence of each distinct family [and] . . . effectively to prevent the communication of contagious disease'. The flats each had a small lobby, living-room, scullery, WC and two bedrooms, all well-planned, self-contained and to a high standard. The building attracted much admiration—'handsome and massive . . . wonderfully compact, airy and convenient premises'. Flats let at 4s–7s a week, depending on size, which was comparable with the rents of many tenements of inferior quality and amenity, but again not yielding the kind of profit which would have attracted commercial investors.

This phase of the Society's activities appropriately ends with its contribution to the Great Exhibition in 1851—a set of cottage flats for four families, described as Prince Albert's Model Cottages, but made so that they could be multiplied vertically and/or linearly if desired. The cottages are interesting, not because they were copied on a commercial scale, but because they represent the ideal of housing reformers in the mid-century. Aesthetically they cannot have been too pleasing with their free use of polychromatic and glazed bricks, but internally they provided quite spacious accommodation, with entrance lobby, living-room, kitchen, scullery, WC and three bedrooms; the living-room measured 150sq ft, the largest bedroom 100 and the two smaller 50. Although some of the planning was strange, with one bedroom opening off the scullery (possibly to give a proper separation from the others), the fittings were of an unusually high standard, with the scullery including sink, rack, dust-shaft, ventilator, meat-safe and coal-bin.[83]

THE QUALITY OF SPECULATIVE BUILDING

Building of this kind was explicitly exemplary, intended to demonstrate ideal standards of construction and amenity well above those currently offered by commercial enterprise. It had all the advantages on its side—royal patronage, philanthropic investors who did not demand the going rate of interest, a dedicated and imaginative architect in Henry Roberts. Against such advantages it is scarcely surprising that the small speculative builder who put up most of the working-class houses of early Victorian England was sometimes found wanting. As Henry-Russell Hitchcock observed:

Workers' housing in cities flowed out of the builders' offices—if the more modest builders ever had proper offices—without benefit of any sort of serious designing. It was therefore something of a vernacular product, like the country cottages of the Middle Ages, although the analogy is one that must not be pushed very far.[84]

The point is an important one. The speculative builder was no innovator in design, building techniques, materials or anything else: he broadly followed existing local trends, building in the only way that a highly traditional and conservative industry knew, usually doing an honest job at the price which the market allowed but sometimes a poor and dishonest one. There is no lack of evidence of sharp, 'scampy' building practice. Improvements went to those who could pay best, as James Hole pointed out:

> In the growth of our large towns it is noticeable that while among the middle and upper classes the newly erected houses are constantly improving in convenience and architectural appearance, there is not a corresponding improvement in the dwellings of the working classes ... Social or sanitary considerations do not sufficiently weigh with the capitalist builder if they involve increased outlay without a corresponding return.[85]

Here was the crux of the problem. The benefits of the age of technology were so far accruing to a small, though growing, section of the community, while the majority inhabited accommodation which was inappropriate to the age of great cities, and which, replicated on a massive scale, produced only ugliness, dirt and disease. The sanitary and structural solutions to many of these problems were already known by mid-century, and were employed by a few, but it was vain to expect the little builder who ran up half-a-dozen back-to-backs a year to be much concerned over proper ventilation, sewerage or water supplies unless a local authority compelled him to be. It was equally unlikely that he would have been a regular reader of *The Builder*, founded in 1842, or persuaded by the arguments of the editor, George Godwin, for the 'agglomerated house' to be produced by methods of system building. 'Something should be done to cheapen [the cost of constructing houses for the labouring classes] by using machinery, as we have already suggested, and producing doors, windows, floors, skirtings, roofs and so on to suit particular plans ... The use of concrete for cottage building has not been sufficiently tried.'[86]

As a practical, informed architect, and through his work as a district surveyor under the Metropolitan Building Act, Godwin knew more than most men about standards of building in mid-century:

> See the mode in which thousands of houses in the suburbs of the metropolis and elsewhere are commenced; without any excavation; the basement floor of thin, gaping boards placed within six inches of the damp ground; with slight walls of ill-burnt bricks and muddy mortar, sucking up the moisture and giving it out in the apartments; ill-made drains, untrapped, pouring forth bad air; and you scarcely need more causes for a low state of health ... We are much disposed to think that the legislature should interfere, and that some properly constituted officer should certify that every new house is built in such a manner as to be fit to live in.

Complaints of this kind recur sufficiently often to suggest that they were not isolated examples. A description of Bethnal Green, written in 1838, similarly criticizes the absence of common sewers, the foundations 'often laid upon the turf or vegetable mould' with no ventilation between the floors and the undrained soil, the roofs badly pitched and inadequately pointed, 'scarcely enough to keep them water-tight', the half-burnt bricks, inferior mortar and warping scantlings.[87] In Liverpool, reported a builder in 1844, 'there are thousands of houses and hundreds of courts . . . without a single drain of any description; and I never hail anything with greater delight than I do a violent tempest, or a terrific thunderstorm, accompanied by heavy rain, for these are the only scavengers that thousands have to cleanse away impurities and the filth in which they live or, rather exist'.[88]

One of the principal reasons for inferior quality and workmanship was the sub-contracting system, by which sections of the work—the bricklaying, carpentry, plumbing and so on—were let out by the builder to other workers at a fixed price known as 'the lump'. Consequently, there was no proper supervision of the work: all that mattered was that it kept within the price, and passed muster in appearance, and even in London, where under the Building Act new houses were required to be passed by the surveyor, Mayhew believed that builders were often hand in glove with the inspectors to pass inferior work.[89]

Under the London Building Acts the external walls of a 'third-rate' house were required to be 9in thick and those of a 'second-rate' house two and a half bricks, but how far short many new houses outside London fell of this standard may be judged from the frequent references to walls only half-brick thick ($4\frac{1}{2}$in) which would have given quite inadequate protection against damp, cold or noise, especially when the bricks were porous or soft from inadequate firing. A fairly common practice on the better, end-of-terrace houses was for slate-hanging on the gable walls as an additional protection. Party walls were often only half-brick thick, and in many cases were either not bonded properly, or even not fixed at all, to the external walls, either because of cheapness or because of the ignorance of unskilled workers. Slate was the most common material used on gable or hipped gable roofs, too often at a shallow pitch of only 30°, again for the sake of economy. Flooring was, as we have seen, often very inadequate, consisting of boards or flagstones sometimes laid directly on to damp earth—a disadvantage which cellared houses at least avoided. Windows, especially those in bedrooms, were another unsatisfactory feature, often extremely small (as little as 2ft by 1ft 6in) and made with one half fixed and only the other opening; again, the high cost of glass before mid-century, the extra timbering and the structural difficulties of providing adequate lintels or segmented brick arches for wider spans seem to have been the main reasons.[90]

LOCAL VARIATIONS IN HOUSING QUALITY

If the standard of housing reflected the unequal distribution of wealth and poverty between individuals, so also did it between towns and regions, and beyond the general factors already listed particular areas had their own special housing problems or advantages. To his general comment that the homes of the working classes were 'comfortless and even unwholesome, ill-furnished and ill-kept, betraying a lamentable want of self-respect in their inmates', G. R. Porter noted the exception of Sheffield, a town which was 'ill-built and dirty beyond the usual condition of English towns', but where 'it is the custom for each family among the labouring population to occupy a separate dwelling, the rooms in which are furnished in a very comfortable manner: the floors are carpeted, and the tables are usually of mahogany: chests of drawers of the same material are commonly seen, and so in most cases is a clock also, the possession of which article of furniture has often been pointed out as the certain indication of prosperity and of personal respectability on the part of the working man'.[91] Here there were few cellars or tenements and little overcrowding, with an average of fewer than five persons to a house. The disease and high mortality were due, not to bad housing as such, but to the inadequacies of water and drainage, and, no doubt, to the polluted atmosphere. Sheffield was not a planned town, the chief landowner, the Duke of Norfolk, having done nothing to control the layout of narrow rows of houses in narrow streets; there was no Building Act until 1867, and no obligation on the part of the builder to construct streets or drains.[92] The relatively good housing record of the town rested primarily on the prosperity of workers in the highly-skilled steel industry and its derivatives, in which Sheffield enjoyed a virtual monopoly. The absence of building controls, and the non-enforcement of restrictive covenants in the building lease, made house-building in Sheffield cheap and attractive, well able to respond to a buoyant, effective demand.

Sheffield was the archetypal, one-class industrial town, avoided by people of wealth or culture who were drawn to the refinements of York, Harrogate or Scarborough. In the two great ports and commercial centres, London and Liverpool, there were all classes, merchant princes and market porters, bankers and book-keepers, unskilled and unemployed—every gradation of extreme wealth and abject poverty. The accommodation of the working classes, as we have seen, reflected these infinite distinctions of income, which inhibited any single solution to the housing problem. Both cities suffered from rapid and sustained immigration; both experienced dislocation caused by commercial development, resulting, not in dispersal, but in increased crowding in adjoining central areas; both had large proportions of the population occupying adapted accommodation such as lodging-houses, tenements and cellars, and both experienced increased overcrowding during the first half-century—in London, from an average of 7·03

Holford Square, Clerkenwell, London, completed 1847. A good example of the persistence in London of the Georgian tradition of square and terrace housing. According to the 1851 Census, the heads of households here were predominantly middle-class – a silk buyer, two company secretaries, a builder, a linen draper, etc. There was an average of 1.25 servants per household (*Greater London Council*)

Design for a pair of villas, 1855. Taken from an influential 'pattern book' of the mid-century, *The Builder's Practical Director*, they illustrate how the Loudon tradition had persisted and been reinterpreted twenty years later. Interesting developments in this modest suburban middle-class house (2 reception rooms, kitchen and four bedrooms) are the elevation of the kitchen to the ground floor and the provision of an internal WC (*Drawing by E. L. Tarbuck*)

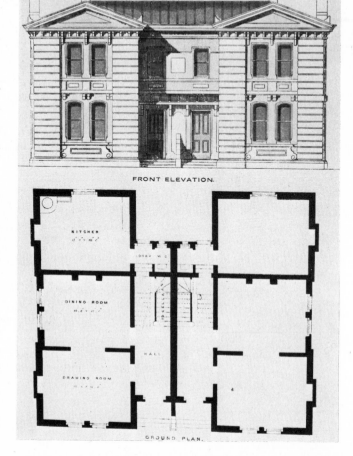

FRONT ELEVATION.

KITCHEN

DINING ROOM

HALL

DRAWING ROOM

GROUND PLAN.

John P— and his cottage, c1874. The cottage, built of mud and thatch, consisted of two ground-floor rooms, each about 9ft square, used as living room and bedroom. The walls were less than 6ft high, and the total height to the roof ridge 10ft: there was no ceiling or upper floor. A family of eight had formerly occupied the cottage; the present tenant paid £2 10 0d pa rent out of his wage of 5/- a week. Frontispiece from Heath *The English Peasantry* 1874

Agricultural labourers' cottages: block of three by J. Birch, before 1892. Accommodation was living room, scullery, pantry, three bedrooms, fuel store and outbuildings. Estimated cost, complete with cavity walls, water supply and drainage, was £380–£430 (*Photographed from RIBA Library*)

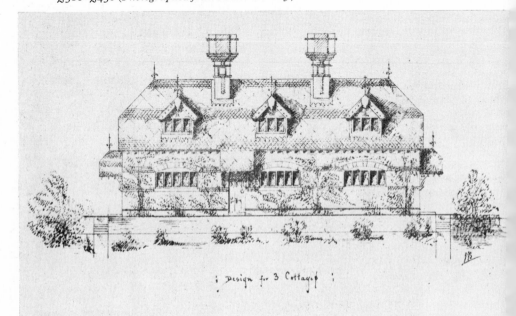

Design for 3 Cottages

Terrace backs: three-storey example in Palmerston Street, Manchester, shows walls of small back yards, outhouse roofs and 'ginnel'. Texture conveyed by brickwork and sets is characteristic of period and place (*C. G. Powell*)

Late Victorian by-law terrace. Accommodation in these York houses was similar to that of the Coventry example in text illustration 10. Typical external features were long unbroken terraces, small front gardens, bay windows, decorative masonry moulding and contrasting brickwork. Backs were more plain, as were the fronts of smaller, cheaper examples. From Rowntree *Poverty and Progress* published by Longman Green 1942, where it is captioned 'the best type of working class house in 1900'

Philanthropic tenements: Beaconsfield Buildings, Stroud-Vale, Islington. The first two blocks were finished in 1879 and accommodated 1100 people. This was the second project to be designed by Charles Barry for Victoria Dwellings Association. Access balconies are visible on one side of each block, and the regimented appearance was scarcely relieved by string courses and other decorative devices. In this respect design was backward-looking compared with the larger LCC Boundary Street scheme fourteen years later (*Illustrated London News*)

Outstanding pioneer: LCC tenements, Boundary Street, Bethnal Green, 1893–1900. 1069 tenements, mostly two- and three-room, were provided on a 15-acre site. Architect in charge Owen Fleming coordinated various others including Rowland Plumbe (*Greater London Council*)

persons per house in 1801 to 7·72 in 1851.[93] In Liverpool housing density, after an initial improvement from 6·78 persons per house in 1801 to 6·05 in 1811, steadily deteriorated to 7·32 in 1851. The greatest overcrowding was in the earliest-developed parts of the port such as Vauxhall Ward, Exchange Ward and Pitt Street Ward, where in particular 'black spots' densities rose to 13 and more per inhabited house. In these areas a majority of houses were back-to-back in narrow courts, sometimes with as little as 6ft between rows, and in total accommodating about one-third of Liverpool's working-class population. Better-off workers lived in 'front' houses which had the advantages over courts of being open at both ends and of a street's width (usually 24ft) between rows; unfortunately, the bulk of Liverpool's cellars were in these houses. Liverpool was stigmatized in the early 1840s as 'the most unhealthy town in England', with a mean duration of life of only 26 years compared with 37 in London and 45 in Surrey, and with 53 out of every 100 children dying before the age of five. Working-class housing in Liverpool was adapted to a low-wage economy—to the low earnings of dock labourers, to underemployment and periodic unemployment, and to a population which by 1851 included 25 per cent of Irish-born whose housing standards had always been, on average, lower than those of English workers.[94]

Nottingham, like Sheffield, was a town dominated by one industry or, rather, group of associated industries—hosiery, lace and bobbin net—but, unlike Sheffield, industries whose fortunes fluctuated widely over the period. Nottingham grew from 'a fair city' in 1750 of 10,000 inhabitants in 2,000 houses, many of them in gardens or orchards, to 28,800 in 1801 and to 53,000 in 1841, two-thirds of whom lived in back-to-back cottages many of which were built in narrow courts on what had once been gardens and cherry-orchards. It has often been argued that Nottingham's basic problem was that the town grew in numbers but not substantially in area: on three sides it was hemmed in by inviolable property rights—on the north and south by common fields and meadows, and on the west by two great estates, Nottingham Park, owned by the Duke of Newcastle, and Wollaton Park, owned by Earl Middleton.[95] Added to this, intense pressure on accommodation in the centre of the town was caused by the rapid expansion of the framework industries at the end of the eighteenth century and the need of workers for housing within walking distance of factories, workshops and warehouses. By 1845, when the Health of Towns Commission published its Second Report, Nottingham was described as having areas of slums and overcrowding worse than those of any other industrial town. But because of the existence of the enforced 'green belt', Nottingham's growth took place mainly by the formation of 'overspill' industrial villages (the later suburbs) two to four miles from the centre—Radford, Sneinton, Lenton, Carrington, Basford, Hyson Green. Many of them, built during the prosperity of the lace trade in the 1820s, when skilled workers could earn from 40s to 80s a week, were described as 'handsome villages' with very few back-to-backs, most of the houses being three-storey terraces, two rooms to a floor, sometimes with an additional loft for storage or extra sleeping accommodation for journeymen.

It is clear from contemporary accounts that such houses in the industrial villages represented a substantial improvement on previous working-class accommodation in Nottingham—more spacious, better furnished, often with private backyards and, as at Hyson Green, with front gardens thirty-five yards long. But the 'twist-net fever' then gave rise to slums in the central area worse than anything known before, to garrets, cellars, lean-to shacks and anything which would provide minimal shelter for men and machines. And as framework-knitting, as opposed to lace-making, moved into increasing depression after 1815, with wages as low as 5s or 6s a week by the 1840s, the standard of living in this trade fell to pitiably low levels. Because of the differing experiences of its two staple trades, the effects of industrialization on Nottingham housing were to raise the standards of some workers—almost certainly a majority—from two or three rooms to four or five, and to lower those of others—a declining minority as time passed—to exceptionally low levels. But even in Nottingham proper, not including the satellite villages, the statistics indicate an improvement of persons per house from 5·7 in 1801 to 4·1 in 1841.[96]

In his careful study of Leeds, another city which experienced extremely rapid growth and, like Nottingham, found its solution in a high proportion of back-to-backs, W. G. Rimmer came to a similar conclusion—that housing conditions did not deteriorate despite a major change in the character of the town. This is not to say, of course, that housing was generally satisfactory. Three-quarters of all houses in 1839 could be described as tiny, dark and ill-ventilated, without piped water, gas or adequate sanitation, and this despite the fact that well over half were new, having been built since 1815. Central areas like Kirkgate, containing the infamous and widely-publicized Boot-and-Shoe Yard, had their rookeries and slums as bad as any in the country, but this town grew easily outwards, with no legal or geographical barriers to expansion, and overall density per acre fell from 341 in 1815 to less than 200 in 1839. The somewhat uncertain statistics of persons per occupied house suggest a remarkable stability—4·6 in 1801 and 4·7 in 1841—with a proportion of between 6 per cent and 8 per cent of unoccupied houses in the later decades. There is certainly no general evidence of serious or increasing overcrowding. Rents rose sharply between the 1790s and the 1840s, often by as much as double, reflecting greatly increased land values, materials prices and labour costs, but wages had also moved up and Rimmer concludes that, given regular employment, workers at the later period could afford at least as good accommodation and food, plus a rather larger margin for other things. In 1839 one quarter of workers earned 20s–26s a week and devoted 8–15 per cent to rent, two-fifths earned 15s–20s and devoted 13–27 per cent to rent, one-third earned 11s–15s and devoted 13–18 per cent to rent. The range is large, and for those at the bottom of the earnings scale it is probable that housing represented an increasingly severe burden, but for a growing proportion of the labour force there were both improving housing standards and bigger surpluses over the necessities of life. Leeds's problem was not a housing problem as such, but the difficulty of attracting capital for 'unremunerative' social overheads like water, roads and sewerage.[97]

THE BEGINNING OF HOUSING REFORM

Such housing progress as there had been by 1850—and one of the objects of this chapter has been to show that some housing progress, both in quantitative and qualitative terms, did occur—took place wholly without intervention by the State. Throughout the decade of the 1840s the battle for public health had arrested the attention of reformers and legislators, but the focus of that attention had been the urban environment as a whole rather than housing in particular. The concentration of interest had been on the relationship between lack of sanitation, defective drainage, inadequate water supply and overcrowding on the one hand and disease, high mortality rates and low expectation of life on the other. Closely related to this central theme were other issues such as the economic costs of ill-health, the social costs of squalor in terms of intemperance, immorality and criminality, and the argument for new legal and administrative machinery for the protection of the public health. Housing was regarded only as one, and that not the most important, of many matters touching on 'the sanitary question'.

Given this emphasis, it was almost inevitable that those recommendations in the Reports of the 1840s which did bear directly on housing should have been lightly brushed aside when they came up against the powerful vested interests of property-owners. The most radical proposals were contained in the earliest Report, that of the Health of Towns Committee of 1840, and the three Bills based upon it in 1841. That concerned with building proposed to appoint surveyors who would have to be notified before any new house was built. It proposed that back-to-backs should be banned, that no cellar be used for human habitation which did not possess a window, a fireplace and an open area, that houses were not to be built in close alleys, that streets were to be at least 30ft wide, that no house was to be built until the site was drained and that drains were to be constructed for houses already built. The back-to-back clauses were dropped in Committee following strong objections from the industrial towns that they would raise the cost of houses, and, therefore, of rent: the rest of the Bill was postponed pending the Report of the Royal Commission of 1844–5, which concentrated on drainage, cleansing and water-supply—the aspects which ultimately became law in the Public Health Act of 1848.

More important than the minimal legislative outcome, the investigations of the decade played a vital part in the education of public opinion, especially at the local level. Although national attempts to remedy housing evils had proved premature, some local authorities began to obtain private Acts and to use permissive powers to bring about improvement in the areas over which they had control. In 1843 the Birkenhead Improvement Commissioners obtained an Act which forbade building in close courts, regulated the sizes of rooms and windows in new houses, and compelled owners to provide privies. Next year, a local Act in Manchester required that every house should have a privy and ash-pit behind it, thus putting an end to the building of back-to-backs. When Nottingham at last obtained an Enclosure Act in 1845, allowing building on the former common lands, 130 of the 1,069 acres were first set aside for public recreation, and strict regulations were laid down for new building on the rest, including requirements that no house should adjoin another on more than two sides, that every house should have three bedrooms, a separate privy and a yard or garden 30ft long. In 1846 a local Liverpool Act made regulations about houses, courts, cellars, effective sewering and draining, as well as appointing the first medical officer of health in the country, Dr W. H. Duncan. These were the real and effective beginnings of housing reform in England, having direct and beneficial effects on the homes of future generations, and demonstrating what local zeal and initiative could accomplish where national remedies had foundered. In the prevailing climate of social values it was impossible to direct national resources on any significant scale to a war on dirt, disease and death, however hard Chadwick argued that money so invested would reap a handsome return. *The Times* aptly summed up the problem:

> A town of manufacturers and speculators is apt to leave the poor to shift for themselves, to stew in cellars and garrets, nor are landlords and farmers apt to care much for cottages . . . Something of a central authority is necessary to wrestle with the selfishness of wealth.

In the absence of that central authority, a few towns by 1850 were just beginning to put their own houses in order.

CONCLUSION

In 1866 James Hole published the first general review of the state of working-class housing. His long list of the causes of the problem, many of which this chapter has touched upon, included the rapid growth of towns and of immigration, the greatly increased cost of land and rents in central areas, public 'improvements' such as railway-building and commercial development which were often harmful to the poor, the migration of the better-off classes to the suburbs, the temptation of builders to put up inferior cottages, the general ignorance of the nature of diseases and the importance of sanitation, the need of the working classes to live near their work and their desire to pay as low a rent as possible. To this he added a number of reasons for the slow progress of housing reform—the inefficiency and neglect of local authorities, the ignorance of ratepayers, the objections to 'centralization', and, hence, the inadequacy of compulsory powers exercised by central government. Clearly, no single, simple fact explained the housing problem. But although Hole recognized in a general way the prevalence of poverty, he did not bring out sufficiently sharply the fact that no one would build for the poorest classes who could not afford to pay economic rents, and that, at its roots, the housing problem was a problem of poverty. The very poor were unprovided for because it would pay no one to do so, and because the day was yet far distant when their accommodation was to be thought of as any kind of public responsibility. The average proportion of working-class income devoted to rent in the nineteenth century was 16 per cent—approximately twice the proportion devoted by the middle classes—but the fraction was inversely proportional to income, and was often much higher among the very poor where a single room would take 1s 6d or 2s a week out of earnings as low as 6s or 8s. Their housing was necessarily residual, for no builder would build for the unemployed, the casual worker, the sick, the widow. The very poor—that fraction of the population which social investigators at the end of the century were to identify as nearly one-third of the population—had no share in the improvements which were accruing to the rest of society. In the standard-of-living equation, their housing experience was simply a perpetuation of existing inadequacies and already low standards into a new environment in which their scale and intensity were further heightened.

4

MIDDLE-CLASS HOUSING

A good house
Is no uncovetable thing: large rooms,
Servants, gay drapery, new furniture,
Nor desired, nor undesirable.
But first take counsel of thy income; wait,
Till prudence speak in the affirmative
Too dear thou purchasest those luxuries
If peace and independence be their price.

'Within the Means', in S. W. Partridge, *Upward and Onward:
a Thought Book for the Threshold of Active Life* (1857)

For that part of the population whose economic resources allowed it to exercise some real choice as to how and where it lived, the home, and its physical expression, the house, were the central institutions of civilized life. Precisely what the proportion of the middle class was in the early nineteenth century it is impossible to know, partly because exact limits cannot be set to its membership and partly because the statistical data are incomplete. What we do know about the class is that it was still small, though growing rapidly in response to the new needs and new opportunities of industrialization. Although it is difficult to discover any century since the Middle Ages when the middle classes could not be said to be 'rising', it is true that the nineteenth offered unprecedented opportunities of material gain, social mobility and, ultimately, political and cultural leadership. To those small numbers of merchants, trading and professional people who, since medieval times, had constituted a group distinct both from 'landed society' above and the 'labouring poor' below them, industrialization added important and vital new elements—capitalist manufacturers employing workers to spin and weave cotton, mine coal and build ships, and new professions, called into existence by the need for bankers and brokers, shippers and insurers, engineers and designers. Added to these, the phenomenally rapid growth of the urban population called for more architects, surveyors and master builders, more doctors and dentists, more teachers, clerks and shopkeepers than ever before.

Out of this amalgam was gradually emerging, not a single class, but a tier of middle classes. At the top were the great industrialists, merchants and bankers, with incomes as large as many of the landed aristocracy. In the middle were the members of the professions, both old and new, the lesser factory-owners and the senior clerks, not yet elevated to 'managerial' designation. At the base were the petty tradesmen, shopkeepers and book-keepers, the little masters of sweated workshops, the Nonconformist clergy, the apothecaries and the craftsmen-retailers in old, unrevolutionized trades—men whose earnings were often little greater than those of skilled workers, but whose habits, tastes and aspirations set them into a world apart. It has been estimated that in 1851 the professions occupied about 150,000 persons, with teaching in all branches adding another 100,000, and the services of central and local government 75,000. Those engaged in merchanting, shopkeeping and financial occupations numbered about 130,000, clerks and commercial travellers about 60,000; 'manufacturers employing capital in all branches', the dynamic, entrepreneurial component of the class, numbered 86,000.[1] We must add to these an uncertain proportion of the 119,000 adult males of independent means and the 141,000 occupiers of land employing labourers given in the Census of 1841[2] whose wealth did not admit them into the charmed circle of landed society. In total, we have a 'middle-class' figure for mid-century of around 6–700,000 income-receivers who, with their wives and families, would account for perhaps 3,000,000 people out of the population of 18,000,000. We are concerned in this chapter, therefore, with the housing of about one-sixth of the English people.

This 'new' class was the most family-conscious and home-centred generation to have emerged in English history. Originating perhaps in the 1820s, a distinctively middle-class family pattern grew up which was in full development by the middle decades of the century; although at first in sharp contrast to the family patterns of both the aristocracy and the working classes, it was one which, in time, the middle classes were largely successful in imposing on the orders above and below themselves. It had certain well-defined characteristics, based upon a set of values and beliefs which were imbued almost with religious authority—the belief in male superiority, from which it followed that man alone was capable of wielding economic, political and legal power, and that wives and children owed only obedience to this God-like creature; the belief that a 'lady' did not work, that her vocation in life was a prudent marriage, and that the primary purpose of that marriage was the procreation of children; and the belief, not seen as conflicting with the last, that, for the wife at least, sexual intercourse was duty, not pleasure, and that the subject of sex must not be allowed to sully the Christian sacrament of marriage. The home, in this view, itself became almost a sacred institution, the pivot not only of domestic comfort but of moral rectitude, the Christian commonwealth in miniature, in which the members of the family would be reared in those principles of honour, duty, industry, thrift and sobriety which would best conduce to their own well-being and to that of society at large.[3]

The rigid statement and enforcement of such a code was of particular importance to a class which, despite its evident energy and enterprise, was still new, insecure and largely unrecognized in political or social status. Many of its members were first-generation recruits, who needed clear guidance on rules of conduct and behaviour. A code would define status: it would serve as a unifying force to combat the enemies without and protect the members within, affording a private retreat behind which the strains and stresses of business life could be washed away, or at least concealed. The home, then, had to fulfil these many functions—to comfort and purify, to give relief and privacy from the cares of the world, to rear its members in an appropriate set of Christian values, and, above all, perhaps, to proclaim by its ordered arrangements, polite behaviour, cleanliness, tidiness and distinctive taste, that its members belonged to a class of substance, culture and respectability. The house itself was to be the visible expression of these values.

The adoption of such a code depended crucially on the economic resources of those seeking membership. A level of income was necessary which would buy food,[4] dress and accommodation of the approved kind, would furnish and equip the home, provide for the education of children and the occasional recreation of the whole family and would still leave a reserve, generally calculated by writers on domestic economy at one-twelfth of income, for saving and unforeseen contingencies. This ability to plan and budget resources for the future was one of the important distinguishing characteristics of the class. Equally important was the ability to employ domestic servants to relieve the women of the family from household drudgery. More than any other single factor, middle-class status was determined by the employment of resident domestic staff, the numbers and functions of whom were carefully regulated in precise accordance with the level of income. Middle-class wealth also commanded the newer services of technology in the search for domestic comfort, making possible piped water in each house, proper systems of sanitation and drainage, gas for lighting and cooking, and a score of other home improvements ranging from the sewing-machine to sprung interior upholstery.

No precise minimum income for membership can be set, but by common convention in the first half of the century it was at least £150 a year—more, that is, than the wage of all but a handful of highly-skilled workers and an income which would normally allow the employment of some domestic help. As if to confirm social usage, the anonymous author of *A New System of Practical Domestic Economy*, probably the most influential treatise of its kind from the 1820s to the 1840s, after discussing in Part I the budgets of working people, began Part II for 'families of a superior condition in life' at an income of £150 a year. The head of the household was now described as a 'gentleman' and there was a servant for occasional charing at £3 a year.[5] Clearly, this was still somewhat marginal, but at £200 a year there was now a resident maid-servant at £9 a year, and at £250 the 'wife' became promoted to a 'lady': such a family had unequivocally 'arrived'.

All the evidence suggests, however, that as the century advanced and what J. A. Banks has aptly described as 'the paraphernalia of gentility'[6] accumulated, this figure had to be raised. By the 1840s there had developed the concept of 'the proper time to marry', and young middle-class men were being strongly urged to postpone matrimony until they had established a position in life and achieved a sufficient income. 'Steel yourself against the tender passion', advised a publication of 1845 to young men of £100 a year, 'for marry you cannot, with any propriety, or hope of providing for a family'.[7] In 1858, *The Times* conducted a lively debate on the question of whether one could marry on £300 a year. The dilemma which now faced young men who did not wish to be accused of an 'imprudent' marriage was well summed up by an article in *The Guardian*:

> People in these days have an acute sense of the duty of not marrying without a competent support; but instead of tempering the idea of competency by habits of frugality and self-denial, so as to render marriage compatible with the means within their reach, they are daily adding expensive appliances for show or comfort to the list of necessaries, and so the upper surface of society rises higher and higher in the scale of luxury . . . It is not generally so much the mere taste for personal enjoyment which leads to this, as the opinion that a certain class of luxuries and scale of expenditure are necessary to the maintenance of a due social position.[8]

Careful household budgeting was, therefore, of prime importance to the class, and manuals of domestic economy minutely allocated income to the major heads of expenditure—food, drink, heating and lighting, cleaning, clothes, education, servants' wages, entertainment, medical and other incidental expenses, taxes, and, not least important, house-rent. The assumption in all the guides of the first half of the century is that the house will be rented, not bought outright or by instalment purchase. At a time when the urban housing market was mainly based on leasehold tenure, and before building societies had developed into major agencies of home-ownership, renting was almost inescapable, but it was, in any case, well-suited to a class which was geographically and socially mobile, and did not necessarily wish to put down deep roots. Freeholds were more often available in country districts and in the new suburban housing estates, but in London and provincial cities middle-class families who had not had the advantage of inheriting property normally rented their houses, taking renewable leases of a year, six months or a quarter.

The handbooks also concur in suggesting that the appropriate fraction of income to be devoted to house-rent was about one-tenth, and, in normal circumstances, should not exceed one-eighth. In many, taxes and local rates are included in this fraction, and in *A New System of Practical Domestic Economy* the invariable allocation to this composite item for those of moderate income is one-tenth—thus, at £150 a year 'Rent, Taxes, etc.' are given as £15, at £250, £25, and at £750, £75. J. H. Walsh's *Manual of Domestic Economy*, first published in 1857, allowed one-eighth of income, to include taxes and repairs,[9] and Mrs Beeton's *Book of Household Management* of 1861 warned that 'the rent of a house . . . should not exceed one-eighth of the whole income of its occupier . . . although there may be many circumstances which would not admit of [this rule] being considered infallible'.[10]

Records of actual middle-class families suggest that, with Mrs Beeton's proviso, this was in fact the kind of fraction that was actually spent on rent. One of the contributors to the *Times* controversy in 1857 detailed his budget for the past year, showing £25 on rent out of an income of £300. He was a respectable London clerk, inhabiting a small house in the suburbs with drawing-room, dining-room, kitchen, three bedrooms and a servant's room. In 1834 the Carlyles, living in what was then unfashionable Cheyne Row, Chelsea, paid £35 a year out of their income of £300 for an unmodernized, eight-roomed Queen Anne house; the only source of water was a basement pump, the servant cooked before an open fire, and lighting was by candle and oil-lamp until the Carlyles installed two gas-jets in 1852.[11] A rent of £100 would command a large, comfortable and well-appointed house in one of the fashionable London squares or inner suburbs like Kensington or Belgravia. At this figure one would expect an impressive hall and staircase, large drawing and dining-rooms, a parlour and study, ample kitchen quarters, four or five main bedrooms in addition to servants' rooms, a coach-house and stabling. Further increases in rent bought additional space and rooms for more specialized functions—a receiving hall, a library, boudoir, billiard-room, schoolroom, nursery, and more elaborate quarters for staff, probably in a separate wing, including kitchen, scullery, stillroom, cellars, butler's pantry, servants' hall and housekeeper's room.

Cost, represented primarily by annual rent, was, then, the first determinant of the form of the middle-class house. In households where prudence prevailed, and the counsels of the textbook-writers were strictly heeded, it was the principal determinant, and the search for status was not allowed to override the arguments of economy. But the Victorian middle classes were blessed, or burdened, with households of a size larger than the average, and it was necessary that their houses should be large enough to accommodate their occupants with decency and comfort. The second determinant of house-form was, therefore, the number and description of its occupants, a subject on which recent local studies of Victorian household structure have begun to throw some light. We know that the average age of first marriage for middle-class men, persuaded by the arguments for postponement, was late—29·9 years for those clergymen, lawyers, doctors, merchants, manufacturers, bankers and 'gentlemen' who married in the period from 1840 to 1870. These men had an unprecedented choice of marriage partners, partly because there were substantially more females than males in the population, and partly because within the middle class itself many potentially marriageable young men were serving the Queen in distant parts of the Empire remote from female association: the result of this was that in 1851 no fewer than 42 per cent of women between the ages of twenty and forty were spinsters. It seems likely, too, that the upper middle classes shared with the poorest stratum of the working classes a high degree of geographical mobility, so that in York in that year only 20·8 per cent of heads of households in the highest socio-economic group were natives of the town compared with 54·3 per cent of the artisans and small shopkeepers.[12]

About family size we know rather more from the statistics of fertility and mortality. Of every 100 women married in the decade of the 1870s, 8 would have no children, 13 either one or two, 18 three or four, 43 between five and nine, and 18 ten or more: the average number of live births per marriage was between five and six. Not all of them, of course, would survive childhood. In 1850, a relatively healthy year without mass epidemics, 146 infants out of every 1,000 in England and Wales died within one year of birth, and as many again would follow them before the age of five: still more deaths would occur in adolescence and early adulthood. All this means that an average of five live births per marriage (and an unknowable number of pregnancies) would probably produce only three adult offspring, though at earlier stages in the family cycle there would be more young children to accommodate.

The statistics cited are for completed family size over a span of childbearing of some 15–20 years, and it is important to distinguish this from household size—that is, the number of persons living under the same roof at a given moment in time. The researches so far published suggest that household size was higher in the middle classes in the mid-nineteenth century than in the working classes, not because the former had more children, but because they sheltered more relatives, lodgers, visitors and domestic servants. In Nottingham in 1851 Class I and II households (professional people, managers, entrepreneurs, farmers, and those living on annuities and investments) had a mean size of 5·12 persons (±0·40) compared with 4·24 (±0·25) in Classes IV and V,[13] while in York in the same year the closely comparable figures were 5·31 (±0·46) and 4·48 (±0·33).[14] The difference lies in the fact that the middle-class house in York accommodated, besides parents and children, an average of 1·15 domestic servants, 0·42 lodgers, 0·41 relatives and 0·21 resident visitors.

Lodgers were slightly more common than this in working-class households, resident relatives and visitors considerably less so, but the most important difference was, of course, in the domestic servants who were statistically insignificant in any classes outside I and II.[15] The middle-class code of conduct required, as we have seen, that the housewife should not, if possible, engage in menial household work, and the manuals of domestic economy laid down the precise numbers and duties of domestic staff in strict accordance with level of income. In *A New System of Practical Domestic Economy* (1824 edition) it is assumed that at £200 per annum there is one resident maid, presumably a very young and inexperienced girl since her wage is only £9 a year; at £250 there is a responsible maid-servant at £16 a year, at £300 two maids, at £400 a horse, requiring the services of an occasional groom, and at £500 the important step is taken of engaging a full-time manservant. At an income of £1,000 there are three female servants, a coachman and a footman, which, with the family of husband, wife and three children assumed in all the estimates, gives an establishment of ten persons.[16]

All this related directly to the size of house which the middle classes deemed necessary and desirable. Since there would be children of both sexes they must occupy two bedrooms, and, as they grew to adulthood, preferably more. Servants also needed bedrooms; two maids might share one, but a cook would expect her own room and menservants must have their own, either in the house or above the coach-house. In larger establishments, servants would also need some provision for their off-duty hours other than the kitchen. At least one extra bedroom would be required for the occasional guest, or the more permanent relative or lodger. Very tentatively, and allowing for infinite variations in the pattern, we might construct a model of what this implied for a middle-class family in terms of housing needs. The husband, a young professional or businessman, has prudently delayed marriage until the required age of thirty and the income of £300 a year have been attained. He rents his first house at £25 a year, a six-roomed terraced house with small drawing and dining-rooms and three bedrooms, the smallest of which is occupied by the single maid. In five years' time they move to a semi-detached house in the suburbs, with four bedrooms so that the two children may normally have separate rooms, and with a somewhat larger dining-room which does not disgrace the monthly dinner-party. In another five years, by which time the husband is forty and his income has expanded to £750 a year, the important move is made to a newly-built, detached villa, perhaps in another town, at a rent of £75 a year. It is a house of 'character' in the fashionable 'Gothic' style, with ten rooms—not counting the spacious hall—a large dining-room and an elegant drawing-room opening to a conservatory, a study, a kitchen and adjoining domestic offices sufficient for the manservant, cook and two maids who are now kept, six bedrooms, the principal one having its own small dressing-room, and, for the first time, a bathroom with a fixed bath and a piped water-supply. The family has 'arrived'. It now has a two-wheeled carriage, the manservant combining the functions of groom and footman and sleeping in the coach-house. The children occupy two bedrooms, the maids two, and there is an extra for visitors and the wife's sister who inclines to longer stays. The lady pays afternoon 'calls' in the carriage: there is a weekly dinner-party, and in the summer a house at the seaside is rented for three weeks or a month. This might well be the last, the family house, or for the few whose incomes continue to expand from the hundreds into the thousands, only another step in the search for status which might end in a mansion in a fashionable London square or even in a country seat.

The third determinant of middle-class housing was location. Where the house was situated mattered a good deal, not only for social and aesthetic reasons but also for more practical sanitary and economic ones. Separation from traffic noise and dirt, and from industrial smell and smoke, became highly desirable as the scale of urban activities constantly increased, but separation from human contamination was even more persuasive. Once it had been shown by the sanitary enquiries of the 1840s how many diseases were spread by human filth, and once the statisticians had demonstrated how widely mortality rates varied in different areas of towns and in different occupations, the poor became unacceptable as near neighbours. In 1841 the average expectation of life at birth throughout England and Wales was 41 years, but whereas in Surrey it was 45 years, in London it was 37, in Liverpool 26 and in Manchester only 24;[17] similar, though not such dramatic, differences could be shown between 'healthy' and 'unhealthy' districts within the same town.

Moral dangers also, it was now known, kept close company with the physical. Again, the statistics showed, or seemed to show, that criminality went with poverty, that vice had its home in the thieves' dens in the poorest quarters of cities, that theft, assault and drunkenness were concentrated here, and that prostitution, the 'Great Social Evil', though its haunts might be in the Strand or Piccadilly, took its patrons back to the rookeries of Seven Dials and Clare Market. The hearts of great cities were no longer places where children could be reared in Christian innocence, where womenfolk could walk without fear or men find peace and ease after the toil of the day.

Yet the movement of the wealthier classes outwards from the town centres was not only an escape from their evils; it was a conscious and positive migration towards a different physical environment and a different set of social values. Fundamentally the better-off classes were drawn out of the cities by a dream or image of a different style of life. Part of that dream consisted of social aspirations. In London, for example, the riverside villages to the west of the built-up area had already become fashionable places of

residence for the aristocracy by the early nineteenth century, with large
mansions standing in landscaped parks. By mid-century 'Imperial Kensington' or the 'Court Suburb' was attracting numbers of professional men,
merchants and capitalists anxious to establish a social position—London's
'pursy' citizens, according to a contemporary account, who were moving
out to populate these 'snug' new suburbs.[18] A building boom, lasting from
1837 to 1856, created Kensington as an upper-middle-class preserve for
what a Town Directory of the period described as 'all those whom education
and intelligence—tested by their professional and commercial pursuits—
have rendered equally deserving of honourable or gratifying mention,
forming as they do the bulk of what is termed good society'.

This physical separation from the centres of towns where business and
commerce were carried on—a separation, that is, of living from working—allowed and encouraged the development of a new kind of social life.
Leonore Davidoff has observed that 'when leading families lived in or very
near the central city, their control over local politics meant that social life
was ultimately tied to the governing of the city. As families moved out to
prosperous suburbs, local social life centred more on charity, the arts and
the marriage market'.[19] Inevitably, it reinforced the growing separation of
the sexes to the point where, for women, the centre of existence became the
home as the basis of social life. It was of the essence of the new code of
conduct that social interaction should be ordered and regulated by a ritual
of 'calls', 'At Homes', teas, dinners and parties, and not left to possibly
embarrassing chance encounters. This therefore implied that the house
itself should be as separate as possible from its neighbours and, at all costs,
from neighbouring areas of an inferior social status. For these reasons,
terraces became increasingly out of favour as the century progressed, and
the detached house increasingly the ideal; the semi-detached was a compromise solution typically employed in the inner suburbs where land costs
were relatively high. Segregation was still further achieved if the house was
situated in a private, unadopted estate which excluded undesirable visitors
by gates, and sometimes a gatekeeper, at each point of access. Such estates
were by no means confined to the suburbs, about 150 existing in central and
western districts of London alone in 1875, mainly in Belgravia,
Marylebone, Mayfair and St Pancras: until 1890 several gated estates were
allowed to block important thoroughfares despite serious public
inconvenience like delays to fire-engines.[20] Where total privacy and single-
class exclusiveness of this kind were not possible, relative privacy was
achieved by siting the house in a spacious garden, building walls round the
perimeter, and protecting the front door behind a carriage-sweep and
shrubbery.

These increased possibilities of social distancing help to explain the
attraction of suburban life for the Victorian middle classes. If it was closer
to the healthy air of the countryside, it was also closer to the life-style of the

country gentry, towards whom the bourgeoisie bore an ambivalent attitude compounded of admiration, envy and contempt. 'The middle-class suburb', it has been said, 'was an ecological marvel . . . it offered an arena for the manipulation of social distinctions to those most conscious of their possibilities and most adept in turning them into shapes on the ground; it kept the threat of rapid social change beyond the horizon of those least able to accept its negative as well as its positive advantages.'[21] For the men of suburbia there were, also, solid economic benefits which accorded well with their business interests—opportunities for speculation in land, for supplying building materials, fuel and food for the new residents, the development of local transport services, and the creation of work for solicitors, architects, surveyors, auctioneers, banks and building societies. It was 'a kind of self-generating expansion, a re-investment . . . in the social overhead capital . . .' For their womenfolk the benefits were less tangible but no less real. Suburban life conjured up images, romantic, even idyllic, of a life remote from the physical ugliness and the moral snares of the city, a life of civilized simplicity and carefully contrived natural beauty which would combine the advantages of urban and rural existence yet be distinctively different from both. Henry James admirably expressed this yearning of the Victorian middle classes for 'a mingling of density and rurality, the ivy covered brick walls, the riverside holiday-making, the old royal seats at an easy drive, the little open-windowed inns, where the charm of rural seclusion seems to merge itself in that of proximity to the city market'.[22] Yet suburbia was an essentially practical solution to the problem of living out of the city without losing control of it.

The suburb clearly responded to some deep cultural need, and more than any other residential planning form it provided the model environment which gradually became the ambition of the majority of English people. Architecturally, it allowed for expressions of personality and individuality in house style and ornament which, in this period, often took the form of the 'Picturesque' (see p. 112), with exteriors heavily influenced by Gothic, Italian, even Greek or Swiss styles. 'The Picturesque was, thus, an anti-civic aesthetic . . . It promoted the gospel of individuality . . . "Rus in urbe" meant every man possessing his own distinctively composed villa amidst his own shrubbery.'[23] If the suburb itself was a rejection of urban values, the suburban house was a rejection of the Georgian terrace in which ten or twenty identical house fronts had been united by common colonnades or central pediments, while externally, instead of overlooking a communal square, the suburban could look from his drawing-room window onto a landscape which at least appeared to be all his own.[24]

London, already in the early nineteenth century the most densely-populated city and the magnet for continuing waves of immigrants, was the first to experience the drift. The London house had been conditioned by economy—the need to place as many houses as possible onto expensive land, and particularly to limit the size of house-fronts to the street. The typical site was, therefore, a long, narrow strip containing an 'area' extending forward partly under the street, the house itself, a narrow rear garden and, perhaps, a coach-house at the back served by a subsidiary road. The plan of the house was all but inescapable with a frontage of up to 24ft, implying two rooms behind each other, with a hall and staircase to the side: such a plan was used equally at Carlton House Terrace and in East End cottages.[25] But in order to provide a sufficient number of rooms on such a site-plan it was necessary to build upwards, so that a typical better-class London house had consisted of a basement for kitchen and servants, a ground floor of dining-room and parlour or study, a first-floor double drawing-room, and two- or three-bedroom storeys above. It was essentially 'vertical living' as opposed to the 'horizontal living' of Paris and other European capitals, but the 'flat' was not an acceptable house-form in England until Henry Ashton's superior apartments were built in Victoria Street in the 1850s. These curious domestic arrangements had surprised a French visitor, Louis Simond, in 1817:

> These narrow houses, three or four storeys high—one for eating, one for sleeping, a third for company, a fourth underground for the kitchen, a fifth perhaps at the top for the servants—and the agility, the ease, the quickness with which the individuals of the family run up and down, and perch on the different storeys, give the idea of a cage with its sticks and birds.[26]

There had been comparatively little private building in London during the French Wars (1793–1815), owing to a shortage of Baltic timber and heavy taxation of building materials, but on the return of peace the capital began to break out of its eighteenth-century confines in the first major suburban expansion. The process occurred, as Sir John Summerson has so admirably detailed, by the development of new 'estates' by a group of men who combined the functions of architects, master-builders and land speculators, negotiating building leases from the Crown, City Companies, charities and private owners, organizing the site maps, designing the houses and erecting them often on a sub-contract basis. James Burton's work in Bloomsbury, on the former Foundling Hospital estate, was the prototype. Between the 1790s and 1817 he dominated Bloomsbury building, his best-known work perhaps being Russell Square (1800–14). So highly-organized were his building operations that the joinery and ironwork for his houses were virtually mass-produced, the design being primarily a matter of assembly. The first known reference to pairs of semi-detached houses occurs about this time on the Eyre Estate, to the north of Marylebone, in 1794. The author of this revolutionary new house-type is unknown, but the Eyre Estate, which was to be developed as St John's Wood, was the first suburb to abandon the terrace in favour of the semi-detached villa. The work of John Nash in the Regent's Park Estate was far more ambitious than that of

Burton, involving, it has been said, the original concept of 'a garden city for an aristocracy': the scheme, executed between 1811 and 1835, included the Inner and Outer Circles, the majestic Nash Terraces, numerous large detached villas within the park, two Park Villages consisting of smaller houses in Gothic and Italian styles, and a working-class end of the estate in Munster Square. But as contributors to the expansion of London housing, both Nash and Burton were overshadowed by Thomas Cubitt, the virtual creator of Belgravia and Pimlico, of Tavistock Square (where the houses were let at £150 a year), Gordon Square, Woburn Place, Endsleigh Street and Place, besides parts of Camden Town, Stoke Newington and Clapham. Although Cubitt was the speculative builder *par excellence*, his work was the antithesis of jerry-building and was characterized by consistently high quality.

The development of the London estates, essentially on Cubitt lines, continued rapidly until the 1870s. Bayswater and Notting Hill were developed by substantial builder-speculators to become 'immense residential strongholds covered from top to toe with Italian ornament'. Hyde Park Gardens (1836) and Leinster Square (1856) were the most imposing of the speculators' works, while the later, mid-century extensions of Paddington, Chelsea and Islington showed a decline in taste and competence when architects of any reputation were ceasing to concern themselves with estate development. The character of the London estates depended much on the interest and degree of control exercised by the ground landlords. Wealthy owners like the Duke of Bedford in Bloomsbury and Lord Grosvenor in Belgravia employed their own permanent staffs to supervise both the building and the subsequent tenants, and maintained high standards for their estates: on the other hand, the Marquess of Northampton neglected his large property in Clerkenwell, built 1815–18, which reaped a large crop of slum tenements in subsequent years.[27]

John Summerson has identified four types of London suburban growth in the late eighteenth and early nineteenth centuries: first, village development at distances of up to about ten miles from the centre (Hampstead, Richmond, Twickenham, Hackney, Bow, Greenwich, Dulwich, Battersea, etc); second, country villa building (individual houses, usually set in substantial grounds, either in the Palladian or, later, in the 'Gothic' ornamental cottage style, and dotted all over the London countryside); third, roadside ('ribbon') development, using the borderlands of main roads, and encouraged by the improved surfacing of roads by turnpike trusts (all round London, but good examples in Islington, Southwark, Camden, Fulham); and fourth, estate development, usually planned by large speculative builders and filling-in between main roads (Hans Town, Somers Town, Camden Town, Kensington New Town, Milner Square).

In provincial towns and cities the middle-class suburb, although it existed as a clearly-defined type of residential area, was usually still so close to the centre that most middle-class men could reach their work by foot. Only from about the 1830s did the shopkeepers, smaller manufacturers and commercial classes begin to move out of the hearts of large provincial towns to an inner suburban belt still within walking distance of their places of business.[28] A mile and a half was sufficient in the 1840s to take one out of the slums of central Manchester to open country and a river sufficiently unpolluted for bathing, while a similar or shorter distance did the same in Liverpool, Birmingham, Bradford and almost every industrial town. Manchester had no need for a cab-stand until 1839: most Leeds manufacturers could still walk to the Cloth Halls within twenty minutes, and fashionable Liverpool society still lived in the large Georgian houses at Everton Hill, only a mile from the busy, disreputable river-front.[29] Some of the really great manufacturing families, like the Drinkwaters and the Phillips of Manchester, had, it is true, moved further out to country houses in park-like estates, where from Prestwick the head of the Phillips family each day endured the inconvenience of a three-mile ride on horseback to Kersal Toll Bar where a four-wheel cab met him to convey him to his warehouse. In Liverpool, where life was more gracious and spacious than in the industrial cities, some of the merchant princes had 'marine villas' as well as town mansions. These were at Waterloo, just clear of the Mersey estuary, where about a hundred white ornamented cottages had been built in a crescent with an esplanade and a hotel. One could travel by omnibus or express canal boat, and husbands would ride back to work in Liverpool along the sea-shore.

This was the extreme social segregation, the regular retreat of a *haute bourgeoisie* to a carefully-contrived, exclusive community, the nearest approach for people still engaged in consolidating their fortunes to a retirement in Harrogate, Tunbridge Wells or Bournemouth. Usually, the physical separation of the classes in provincial towns was much less distant, though the social segregation no less complete. In Leeds, for example, the working classes lived in certain well-defined areas of the town, the North, North East and Kirkgate wards and the rapidly growing out-townships of Holbeck and Hunslet, while the middle classes inhabited the healthier and more pleasantly-situated districts in the Mill Hill, West and North West wards.[30] Frederick Engels described the same characteristic in Manchester in the 1840s: first, a commercial centre, about half a mile square, of offices and warehouses, practically without permanent residents but intersected by main thoroughfares occupied by shops of 'dazzling splendour'; next, a primarily working-class area, surrounding the commercial centre in a belt approximately one and a half miles wide; third, a middle-class area of regularly laid out streets in Chorlton and Cheetham Hill; and finally, an upper-middle-class area 'in the remoter parts of Chorlton and Ardwick, or on the breezy heights of Cheetham Hill, Broughton and Pendleton, where they live in villa-like houses surrounded by gardens'.[31] Omnibuses, running every fifteen or thirty minutes, connected these outlying suburbs to the commercial centre by the shortest possible routes, and although they necessarily ran through the working-class belt the passengers were totally oblivious of them since the slum areas were fronted and concealed by respectable shops along the main roads which 'serve the purpose of hiding from the eyes of wealthy gentlemen and ladies with strong stomachs and weak nerves the misery and squalor that form the completing counterpart, the indivisible complement, of their riches and luxury'.

Location, size and rent were clearly important influences on the middle-class house, yet they were almost certainly not the major considerations. To a large degree the choice of a house was unconscious and irrational: it 'appealed' because it seemed to give physical expression to a set of values which the occupier felt it was important for him to communicate to his family, his friends, relations and society at large. Better than any other symbol, the house conferred and announced status, and to a class whose familial origins and sources of wealth might be dubious, social goals held primacy over more rational considerations of size, location and cost.

In their suburban villas those whose incomes depended on the economic exploitation of the machine age could escape to romantic dreams of 'Merrie England', happily following Pugin in his hatred of the ugliness and ungodliness of the industrial age. The escape into the past—expressed in a self-conscious revival of earlier, especially Gothic, styles of architecture, furnishing and decoration—was also influenced by social imitation. If the working-class way of life was to be condemned and shunned, that of the gentry and aristocracy was, at least in some respects, to be admired and cultivated. They were still the arbiters of taste and fashion: their country houses and the life-style that went with them were still models to be aspired to, provided always that one could ignore their political and sexual irregularities. But there could be no doubt that landed society possessed gentility, and those who were assuming gentility for the first time needed a legitimizing ideology and a house that would characterize it. The cost and size of a country mansion and surrounding estate of some hundreds of acres were obviously inappropriate for most of the middle classes, but its plan and organization were important influences on the modest suburban villa. The middle classes felt the same need as the aristocracy to have as large a house and establishment as possible in order to entertain and interact in a civilized way, and also to fulfil their social duty to provide employment for household staff, tradesmen and other dependants.[32]

The great aristocratic house had itself already undergone change since the eighteenth century. A house like Lord Derby's in Grosvenor Square, designed by Robert Adam in 1773, has been described as 'devised for the conduct of an elaborate social parade', not built for domestic life so much as for the public life of politics, government and the law.[33] Country houses of the mid-nineteenth century, while retaining the great halls, receiving-rooms and galleries necessary for public, ceremonial occasions, had increasingly recognized the need for household privacy by providing family suites and, sometimes, separate family wings.[34] Private life and public life had, in any event, become increasingly differentiated as the apparatus of government had become enlarged and institutionalized. For the Victorian middle classes the separation of home from work, of business and professional life from the domestic life of family and friends, meant that privacy became an outstanding requirement in their homes. Together with respectability and confident solemnity, privacy was the leading characteristic of middle-class home life. It implied that the house itself should, desirably, be structurally separated from others and well-screened from the road: if this were impossible, as in the inner suburbs of cities, the compromise was pairs of semi-detached houses, unified by roof-line, gables or pediments to resemble one large house, nearness to the street being overcome by blinds or curtains of Nottingham lace. In this, as in so much else, the Victorians were ambivalent and illogical. The bay-window was important in order to distinguish the house from a flat-fronted, working-class terrace, but the bay-window invited prying eyes as well as sunlight which faded the carpet and upholstery, and therefore needed to be screened by inner curtains and floral displays.

Inside the house, privacy was again of central importance. Domestic life was to be controlled and regulated through categorization and segregation, so that specific functions would be confined to specific spatial areas. Bedrooms, kitchens, servants' rooms, bathrooms and sculleries spoke for themselves; dining-rooms were strictly for dining (and, commonly, family prayers), drawing-rooms for ceremonial social occasions, leaving a parlour or family room as necessary for everyday living. Larger houses would have still greater differentiation—studies or libraries, billiard-rooms, conservatories, smoking-rooms and morning-rooms, besides boudoirs, dressing-rooms, and day and night nurseries. Even in a moderate-sized house these requirements often implied two staircases and in a large house, three or more, besides innumerable doors, passages, hallways and vestibules designed to isolate family from servants, guests from tradesmen, males from females. Translated into the diminutive scale of the suburban villa, the concentration on privacy often produced a bewildering plan, a succession of small rooms, and much 'wasted' space.

The home was also seen as having a strong moral purpose, indeed, as the very centre of moral goodness, inculcating Christian love, truth and obedience and preserving the social and sexual respectability associated with such virtues. This view of the home was admirably expressed by John Ruskin:

> There is a sanctity in a good man's house . . . I say that if men lived like men indeed their houses would be temples—temples . . . in which it would make us holy to be permitted to live . . . When men do not love their hearths, nor

reverence their thresholds, it is a sign that they have dishonoured both, and that they have never acknowledged the true universality of . . . Christian worship . . . Our God is a Household God, as well as a heavenly one.[35]

To the architects of the Gothic Revival, especially to A. W. N. Pugin, it followed that buildings themselves should reflect Christian principles and purpose and the social 'propriety' ordained by God. 'Propriety' he interpreted to mean that 'Every person should be lodged as becomes his station and dignity, for in this there is nothing contrary to, but in accordance with, the Catholic principle'.[36]

The Christian justification for hierarchical housing was carried to extreme lengths in the work of Anglican architects such as William Butterfield at the village of Baldersby St James in Yorkshire, where from the church, the focus of the village, to the parish school facing it, down through the various kinds of housing, there was a conscious and carefully-controlled grading of size and decoration until the humbler dwellings ultimately merged into farm outbuildings and cow-sheds. In the largely unplanned growth of the towns social grading could not always be so nicely defined as this, though innumerable external features—width of house frontage, depth from road, height and type of windows, brickwork, mouldings, decorative plasterwork, wrought or cast-iron in railings and canopies, door panelling and furniture—could be used as signals of the status of the occupant. A line had to be carefully drawn, however, between extreme ostentation which might pass for vulgarity, and those distinctions which it was not only permissible, but a social duty, to employ.

Privacy, respectability and distinctive social identification were the leading external characteristics of the middle-class house. Internally, and additionally to these, were the characteristics of comfort and accumulation. The importance which the Victorians attached to their homes is evidenced by the amount of time, energy, thought and expense which they lavished on them, carried to the point where home and family—regarded as inseparable—came to be regarded as the central life interests. This is what most struck the American observer, R. W. Emerson:

> If he is in the middle condition he spares no expense on his house . . . Within it is wainscoted, carved, curtained, hung with pictures and filled with good furniture. 'Tis a passion which survives all others to deck and improve'.[37]

Ruskin was right to describe such homes as 'temples', though whether they were temples to God or to Mammon is debatable. They were, indeed, treasuries filled to overflowing with large and solid furniture, with floors heavily carpeted and with walls so obscured by pictures, draperies, shelves and mirrors that little of the patterned wallpaper was discernible, and with a multiplicity of small objects possessing either use, ornamental effect or ritual significance. Some of these, like the silver and silver-plated ware, combined all three, but many more purely ornamental curiosities had a use quite insignificant compared with their importance as display objects. Enormous ingenuity was also employed in disguising everyday objects like coal-scuttles into more 'polite' forms, usually by the heavy application of 'Gothic' or 'Classical' decoration. Novelty and imitation of the past were important ingredients in Victorian taste, combining, as it were, the practical advantages of technology with a rejection of utilitarian values.

Solid comfort and a cosy clutter were the leading characteristics of the Victorian interior. It could easily descend into a mean, depressing respectability or into crude, vulgar showiness, but it is wrong, as A. E. Richardson has reminded us, to judge the typical interior by the standards of the junk-shop or the seaside boarding-house.[38] Few middle-class houses would be furnished entirely in the new post-1830 styles, but would probably contain some Georgian and Regency pieces inherited as heirlooms even if now regarded as somewhat unfashionable. Comfort also included warm and adequately-lit rooms, well-upholstered easy chairs (coil-sprung from the 1830s onwards), tidiness and punctuality, especially at such ritual occasions as family prayers and mealtimes. It also meant, very importantly, scrupulous cleanliness and highly-polished surfaces—of furniture, windows, looking-glasses, silver and brass, glassware, fire-irons and hearths—which would reflect light and give visual brightness to the interior. This was, no doubt, optically desirable at a time when artificial lighting by candle, oil-lamp and, latterly, gas-jet, was still inadequate, but cleanliness and polished surfaces also possessed social and psychological significance as indicating a conquest of the environment, an announcement to the world that here at home lightness and order triumphed over the forces of darkness and chaos without.[39] Their victory, and, indeed, the whole 'philosophy of comfort', depended, as we have seen, on an abundance of personal service, without which the inconvenient houses with their multiplicity of rooms, long passages and staircases, and accumulations of furniture, hangings and knick-knacks would quickly have degenerated into dirty, dilapidated warrens. It is a question whether a large house was needed to accommodate the numbers of domestic servants, or whether a large domestic staff was necessitated by the large house. Probably both were true. A family needed to have as large an establishment as possible in order to entertain and interact in a civilized way at occasions such as dinner-parties, but at the same time one was providing employment for the sons and daughters of the poor, and thereby fulfilling a social duty.

An influence which runs through these attitudes is the increasing feminization of the Victorian house. Shut out from so much of public life and released from domestic drudgery by their servants, middle-class women turned their energies to home-making as no generation before had done. Their husbands' work had now been clearly separated from the home, and now that it no longer had to serve as shop, workshop or office it could be devoted to essentially female purposes—the care and nurture of children, the entertainment of friends and guests, the management of familial and matrimonial affairs. Thus, the home became a stage for the playing-out of roles and the conduct of an accepted pattern of social intercourse. In gaining admission to society, 'the roof is an introduction', so that to be presented to a stranger at a dinner-party was a guarantee of respectability which could then be developed in the ritual of 'calls': if acquaintance ripened, it would be recognized by invitation to a dinner-party, the apogee of the social scene, where strict formality, hierarchy and precedence prevailed. In the enforcement of these social codes, which centred on the home, women were the arbiters and executants.[40] In larger houses, it is true, it was possible to divide the accommodation into male and female 'territories'—for the former, studies, libraries, billiard and gun-rooms (sometimes arranged in a self-contained suite), for the latter, drawing-rooms, boudoirs, sewing and music-rooms—but in the average-sized house such extravagant use of space was not possible, and the male preserve was usually restricted to a small study and a dressing-room off the principal bedroom. The rest of the house, with the possible exception of the dining-room, which might be regarded as 'neutral', was essentially female territory where men moved circumspectly, and stepped out of line at their peril.

How were these characteristic values of middle-class home life translated into shapes on the ground? They were, necessarily, mediated through builders who, because they generally built speculatively, had to respond to what they believed clients wanted. In few cases was the ordinary middle-class house individually designed by an architect to a client's order. A large speculative builder might employ an architect to draw designs for a suburban estate development, but more commonly builders drew their own 'draughts', or they copied or adapted plans from one of the many pattern-books of house designs that were available. In choosing the patterns most likely to appeal, they would necessarily follow the broad trends in architectural style which succeeded each other rapidly throughout the period, adapting, simplifying and often crudifying. Where the scope for changes in plan was small, 'architectural style' might mean little more than the shape of windows and applied decorative features which would give a distinctive appearance to the exterior of a house the internal organization of which followed a standard plan. Architecture in the proper sense of the word—in the sense that Pugin understood when he ordained that 'there shall be no features of a building which are not necessary for convenience, construction and propriety'—was not a principal determinant of middle-class house form.

Style, however, was, and what was evidently and eminently fashionable in the first half of the nineteenth century changed rapidly—far more so than in the whole century which preceded it. Essentially, the ordered symmetry of the Georgian period gave way to a variety of styles the keynotes of which were individuality and romantic reaction to classicism. To an age which prided itself on individualism, the regularity of Georgian house design was increasingly unacceptable. In particular, the London Building Act of 1774, which categorized houses from First Rate to Fourth Rate according to their floor area and value, and laid down for each a code covering structural requirements, ornament and detail, became increasingly unpopular under its nickname, the 'Black Act'. Intended to prevent dangerous structures and to reduce fire risks, the Act became associated with municipal interference as well as architectural monotony, and largely accounted for the contemptuous dislike with which many Victorians subsequently viewed the Georgian period. G. Laurence Gomme echoed a widely-held view when he wrote of 'the gloom and incompetence in matters of art which characterized the Georgian period of history. There [was] . . . no new inspiration to add picturesque details to the bricks and mortar which took the place of green fields and trees . . . The Georgian spirit of architecture was against art, and declared for so-called utilitarianism, as if utility could exist without the element of art'.[41]

The breakaway from classical restraint began in earnest with the 'Picturesque', usually dated from the 1790s. It was essentially part of the Romantic Revival, aiming at structures sited pictorially within a landscape which would give the effect of a controlled wilderness. The Picturesque was, therefore, mainly a rural or suburban form which could not easily adapt to the town. It was particularly associated with Humphrey Repton, the landscape gardener, and with Paul Nash, its characteristic building types being the 'villa' (for example, Cronkhill, Salop) and the cottage—rediscovered in the period as a decorative toy to adorn an estate and to provide accommodation for farm servants (for example, at Blaise). The essence of the style was a combination of freedom and imitation, either of earlier, modified English forms such as castellated Gothic, or of continental styles from Italy, France, Switzerland and even India. The Italian balcony, the Indian verandah and the Turkish dome (as in the Brighton Pavilion) all became incorporated as picturesque features of the English country house and, with more restraint, in the Regency villas of suburban areas, watering-places and seaside resorts. The Repton villas at Kingston, Surbiton, Southgate, Dulwich and Bromley, the Nash 'villages' in the Regent's Park scheme and the housing developments in middle-class suburbs such as Edgbaston, Jesmond and Sefton Park all indicated the same revulsion against an urban aesthetic, against order, uniformity and control.[42]

The Picturesque was succeeded by a Greek Revival dating from about 1804, and associated with architects such as Robert Smirke and William Wilkins. Characteristically employed for large public buildings like museums, universities, theatres and clubs, the style was not so easily adapted to house building, though it was used in suburban 'villa' development by John Nash and others. Frequently such houses would be built in pairs, and sometimes in threes, giving collectively the appearance of one substantial villa and allowing the use of larger architectural features than would be possible on small individual houses. But much the more important influence on style after about 1820 was the 'Gothic'. In some respects, it had never totally disappeared, for there had been some 'Gothic' churches built in the seventeenth century, and Walpole's 'Strawberry Hill' Gothic of the mid-eighteenth century had ultimately merged into the Picturesque. The beginning of the serious Gothic Revival can be dated at around 1830, and was to be epitomized in the publication in 1836 of A. W. N. Pugin's *Contrasts*, a book which illustrated the ugliness and inhumanity of the industrial town compared with the idealized beauty and spaciousness of its medieval counterpart. The Gothic Revival quickly became an exceedingly powerful influence, affecting not only the Catholic and High Anglican churches, but having the support also of Evangelicals and Nonconformists and of the 'Merrie England' party who followed Cobbett and others in believing that industrialization was not only destroying the natural beauty of the land but was breaking up the natural orders of society as well as breeding paganism and vulgarity. To restore the 'natural' architecture of England would also be to restore her natural morality and society.[43]

These stylistic influences were communicated and popularized mainly by the compilers of architectural copy-books, of whom John Claudius Loudon (1783–1843) was easily the most successful and well-known. The son of a Scots farmer, Loudon became a professional author and encyclopaedist in the 1820s, publishing successively large works on gardening, agriculture and plants before producing his *Encyclopaedia of Cottage, Farm and Villa Architecture and Furniture* in 1833. It was, in fact, from landscape gardening and the design of conservatories and hot-houses (his invention of curved wrought-iron glazing bars made the glazed curvilinear roof a practical possibility) that he derived his interest in buildings, and, particularly, in 'villas' suited to a rural or suburban setting. His chief importance was as a purveyor of architectural styles for villas, farmhouses, cottages and inns, and for their interior decoration and furnishing. His *Encyclopaedia* contained over 2,000 illustrations of elevations, plans and details of houses in many varieties of 'romantic' style, from which it was possible for the client to select 'a small Grecian villa or casino', 'a villa in the Old Scotch Style', 'Old English' houses of stone or rubble-work, 'castellated Gothic', a wooden Swiss chalet, or even a two-roomed 'Italian Gothic' cottage suggested as being suitable for a childless country labourer and his wife.[44]

The naïvety and absurdity of some of Loudon's designs were too much even for a committedly imitative generation. The suggestion that a castellated Gothic villa for a small family should be sited 'on a bold, commanding, rocky prominence', and that the 'ornamental architectural appendages which accompany it should either be in some degree marked by the lines and finish of fortified walls, or should imitate their ruins', was dismissed by Pugin as 'a mere mask, and the whole building an ill-conceived lie'. But the less extreme designs were widely copied and adapted by speculative builders throughout the middle decades of the century, and Loudon's revival of vernacular features like half-timbering, casement and latticed windows, thatched roofs and so on were to leave enduring marks on subsequent house-building. More than any other individual he was responsible for the break-up of the long Georgian domination of English house style and for what John Summerson describes as 'the descent into chaos'. From one point of view, the English bourgeoisie had abandoned 'taste' for 'fashion' and had lapsed into a sentimental antiquarianism: from another, they had rejected their dependence on traditional, aristocratic dictates, and had announced their individuality in a variety of distinctive architectural styles.

In any case, the great majority of speculative builders did not adopt Loudon's designs *in toto*, which would often have meant expensive and unfamiliar building, but took a few features which, they hoped, would stamp a particular character on an otherwise standard house—a pillared and pedimented porch, bay-windows to the ground floor, a castellated parapet, a half-timbered gable or mullioned windows, or merely some decorative brickwork, stucco or plaster. The result might be considerable elegance (as in Cubitt's houses at Clapham Park), vulgarity (as in 'Camden Town Gothic'), or, more commonly, something between the two. Life in such a house, adequately serviced by a domestic staff, could bring to the middle classes new standards of comfort, order and even elegance not very different from those formerly enjoyed only by the small and privileged class of gentry. A letter written by the daughter of a vicar whose income was about £800 a year describes a house and a life-style which many of those in the 'middling ranks' of society would have recognized as very like their own:

In 1847 we came to live in Hertfordshire . . . The Vicarage was an attractive red-brick house, built by my father, who spent, I believe, far more than he could afford in extras not covered by the Church grant. There was a park-like field, a small flower garden and excellent kitchen garden, stables and piggery. We kept poultry but not cows. The house contained a tiled entrance lobby and oak-floored hall, dining-room, drawing-room and study, three best bedrooms and two dressing-rooms, two servants' rooms and two nurseries. These latter were in a wing approached by a baize-covered swing door, and back stairs led down to the kitchen, pantry and a small parish room, which were approached from the hall by another baize-covered swing door . . . there were no bath rooms then, and all hot and cold water had to be carried from the kitchen and scullery. But we all had baths each day in spite of that. Oil lamps and candles were used for lighting. Our drawing-room was papered with a buff and gilt Fleur-de-Lys patterned paper. There were book shelves and pier glasses and wool-work ottomans and an upright grand piano with faded red silk fluted across the front and a very fine harp. The harp was a popular instrument in my mother's youth. The carpet was red with a buff pattern, and my mother had a davenport (a small writing-table) sacred to her own use. In the best bedrooms there were four-post beds with damask curtains, though brass beds were by then becoming fashionable . . . After the nurse left, our household consisted of a cook, house-parlour-maid and a girl. Their wages were £18, £16 and £6.[45]

Trollope's Archdeacon Grantly had considered a dining-room 16ft by 15ft quite impossible because it would only accommodate a round table, which he associated with oak and Dissenters and calico-printers who, he imagined, chiefly used them. But the interior of the middle-class house, its use and furnishing, we leave until a later chapter.

PART II: 1850–1914

5

HOUSING THE LABOURER

The housing of the rural worker posed a problem for Victorian humanitarians and legislators which raised, in miniature, many of the fundamental issues that ultimately had to be faced on a larger scale in national housing policy. The justification for devoting a chapter to the housing of what was, after all, a declining section of the population is that for the first time public opinion was brought face to face with a problem that defied traditional remedies and prompted radical, uncomfortable alternatives.

The truth behind the Victorians' sentimental image of the countryman was that agricultural labourers existed at the lowest standard of life of any fully-employed section of the community, that they were, in general, miserably rewarded for long and arduous work, that they were ill-fed, ill-clothed and ill-housed and, until late in the century, uneducated, unenfranchised, unorganized and unrepresented. 'The constant wonder is', wrote the Rev Sidney Godolphin Osborne, 'that the labourer can live at all'—the paradox perhaps explained by Canon Girdlestone's rejoinder that labourers 'did not live in the proper sense of the word, they merely didn't die'. But it was difficult for urban England, struggling with its own problems of dirt, disease and overcrowding, to recognize that a man who spent his days in the open air, had a home provided free or at a nominal rent, and could often grow at least some of his own food, could be poorer than the poorest industrial worker. One needed to penetrate, as Francis George Heath had done in 1873, behind the whitewashed walls and thatched roofs half-hidden by orchards and festooned in creepers—beyond, that is, the threshold where Mrs Hemans had not stepped. In a row of eighteen such pretty dwellings in a hamlet near Minehead, he caught sight of a child without shoes sitting on the doorstep of 'Rose Cottage'. The father of this family of five children—the eldest a boy of $9\frac{1}{2}$—earned 10s a week as a carter and three pints of cider a day as a 'privilege'; on this, he somehow supported his wife, his children, and his bedridden mother of 93, the only other source of income being the earnings of the eldest child—5d a day. The cottage consisted of one wretched living-room and two small bedrooms above, one occupied by the old lady, the other by the parents and five children; there was a tattered bed which filled most of the small floor-space, and three of the children had to sleep on a pile of rags at its foot. The one tiny window had several of its panes broken, but repair was the tenant's responsibility, and there was never any spare money. The rent had formerly been £2 2s 0d a year, but the new squire had raised it to £3 5s 0d, and additionally, and ironically, there was 10s a year for rates—poor-rate,

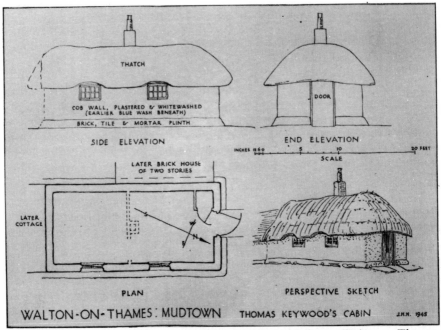

6   Near the minimum: simple cob and thatch cottage, Mudtown, Walton-on-Thames. Two-room cottage built c 1830 representative of low-quality building widely prevailing in late nineteenth century. Internal size 21ft × 9ft 3in (6·4 × 2·8m) (*Surrey Archaeological Collections*)

school-rate and gas-rate for the parish of Minehead. 'The poor folks wondered, naturally enough, why they had to pay a gas-rate when there was no gas within more than a mile of them . . .'[1]

The labourer's cottage, like his food, his dress, and every other aspect of his material well-being, depended ultimately on what he could afford to pay, and hence on his general economic position. That position bore little direct relation to the state of the agricultural economy of which he was an essential, though almost unrecognized, part. On the contrary, during the so-called 'golden age' of farming prosperity between the repeal of the Corn Laws in 1846 and the onset of agricultural depression in the early 1870s, his standard of life was probably at its lowest, while in the period of falling profitability in the 1870s and 1880s he was often able to make some significant gains. His position depended much more intimately on local factors and personal circumstances. Long before Seebohm Rowntree identified the 'cycle of poverty' through which many industrial workers would pass at different periods of their lives, George Bartley in *The Seven Ages of a Village Pauper* (1874) had shown how the agricultural labourer's standard of life varied between his childhood, his marriage, the raising of his family, and his old age, and how, at numerous critical points in his life-journey, he would be forced to apply to the Poor Law Guardians for relief. In the anonymous village of 1,450 inhabitants twenty-four miles from London on which he based his investigation, one in every eleven were officially paupers on Lady Day, 1873, but three-quarters of all would probably receive public relief at some stage of their lives.[2] The same man who might be moderately comfortable in middle life when he was at full strength and when his children were contributing to the family budget might well end his days in the workhouse or, at best, dependent on niggardly charity.

A second important variable was the nature of employment. Among farm workers there were many degrees of skill and responsibility which were rewarded by different levels of pay and 'perquisites'; and, in particular, there was usually a sharp distinction drawn between farm servants and day labourers. The former were key men, mainly concerned with the stock—cowmen, shepherds, horsemen, waggoners and so on—who were paid anything from 1s to 3s a week extra, were generally hired by the year, had a free cottage (or, as in Cumberland, were boarded in the farmhouse) and suffered no deductions of pay for days lost in bad weather. Cottages on farms were included as part of the farmer's holding from the landlord, and were used to accommodate these men who needed to be on the spot and available for extra and irregular work. Day labourers, on the other hand, were mainly employed on field work, which was necessarily seasonal in demand. They had no security of employment, being generally hired by the week or even by the day. They had few, if any, perquisites, and since they were only paid for work done, could expect to lose a proportion of their wages, especially in winter. Their opportunities of regular employment were, in any case, diminishing as machinery began to take over such tasks as threshing, and as farmers increasingly contracted work out with peripatetic agricultural 'gangs', consisting largely of women and children under the control of a 'gang master', and consequently needed to keep a smaller permanent labour force. Above all, the day labourer, as a supposedly free agent in the labour market, was not provided with accommodation, and had to make his own arrangements with proprietors in a village or market town at some distance from his work.[3] This contrast between the housing experience of farm servants and day labourers was fundamental to the whole problem of rural accommodation.

The contrast between the labourer's position in the 'low-wage' counties of the South and South-West and the 'high-wage' areas of the North and North-West, which was discussed in chapter 2, also continued to be of major importance in the later part of the century. An official enquiry in 1872 showed a range of day labourer's wages from 10s 4d a week in Dorset to 20s 6d in Durham, the mean being supposedly 14s 8d,[4] though it was in that same year that Joseph Arch's newly-formed Agricultural Labourers' Union was demanding an increase in the Warwickshire labourer's starvation wage of 12s a week. By the first decade of the twentieth century further gains had been made in many parts of the country, though there can be no exact statistics where 'allowances', 'days lost' and, for some, the value of a tied cottage were all involved in the calculation. A Board of Trade Report for 1903 calculated an optimistic average wage, including all extra earnings, of 18s 6d a week, though a detailed survey by H. H. Mann of the Bedfordshire village of Ridgmount in 1904 gave 14s 4d and another by C. R. Buxton of Oxfordshire villages in 1912 gave only 10s–12s. What such wages meant in terms of purchasing power was highlighted by Seebohm Rowntree in 1913, extending his earlier survey of urban poverty into the countryside and demonstrating that only in five northern counties (Northumberland, Durham, Westmorland, Lancashire and Derbyshire) was the wage sufficient to maintain a family of average size in a state of 'mere physical efficiency', calculated on the minimum nutritional requirements.[5] His stark, scientific findings seemed to belie the conclusion of the Royal Commission on Labour of 1894 that 'his [the labourer's] standard of life is higher, he dresses better, he eats more butcher's meat, he travels more, he reads more and he drinks less . . .'[6]

In one respect, at least, the judgment was correct—the labourer undoubtedly travelled more. One of the main causes of what improvement there had been was that the labourer had made himself a scarcer and more valuable commodity on the rural labour market by a massive flight from the land to the towns, to the colonies and to America. Between 1851 and 1911, during which time the population of England and Wales doubled from 17,928,000 to 36,070,000, the number of agricultural workers fell from 965,500 to 643,100.[7] During the last thirty years of the century labourers were leaving the land at the rate of 100,000 every decade to go navvying, to join the army, the navy or the police, to seek whatever labouring work the towns had to offer or to go, often with assisted passages, to new lands which gave men without capital the opportunity of a stake in the soil. The reasons which prompted labourers to exchange their secure poverty for the uncertainties of life elsewhere were many, various, and in the end individual, but one of the investigators for the Royal Commission on Labour in 1893 believed that what the rural labourer wanted was greater independence, and that he did not leave the land when he had a decent cottage at a fair rent, a good-sized garden or allotment, and the hope of one day gaining a smallholding of a few acres. What was resented was the old, semi-feudal relationship, the stigma of dependence on the goodwill of the landlord or farmer, and the insecurity of a tied cottage which often made a labourer prefer to rent high-priced accommodation in a village several miles from his work. Others blamed the scarcity of cottages as a main reason why young people left the land because of the difficulty of marrying and setting up home and their refusal to share already overcrowded accommodation with parents and younger children. Similarly, the Report of the Land Enquiry Committee of 1913 ascribed the drift to inadequate housing, long hours, monotonous work, the lack of a Saturday half-holiday and, above all, the lowness of wages. Trade unionism, it was noted, was least effective among the lowest-paid workers, and it was suggested that the recent Trade Boards Act should be extended to farm workers in order to guarantee a minimum living wage.[8]

It was precisely this growing public concern over the depopulation of the countryside which promoted rural housing to an issue of national importance. From the early 1870s to the outbreak of World War I dozens of reports, books, investigations, and articles in learned and periodical journals deplored the flight from the land, sometimes in sentimental, emotional terms, but more often on the basis of a supposedly scientific argument that the preservation of the countryman was essential to national health, vigour and character. It was widely believed—and statistics were quoted to support it—that the countryman was fitter than the townsman, and that his continued presence on the land was necessary for the maintenance of national physique: in 1906–10, for example, the general death rate in the towns was 16 per thousand compared with $12\frac{1}{2}$ in rural districts, the infant mortality rate 127 per thousand as against 98. The anxiety was expressed that by now country dwellers had 'given up their best' and that the previous 'reinforcement of the anaemic town dwellers by countrymen'[9] was rapidly coming to an end. It was a well-known fact that it had been the youngest, fittest, most intelligent men and women who had emigrated to the towns and the transatlantic prairies, leaving an ageing and degenerating stock behind them. Further statistics were adduced to show that the greatest poverty in the towns was among the town-bred workers, not the country-bred, and that in 1906, 66 per cent of the Metropolitan Police Force were country-born, and of the Glasgow Police no fewer than 91 per cent. Where was the next generation of recruits to come from? And, more serious still after Britain's near-defeat in the Boer War (1899–1902) and the rejection for military service of 40 per cent of volunteers on medical grounds, where were the future armies and navies to come from, on whom Britain depended for the maintenance of her world power and empire? The newly-awakened concern for 'national efficiency' which was shared by groups as divergent as Liberal Imperialists and Fabians, and which became a major political influence in the years before 1914, had at last forced the question of the labourer's condition, and specifically the labourer's housing, onto public attention.

The problem was how to anchor the surviving peasantry to the soil, and, if possible, win back some of the enterprising emigrants from the over-crowded towns and cities. Higher wages—if necessary negotiated by Agricultural Trades Boards—better educational opportunities, public provision of allotments and small-holdings, increased mechanization on large farms leading to a demand for higher skill, would all help, it was believed, but there was universal agreement that improved housing was central to the problem. The labourer needed a secure, comfortable, sanitary cottage, with sufficient bedrooms to ensure decency for his larger-than-average family (closer to five rather than the four of urban districts in 1901) and with enough garden to grow his own vegetables, otherwise he would continue to desert for better opportunities elsewhere. Existing cottage accommodation was inadequate both in quality and in quantity, an investigation of 1913 showing that in 1,400 out of 2,700 parishes there was an actual shortage, and estimating that 120,000 new cottages were urgently needed either for replacement or addition to stock.

It had long been known that, given the labourer's low wages, a rent in the range of 1s 6d to 2s 6d a week was all, or more, than could reasonably be demanded, but that this would not yield anything approaching the 8–10 per cent a year profit which a builder or investor expected to make out of real property. This was the root cause of the problem. Here was a large class of labour, hard-working, patient and socially desirable, which could simply not afford the economic rent which would enable them to occupy the kind of accommodation which the community had decided was minimally accept-able. The result was that cottages were frequently let at rents at which it did not pay to build new ones. Much of the discussion in the earlier part of the period was either about the possibility of cheapening costs of construction by changes in building methods, or about the humanitarian responsibility of landlords and farmers in effect to subsidize the accommodation of their workforce by devoting as much care and expense to it as they did to the accommodation of their livestock. As early as 1863 the Rev Dr Begg was telling the influential National Association for the Promotion of Social Science that rural labourers were in a quite different position from town workers in that, as a rule, they were 'entirely at the mercy of tenants and landlords, and unless good cottages were provided for them, they could not obtain them by any efforts of their own'. Inspectors should be appointed, on the analogy of factory and mines inspectors, to survey all rural cottages. Landlords were the only large class of people in the country to whom the principle of control had not been extended, and considering how helpless the labourers were 'they, of all others, require some public and authorita-tive interposition on their behalf'.[10] Begg was already pointing the argu-ment forward. By 1914 it had become abundantly clear that both market forces and philanthropy had failed to solve the problem of the labourer's dwelling, and that local authorities, operating the complicated and inadequate Housing Acts of 1890 and 1909, were equally powerless. William Savage, who as Medical Officer of Health for Somerset, knew the rural housing problem intimately, summed up the dilemma and its solution: private enterprise looking for profits could not supply the deficiency; the closure of unfit houses only aggravated the problem for the remainder; building by local authorities meant, in effect, a subsidy to the farmers who paid low wages, but to raise wages would be to raise the cost of food. The only solution was direct state assistance by the Exchequer, a national subsidy to aid private builders and local authorities, and, at the same time, a gradual improvement in wages.[11] The case for state subsidization of housing was openly declared, if still not generally accepted.

In turning to the actual condition of labourers' housing we select two periods for comparison—the 1860s and the end of the century—for both of which there is abundant contemporary evidence. To read through the pages of the official Reports of the 1860s is to journey through almost unbroken misery and wretchedness, relieved only rarely by bright spots where philanthropic landowners had erected a few neat, model cottages. In general, the accounts are of crazy, dilapidated hovels, many containing only one bedroom into which large families, grandparents and even lodgers were crowded indiscriminately, of whole families ill of fever and lying in the same room with a corpse, of holes in roofs and ceilings, damp walls, saturated floors and rooms filled, not by furniture but only by smoke. Writing of this period with outraged emotion, Richard Heath described the 'innumerable miseries which rendered these miserable homes still more miserable—the toilsome journeys to work, often many miles a day—the occupation of the mothers in the fields—the corruption of the young by the ganging system; all these causes assisted to destroy domestic affection—the one humanizing influence left to the labourer amidst all his trials and temptations'.[12]

In 1864 Dr John Simon, the pioneering Medical Officer of the Privy Council, commissioned the first national enquiry into rural labourers' dwellings, carried out by Dr H. J. Hunter, and published the following year.[13] His surveys covered 821 country parishes in which between the census years of 1851 and 1861 the population had increased from 305,567 to 322,064. The number of cottages, however, had fallen from 69,225 to 66,109, with the result that the average number of persons per house had risen from 4·41 to 4·87. Dr Hunter then made a detailed investigation of the structure of 5,375 typical cottages, particularly with respect to bedroom accommodation. In total, the 5,375 cottages possessed 8,805 bedrooms which had to serve for 13,432 adults and 11,338 children, an average of almost three persons per room; 2,195 cottages (40·8 per cent) had only one bedroom, 2,930 (54·5 per cent) had two, and only 250 (4·7 per cent) had more than two. The single-bedroom cottages contained an average of four persons per room. The average air-space per person over all the sample worked out at 156cu ft, whereas the law required a minimum of 250cu ft in common lodging-houses, providing only temporary accommodation, and 500 in workhouses and other Poor Law institutions.

The national statistics are made more pointed by examples, taken almost at random from the Report, of the situation at local levels. At Gayhurst in Buckinghamshire in 1851, eighty-eight people had occupied twenty-three houses; ten years later 129 persons occupied twenty-one. At Charlton Marshall in Dorset cottages had fallen from 167 to 124 while the number of occupants had risen from 463 to 553. In fifty-five Somerset parishes investigated there had been an increase of 2,018 people in the previous ten years but a decrease of 325 houses. The inevitable result of such changes was increased overcrowding of accommodation, and especially of bedrooms. A row of twelve cottages at Langtoft in Lincolnshire each had only one bedroom (12ft 2in by 9ft 5in), and these bedrooms contained thirty-eight adults and thirty-six children, an average of more than six per room, while in the strawplaiting district of Bedfordshire ninety-four one-bedroom cottages contained 264 adults and 210 children, or an average of five per room. On this and much similar evidence Dr Simon came to the conclusion that the state of labourers' housing, despite the prosperity of agriculture at the time, was seriously deteriorating, 'house-room being now greatly more difficult for him to find, and, when found, greatly less suitable to his needs than perhaps for centuries has been the case. Especially within the last twenty or thirty years the evil has been in very rapid increase, and the household circumstances of the labourer are in the highest degree deplorable'.

The main cause of the problem, Hunter believed, was the unfortunate distinction between 'closed' and 'open' parishes. As we have previously seen, the distinction had long existed, but it became more evident as estates were increasingly concentrated into fewer hands in the middle of the nineteenth century, and was exacerbated by the fact that until 1865 poor-rates were levied on the house-property in each parish so that it was strongly in the interests of a landowner to demolish any accommodation which was not absolutely necessary for the farming needs of the parish. The evil of this was, as James Caird pointed out in 1852, that a proprietor was often able to drive a labourer out from the parish in which he worked to a distant 'open' village from which he would have to walk perhaps an hour in each direction. Cases were quoted of labourers walking forty and fifty miles a week, and of some farmers actually providing donkeys to prevent their labourers being too tired for their work.[14] The other side of the coin was, of course, that they were then crowded together in the 'open' parishes, suffering from high rents and dangers to health and morality, while the 'closed' proprietors preserved a tidy estate of improved or model cottages for their essential farm servants only. The image of a contented and obedient peasantry was maintained by the disciplining of a village by eliminating uncontrolled dwellings and undesirable labourers. 'In the close village', wrote Dr Hunter, 'the scene is beautiful, but unreal; without its open neighbour it could not exist . . . It is a hiding away of the cottage population in certain villages, and this is effected by unsparing destruction in others.'

Throughout the 1860s detail was piled upon detail to elaborate and confirm Dr Hunter's findings. To attempt to summarize the mass of evidence would add little to the picture, and it is more revealing to focus on two or three counties which are representative of differing agricultural areas. East Anglia was typical of prosperous, 'high farming', and Norfolk had long been known for its 'improving' landlords and model techniques. The housing of the labourer here, however, could be either very good or very bad. In 1863 the *Norfolk News* published a week-by-week survey of cottages carried out by a Mr Clarke which uncovered housing evils as bad as any in the country:

A stranger cannot enter the village [of Saxlingham] without being struck with surprise at the wretched and desolate condition. Look where he may, he sees little else but thatched roofs, old, rotten and shapeless, full of holes and overgrown with weeds; windows sometimes patched with rags and sometimes plastered over with clay; the walls, which are nearly all of clay, full of cracks and crannies . . . internally, they are quite as bad as far as their state of disrepair . . .

At Corpusty fever had recently broken out. A typical cottage here contained

. . . two small, wretchedly ventilated and almost dark bedrooms, with slanting roofs coming down almost to the floor. This miserable hovel was occupied by J.R. and his wife, five children and their grandfather, besides an illegitimate child of one of the daughters . . . In one of the upstairs rooms sleep father and mother, while in the other, measuring only 11ft 6in by 7ft 6in, sleep son eleven, daughter thirteen, daughter seventeen, son twenty, and daughter twenty-three, as well as the child of the eldest daughter . . . [15]

Perhaps it was that Mr Clarke was only looking for the bad cottages—as some correspondents suggested—and found them. But he was fully vindicated a few years later when a Royal Commission on the Employment of Children, Young Persons and Women in Agriculture rightly devoted much space in its massive Reports to the circumstances of home life and the condition of cottages. The Rev James Fraser, who was responsible for the Norfolk enquiry, studded his report with such comments as 'It is a hideous picture, and the picture is drawn from life', and 'It is impossible to exaggerate the ill-effects in every respect, physical, social, economical, moral, intellectual . . . Modesty must be an unknown virtue, decency an unimaginable thing, where, in one small chamber . . . father, mother, young men, lads, grown and growing-up girls—two or sometimes three generations—are herded promiscuously'. Much cottage building had been done in recent years by some great landowners, but the complete remedy did not lie with them. Many cottages belonged to small proprietors, too indigent to spare anything for their improvement, some to absentee and embarrassed landowners, some to mortgagees, many to speculative builders, especially in the 'open' parishes. 'It is estimated that the proprietorship of less than half the cottages in Norfolk is in the owners of the soil.' At the root of the problem were the wretched 'open' villages like Docking, 'into which have been poured remorselessly the scum and off-scour of their "close" neighbours', and for such places the only remedy was a Building Act, a system of inspection and limitation of the number of occupants in relation to cubic capacity. Rents in Norfolk ranged from £2 12s 0d to £7 a year, often the cheapest being the best model cottages and the highest some of the worst speculative building in 'open' villages. Lord Leicester charged only £3 3s 0d for his model dwellings, and had adopted the excellent practice of letting direct to the labourer, which gave some protection and security of tenure against the farmer-employer.[16]

An agricultural region of very different character, Northumberland and Durham, was surveyed by Mr Henley. Here was more pastoral farming, requiring the constant attendance of hinds and shepherds, who were usually hired by the year and received cottages as part payment. There had been much progress during the last thirty years by great landowners, the Duke of Northumberland having built or improved 931 cottages, and Earl Grey and Mr Creswell also having been prominent in the 'model' movement. Farmers were now becoming reluctant to take a farm unless there was suitable cottage accommodation, since otherwise they had to pay higher wages or be content with second-class labour. The old style of accommodation, still prevalent in the unimproved areas, was a single large room about 18ft square, built of rough stone, with an earth floor, no ceiling or upper storey, and with accommodation for a cow at one end. Everything had to be brought in by the hind when he took possession—fixtures, shelves, partitions, a fire-grate, even, sometimes, the one tiny window which fitted into a space provided. Such places accommodated eight, ten or eleven persons, sleeping in box-beds which a local surgeon described as 'very injurious . . . sort of coffins for the living'. It was said, however, that even in 1867 the preference was still for one large downstairs room where a fire was kept burning constantly, and warmth was gradually built up through the long winter. Parents and the younger children would sleep here, but ideally there should be one or two separate bedrooms for older children, also on the ground floor: this arrangement was thought to be very preferable to the designs adopted by the Cottage Building Society in 1847, which provided only one room, a loft, and very inadequate sanitary arrangements. One good feature that Mr Henley admired, however, was that in contrast to the exteriors of the old cottages, housewives generally lavished great attention on the interiors, keeping them bright and clean, furnishing them well, and even hanging calico 'ceilings' between the roof beams.[17]

From every part of the country the evidence was assembled. A few counties emerged from the scrutiny with relatively good reputations—Yorkshire, Lancashire and Derbyshire being the best, Leicestershire, Shropshire, Gloucestershire and Worcestershire bad, Dorset, Wiltshire and Somerset competing for the worst. The South-West generally was a region of 'wholesale neglect', suffering from the lowness of wages which Caird had noted, and from the scarcity of great 'improving' landowners. We select Dorset as representative of the region, where the cottages were described as 'a byword and a reproach'. Wages then still stood at only 8s and 9s a week, or 10s for a cowman having Sunday work. A labourer in Piddletown paid 2s a week rent out of a wage of 8s 6d, and rents for new, substantial cottages went up to £7 a year. A few landlords had done much for their own villages, the example having been set by Henry Charles Sturt of Critchell, who since the early 50s had been building three-bedroomed cottages for families and some, on one floor only, for old people. But in the many 'open' parishes housing of a virtually medieval kind was still prevalent.

> The Dorset cottage is usually built of mud, with a thatched roof. Many have only one bedroom; three is a luxury to which few can lay claim. Enter one; a more dreary place it would be difficult to imagine. There is no grate, but a huge open chimney, with a few bricks upon the hearth, on which the miserable inhabitants place their fuel—sometimes nothing but clods of peat, emitting wretched, acrid vapours. Owing to the low, open chimney, the house is constantly filled with smoke, rendering the ceilings, where they have them, black and dingy enough.

Dr Aldridge stated at a meeting of the Farmers' Club at Dorchester in January 1867 that 'the cottages at Fordingham were so bad that he ventured to say that they would not put their animals in such places . . . In many of these cottages one could not stand upright, and the smoke, dirt and filth together made a state of things not to be equalled in St. Giles's'.[18]

The picture of rural housing in the 1860s was, then, a patchwork of good, bad and terrible, of crumbling mud and thatch survivals from an earlier age interspersed here and there with tidy new brick and tile cottages on model estates, heightening the contrast between 'closed' and 'open' parishes. In these prosperous days for farming, when, as Lord Sidney Godolphin Osborne reported, 'the first thing you hear after breakfast, on paying a visit to a country neighbour, is "Come and see my new cottages"', it was still possible to believe that enlightened self-interest, encouraged by the equalization of poor-rates and by the possibility after 1865 of borrowing from the Inclosure Commissioners for cottage improvement, would, in time, solve the problem. The problem was not seen as a national one so much as a local, individual and moral one. Overcrowding in cities had begun to receive some attention, pointed out the Rev John Montgomery, but in the rural areas hardly at all, yet it greatly contributed to 'the mass of accumulated misery and corruption which they contain ... If human beings are crowded together, moral corruption takes place as certainly as fermentation or putrefaction in a heap of organic matter'.[19] The simile was powerful, if hardly polite. Yet the Rev James Fraser, after alluding to the physical effects of bad and insanitary accommodation—fevers of all kinds, catarrh, rheumatism, scrofula and phthisis—returned to the moral consequences of overcrowded bedrooms as 'fearful to contemplate ... The whole atmosphere is sensual, and human nature is degraded into something below the level of the swine'. In Norfolk, it was reported, one child in every ten was illegitimate, and in Gloucestershire, according to Canon Girdlestone,

> When young girls are brought into contact with men by overcrowding in that sort of way, and by going to offices [privies] which are exposed to public view, the fine edge of modesty must, of course, be very much blunted; and there is no doubt that that does lead ... in the end to immorality, to communication with each other before marriage, and such like.

A few observers in the 1860s had begun to see the wider implications of 'cottage herding'. The closed circle of bad housing and living standards, drink, poverty and pauperism has already been noticed. Others identified another vicious circle of bad housing leading to low rents, low wages and low standards of living, and argued that employers who did not provide decent cottages only got bad, inefficient labour, and paid dearly for it in the end. It was also claimed with some force that the notorious 'gang system' was in part due to the shortage of cottages, and therefore of sufficient permanent labour, on the farms. This mounting concern over the cottage question, in which the rural clergy played a leading part alongside doctors and sanitary reformers, was beginning to have noticeable effects on the rate of new building and improvement, and in Suffolk alone it was reported that one landowner had spent £10,000 and another £8,000 on cottages within the previous ten years.[20] But shortly after this the prosperity of much of English agriculture was undermined by the onset of depression in 1873. In the face of mass imports of American wheat, followed in the next decade by imported frozen meat, farming rents and profits slumped badly, much land went out of cultivation, and a general loss of confidence spread over the countryside. Such conditions were hardly conducive to agricultural investment of any kind, least of all, perhaps, to labourers' housing, and for the next twenty-five years or so cottage building on many estates virtually came to an end. Those 'nine-tenths of landowners in the south of England' who, in 1871, were reported as 'busy at improvement'[21] were now precisely those who were most busy at economy and retrenchment.

From the dismal record of the 1860s to the end of the century is but a short step, and in many cases the actual descriptions of cottages were almost identical. The structural condition was often still as bad as ever—bare thatch, wattle and daub walls, earth floors and ladders to the single, upstairs room—and overcrowding in bedrooms equally persistent. Mr Selby, an agent of the Agricultural Labourers' Union, testified before the Royal Commission on the Housing of the Working Classes in 1884 to cases in Wiltshire of seven and nine persons sleeping in one small bedroom and to numerous Essex villages where one bedroom was the general rule. The Rev C. W. Stubbs described his parish of Granborough, Buckinghamshire, as containing 50 cottages, 17 of which had only one bedroom, 32 two, and only 1 more than two, and in some the rooms were no more than 8ft square. Several union witnesses made a strong complaint about tied cottages, and the fact that labourers were sometimes turned out at a week's notice. 'There is evidence from different parts of England', said the Report, 'that there is more dissatisfaction among the labourers with regard to this part of the cottage question than about anything else; the insecurity of the tenure is felt more severely even than the misery of the accommodation.'[22]

By the 1880s the quality and tenure of cottage accommodation was being articulated by labourers themselves for the first time. Their emergence into the political arena was due, in part, to improved education and to rising standards of living and expectation but, more importantly, to the extension of the franchise to the rural worker in 1884. Although Lord Ernle's claim in 1912 that 'from that moment politicians have tumbled over one another in their eagerness to secure his support' was exaggerated optimism, it is true that from now on governments were increasingly conscious of, and responsive to, the needs of a new and significant body of workers whose supposed traditional attachment to the Conservative cause might be in doubt. Security of tenure was, as the Royal Commission pointed out, a more sensitive issue to the labourer than a mere shortage of bedrooms or privies, and had been in the programme of the National Agricultural Labourers' Union since its formation in 1872. Joseph Arch was now arguing strongly for 'cottage right' as well as 'tenant right'. When cottages were let with the farm, the labourer was 'bound hand and foot' and dared not move to higher-paid employment such as railway work: he should have a proper tenancy agreement and proper notice to quit—not eviction after a week or a day.[23] But after the Agricultural Lockout of 1874 the union's influence and membership were in decline, and some landowners who had followed Lord Leicester's good example of letting direct to the labourer now changed their practice in the belief that the farmer needed more protection. In this respect, there was some justification for the view of the Kent Agricultural Labourers' Union who at their formation had refused to make cottage improvement one of their objects on the ground that it could only give greater control to the landlord.

The situation at the end of the century can best be gathered from the voluminous reports of the Labour Commission, 1892–4, and especially from the *General Report* of William Little. His comments show that in respect of numbers the situation had improved somewhat during the last twenty-five years, but that qualitatively there had been no radical progress:

> The supply of cottages is not now generally defective in respect of numbers, owing partly to the decrease in the rural population and partly to the large number of cottages which have been built by large landowners and others who can afford to build without an expectation of a profitable return for their outlay . . .
>
> The distribution of cottages is irregular, and their situation often very inconvenient for the inhabitants . . .
>
> The accommodation provided in respect of the number, size and comfort of the rooms, the sanitary condition and the water supply are lamentably deficient generally, and require amendment . . .
>
> The rent paid for cottages hired by labourers varies from 9d to 7s a week, the most usual sum charged being apparently about 1s 6d a week, or £4 a year . . .
>
> That rent has generally no relation to the size of the cottage, the cost of its construction, the accommodation which it affords, its condition as regards repair or sanitary arrangements, or to the earnings of the occupant . . .[24]

Although so much here was familiar, change was evidently beginning to overtake the countryside in some respects. In areas where there was still a scarcity of housing, the reasons were put down partly to the higher standards now expected, the demand by townspeople for country cottages and the increased longevity of labourers themselves. The labourer was at last beginning to think of more than minimal shelter and, conscious of his own scarcity, was abandoning the very worst pest-holes for work which would offer him acceptable accommodation. In some places cottages visited by the Commissioners in 1893 were described as 'little palaces', but others they regarded as suitable only for the inferior class of livestock. The contrast between good and bad was sharper than ever—between the new, model cottages with their three bedrooms, proper sanitation and water supply, and good gardens which enlightened landowners were building again by the 1890s, and the old, decayed 'one up and one down' shacks which were unchanged since the eighteenth century, some with clay walls no more than an inch thick in places, with damp brick or earth floors, tiny, rickety windows and a complete absence of such conveniences as ovens, coppers or sinks.[25] Plenty of one-bedroomed cottages were still reported in Norfolk and Suffolk, throughout the Midland counties, the South-West and, less commonly, in the Home Counties, and landlords sometimes found resistance to improvement in areas where the bad was so familiar. Families provided with a new, three-bedroomed cottage sometimes did not use the third, or used it as a granary or lumber-room: there was sometimes a preference for ladders rather than staircases as requiring less space. Ventilation was provided but not valued, it was said, and drainage and sewerage were being forced on an unappreciative peasantry.

We may, tentatively, summarize the accommodation change between 1850 and 1900 as a change from one living-room and one or two bedrooms to a living-room plus a kitchen or scullery and either two or three bedrooms. There had also generally been improvements to fittings such as cooking-ranges, ovens, boilers and WCs, though much still remained to be done in the provision of such amenities of comfort. In this respect it is useful to examine the recommendations of 'model' designers as representing what were regarded as something like ideal standards for their time. A posthumous edition of Loudon's now-famous *Encyclopaedia*, edited by his wife in 1857, contained more than eighty designs for cottages and lodges, many of them in some variety of 'Picturesque' style—Gothic, Tudor, Classical and so on. The 'simplest' of them contained a 'parlour' 10ft 6in by 7ft, a kitchen 11ft by 7ft, a back kitchen 11ft by 10ft, a larder, separate men's and women's WCs, and four bedrooms, the smallest of which measured only 10ft 6in by 4ft 6in and 8ft by 4ft. The back kitchen was unaccountably at a lower level, approached by a set of steps, and the general design, with its multiplicity of small rooms, highly inconvenient. The author added that 'the beauty of such a dwelling would be greatly heightened by the addition of a terrace parapet and by ornamental chimney tops'.[26]

But Loudon represented an earlier, romantic tradition which was now coming to be abandoned in the face of economic and technical realities. The Picturesque might still be used for lodges, gardeners' cottages and other architectural adornments to the estate—a late example of very ornate designs being C. J. Richardson's *The Englishman's House* in 1870—but in general the trend was now towards simple plans which could utilize mass-produced materials such as brick, slate and tile. This trend was also encouraged by the fact that great landowners like the Duke of Bedford, whose estates were scattered over many parts of the country, adopted a common 'estate style' which was widely publicised in the architectural and agricultural press. The Bedford cottages all contained two ground-floor rooms—a kitchen provided with a cooking-range and a scullery containing a copper—and either two or three bedrooms, one of them fitted with a fireplace; there were outbuildings including a WC, and an oven common to each block of cottages. Built of 9in brick walls, the cottages cost in mid-century £90–£100 each and, let at 1s–1s 6d a week, were claimed to show a profit of 3 per cent. They probably represented the most economic building costs, for the Duke had virtually organized mass-production methods, keeping a hundred workmen permanently employed and making windows, doors, staircases and fittings to standard patterns. Even so, by 1885 rather higher standards and increased building costs had raised the price to £500 a pair, and had lowered the profit to $\frac{1}{2}$ per cent.

In these circumstances it was not surprising that the numerous cottage societies and awards for model designs should sometimes concentrate on cost-reduction rather than amenity. The designs advocated by the Labourer's Friend Society were extremely simple: built in pairs, they consisted of a porch, a kitchen 15ft by 10ft, a pantry, a closet under the stairs, and two 'good' bedrooms 13ft 3in by 8ft 6in and 10ft 4in by 6ft 2in; there was an external privy and a pigsty.[27] A more generous design by George Arnold, who was awarded the cottage prize by the Royal Agricultural Society in 1855, provided porch, living-room 13ft by 11ft 4in, scullery 14ft by 6ft, pantry and three bedrooms (the smallest 8ft by 7ft); they were constructed of rubble masonry 1ft 8in thick, with slated roofs, and were estimated to cost about £160 a pair.[28]

Something like this remained the ideal throughout the rest of the century, varied only in detail. A second living-room—a 'parlour'—was extremely rare in designs for labourers' cottages. Where there was anything more than the one, all-purpose room, the division was usually between 'kitchen' and 'scullery' or between 'living-room' and 'kitchen', the first arrangement separating washing functions and the second cooking. The extreme size of the living-room seems to have been about 15ft by 12ft, the size used by Miss Martineau in her Westmorland cottages costing £117 each and rented at £7 a year.[29]. Again, more than three bedrooms was quite exceptional, though it seems clear from the Labour Commission of 1893 that by then three bedrooms had become normal for new building, and there were a few instances of four-bedroomed cottages like those built by Lord Leconfield at North Stoke in Sussex. The most important changes in cottage-building standards achieved by the end of the century lay in the general provision of a third bedroom and a (usually external) WC, due partly to the increasing anxiety about moral and sanitary matters and also to the requirements laid down by the Inclosure Commissioners who, since 1845, were empowered to lend public money to landowners for estate improvement. Their requirements for cottage building included a proper separation of the sexes for sleeping, an avoidance of unnecessary decoration, adequate sanitary arrangements, well-made bricks and properly-seasoned timber. Some model designs went to considerable lengths to ensure this sexual separation, one suggesting using the roof-space as a loft-bedroom for boys,[30] another recommending that the third bedroom should be in a ground-floor annexe—partly because there would be insufficient space for three adequate-sized bedrooms over the ground-floor plan, and partly because, if the room was used as a boys' and guests' bedroom, 'any evil result from taking a lodger seems to be effectually provided against'. The girls were to be accommodated in the second upstairs bedroom, leading off the parents' room.[31]

By the 1880s there was clearly a consensus of opinion about what constituted an acceptable standard of housing for the labourer, but, as always, the great impediment to improvement was the cost of building set against the labourer's pitifully small wage. The pretty Alexandra Cottages which the Prince of Wales built on his Sandringham estate cost £195 each and showed only 1½ per cent on capital; few landowners were able or willing to emulate his generosity, especially during the lean years of the depression. One landowner who had had several of his thatched roof cottages condemned made a strong defence of them to a meeting of the Statistical Society on the ground that they 'encouraged ventilation'.[32] The average cost of the Inclosure Commissioners' cottages in the 1860s was £143, and on the generally accepted assumption that the labourer should not be expected to devote more than one-seventh of his earnings to rent, this meant only 1s 3d out of a wage of 9s, or 2s out of a 14s wage. Even at this above-average level it would take thirty years to recover capital, not including interest and repairs. Unfortunately, cost-reducing building methods were not well adapted to labourers' cottages, which were usually built only in pairs or in small rows in scattered and sometimes remote places. This partly explains why the proposal by Benjamin Nicholl to use 3in pre-cast concrete slabs for walling was apparently not exploited commercially, though he claimed in 1867 that by this method he could build three-bedroomed cottages for £85 which, rented at 1s 6d a week, would pay a reasonable return of 5 per cent.[33]

By the end of the century the problem of rural housing had reached an impasse. Speculative building for the labourer—as opposed to the retired or weekending townsman—had practically come to a stop, dictated as it was purely by market forces. 'Philanthropic' building by landowners, though it had made important contributions in restricted areas, fell far short of national needs, and in any event never recovered its former momentum after the depression. The problem that remained was both quantitative and qualitative—an absolute shortage of houses estimated at around 120,000, and a much higher, though incalculable, number of dilapidated, insanitary and overcrowded cottages. Evidence continued to accumulate down to 1914 on both aspects, from official enquiries such as the Select Committee on the Housing of the Working Classes Acts Amendment Bill, which concluded in 1906 that the 'house famine ... is incontestable', and from private investigations like those of Francis George Heath, F. E. Green, Rider Haggard and Seebohm Rowntree[34] which amplified and quantified the persistence of rural poverty and inadequate living standards.

With the acknowledged failure of private enterprise, attention in these last years turned increasingly to the possibilities of public reform and provision. The Public Health Act of 1875 had given local authorities powers to inspect property, to condemn as nuisances any premises which were so insanitary or overcrowded as to be dangers to health, and to forbid the use of houses proven to be unfit for human habitation.[35] Its primary concern was with sanitation and sewerage, in which respects some improvements were made, mainly in new building, but Joseph Arch records that he once called in the Nuisance Inspector to his village of Barford in Warwickshire who prevented the overcrowding and 'indiscriminate sleeping' in bedrooms by compelling the farmers to build some new cottages. Individual initiative, it seems, could occasionally achieve much, but few labourers had the power of Arch, who owned his own cottage and was independent of employers. The 1890 Housing of the Working Classes Act was again more concerned with urban than with rural housing, but Part 3 of the Act was potentially of great importance since it empowered local authorities to acquire land and to erect or convert buildings suitable for dwelling-houses for the working classes; the Public Works Loan Commissioners were given power to make advances for the purpose. In fact, this part of the Act achieved practically nothing, as its adoption by local authorities was only permissive, and only eight rural authorities did adopt it in the nineteen years of its existence. Somewhat greater success attended the Housing, Town Planning Act of 1909, which made systematic survey of rural housing obligatory, simplified the procedure for dealing with unfit houses, gave additional powers for the compulsory purchase of land and extra encouragement to local authorities to build by lowering the interest rates on loans from the Public Works Commissioners. It also invoked for the first time the power of a central body, the Local Government Board, which, on complaint made that the local authority had failed to exercise its powers, could compel it do do so: inactive, niggardly or recalcitrant local authorities were at last under a degree of public supervision and control.

Although a considerable advance on earlier measures, the 1909 Act still did not achieve any substantial building programme. Since building was a charge to local rates, it was at the mercy of all the arguments of economy, and all the powers of vested interests to which local government was notoriously subject. Some effort was directed towards improvement of property 'unfit for human habitation', and between 1909 and 1912, 15,000 notices for improvement were satisfactorily complied with and 5,000 cottages were compulsorily closed. But medical officers of health were often reluctant to issue closing orders in areas of housing shortage on the ground that to further reduce accommodation would only drive the labourer and his family into the town or into the workhouse. In almost half the villages investigated by the Land Enquiry Committee (366 out of 803) no new cottages had been built during the previous ten years, and between 1909 and 1913 loans to local authorities were sanctioned for the building of only 470 cottages—one-tenth of those demolished under Closing Orders. Six were built throughout Bedfordshire and, rented at 4s a week, were available only to better-paid workers like mechanics and gardeners.[36]

Such was the position on the outbreak of war in 1914, which finally ended any hopes that the 1909 Act might bring about a radical improvement in the housing of the rural worker. Already, before that war had made 'homes for heroes' a political issue, it was clear to most informed observers that the rural housing issue could not be solved without the direct involvement of the state and a major commitment to public expenditure. Almost unconsciously the problem of housing the rural labourer had prepared the way for a state housing policy of infinitely greater scope and implication.

6

HOUSING THE MULTITUDE

In the England of 1850 the industrial town was still new, untypical, its future problematic: by 1914 there could be no doubt that, for better or worse, England was an urban society—indeed, 'the' urban society of the western world—and that solutions had to be found to the manifold problems arising from a process which was now permanent and irreversible. Housing was at once the most obstinate and most controversial of those problems. Cities could be paved and drained, watered and sewered: technology and knowledge now existed by which the urban environment could be vastly improved and towns made fit places to live in. Given a willingness on the part of individuals, municipalities and governments to invest in unremunerative social overheads, they might even become new centres of civilization and culture with facilities for human development enjoyed till now only by the few.

But the basic need of the urban multitude for housing was of an order different from the mere provision of drains and dust-carts, parks and public libraries. The assumption that market forces would always meet need—that the supply of houses would naturally and inevitably move in step with demand—was only reluctantly abandoned towards the end of the century as social investigators disclosed the continuing horrors of slums and overcrowding and political economists identified sections of the population who, by their own efforts, could never attain a satisfactory standard of accommodation. How, and by whom, were they to be housed? Could, and should, the great cities somehow continue to make provision for ever-increasing numbers, or did the answer lie in the development of suburbs, new towns, or planned 'garden cities' which, dreamed Ebenezer Howard, would combine 'all the advantages of the most energetic and active town life with all the beauty and delight of the country'?[1] Above all, whatever the solution, who ultimately would pay the cost of housing the multitude?

The statistics of urban growth were astonishing, to some exciting, to others alarming. Using C. M. Law's recalculations of the census data, in 1851 the urban dwellers of England and Wales numbered 9,688,000 or 54 per cent of total population; by 1911 they were 28,468,000 or 79 per cent of population.[2] Over the years 1851 to 1911, when total population doubled, the urban population grew by three times, and over the longer span 1801 to 1911, the total population increased just over four times while the proportion classified as urban increased nearly nine and a half times.[3]

Moreover, by the end of the century the English people had become not merely a nation of town-dwellers, but one of great city-dwellers. Towns grew differentially, some mushrooming, some moving forward by steady increments, some spurting for a while before stagnating, a few actually declining, but the end result of all these processes was that the English population eventually became concentrated in a relatively small number of great cities and conurbations. In 1801 there had been only one city, London, with more than 100,000 inhabitants; in 1851 there were 10, and in 1911, 36. By 1911, 15,812,000 people, or 43·8 per cent of the total population, lived in cities with more than 100,000 inhabitants, compared with 24.8 per cent in 1851 and 11·0 per cent in 1801.

Considering the scale of such changes, and the irregularity of their occurrence, it is remarkable that in the long term house-building proceeded as closely in step with demand as it did. A building 'industry' which was still small-scale, traditional and unrevolutionized in its methods and in no way equipped to make nice calculations about demographic trends or the movement of interest rates provided accommodation between 1851 and 1911 for almost nineteen million new town-dwellers at generally improved standards of construction, amenity and comfort. Overall, new housing was provided at a slightly faster rate than population increase, so that the ratio of persons per dwelling—one important, if crude, measure of housing standards—declined at every census except 1881 from 5·46 persons in 1851 to 5·05 in 1911.[4]

Stated thus, the movements of population and house-building seem a regular progression, marching neatly in step one with the other, but this was unfortunately not so. The number of houses built annually was subject to marked and sometimes rapid fluctuations while the rate of population increase was much more regular; consequently, the 'fit' between the two series was not always nearly so close as a long-term view might suggest. Between 1860 and 1970 the annual rate of house-building per thousand of the population varied between low points of 1·9 per thousand in 1861, 2·4 in 1886, 2·3 in 1890 and 1·3 in 1912–13, and high points of 4·7 in 1876, 4·4 in 1898, and 4·1 in 1901–2. If these figures were shown diagrammatically the peaks and troughs which have characterized building activity over the last hundred years would be clearly seen.[5]

The statistics so far quoted are based on the researches of B. Weber, who has used the plans which were required to be submitted to local authorities enforcing building by-laws in thirty-four towns from 1856 onwards to construct an index of residential house-building.[6] He shows that two kinds of

TABLE 3

House-building in Britain, 1890–1913
(1900–1909 = 100)

	Great Britain	Cotton towns	Liverpool	Manchester	Sheffield	Barnsley, Doncaster, Wakefield	North-East	Birmingham	Leeds
1890	58	145	94		46	104	79		79
1891	61	132	64	32	35	138	74		37
1892	63	111	76	47	40	118	79	47	86
1893	71	131	58	42	42	177	84	54	87
1894	72	119	65	43	32	137	87	50	89
1895	75	118	46	62	27	112	87	55	78
1896	89	147	62	97	54	173	124	58	76
1897	101	167	81	112	74	191	125	59	88
1898	122	172	102	141	116	113	154	59	109
1899	123	142	121	161	136	124	124	66	133
1900	112	135	81	126	147	73	125	71	140
1901	111	110	101	103	108	81	114	58	139
1902	115	99	106	97	101	88	141	116	101
1903	118	85	112	92	105	125	136	122	118
1904	107	80	99	99	100	117	114	127	133
1905	99	85	100	97	97	110	116	89	111
1906	96	84	112	106	95	91	104	84	125
1907	89	99	106	105	86	93	87	105	52
1908	77	107	84	85	85	100	84	110	42
1909	76	117	99	90	75	121	72	101	38
1910	68	111	78	77	64	108	67	87	27
1911	58	94	56	51	44	123	54	63	23
1912	47	80	40	36	36	114	40	41	16
1913	43	77	35	34	26	105	33	39	

fluctuations bedevilled the course of house-building—short-term fluctuations of 5–7 years' duration, associated with the business cycle, and long waves of twenty-five years or more, the latter being particularly characteristic in the second half of the century. One long cycle reached its peak in 1876, followed by a decline in activity until the mid-nineties, after which there was another up-turn reaching a double peak in 1898 and 1903. This was succeeded by another down-swing, and by 1914 the level of activity was lower than at any time since the early 1860s. These calculations are by no means abstract, for in personal terms they meant that the housing opportunities for families depended to an important extent on the point of time at which they entered the housing market.

They depended too, probably to an even greater extent, on locality. The building index for Britain as a whole conceals major variations in different towns and areas, some of which followed the national trends closely while others moved in independent and sometimes contrary directions. Table 3 indicates these variations for a range of towns over the period 1890–1913.[7] It is clear that the Lancashire towns, for example, followed a very individual course, showing a high level of activity throughout the period with peaks in the late eighties, 1898 and 1909, whereas the national peak of 1903 actually represented a trough for several towns. In Liverpool, building continued at a high level until 1909; Manchester experienced twin peaks in 1899 and 1906; the Yorkshire mining towns, Barnsley, Doncaster and Wakefield, were building busily right up to 1914. In the holiday resorts, with the exception of Brighton, very active building also continued until 1914, while in Coventry, under the impetus of the motor-car and bicycle boom, twice as many houses were built in 1911 as in the national peak year of 1903. London, on the other hand, followed the national trend closely, with a major down-turn in activity after 1903 both in the older areas of inner London and, more surprisingly, in the 'outer ring' suburbs despite a continued rapid rise in population there. It seems likely that the boom of speculative building at the turn of the century was considerably in excess of demand, resulting in a large number of empty houses which had to be occupied before building activity revived.

This kind of consideration suggests that fluctuations in house-building were determined to an important extent by local conditions such as the state of trade, the prosperity or otherwise of local industries, the level of wages and, perhaps above all, the number of 'empties' on the market. The evidence of trade journals indicates that builders often made use of the number of 'empties' as an indicator of the state of local demand, and regulated their activities accordingly, but as both the market forces and the state of knowledge were imperfect, and because houses took some months to complete, there could often be a considerable lag between a rise in the number of empties and a fall in activity. Thus, in Nottingham where building had been active until 1911, empties at 9 per cent then indicated a saturated market, and activity fell sharply in the next three years, yet in other towns where there were high proportions of empties in 1901–3—Macclesfield (12·6 per cent), Exeter (9·4 per cent), Bristol (9·3 per cent) and Liverpool (8·8 per cent)—house-building continued at an even greater rate than in the previous three years.[8]

Over the whole country, as we have seen, house-building more than kept pace with population, to produce a gradually falling number of persons per house. Yet the housing evil which aroused the greatest concern among reformers, moralists and, ultimately, legislators, was the extent of over-crowding in the great towns, an evil which seemed to resist all attempts to remedy it, and which apparently grew worse rather than better with the passage of time. The Royal Commission on the Housing of the Working Classes in 1885 was convinced that overcrowding had worsened in some inner areas of London as street improvements and commercial expansion had reduced the number of dwelling-houses. Thus in Holborn and the City the number of persons per dwelling increased from 9·5 in 1851 to 9·7 in 1881, and in the East End from 7·2 to 7·9. To this extent, overcrowding persisted because of a maldistribution of houses—or of people—from one area to another, and because of a maldistribution between one income group and another. It was perfectly possible for national standards to improve while some local standards deteriorated, or for the higher-paid, regularly-employed working classes to live in increasing comfort while the poorest became increasingly overcrowded.

One of the difficulties in the discussion is that although overcrowding received statutory recognition as early as 1855 in the Nuisances Removal Act, it was at first used only as a crude measure of people per house, irrespective of the number and size of rooms or the ages of the occupants. Evidence was gradually accumulated, largely through the efforts of local medical officers of health, that death rates were directly correlated with occupancy rates, and as early as 1858 the medical officer for the Strand was pointing to much wider implications:

> So long as twenty, thirty, or even forty individuals are permitted—it might almost be said compelled—to reside in houses originally built for the accommodation of a single family or at most of two families, so long will the evils ... of ignorance, of indecency, immorality, intemperance, prostitution and crime continue to exist almost unchecked.[9]

John Simon also reserved his greatest condemnation for the moral consequences of dense living conditions:

> It almost necessarily involves such negation of all delicacy, such unclean confusion of bodies and bodily functions, such mutual exposure of animal and sexual nakedness, as is rather bestial than human.

Overcrowding first received a technical definition in 1891, as a room containing more than two adults, children under ten counting as a half, and those under one year not counting at all. It was a tolerant minimum, which allowed a three-roomed house to contain four adults, four children and any number of babies without falling foul of the definition. Even so, on this basis in 1891, 11·2 per cent of the population of England and Wales, consisting of 3½ million people, was overcrowded; in 1901, 8·2 per cent, and in 1911, 7·8 per cent. As always, the national averages concealed wide regional and local variations. In 1901 the range of overcrowding lay between 0·6 per cent in Bournemouth and 1·0 per cent in Leicester, and 30·5 per cent in Newcastle and 35·5 per cent in Gateshead. London overall had a high 16·0 per cent, but Finsbury had 35·2 per cent. Despite the good effects of railways and tramways after the 1880s which were allowing better-off workers to remove to the less cramped houses of the suburbs, and despite the slum demolition programmes which some local authorities were actively pursuing by the end of the century, overcrowding remained the most critical and most persistent aspect of the housing problem.

Clearly, it is important to understand the factors which determined the irregular course of house-building, and the problem has engaged the attention of numerous economic historians. E. W. Cooney in 1949 was the first to suggest that the 'long waves' of twenty or more years which characterized building in the later nineteenth century bore an inverse relationship to the cycles of activity in America, and that this phenomenon was due mainly to the migration of capital between the two countries in search of the more profitable investment. On this argument, the slump in house-building in the 1870s was due to the competition of foreign, especially American, investment for funds, and in future building had to take place predominantly when foreign investment was unattractive and low. The last great internal speculation, Cooney argues, was the railway boom of 1866, and thereafter foreign investment became the chief regulator of the course of the British economy.[10] Meanwhile, as we have seen, B. Weber's attempt to compile a national index of house-building from local data revealed variations which sometimes ran contrary to the national pattern, while S. B. Saul showed that these were particularly marked in the period 1890–1914. While admitting that building activity was obviously affected by the availability of short-term loans, he believed that for the most part it was internally and positively determined, rather than a residual activity which was part of an Atlantic economy. Most subsequent scholars have believed that domestic factors have generally been the powerful determinants of building activity, and have stressed the significance of demographic factors such as the population cycle, and the state of national and local industrial production.[11]

Overcrowding continued, therefore, partly because of maldistribution of existing houses in relation to where people 'wanted' to live—their choice often very limited by work opportunities—and partly because building rates and building costs were uneven in different parts of the country. A further factor which must be taken into account, especially in London and some other larger cities, was the actual destruction of houses for street improvements, commercial expansion such as offices and shops, and the construction of railway lines, sidings and termini. Despite the view of many contemporaries that, by cutting through some of the worst slums and rookeries, such developments were greatly to the public good, large numbers of people were displaced and forced to find, or create, similar accommodation elsewhere. H. J. Dyos has conservatively estimated that between 1850 and 1900 railway-building in London alone displaced about 80,000 people, and that its effect was first to increase overcrowding in central areas and later, when saturation density was reached, to extend it to adjacent 'overspill' districts. Re-housing of displaced people was not legislatively required until 1885, and at least until then the typical public attitude towards displacements of the poor, whatever the cause, was well expressed by *The Times*:

> If the working people of the city are compelled to find room at a greater distance from their work, there will be builders and speculators ready to supply their wants. This is not an affair for railway companies . . . Government has nothing to do with providing dwellings for the poor . . . We accept railways with their consequences, and we don't think the worse of them for ventilating the City of London. You can never make these wretched alleys really habitable, do what you will; but bring a railway to them and the whole problem is solved.[12]

The removal, by whatever means, of overcrowding and slum living was already being seen as the necessary cure for disease, crime, prostitution and immorality, but the medical officers of health, whose knowledge of conditions on the ground was greater than most people's, knew only too well that demolition without re-housing only removed the problems elsewhere. The medical officer of health for Hackney spoke for many when he reported that if he were to carry out the overcrowding clauses of the 1866 Sanitary Act, he would compel 10,000 people to sleep in the streets, and he and his colleagues were among the first to call for powers to build as well as demolish, and for state housing for the poor. As early as 1874 the Royal College of Physicians, in which the medical officers were active, presented a remarkable petition to the Prime Minister which condemned philanthropy, laissez-faire and 'enabling powers' as useless. Within a few more years they were beginning to view overcrowding and the housing problem generally in a wider context—as part of the greater problem of poverty, 'What', asked the medical officer for Kensington in 1890, 'are the main causes of overcrowding? Poverty and high rents.' With that dawning recognition interest was beginning to shift from the external environment, with which the nineteenth-century reformers had been so preoccupied, towards the personal problems arising from individual and collective poverty.

RENTS AND EARNINGS

So far, we have considered some of the factors which determined the availability of housing at the national, macro-economic level, but the access which individuals and families had to the total housing stock depended crucially on their own economic position, and specifically on how much rent they could afford to pay. Although the possibility of house-ownership through building societies was beginning to be available to some of the better-off working classes in the second half of the century, the numbers concerned were still so few—no more than 6 per cent of York's working class in 1900, for example, of which the largest number were widows, retired persons, artisans, clerks and shopkeepers[13]—that for the vast majority of people before 1914 the payment of weekly house-rent was normal, inevitable, and the largest single fixed charge in their budget.

Unlike the middle classes who, in theory and often, it seems, in practice, could safely allocate 8–10 per cent of their earnings to rent, the working classes generally enjoyed no such certainty. Numerous attempts to measure the average proportion of working-class income expended on rent offer a bewildering choice ranging from 9 per cent calculated by the British Association in 1881,[14] to 11·8 per cent estimated by the US Commissioner of Labour in 1890–1 on the basis of a survey of 455 workmen's families,[15] and to 14·9 per cent which Seebohm Rowntree found to be the average proportion of income paid by all wage-earners in York in 1900. Incidentally, the US survey, which was made on a comparative basis, showed that British expenditure on rent was higher as a proportion than that paid in France, Germany, Belgium or Switzerland, though lower than that in North America (15·1 per cent) where amenities in workmen's apartments often included such luxuries as bathrooms, hot and cold water and electric light.

In the tight budgets of the working classes, rent necessarily took second place to food which, in most contemporary estimates, absorbed between half and two-thirds of all earnings. One of Rowntree's labouring families, earning 18s a week, spent 10s 6d on food, 3s 3d on rent and 1s 8d on coal and light. A Stepney painter earning £1 a week paid 10s 9d for food, 5s 3d for rent, and 1s 11d for fuel and light, while in the budgets of skilled workers earning 30–35s a week rents rose to 6s 6d a week. A careful, managing housewife, on receiving the weekly pay-packet or whatever her husband allowed her from it, first set aside money for the fixed expenses like rent, coal (usually 1cwt a week at around 1s 3d), clothing club and insurance, and then bought her food, adjusting the more expensive items like meat according to what was left out of an often varying total. Food could be economized on, the purchase of new boots or household replacements postponed for a while, but rent had to be paid and repayments kept up at the risk of fearful consequences. The constant contemporary references to 'moonlight flits' to escape from debts to landlords and other local creditors partly explain the frequent changes of residence which the poorest classes made.

Housing reformers frequently argued that if only the working classes could be persuaded to devote a rather larger proportion of earnings to accommodation the scarcity of houses in many areas would be solved by the operation of market forces, and the lives of the poor transformed by comfortable, moral homes. Such arguments were usually linked with a condemnation of housewives for mismanagement and of their husbands for drinking, gambling and other unnecessary expenditure. In many cases, complained James Hole in 1866, families live in miserable dens who could well afford comfortable houses, and it was by no means always the poorest who inhabited the worst accommodation. 'There are numberless instances of labouring men systematically spending sixpence and upwards per night (equal to the rent of a good cottage) at the public-house . . . more than ample . . . to transform every hovel in the kingdom into a little palace.'[16] The fact was, of course, that given the low levels of opportunity, education and expectation of many working people, the cycle of poverty—of which intemperance was too often a part—was all but unbreakable, and a comfortable home and family life in middle-class terms were beyond their experience and aspiration. In any case, it was by no means certain that higher rent would automatically bring better accommodation. In evidence to the Royal Commission on the Housing of the Working Classes in 1885, Jesse Collings argued that the supply of accommodation in central areas of London and other cities where the poor chiefly congregated was fixed or nearly so, and because of increasing pressure families who used to occupy two rooms were often now compelled to manage with one, at the same rent. Even an increase in sobriety and thrift, so much to be desired, would in present circumstances only increase rents still further, 'and the money results of improved habits on the part of the people would go into the house owners' pockets'.[17]

The important question, however, is not how much rent was paid by the statistically average working-class household, but by actual individual families, and here the evidence indicates variations so wide that the average becomes almost meaningless. A detailed enquiry among twenty working-class families in Birmingham in the early eighties showed average wages of 27s 6d a week and an average rent of 6s or 23·7 per cent: closer examination, however, showed that the proportion ranged from 15·6 per cent to 33·3 per cent.[18] In fact, rent was usually inversely proportional to income, the poorer devoting a larger share to it, while better-off workers could enjoy a higher standard of accommodation for a smaller fraction of their earnings. The Royal Commission heard that in poor areas of London like Clerkenwell, St Luke's, St Giles's and Marylebone, the average rent for a single room was 3s 11d, for two 6s and for three 7s 5d; out of 1,000 families here, 46 per cent had to spend between a quarter and a half of their earnings on rent, 88 per cent more than one-fifth and only 12 per cent less than this.[19] Among the relatively well-paid and homogeneous ironworkers of Middlesbrough, Lady Bell found a range of rents from 3s 6d to 7s 6d a week, the cheapest being for old, insanitary cottages on low-lying land near the river, the more expensive situated in newer quarters of the town, built in wide, airier roads and having more accommodation.[20]

The most detailed of these studies relating rent to earnings was that carried out by Rowntree in York in 1900. Although for all wage-earners in the town rent took an average of 14·9 per cent of income, the range was from 29 per cent in the poorest group with earnings of less than 18s a week to only 9 per cent in the wealthiest working-class families with incomes of more than 60s. Rowntree estimated that only his Group D, with earnings of more than 30s a week, could afford to house adequately a family of more than four children. Large proportions of the poorer groups were occupying not houses, but rooms, at an average rent of 1s 7d for one room, 2s 6d for two, 3s 6d for three and 4s 7½d for four. York, with its variety of industries and employment opportunities, was reckoned to be a prosperous town with relatively good housing: in 1891 only 6·4 per cent of its people were 'overcrowded' compared with 10 per cent in Liverpool, 16·1 per cent in Leeds, 19·1 per cent in London and 35 per cent in Newcastle.

Sub-letting by the poor themselves of such a saleable commodity as space was a natural response to high and rising rents. Equally, for a family whose earnings were either very small or irregular, the renting of one or two rooms from a fellow working man represented a substantially lower order of commitment than an obligation to a landlord. A survey of 30,000 working men in different parts of London in 1887 showed that accommodation increased in step with wages and security of employment. Half the dock labourers occupied no more than a single room, whereas 99 per cent of policemen managed at least two. In the very poor district of St George's-in-the-East half of all families existed in single rooms, while in Battersea two-thirds of all families earned more than 25s a week and rented three rooms or more.[21]

Mrs Pember Reeves in *Round About A Pound A Week* (1913) described how sub-letting operated in London. A family would rent a small, four-roomed house at 10s or 11s a week, would let one room at 2s–3s—probably the ground-floor front room so that the sub-tenant would have access without disturbing the rest of the household—and retain the rest for its own use. Alternatively, in a six-roomed house rented at 14s or 15s, two rooms might be let at 6s–7s, or if the house were split horizontally the whole of the upper floor might be let. Again, if it had a basement, preferably with its own entrance from the area, two rooms could be let here at about 5s 6d a week. In these various ways the principal tenant kept down her own rent obligation to around 7s or 8s a week with the advantage of a whole house over which she could retain control and supervision.[22]

Every tenant in the later nineteenth century knew that the rent he had to pay was rising steadily—not week by week, or even month by month, but perceptibly enough over the years. An index of urban house-rents in England and Wales compiled by H. W. Singer shows a rise from 100 points in 1845 to 185 in 1910, with particularly sharp increases in the mid-sixties, throughout the seventies and at the turn of the century.[23] Again, although the trend was a national one, it varied greatly in different towns and different districts of the same town, indicating that local forces of supply and demand were superimposed on the general curve. London experienced the greatest increases, and by the time of the Royal Commission housing in central areas had already reached critical proportions. A single room which had cost 2s 6d in the 1850s now let at 4s 9d, and two rooms at 7s 6d were often beyond the means of semi-skilled workers. In Hackney rents jumped by as much as 33 per cent between 1894 and 1902 alone, mainly as a result of rapid rises in the costs of land and building materials.[24] In 1848 the Statistical Society investigated wages and rents in St George's-in-the-East, and, by good fortune, the same area was included in a Board of Trade enquiry in 1887. The comparison between the two is revealing, and indicates that for some workers increases in wages over the period were eaten up by the rent rises.[25]

Provincial rents showed similar, though generally less dramatic, movements. In Sheffield in mid-century the normal rent of a back-to-back cottage with cellar, living-room, chamber (bedroom) and attic was 2s 6d. It cost between £60 and £75 to build and paid a return of 6–7 per cent after deducting all costs of servicing and collection. By the 1890s the cheapest cottage in a poor district had risen to 3s–3s 6d, and a better house was 5s, while by 1914 no new cottage could be let at less than 5s, and some were as much as 7s. Like many other towns, Sheffield had some very bad housing at the same time as 5,000 'empties', a sure sign of a lack of effective demand.[26] Leeds was reckoned to be a low-rented town. Here, the small, old back-to-backs with only one room down and one up let in the 1860s at 2s–3s; newer, superior houses with a living-room on one side of the door and a scullery on the other, two bedrooms above and an attic bedroom let at 3s 9d–5s 6d. By 1908 the two-roomed were 3s–3s 6d, and the superior, five-roomed houses 5s–6s 6d.[27]

This movement of rents was an important exception to the generally falling prices of the seventies and eighties, and prevented many working people from taking full advantage of a rise in real earnings which would otherwise have benefited their standard of living greatly. Rent increases in a poor area sometimes absorbed the whole of the increase in wages, though this does not take into account the substantially lower food prices of the period of 'the Great Depression'. Leone Levi, normally optimistic about the improvement in the standard of life of the worker, believed that between 1857 and 1884 'what is gained in the cost of food goes mostly in additional house rent', and another contemporary, Edith Simcox, calculated in 1885 that three-fifths of the wage increases over the previous half-century had gone to rent. A precise comparison is impossible, partly because food prices continued to fall well into the nineties and, more importantly, because standards of accommodation had themselves improved and like was not being compared with like; but the fact remains that advances in the standard of living would have been more spectacular than they were had it not been for the marked upward drift of rents.

The Royal Commission of 1885 heard with dismay that while rents in central London were soaring, wages remained static, that 4s was being paid for a single room in St Pancras, 5s off Tottenham Court Road, the same in Notting Hill, and 4s 6d–6s in Spitalfields. The main reason, it believed, was the necessity of the poor to be near the range of casual work which existed in the city centre, and to be strategically placed so that they could seek employment in any direction. No matter what the cost and quality of accommodation, they were inevitably tied to locations where a day's work might be picked up if a man were on the spot at 5 or 6 am, and where his wife and daughters could work as charwomen, seamstresses and at sweated domestic industries not available in the suburbs. Cheap markets meant that food prices were lower here than further out, while debts to local shopkeepers also tended to fix the poor to areas where they were known and could obtain credit. There was a natural reluctance to move away from friends, neighbours and relatives who could provide a network of support at times of crisis, which would be absent in an anonymous new suburb. Again, certain areas experienced particular pressure from immigrants, such as the Jewish colonies in Spitalfields and Whitechapel. But the Royal Commission rightly pointed to the fact that in many central areas accommodation was actually being diminished, and, ironically, the removal of bad property was often aggravating the evils it was supposed to remedy. Demolitions in the area of the Mint under the Torrens Act caused local rents to double: St Luke's had never recovered from the demolitions caused by the building of 'Peabody Town', but the poorest classes who were dispossessed failed to get accommodation there. The Commissioners found themselves in the embarrassing position of having to condemn socially desirable things like railways, schools and model tenements for the ill-effects they entailed on some of those they were intended to benefit.[28]

Behind these reasons for high rents also lay the high profits which were being made from rack-renting in central area properties. The leaseholders of most house-property in the poorer districts were not large capitalists but small businessmen, shopkeepers or publicans—according to the medical officer for Limehouse in 1881, 'People who have saved a little money; people who have been in trade; they are not a nice class of person as a whole'. Much dealing was done by such men in 'fag-ends' of leases which had only a few years to run: these would be re-let to middlemen—'house jobbers', 'farmers' or 'knackers'—who were under a fixed obligation to the ground landlord and made their own profit by overcrowding and charging extortionate rents. Houses would be broken up for sub-letting, families who had formerly occupied two rooms would be forced into one by threat of eviction, and by such means the income from a house was often raised from £30 to £80 a year in a short time. With such a multiplicity of relationships ground landlords might know little or nothing about their property, their tenants or the rents they paid. Middle-men were supposed to repair, but responsibilities could easily be avoided where so many interests were involved. Evidence was given to the Royal Commission that one house jobber received £100 a year in rent from a subdivided house in Clerkenwell, but paid to the landlord, Lord Northampton, only £20 a year; the agent to the estate allowed that middlemen's profits of 150 per cent were not uncommon.

By the end of the century the structure of rents throughout the country showed vast variations. At the lowest level of all it was still possible in parts of London to find some single rooms at around 1s 6d a week, a rent which had remained unchanged throughout the century and which, as Enid Gauldie has pointed out, really lay outside the normal housing market.[29] These would be small, dilapidated rooms in slum areas like St Giles's, quite unsuitable for a family and probably unfit for any human habitation. Two rooms in a model block like Peabody cost 5s 6d upwards, the same as for a new four- or five-roomed cottage in the London suburbs. For three rooms in the centre 8s or 9s would be necessary. A four-roomed LCC cottage in 1914, built outside the County of London, varied from 6s 1d to 8s 11d, while a three-roomed flat in the centre was from 6s 7½d to 12s 3d. Westminster borough council provided flats at 3s for a single room, 9s for three rooms and 12s 6d for four.[30]

Given this wide disparity of rents between the centre and the suburbs—that what was paid for two rooms in one would buy a cottage in the other—it seemed remarkable to many contemporary observers that the working classes did not take greater advantage of these opportunities of healthier, cheaper and more pleasant life away from the overcrowded city centres. Some of the reasons why the poorest workers found themselves virtually imprisoned in traditional, well-defined areas of the cities have already been discussed. But movement to the suburbs was crucially dependent on cheap transport by tram or by workmen's fares on the railways which were not generally available before the Cheap Trains Act of 1883, and even after this the economics of suburban living were not always in favour of the commuter. A survey carried out by the LCC in 1900, based on the costs of third-class travel from Waterloo Station, showed that rents progressively declined from 8s 1d for two or three rooms in the immediate vicinity to 6s 9d for the same accommodation at Vauxhall and only 5s 6d for a whole cottage at Sunbury, but here 5s a week had also to be paid for fares.

Earlier starts—or later arrivals—for work, the somewhat higher costs of food in the suburbs and the more limited opportunities for women's employment tended to limit suburban migration to more highly-paid workers with well-established jobs which did not require a daily or weekly search for work.

The gap between central London and provincial rents was even wider, and illustrates how much better off in terms of accommodation was the man with regular employment in the Midlands or North of England. Some parts of great cities like Manchester and Liverpool exemplified, on a lesser scale, the problems of London, but even here most families inhabited houses, not rooms, and paid only about half of what comparable accommodation would have cost in the capital. In Leeds at the end of the century a superior 'through' house, representing the upper level of working-class aspiration, could be had from 5s 3d to 6s. In Liverpool the Hornby Street development of tenement blocks built by the Corporation provided one-roomed flats at 2s 6d, rising to 5s 3d for the largest, four-roomed flats on the ground floor, while in Birmingham Corporation's redevelopments new four-roomed houses let at 5s 3d.[31] In Sheffield the first workmen's garden suburb was started by the Corporation at High Wincobank in 1906 with cottages at 5s–7s and 'exhibition houses' at 6s–10s.[32] A Board of Trade enquiry of 1903 found that the average rent paid by the working classes in Manchester, including that of rooms in Corporation and Trust tenements as well as whole houses, was 3s 9d a week, and in Liverpool 3s 8d.

Within this local framework, what an individual family paid for rent depended crucially on its size, and particularly on the number, age and sex of children. At the lowest levels of poverty, in the slums and rookeries, large families might be prepared, or obliged, to flout morality and social convention by herding into a single room, but whenever possible English respectability demanded the separation of living and sleeping, and of the sleeping of older children of different sexes. Rowntree estimated that 22 per cent of the poverty in York was directly ascribable to over-large families and the effect which every additional child had on depressing a slender family economy.

Family size had a direct effect on the number of rooms for which rent would have to be paid. Mrs Reeves estimated in 1913 that with one, two and even three children a family might still manage in a single room, costing in London 3s 6d to 5s according to size; four or five children necessitated at least two rooms, costing 6s–7s, and six children meant three rooms at 8s–9s. In one of the cases she investigated, a bus conductor with five children was paying 9s a week rent out of his wage of 18s.[33] A family like this, with many closely-spaced children not yet old enough to work, was especially unfortunate, and in the most critical stage of the poverty cycle. But the important general point is that the 'fit' between inflexible house types and families which expanded and contracted much more than now was inexact and inadequate, involving excessive crowding at some stages of life and under-use of space at others.[34] Demographic factors such as these were not seriously considered in the design of Victorian house-plans, which continued to be determined principally by the economics of building operating within a set of customary local usages. To these we now turn.

OTHER FACTORS INFLUENCING HOUSING QUALITY

Individuals and families occupied not the accommodation that was necessarily appropriate for them in terms of family size or, in many cases, in terms of their income, but the accommodation which happened to be available in the area in which they needed to live. The housing experience of working-class families in the second half of the century therefore varied widely, the same rent often buying very different standards of comfort in different parts of the country. Although by the end of the century the general development of working-class housing was towards more standardized forms, determined largely by legislation, distinct regional types continued to characterize different geographical areas—the through terrace of the South, the back-to-back of parts of the Midlands, Yorkshire and Lancashire, the 'up-and-down' flat of Tyneside, the divided, tenemented house of London, and so on. Many of these were, of course, inheritances from the past, and towns which were struggling to raise their housing standards often had to contend with a dead weight of old, inadequate property which continued to stamp its character on an area long after new building of the same type had been outlawed. What had been barely tolerable building practice in the 1840s was often unacceptable by the 1880s, but the useful life of houses was generally considerably more than forty years, and the attack on the slums was a painfully slow process.

How very varied the housing experiences of the working classes were came to light fully only in 1908 in an official enquiry into Working Class Rents, Housing and Retail Prices.[35] The enquiry investigated the proportions of people in the principal towns of England and Wales occupying one room, two rooms, three, four, and five or more; the results for some selected towns are shown in Table 4. Thus, throughout the country as a whole, 18·0 per cent of the population lived in three rooms or less, in London 38·8 per cent did so compared with 57·6 per cent in Gateshead and a mere 4·0 per cent in Leicester. In Bristol 84·8 per cent of the population occupied four- or five-roomed houses, in Nottingham 87 per cent, but in Newcastle only 46·7 per cent. In Derby more than four-fifths of the population lived in houses with five or more rooms, in Bradford less than two-fifths, and in Jarrow only one-fifth. Clearly, vast differences existed in the accommodation of the working classes, depending largely on the types of building in different towns and regions. These variations were confirmed in a detailed study of four towns—Northampton, Warrington, Stanley and Read-

ing—carried out in 1915.[36] In Northampton the six-roomed house predominated, accounting for 62 per cent of all working-class houses; in
Reading the five-roomed house was most typical, again accounting for 62
per cent; the four-roomed house predominated in Warrington (50 per cent),
while in Stanley, a small coal-mining town, the commonest type (41 per
cent) had three rooms and as many as 19 per cent had only two.

TABLE 4

*Percentage of total population in 1901 occupying
tenements of one, two, three, four and five or more rooms*

Town	Total population	Percentage of total population occupying tenements of:				
		One room	Two rooms	Three rooms	Four rooms	Five or more rooms
England and Wales	32,527,843	1·6	6·6	9·8	21·9	60·1
Birmingham	522,204	0·3	2·4	29·4	13·0	54·9
Bradford	279,767	1·2	13·6	27·4	20·8	37·0
Bristol	328,945	1·6	5·7	7·9	10·5	74·3
Derby	105,912	0·2	1·4	2·3	10·8	85·3
Gateshead	109,888	5·2	26·3	26·1	23·4	19·0
Jarrow	34,295	3·3	31·0	24·5	18·9	22·3
Leeds	428,968	0·4	9·5	16·0	25·0	49·1
Leicester	211,579	0·1	2·4	1·5	9·0	87·0
London	4,536,541	6·7	15·5	16·6	15·2	46·0
Manchester	543,872	0·8	4·0	3·9	40·0	51·3
Newcastle-on-Tyne	215,328	6·0	23·9	23·4	19·1	27·6
Nottingham	239,743	0·4	1·9	10·7	15·3	71·7
Sheffield	380,793	0·4	4·0	18·8	23·2	53·6
York	77,914	0·8	5·5	5·0	24·0	64·7

Quality of building construction also varied greatly, and complaints of
the sharp practices of jerry-builders continued to be heard frequently,
especially during the third quarter of the century.[37] Engels in 1844 had
complained that the neat appearance of new cottages in Manchester was 'all
pretence, a pretence which vanishes within the first ten years . . . I have seen
many a cottage . . . some in process of building, whose outer walls were but
one half-brick thick . . . As such cottages are often built but twenty or thirty
years before the expiration of the term, it may easily be imagined that the
contractors make no unnecessary expenditure upon them.' The
niggardliness of the original construction, the neglect of repairs, the frequent change of occupants and the ravages of the tenants sometimes

brought about the complete ruin of houses well before forty years, Engels argued, citing the example of Ancoats where many houses built at the beginning of the century were already uninhabitable.[38] The most common faults seem to have been inadequacy of foundations, porous bricks, external brickwork of only $4\frac{1}{2}$in instead of at least 9in, unseasoned timber, floors whether of timber or stone laid directly on the earth, improperly flued chimneys, and sometimes the complete absence of a trapped drainage system. Some of these failings began to be dealt with after the Public Health Act of 1875 and the adoption of local building by-laws, but even at the end of the century evasion was still widely practised, especially in new suburban areas which had not come under proper administrative control. Some of the new districts of London, on which the housing reformers had pinned such high hopes, were already being described as 'embryo slums' before the end of the period. The *Lancet* had warned as early as 1874:

> It is difficult to understand the argument of those who contend that the labouring classes ought to live in the suburbs—i.e. in unhealthy, cheap, undrained districts, often beyond the pale of sanitary legislation, and in adulterated houses whose foundations were rotten, whose walls were scarcely weatherproof, and whose owners but too often belong to the most unscrupulously dishonest class to be found among us.[39]

Even when systems of building inspection were long-established, as in London, a satisfactory report on unsatisfactory workmanship might be procured by bribery and corruption. Walter Besant quoted in 1901 the evidence of a man who twenty-five years previously had been an apprentice in the building trade: 'For a house like this it was £15 to the inspector; for one of the smaller houses it was £10.'

Nevertheless, the general adoption of building controls after 1875 did bring major improvements to the layout, construction and amenities of working-class housing, and what is sometimes almost contemptuously designated 'by-law housing' was the first important attempt top bring planning into the urban chaos. Before 1875 most towns had had no general powers over building, either over the construction of individual houses or over the development of new areas. The exceptions to this were those towns which had voluntarily adopted limited powers under private Acts of Parliament, and London, which ever since the Building Act of 1774 had controlled the construction of party walls and other matters by establishing four classes of house based on size and value. The extension by the Metropolitan Building Act of 1844 laid down minimum widths for new streets, alleys and mews, and provided that every new dwelling-house should have an open space at its rear of not less than 100sq ft: here, for the first time, spatial characteristics and environment were to be considered. Later Acts in 1855 and 1878 regulated, at least in theory, the construction of foundations, the quality of materials and the height of ceilings.[40]

Several provincial towns had begun to regulate particular aspects of building by private Acts or by passing by-laws under other statutory authority such as the Public Health Act of 1858. As we saw in Chapter 3, much of this early control had been concerned with banning or at least regulating back-to-back building: thus, Manchester had made their building illegal in 1844, Liverpool in 1861; and Bradford in 1860 had limited their construction to a maximum of two pairs by specifying open space at the rear or side of every house. The Leeds Improvement Act of 1842 had given the council power to compel a proper privy for each newly-erected house, but James Hole pointed out in 1866 that no summons had been issued for many years.[41] In this year a reluctant council passed a by-law which restricted future back-to-backs to blocks of not more than eight (four front and four back) with yard privies to be placed between each block. Although Leeds clung to the back-to-back longer than any other town, continuing to build them into the 1930s, one good effect of the 1866 by-law was to widen the spaces between blocks and lead to larger, intercommunicating streets in place of the ill-kept courts and culs-de-sac which had characterized earlier building.[42] Manchester prohibited cellar-dwellings by a local Act in 1853, and in 1867 drew up regulations which concerned room sizes, window areas and the provision of every new house with a small private yard. The most common purpose of the by-laws of the 1860s was, however, to regulate the areas of open space about houses and the width of streets to the faces of opposing buildings, so that better ventilation and natural lighting would be ensured.

Some control over the spatial aspects of housing was, therefore, beginning in some towns in the middle decades of the century, though it was partial, irregular and often evaded. Important extensions of building control came in the last quarter of the century, still under the aegis of public health authorities, partly because the matters they concerned themselves with were, in a broad sense, health matters, and partly, no doubt, because extensions of sanitary laws were politically an easier way of dealing with housing evils than a frontal attack on the rights of property. The Sanitary Law Amendment Act of 1874 allowed local authorities to lay down regulations concerning paving and drainage of premises and the ventilation of rooms. More important, the Public Health Act of 1875 gave local authorities a series of powers to control the sanitary and housing conditions of their districts. In particular, section 157 allowed them to make by-laws governing the layout, width and construction of new streets, the construction of new buildings, the space around them and the sanitary provisions relating to them. Two years later the responsible central authority, the Local Government Board, issued a set of model by-laws for the guidance of local authorities.[43]

In order to make such by-laws effective, local authorities were empowered to require developers to give notice of their activities, and to deposit plans: they could also inspect building work and might remove, alter or demolish work which contravened their regulations. Finally, the Public Health Amendment Act of 1890 concerned itself in greater detail with the construction of houses, allowing local authorities to control the structure of floors, hearths and staircases and the height of rooms, and to forbid the use of rooms built over privies or cesspools and houses erected on ground filled with offensive matter.

Extensive as these powers were, their usefulness was limited by three factors. First, the adoption of by-laws by local authorities was permissive, not mandatory, and unwilling councils could for long decline to invoke them, despite the persuasive efforts of the Local Government Board. Second, towns which had already passed local Acts could continue to operate them, although they might be considerably less stringent than the model by-laws. And third, the new regulations naturally only applied to new building, leaving untouched the problems inherited from the past. In the hands of an energetic council they meant that future slums could be prevented, that houses would be constructed to minimum standards of space, materials and amenities, and so sited in relation to other buildings as to ensure adequate light and ventilation. In the model by-laws of 1877 new streets over 100ft in length were to be at least 36ft wide and open at one end throughout their full width and height. Every new house was to have an open space at the rear exclusively belonging to it of at least 150sq ft. Windows must have an area at least one-tenth of the floor space, and at least half the window must be openable. Other regulations governed the provision of satisfactory drainage and the means of access to privies which would enable their contents to be removed without being carried through the house.

'By-law housing' of the period 1880–1914 has been the object of much criticism on account of its monotony and the fact that builders almost inevitably built down to the lowest standards permitted. Indeed, by-laws were opposed in a number of towns on the ground that they would materially raise the costs of building and, hence, of rents, and would therefore be a disservice to lower-paid workers. These considerations had to be finely balanced, and it is scarcely surprising that aesthetic values were often sacrificed to improved standards of construction and sanitary convenience. Typically, the 'by-law housing' which spread over large areas of working-class suburbs in London and provincial towns in the late nineteenth century consisted of repetitive terraces of four, eight or more houses, intersected by passages or tunnels ('ginnels' in the North) which gave access to small, walled private yards containing a privy and, perhaps, a coal-house, and set in long, parallel, treeless streets from whose pavements the front doors usually opened directly. In those of a better class there might be a tiny front garden with palings to separate the house from the pavement, a bay-window and a small rear garden in place of the paved or cemented yard, but in either case the outstanding characteristic was that of a through terrace house with a 'tunnel-back' replacing the 'back-to-back'.

To this extent, 'by-law housing' represented a distinct advance in working-class housing standards. Environmentally, it produced wider, connected streets in place of enclosed courts and back alleys which led nowhere, lower housing densities, airier and lighter houses, and, possibly most important of all, a private patch of rear territory which could accommodate an individual privy. The regular removal of 'night soil', neutralized by

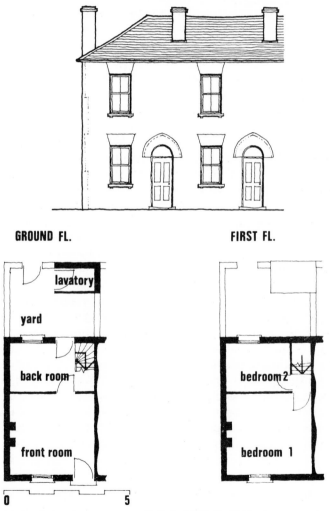

GROUND FL. **FIRST FL.**

lavatory

yard

back room

front room

bedroom 2

bedroom 1

0   5

7   Plain and simple two-storey terrace. Built in Willis St, Salford, apparently early in the second half of nineteenth century. Two rooms down and two up. Front room and Bedroom 1 11ft × 10ft (3·4 × 3·0m), Back room and Bedroom 2 11ft × 6ft (3·4 × 1·8m). Drawing by C. G. Powell

earth or ashes, largely determined the new ground plan of a through house—a back yard containing the closet at an appropriate distance from the dwelling, with an alley separating the backs of the yards and giving access by an individual gate for refuse collection. Compared with the broken and overflowing cesspools of mid-century, often shared by the occupants of a dozen or more houses, this was the beginning of a sanitary revolution. By the end of the century the spread of water-borne sanitation was allowing the closet to be incorporated into the building of new houses, usually as part of the scullery annexe, with even more privacy and convenience for its users. This development made possible major modifications of the first-floor plan, with additional space for a third bedroom and, even, at the top end of the working-class scale, a bathroom.

Internally, the effects of by-laws also brought important gains. Sounder constructional methods and materials meant better insulation from cold, damp and noise; higher ceilings (usually a minimum of 8ft 6in) and larger window openings gave greater light and ventilation, especially in bedrooms; timber flooring increasingly replaced stone flags; staircases became less steep and tortuous; and there was better provision of fireplaces, sinks, coppers and iron cooking-ranges which usually combined an oven and water-heater. By the 1890s individually piped water supplies to working-class houses were common in many towns, though not yet universal, and gas for lighting and cooking on the penny-in-the-slot system was making much progress. Finally, the through terraced house almost invariably provided a considerably larger floor area than its predecessor. The mid-century back-to-back typically had external measurements of 15ft by 15ft in Leeds, or 17ft by 14ft in Oldham, a total of around 450sq ft on two floors. A typical four-roomed terrace house measured overall about 16ft by 24ft or 760sq ft. It is true that some extremely small four-roomed terraced houses were built, such as those in Willis Street, Salford, which had a floor area of only 360sq ft (the scullery was a mere 8ft by 6ft), but by the period of 'by-law housing' a minimum of around 12ft by 12ft for the living-room and 12ft by 10ft for the kitchen produced houses of at least 570sq ft upwards. The addition of a single-storey annexe containing scullery and WC, as in Little Albert Street, Easton, Bristol, provided 670sq ft, while nearby houses with a full two-storey annexe providing a third bedroom occupied 850sq ft. This type of house, usually occupied by skilled and better-paid workers in the years before 1914, had a front door leading not into the front room, but into a lobby or passage about 3ft wide, a front parlour 12ft by 9ft, a kitchen of the same size, and a scullery 10ft by 6ft. Stairs led from the lobby to three bedrooms, two of which measured 12ft by 12ft and the third 10ft by 6ft. Such a house, with its 'hall', internal WC and small rear garden in addition to the yard, was eminently 'respectable' in the south of England, and 'superior' in the north. It gave the desired separation between washing in the scullery, cooking and living in the kitchen and display in the parlour,

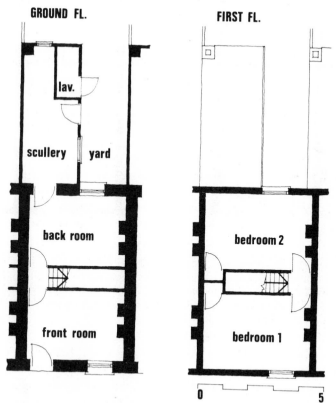

7

GROUND FL.

lav.

scullery | yard

back room

front room

FIRST FL.

bedroom 2

bedroom 1

0   5

8   House with single-storey rear annexe projection in Little Albert Street, Bristol. Three rooms down and two up. Front room 12ft 6in × 8ft 9in (3·8 × 2·7m), Back room 12ft 6in × 9ft (3·8 × 2·7m), Bedroom 1 and Bedroom 2 14ft × 9ft 9in (4·3 × 3·0m). Drawing by C. G. Powell

which could be further refined by using a gas-cooker in the scullery and reserving the kitchen for family living. Upstairs, the three bedrooms gave just sufficient separate space for parents, boys and girls, provided the family was not over-large. A working-class house much larger than this was very rare, the most likely possibility being a three-storey house with basement accommodation and two rooms to each floor, giving a total of six full-sized

9   House with two-storey rear annexe projection. Three rooms down and three up. Annexe bedroom opens off another. This example, also in Little Albert Street, Bristol, had similar but slightly more grand street elevation to single-storey annexe type. Front room 11ft 9in × 9ft (3·6 × 2·7m), Back room 11ft 6in × 9ft (3·5 × 2·7m), Bedroom 1 12ft 3in × 11ft 9in (3·7 × 3·6m), Bedroom 2 12ft 3in × 11ft 6in (3·7 × 3·5m), Bedroom 3 10ft × 6ft (3·0 × 1·8m). Drawing by C. G. Powell

rooms. An example in Morley Terrace, Barton Hill, Bristol, had six rooms all 15ft by 12ft and a total superficial floor area of 1,250sq ft; but a house as large as this, with a separate entrance to the basement from the garden side, lent itself easily to subdivision, and was unlikely to be occupied by a single family.

   'By-law housing' was especially appropriate for the development of new areas where the rectilinear layout of streets and terraces could be imposed over open land. It therefore fitted ideally—both spatially and chronologically—into the pattern of suburban development which most large towns were experiencing in this period, and especially from the 1870s onwards. In London, because of its great size and the congestion of its central areas, working-class suburban development began earlier than elsewhere, and from the mid-century onwards rapid growth occurred along the lines of the railways, especially in north and north-east London where the Great Eastern Company offered the most comprehensive system of workmen's trains. Between 1851 and 1891 Willesden grew from 3,000 to 114,000, West Ham from 19,000 to 267,000 and Leyton from 5,000 to 98,000, and with the further extension of cheap travel after the Act of 1883 a ring of working-class suburbs began to encircle London, though broken to the south and west by enclaves of a higher social status. In 1905 a twopenny ticket carried a passenger eleven miles to the north of London, twelve miles to the west, twenty-one miles to the east but only eight miles to the south. By then approximately 13,000 families a year were leaving the inner circle for the suburbs and, the LCC estimated, about 820,000 workmen were making extensive journeys to their work each day.[44] The growth of suburbs did not solve London's housing problem, as some sanguine reformers had hoped, mainly because their economic advantage had declined by the end of the century as land values rose and as building by-laws increased the standards and costs of suburban housing, but they played an important part both in easing the housing crisis of the period and in sharpening the contrast between those who were increasingly well-housed and those who were still condemned to life in the slums.

Outside London, suburbanization tended to be later and slower, though it followed a similar pattern. Because of their smaller scale, the suburbs of provincial cities typically lay at distances of only two or three miles from the centre rather than from three to eight or ten, and their development as working-class dormitories depended more on internal urban transport, and especially on the tram, than on the railway. The important development of the electric tramway located this type of suburban growth from the eighties and nineties onwards. Thus, in Sheffield rapid new building took place at the end of the century in districts such as Meersbrook, Millhouses, Sharrow, Fulwood, Eccleshall, Walkley, Tinsley, Catcliffe, Hillsborough and Norton, several of the new estates being deliberately located round the tram termini. A local councillor in 1898 expressed the opinion that corporations trying to deal with their slum problems would see 'the ultimate connection there was between an adequate, efficient and cheap tramway service and the question of the housing of the working classes'. Like many other councils, Sheffield corporation took over the tram system in 1896, and continued to extend it down to the outbreak of war.[45] Similarly, in Nottingham internal transport was transformed in the last two decades of the century. The industrial villages which had grown up at

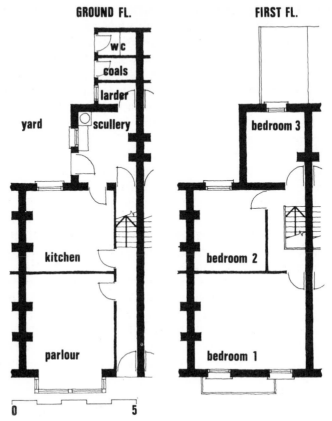

GROUND FL.

wc

coals

larder

yard

scullery

kitchen

parlour

FIRST FL.

bedroom 3

bedroom 2

bedroom 1

0   5

10   Ultimate development of rear annexe projection; an example at Longford, Coventry, 1911. Third bedroom reached off landing. Parlour 12ft × 11ft (3·7 × 3·4m), Kitchen 11ft × 10ft (3·4 × 3·0m), Bedroom 1 14ft × 12ft (4·3 × 3·7m), Bedroom 2 10ft × 9ft (3·0 × 2·7m), Bedroom 3 8ft 6in × 7ft 6in (2·6 × 2·3m). Drawing by C. G. Powell based on information in *The Houses of the Workers* by A. Sayle, published by Fisher, Unwin in 1928

distances of two to five miles to the north and west of the city in the early part of the century retained an almost independent existence until daily omnibus services to Beeston and Arnold began in 1853. In 1886 a group of local businessmen formed the Nottingham Suburban Railway between Nottingham and Daybrook with the object of improving passenger transport for some 40,000 people living to the north and east of the town, but by then, tramways, which had begun in 1874, were already beginning to offer a more convenient alternative. Routes were extended in the 1880s to Hyson Green and Carrington, and further developments took place after 1897 when the Corporation acquired the system.[46] The growth of artisan suburbs such as Sherwood, situated at one of the tram termini, was particularly rapid at the turn of the century, and coincided with the period of 'by-law housing' development. Thus important advances in housing standards for better-paid workers towards the end of the century were often the result of controlled private building in new suburban areas, bringing their residents for the first time into acquaintance with standards of space and hygiene which until then had been the prerogative of the middle classes. Coinciding with important advances in real earnings during the seventies and eighties which made possible higher standards of nutrition,[47] furnishing and domestic comfort generally, this period was, for a substantial section of the working class, the beginning of major changes in the pattern of home and family life.

PROVINCIAL HOUSING STANDARDS: THREE CASE-STUDIES

Having discussed some of the general factors affecting housing standards, we may turn to the experience of some particular cities in the later nineteenth century. Birmingham, Nottingham and York represent towns of very different size, and dependent on very different industrial bases.

Birmingham had a long and large inheritance of back-to-backs—no fewer than 42,000 remaining in 1914, many of them still in enclosed courts, although by then the Housing Department under the guidance of J. S. Nettlefold was busy opening them up by removing the end houses. Birmingham at least had no cellar-dwellings, and few tenemented houses: the tradition was for every family to have a separate dwelling, even if this was of the back-to-back variety. Working-class houses in Birmingham in the later nineteenth century consisted of four basic types, three of them back-to-back and the fourth a through terrace. The illustrations indicate these variations, Type 1 consisting of a living-room with two bedrooms above in a three-storey house, Type 2 of two storeys and having the first floor divided into two small bedrooms, and Type 3, larger, having a narrow hall from which led the staircase, two bedrooms on the first floor and an attic bedroom above. Type 4, occupied by better-paid artisans, was the conventional through terrace, with hall, front parlour, back kitchen and washhouse or scullery annexe; on the first floor were two bedrooms, with two more attic bedrooms above them. Very few of these houses had internal water or drainage, but otherwise Types 3 and 4 at least provided adequate bedroom accommodation.

It was, no doubt, a house of Type 4 which a French visitor to Birmingham, Paul de Rousiers, described in 1895:

While I was alone in the parlour I had time to look at it well. The room was nearly square, about 12ft each way, and well lighted by a window looking on to the street. The floor was covered with carpets, and from the middle of the ceiling hung a chandelier with three burners. The wall opposite the door was occupied by a white marble mantelpiece with a cast-iron grate; over the fire was an overmantel of wood. A suite upholstered in horse-hair looked like good solid family furniture, and consisted of six chairs, a sofa, and a low chair. There were two tables, covered with cloths. One stood in front of the window, and held a china flower-pot in which a fern was dying, the other was covered with books and albums. A mahogany chiffonier with glass panels and shelves completed the furniture. Photographs were scattered about on the mantelpiece and tables, and there were two or three indifferent pictures on the walls.[48]

Here was gentility almost of middle-class standards. The parlour suite had cost Mr Brown, who owned his house, twenty-two guineas on his marriage twenty-seven years ago: it was still in good condition, he explained, not like the cheap, 'showy' suites made up in Whitechapel of unseasoned wood which could now be had for six guineas. The chiffonier had cost fifteen guineas, the overmantel seven guineas and the marble fireplace six guineas. In the 'sitting-room' (not 'kitchen'), 'where we have meals and where we spend most of our time', there was also a marble mantelpiece, less elaborate, at four guineas, solid chairs which had cost £1 5s 0d each and a sofa at seven guineas. There was also a very convenient 'kitchener', 'a marvel of ingenuity' which was capable of cooking the family meals, providing constant hot water, drying linen and heating irons; it had cost £8, but burnt only about 2s worth of coal a week.

Few working men anywhere could aspire to these standards, though in this city building clubs and freehold land societies were making an important contribution to home-ownership by the working classes.[49] But all benefited after 1876 when the Birmingham by-laws began to break down the court system and to control the standards of new houses. A careful analysis of the plans of over 500 of these, built between 1878 and 1884, has been made by S. D. Chapman and J. N. Bartlett, which reveals much about the effects of by-law legislation at this time. The houses, all of which had a total living area of less than 800sq ft, were almost invariably built in terraces, access to the rear being through a tunnel or passage at ground level between blocks. About half had a ground-floor bay window for appearance and greater light, and 40 per cent had a small front garden averaging 50sq ft. The average area of the houses was 658sq ft, excluding cellars and external privies. Only 12 per cent were of three rooms only; the great majority contained four or five rooms—two on the ground floor and either two or three bedrooms—while six-roomed houses, accounting for 14 per cent of the sample, had a third ground-floor room, providing either living-room, kitchen and scullery or parlour, living-room and kitchen. The average room sizes in all the houses were comparable with those of a small modern suburban or council house—132sq ft for the living-room and parlour, 100sq ft for the kitchen and 60sq ft for the scullery; 60 per cent of the houses had a cellar, used for storage space. Upstairs, all houses had at least two bedrooms, measuring 113sq ft and having tall, 9ft ceilings; half also possessed a third, attic room of approximately the same size. The greatest disadvantages of these houses lay in their sanitary provisions. Only

46 of the 500 houses had internal WCs, and of the predominant external privies one-third were still shared between several families. Only 9 per cent of houses had a wash-house, and none had a bathroom. Also lacking by modern standards was a separate lobby, as most front doors still opened directly into the front room. But with these exceptions the by-law houses of the eighties represented a marked improvement on their predecessors, possessing through ventilation, more rooms (typically four or five rather than three or four), larger rooms, higher ceilings and improved sanitary services. The average number of persons per house in Birmingham in 1881 was only five. These new houses, built in the suburbs, were in sharp contrast to the older, three-roomed back-to-backs which still housed 30 per cent of the city's population in 1901, and which were almost universal in the central districts.[50]

Another town with a large inheritance of back-to-backs was Nottingham, where in mid-century between 7,000 and 8,000 of its 11,000 houses were of this type. Indeed, the sanitary reports of the 1840s had believed that slums and overcrowding were worse here than in any other industrial town, commenting that 'the entire quarter occupied by the labouring classes forms but one great nuisance'.[51] Only in its excellent supply of water, the creation of Mr Hawkesley, the engineer of the Trent Water Works, could the town boast any reputation, but housing in the central area was extraordinarily cramped and inferior. The houses had usually only two or, sometimes, three rooms, each about 11ft square, built in successive storeys. Almost all were back-to-back, in narrow courts closed at both ends, and, unlike the arrangement in Leeds and most other towns, the rows were built at right angles to the streets rather than parallel to them.

To the city's credit, when the enclosure of the common lands was at last forced through against the vested interests of burgesses, owners of slum property and site values, in 1845, strict and enlightened regulations governing the development of the new building land were laid down. No house was to be built without a private garden or yard, a separate privy, and at least three bedrooms, and it was not to adjoin another building on more than two sides. Streets were to be at least 36ft wide, alleys and courts 20ft; cesspools were not to be within 10ft of a house.[52] Despite some evasions, there is no doubt of the gradual improvement of Nottingham housing in the second half of the century under the influence of controlled building. The regular reports of the Sanitary Committee, first appointed in 1849, testify to slow but distinct progress. In his *Report on the Sanitary Condition of the Borough* in 1873, the medical officer of health, Edward Smeaton, was able to point to the fact that while in the Old Town the death rate per thousand was still 31·2, in the Meadows, where houses had chiefly been built to comply with the terms of the 1845 regulations, it was 20·9, in the more elevated district of St Ann's 17·6, and in the 'villa residences and superior class houses' of Sherwood only 14·9; the death rate for children under five ranged from 13·2 down to 4·8.[53] Shortly after this, in 1876, the Corporation began to make its first direct attack on the slums by rehousing some of the very poor in the Victoria Dwellings, Bath Street. This was a block of one-, two- and three-roomed flats for ninety-three persons, built on the plan of similar London model dwellings, and paying only a nominal return of 2–3 per cent per annum. Town improvement began in the next decade with the building of Gregory and Radford Boulevards, 60ft wide, tree-lined avenues which provided useful social as well as transport amenities, while the opening of King and Queen Streets in the city centre in 1892 demolished some of the notorious rookeries between Market Street and Parliament Street.

By the end of the century house-size had undoubtedly increased, the five-roomed house now accommodating 72 per cent of the town's population. In these, the front door opened directly from the street into the parlour, commonly about 12ft by 11ft, behind which were the kitchen and scullery; stairs from a corner in the kitchen led to two or three bedrooms above, depending on whether the scullery annexe was single or double-storey. The houses had private yards, containing the WC and coal-shed. They were built in terraces of about eight houses, entrance to the rear yards being through the usual tunnel and back alley. Above these in the hierarchy were some six-roomed houses principally occupied by white-collar workers, but including some foremen and highly-paid artisans. These were characterized by a front door which opened into a narrow hall, giving separate access to the parlour, kitchen and staircase. One type had its six rooms two to a floor, thus providing four bedrooms, the other type, on two floors only, having three living-rooms and three bedrooms. In some of the three-storey houses bathrooms had been built out over the scullery. Cooking and lighting by gas had made much progress in the city since the Gas Department first began to instal automatic meters in 1892; by 1906, 23,753 had been supplied.[54]

By 1914 Nottingham was on the way to recovering the reputation of 'a fair city' which it had enjoyed in the eighteenth century. The death rate, at 16·1 per thousand in 1906, was only two decimal points higher than the average of the great towns, while overcrowding at 3·65 per cent was well below the national figure. The heavy inheritance of back-to-backs was being overshadowed by the newer terraced housing, offering substantially larger accommodation in decent, if dull, by-law streets. Though the destruction of the central slums was a slow and difficult process, not completed until the 1930s, the Corporation took early initiative after the Artisans' Dwellings Act of 1875 in designating insanitary areas and preparing schemes of public rehousing—the Broad Marsh being the first area to be so designated. Some council building of compensatory dwellings also began in the seventies and eighties in three areas off Forest Road, St Ann's Street and Hunger Hills Road.[55] Housing and sanitary improvements such as these, the provision of recreational amenities such as the Forest, the

Arboretum, the Central Library and numerous public walks, coupled with a steady advance in prosperity and standards of comfort, were, by the end of the century, beginning to transform Nottingham into one of the more pleasant provincial cities.

In York, surveyed by Rowntree in 1900, four-roomed houses constituted 29·5 per cent of the total stock, five-roomed 24·3 per cent, but there were still substantial proportions of three-roomed (8·3 per cent) and even two-roomed (9·2 per cent) dwellings.[56] All but a tiny fraction of families were, however, able to occupy a separate house, only 391 families inhabiting tenements. Rowntree divided the working-class housing of York into three categories. The best were occupied by well-to-do artisans and housed 12 per cent of the working class. They were situated in the newer parts of the town, in wide streets of 30–35ft, which occasionally had been planted with trees. The houses had frontages of 15–17ft, behind small railed gardens of 10–12sq yd, and were also characterized by bay-windows. Inside, they had five main rooms plus a scullery–sitting-room, kitchen, and three bedrooms above. They had some pretensions to style as well as comfort: ornamental mantelpieces of imitation marble, overmantels and pianos in the parlour—'chiefly used on Sundays, or as a receiving-room for visitors who are not on terms sufficiently intimate to be asked into the kitchen. Occasionally it is used by the husband when he has writing to do in connection with friendly or other societies, or by the children when practising music'. The real living-room was the kitchen, made homely and comfortable by its large open grate and good oven in which bread was baked, the linoleum and hearthrug, the sofa and china ornaments on the mantelpiece. A great advantage of such houses was the scullery, containing the sink, water-tap and copper, which made it possible to banish washing from the living-rooms.

Rowntree's 'class 2' houses, occupied by those earning modest but regular wages, accommodated 62 per cent of York's working class. They were situated in narrower streets which often had a dull and dreary aspect. Some houses in this class were smaller versions of 'class 1' houses, lacking the front garden and bay-window, on a narrower frontage of about 13ft and with rooms consequently smaller; often there were only two bedrooms, the scullery being a single-storey lean-to. The 'parlour' was often used as a store-room for bicycles and perambulators rather than as a ritual receiving-room, and the small back yards usually contained a midden privy rather than a water-closet. But the majority of houses in class 2 were of a more inferior kind, the street-door opening directly into the front living-room which was, in fact, the kitchen, fitted with open range and oven; the small back room, about 9ft by 12ft, was the scullery, with sink and copper, and with a staircase leading to the two bedrooms. Many new houses of this type were still being built in 1900, often with very thin walls and 'green' timber, and were, according to Rowntree, destined soon to degenerate into slums.

'Class 3' houses contained 26 per cent of York's working class. Here lived the 'struggling poor' in gloomy houses in narrow streets which had been run up before the advent of by-law control. Some were inferior versions of class 2, containing only one all-purpose living-room and two small bedrooms, or sometimes only 'one up and one down'. Below these, the houses gradually descended into the slums, often consisting of tiny back-to-backs in courts and alleys, sharing water-taps and midden privies. Even in these poorest districts a few houses were kept tidy and clean, but the great majority were dirty and dilapidated, with broken windows, damp walls, uneven brick floors and decayed plaster. Some were old houses of two, three or four rooms; others single rooms in larger, tenemented houses. Details of some of these were recorded by the local sanitary inspector:

House No. 2. Three rooms. Four persons. House dirty in the extreme. Ceiling almost black. Wall-paper begrimed with smoke and dirt. Rain coming through ceiling. Brick floor uneven and in holes; partially covered with filthy carpet.

House No. 4. Two rooms. Seven inmates. Walls, ceiling, and furniture filthy. Dirty flock bedding in living-room placed on a box and two chairs. Smell of room from dirt and bad air unbearable, and windows and door closed. There is no through ventilation in this house. Children pale, starved-looking, and only half clothed. One boy with hip disease, another with sores over face.

Courtyard. Entered by passage 4ft 9in wide. Yard partially cobbled. Six houses join at one tap and one water-closet. Five of these are back-to-back houses, and the sixth is built back-to-back with a slaughter-house. This slaughter-house (which has a stable connected with it) has a block of houses adjoining another of its sides, and the front of the building is separated from a row of houses by a street only 16ft wide.

At the end of the century York still had about 12 per cent of back-to-backs, the building of which had been prohibited since 1870. Midden-privies, of which there were many, were gradually being replaced by water-closets, and the health of the city's inhabitants benefited from the large 'strays' and promenades constructed by the riverside and on the old walls. The death rate of 13·7 in 1906 was considerably below that of any of the larger Yorkshire towns.

THE HOUSING HIERARCHY AT THE END OF THE CENTURY

Enough has been said of individual towns to indicate that, despite the variety of inheritance and subsequent building activity, certain characteristics of working-class housing had emerged by the end of the century. At the top of the hierarchy, and generally available only to skilled workers with good wages or to those whose children were working and contributing to family earnings, were recently-built houses in the suburbs or newer parts of towns, containing five or more rooms and set in small front and rear gardens. They were distinguished by the possession of bay-windows and by 'architectural' decoration on the house fronts such as coloured string courses, plinths, eaves details, ceramic tiles and coloured glass door panels. Internally, such houses were immediately recognizable by their front parlours containing objects such as pianos, chiffoniers and marble fireplaces which were, for the class, expensive luxuries.

The parlour has evoked much critical comment both from contemporaries and from subsequent observers of social differences. 'The women are proud when they can exhibit a parlour to Sunday visitors', wrote Allen Clarke in 1899 with reference to Bolton. 'It is shut up six days of the week, and is only kept for brag. Ostentatious superfluity in the idea of the artisan's wife is, as with those in higher grades of society, a sign of superiority.'[57] The fact that a room could be so set aside for deliberate under-use, though perhaps irrational, was an indication of the ability to afford a surplus, and placed workers in Midland and Northern manufacturing towns in a distinctly better accommodation position than their fellow-workers in London. For this reason W. A. Abram came to the optimistic conclusion that 'No operative population in the world [is] so well and cheaply housed as are the factory workers in a Lancashire manufacturing town of the second or third magnitude'.[58] The possession of a parlour, appropriately furnished with ritual objects in what was considered to be 'good taste', was an important part of the struggle for achievement and respectability, and of the search for identity by people who instinctively modelled their behaviour on their social superiors. Whether used or not, the parlour announced to the family, to neighbours and to visitors who first glimpsed it through its Nottingham lace curtains, a triumph over poverty and a challenge to the external environment which was too often one of dirt, squalor and social disharmony. Outside, the houses might appear dull and monotonous, in mean streets the starkness of which was often shrouded by grey, smoke-laden skies, but inside the home, and especially in the parlour, the environment could be controlled and order, comfort and even beauty created. In this respect cleanliness and brightness within the home were essential requirements: the bright surfaces of linoleum, polished furniture, mirrors, brass ornaments and starched or glazed fabrics helped to reflect what light was available from outside, from oil- or gas-lamps and from the open fire, and were part of the aesthetic symbolism to which the class unconsciously aspired.[59] Similar motivations underlay the regular Saturday morning sweeping and scrubbing of the pavement to the full width of the house, the ritual 'whitening' of doorsteps and window sills (in fact, the stones sold for this purpose were more often yellow, blue or grey) and the polishing of door furniture. The round of weekly chores in preparation for the day of rest appropriately ended here, with the world shut out behind a clean house-front.

Below such houses as these, with their emulation of middle-class standards, were the houses not of the poor, but of the bulk of the working classes, usually the regularly-employed, semi-skilled factory and mining populations. Infinite gradations of comfort and discomfort were to be found here, depending on a variety of personal and familial circumstances—the number and age of children, the possibilities for extra earnings, the carefulness of the housewife and the sobriety of the husband. But, in general, these houses were characterized by the absence of a front garden, a separate hallway and a ritual parlour, fewer and smaller rooms, and a lower standard of possessions. By the end of the century such houses were generally in through terraces though, as we have seen, back-to-backs were still common in some towns, the outstanding case being Leeds where, in 1886, they formed 71 per cent of the total housing stock. By now, new back-to-backs were almost restricted to Yorkshire, having been all but discontinued in Lancashire, the Black Country and the Potteries, but their popularity in the West Riding was partly explained by the considerable extent of home-ownership by the working classes, among whom it was a common practice to build a block of four back-to-backs on a plot 10yd square, living in one and paying off the mortgage from the rents of the other three. Even in these survivals from an earlier age there had, however, been some changes in design, the cellar kitchen being abandoned in favour of dividing the ground-floor room into a small 'parlour' and even smaller kitchen, and greater ceiling heights being provided.

Many of the houses in this class were clean and well cared for, though their furnishing was usually dreary and utilitarian. The status symbols which were aspired to were much the same as in the artisan class—the piano, the overmantel, the full-drape curtains to the front window, and display objects such as pictures, ornaments and fireside utensils—but their achievement much less common. Allen Clarke thought that among Bolton cotton-workers 'there is one piano in about every hundred of the operatives' houses, and then only got when all the children are growing up and working, and generally on the hire system'. A pair of American rocking-chairs was more common than an upholstered suite, a home-made rag hearthrug on the linoleum more likely than a carpet. Few families in this class would be able to enter matrimony with a houseful of new furniture, despite the big reductions in cost which had come with mass-production. By the end of the century a basic 'house of furniture' for 'one up and one down' could be bought, cash, for twelve guineas. Its contents give a good indication of what such households might ultimately acquire, the absence of a wardrobe in the bedroom being suggestive (see opposite page):[60]

Display was necessarily less ambitious in such homes, though nonetheless important. A velvet plush cover with tasselled ends might conceal a cheap, deal table-top. The bedding and underclothes which often had to be strung across the street to dry should be as good as possible because they were a

	£	s	d
One leather couch or sofa	1	6	0
One hardwood armchair		9	6
One hardwood rocking chair		9	6
Four best kitchen chairs		15	6
One square table		10	6
$3\frac{1}{2} \times 4$ yards oilcloth		14	0
One cloth hearth rug		4	9
One kitchen fender		6	6
One set kitchen fire-irons		4	6
One ashpan		2	11
One full-size brass-mounted bedstead	1	12	6
One double woven wire mattress		14	6
One flock bed bolster and pillows		16	6
3ft 6in. enclosed dressing table with fixed glass	1	15	0
Ditto washstand with tile back	1	9	0
Two cane seat chairs		7	0
$2\frac{1}{2} \times 4$ yards oilcloth		10	0
Two bedside rugs		3	10
	12	12	0

public demonstration of one's economic position. For these struggling, respectable families the important things were to avoid any suspicion of poverty, and to preserve the highest standards of cleanliness in the home. The cult of cleanliness was, perhaps, most highly developed by these housewives whose possessions were comparatively few and worthless, but who lavished on them an endless labour of washing, cleaning, scouring and polishing.

A house-type which deserves separate mention was the miner's cottage, often situated in a village colony, and transitional in character between urban and rural forms. On steep valley slopes they were sometimes built in long, single-storey rows, but more often, as in the Yorkshire villages around Barnsley and Morley, they were small, two-storey cottages, sometimes back-to-back and sometimes in through terraces. In either case, the accommodation was extremely sparse, usually consisting of only one up and one down—the 'house' which was the all-purpose living-room, and one bedroom which accommodated the whole family in two or three beds. Some houses had a cellar, with stone steps leading down under the staircase, though it was not normally used for habitation. The living-room usually had a flagged floor, and its central feature was the large fireplace, generally on the wall opposite the staircase. To one side of this was a cupboard, to the other an iron copper with firebox beneath, and beyond this the sink, made from a block of fine-grained sandstone about 3ft by 1ft 6in by 5in deep. There might be a shelf over this, and a cupboard below. The fireplace contained a cast-iron fire-grate with an oven to one side and a water-boiler, emptied by a 'lading-can', to the other. The furnishing of these cottages was usually equally sparse—a steel fender and fire-irons, a hearthrug made by the housewife of 'clippings' sewn on to hessian, and ideally renewed every Christmas, a central table, usually of deal but if of mahogany having its legs protected on weekdays by old woollen stockings, a few plain wooden chairs or stools and a couple of more comfortable ones by the fireside, often including a rocking-chair. There might be a small sideboard or cheap chest of drawers, often painted. Upstairs there was little room for anything more than the bedsteads—blackened iron rather than brass—a cradle, and a blanket-box or drawers. Lighting was by candle or oil, a hanging brass oil-lamp suspended from the wooden ceiling by three chains being a considerable source of pride and shown off to admiring neighbours.[61]

The line between such houses and those of the poor was a thin one. In 1891, 16 per cent of the national housing stock consisted of dwellings of one or two rooms, and although some of their occupants earned as much as, or more than, the 'respectable', the majority were poor, because of unemployment, low or casual earnings, larger-than-average families, old age or the death of the principal earner. Slum areas, characterized by their overcrowding, dirt, squalor and crime, were to be found in all large towns, sometimes in relatively small, localized pockets as in Nottingham, sometimes spreading over extensive areas, as in Salford. By the century's end many had been identified and some had become the object of remedial policy, though all too often the clearance of one area only created a new slum in another. In 1889 Robert Blatchford asked, 'Where are the slums of Manchester?', and answered himself. 'They are everywhere. Manchester is a city of slums.' He went on to describe the masses of back-to-backs, courts and alleys which were unchanged from half a century earlier except for their increased dilapidation. The average size of rooms here was about 10ft square, many no more than 8ft; ceilings were often only 6ft high; in winter they were damp, cold and draughty, in summer so airless and infested with vermin that their inhabitants sometimes sat out all night on steps and pavements.

> The [wall] paper is black with the grease and grime of years, the plaster is cracked and crumbling, the ceilings are rent and swollen and foul, the woodwork is paintless, the roofs are broken, the walls damp, the doors and windows warped and shrunken, the rotten bricks and lath and plaster are reeking with pollution . . .[62]

From East London, from parts of Bristol, Hull, York, Leeds and many other towns, came closely similar reports of slum conditions towards the end of the century. Their accounts of the dirt and dilapidation of homes, the lack of possessions, the 'bed-bugging' and the twice-weekly visits to the pawnbroker are sufficiently familiar not to require repetition.[63] Like poverty itself, the slums had always been with us, but the awakened concern which made housing the most debated social question from the 1880s onwards was partly due to the demonstration of the real extent of destitution by the surveys of Booth, Rowntree and others, and partly to the discovery that the profit motive could not supply for all people a standard of accommodation which the public conscience had come to regard as acceptable. The fact that many of the working classes had raised their standards of accommodation during the latter half of the century tended to obscure the issue, for it was all too easy to argue that what some had done others could do, and that the natural process of 'filtering up' would in time eradicate the problem. Some reformers, like Octavia Hill, believed that the remedy lay in the hands of the poor themselves, once properly instructed how to manage their resources: others argued that the responsibility lay with individual employers or with philanthropic agencies to demonstrate that the provision of adequate housing for the poor need not be a financial loss, even if it brought little gain. By the century's end it was becoming clear to many that none of these solutions was adequate to deal with the scale of the problem, and that provision would have to be treated as a collective responsibility, supported if necessary by state subvention.

HOUSING REFORM

The various forms which this search for a solution took have been described elsewhere[64] and need not be recapitulated here. What is important for our purpose is to show what results the ideas produced in terms of built form, because these represented, in varying degrees, models of working-class housing for their period, and also because some at least had enduring influences on subsequent building. We may group the movement for improved dwellings under three heads: the work of charitable and semi-charitable societies and companies, that of individual employers, and, at the end of the period, that of local authorities.

As we saw in Chapter 3, two important voluntary bodies were already in existence by 1850, building dwellings in London which were intended to serve as examples for speculative activity. Of these, Shaftesbury's society—the Society for Improving the Condition of the Labouring Classes—produced little more after its demonstration of 'Prince Albert's Model Cottages' at the Great Exhibition in 1851. It had, by then, already demonstrated the principal types of accommodation suitable for working-class families and individuals, and in subsequent years it concentrated on renovation and conversion of lodging-houses. Its achievement in terms of the numbers housed was, therefore, negligible—453 families and 260 single persons by 1875—although eight other societies based on its principles had been formed in provincial towns where they had some small effect in propagating the gospel of improved dwellings.

The other important society of this period, the Metropolitan Association for Improving the Dwellings of the Industrious Classes, continued a rather more active building programme, both of multi-storey blocks and of cottages. The Association's last and largest development was in Farringdon Road in 1874 where five 6-storey blocks provided 260 dwellings and a number of shops. By then, it had built accommodation for 1,122 families, and continued to pay its limited dividend of 5 per cent per annum until the end of the century. Like Shaftesbury's society, it inspired the formation of at least half a dozen other groups in various parts of London providing smaller amounts of accommodation.

The societies had thus demonstrated their principal belief—that sanitary accommodation could be built in central sites in London and made to pay a modest return on capital. Miss Angela Burdett-Coutts's purely philan-thropic development at Columbia Market in 1861, which aimed at housing some of the poorest, paid only 2·2 per cent. The problem was to attract suf-ficient investors to build in quantity on central area sites, a problem which the new trusts and companies formed in the sixties attempted to meet in different ways. Unlike the earlier societies, the intention of 'five per cent philanthropy' was not merely exemplary, but, on the basis of a dividend which would reward the pocket as well as the conscience, to build on a scale sufficient at least to relieve accommodation pressure in central London.

The Peabody Trust, which began in 1862 with a gift of £150,000 from the American merchant George Peabody, concentrated on multi-storey blocks providing one-, two- and three-roomed apartments, usually with shared sinks and WCs; by 1887 the Trust had provided 5,014 dwellings. Sydney Waterlow's Improved Industrial Dwellings Company was launched in 1863 with an initial capital of £50,000 and shareholders who included bankers, merchants, MPs and lawyers. It, too, built in blocks of 5–7 storeys, providing self-contained flats mostly for artisans. By 1871 1,000 dwellings were occupied, and the company was accumulating profits over and above the 5 per cent dividend paid. It worked from standard plans, prepared by a surveyor rather than an architect, which could be adapted to any site, and employed its own builders and carpenters who made up standard joinery and fittings. Like the other societies, the Company did not build for the poorest workers, Waterlow explaining his philosophy:

> The wisest plan in dealing with the question is to attempt, in the first place, to meet the wants of that portion of the working class most worth working for—those earning from £1.5s to £2 per week; and that as the pressure on this class is lightened, and better accommodation provided for their use, the class immediately beneath them will shift into the quarters from which they gradually migrate; that this will be repeated until at least the lowest of all—those comprising what may emphatically be called the lower orders, and who are least likely to appreciate the comforts of a decent home—will slowly, but surely, receive their share of the benefits enjoyed proportionately by those above them.[65]

Two further agencies require mention. The Artisans, Labourers and General Dwellings Company was formed in 1867 primarily to develop suburban cottage estates, the first being at Lavender Hill and later ones at Noel Park, Hornsey, and at Streatham Hill. Rents of 7s–13s a week secured a good return of 6–7½ per cent, but again restricted occupation to better-paid workers. Considerably later in the field, the East End Dwellings Company, formed in 1884, represented a different philosophy of providing minimal standards of housing for some of the poorest unskilled and casual labourers. Its first block in Stepney, Katharine Buildings, offered 281 single rooms, with shared water and WCs on the landings, at rents of 1s 6d–2s a week.

By the time of the Royal Commission of 1885 model societies of one sort or another had been in existence for more than forty years, and it was possible to make some assessment of their contribution. Nearly all the twenty-eight or more associations were paying between 4 and 5 per cent dividend, and so had demonstrated that improved dwellings could be reasonably remunerative. It was estimated that about £6,500,000 had been spent in total, and that 29,700 families, or 147,000 persons, had been housed on 254 sites in London. Yet, impressive as this seemed to some, the total number housed represented a mere 4 per cent of London's population, and, because of its relatively high standards and levels of rents, 'five per cent philanthropy' did not provide for those many workers earning less than £1 or so a week. Single rooms, averaging 2s 1¼d a week, were not usually let to families for fear of overcrowding, and two rooms, at 5s 6d upwards, were beyond the reach of many, quite apart from the rigorous restrictions on use to which tenants were subject. Considerable evidence was presented to the Royal Commission on the unpopularity of block tenements, due partly to the regulations and absence of sheds and workshops, but mainly, reported Lord Compton, because they were regarded as 'a sort of prison: they look upon themselves as being watched'.

The significance of the movement lay not in the quantity of its achievement, but in the development of improved housing standards. The congregation of many self-contained dwelling units in a single building was an innovation in English house design, though well known, of course, in Scotland and on the Continent. It was one possible solution to the problem of housing large numbers of people who needed to live close to their work in central urban areas where land values were high and the traditional method of lateral extension was impossible. In its blocks the Metropolitan Association housed 1,000–1,600 persons to the acre compared with what were regarded as high densities of 237 in old, overcrowded property in Westminster and 304 in Spitalfields, yet the statistics showed mortality rates considerably lower than in adjacent areas or in the country as a whole.

Aesthetically, a frequent complaint of contemporaries was of the 'barrack-like' appearance of the blocks, which had to be designed within strict cost and space limits by men who had had no previous experience of this type of building. Professor Pevsner has described the era of Peabody Buildings as 'truly humanitarian in its pretensions, yet depressing in its results'. The unrelieved façades and long rows of windows often gave a dreary, institutional appearance which was difficult to avoid with relatively low buildings. Internally, the accommodation in most blocks was carefully worked out, convenient and comfortable, with well-shaped and well-ventilated rooms. Space standards were almost always an improvement on existing living conditions, though considerably short of those of contemporary local-authority housing. Dr W. V. Hole has calculated that the overall area of the flats shown at the Great Exhibition was approximately half that recommended for a three-bedroomed flat a hundred years later.[66] The chief advantages of model dwellings lay in the fact that they were usually self-contained and had a much higher standard of services than was to be found in subdivided houses. A well-fitted kitchen or living-room, a water-supply, a dust and refuse-chute, proper cooking and water-heating arrangements, a wash-house and a water-closet were inestimable benefits, and introduced a section of the working-classes to standards of decent comfort which until now had been unavailable.

Multi-storey tenement flats were one possible solution to the problem of accommodation in central urban areas, especially in the great cities, and as such were to be an important influence on twentieth-century concepts. Another, quite different, solution, which involved dispersal rather than redevelopment, was the answer of a number of industrial employers who established planned model communities partly to serve their business interests and partly through a genuine concern to raise the material and moral well-being of their workpeople. Examples of such activities by individual employers and by railway companies in the first half of the century have already been discussed (Chapter 3), and it is clear from the Report of the Factory Commission of 1833, which listed 168 of the 881 large firms which made returns as providing some houses for their workers, that the practice was already well-established, particularly in the textile areas of the West Riding and Lancashire. In the second half of the century several schemes were pioneered which were larger both in scale and in concept, sometimes involving the total planning of new communities on utopian lines, and designed not only to ensure to the employer an efficient and contented labour force, but to point the way towards a new relationship of capital and labour and the creation of a new kind of physical environment in which men and machines could live harmoniously together.

It is with the housing standards rather than the wider planning concepts of such schemes that we are concerned here. Edward Akroyd, the successful Halifax worsted manufacturer, built two model villages at Copley (1849–53) and, more ambitiously, at Akroydon (begun 1859) both of which eventually became absorbed as Halifax suburbs although originally built on practically virgin land in the Yorkshire dales. His development at Akroydon has sometimes been regarded as the real forerunner of the garden city concept. The social purpose of the experiment was here paramount: 'A clean, fresh, well-ordered house exercises on its inmates a moral no less than a physical influence, and has the direct tendency to make the members of a family sober, peaceable, and considerate of the feelings and happiness of each other . . .' No less an architect than George Gilbert Scott was retained to design the village in the 'Domestic Gothic' style which Akroyd specified because it was 'the original style of the parish of Halifax' and because 'this taste of our forefathers pleases the fancy, strengthens the house and home attachment, and entwines the present with memories of the past'.[67] Akroydon was built round a village green, on which stood one of Scott's medieval crosses, though some features of his planning, such as the dormer windows in the cottages, had to be changed when occupants found them antiquated and inconvenient. The houses, which were built of stone with slate roofs, were of various types and sizes, but the earliest contained a generous-sized living-room 15ft by 13ft, a scullery or wash-kitchen, a main bedroom 15ft by 11ft and a children's bedroom 11ft by 6ft 6in; later some larger houses with a parlour and a third bedroom were built. All had small, individual back yards, separated from the next row by a back lane in what was later to become the conventional by-law manner. Like these, Akroydon adopted the rectilinear urban plan of street, backyard and back lane, but on a rural site which could have allowed more flexibility.

Bromborough Pool on the Wirral peninsula, begun in 1853 by Price's Patent Candle Company, probably has a better claim to be regarded as the first garden village. It was a small development, numbering seventy-six houses by 1858, but they were remarkable for the time in being either semi-detached or in terraces of four, in having front and rear gardens and water-borne sanitation. The whole layout was wide and spacious, and the provision of gardens and open spaces unusually generous. The houses contained a living-room 12ft by 10ft 8in, kitchen 9ft 5in by 7ft 1in, scullery 8ft by 7ft 6in, and either two or three bedrooms above.

The best-known of this mid-century phase of employer housing was, however, Saltaire, the creation of the Bradford alpaca manufacturer, Titus Salt, and conceived on a massive, baronial scale executed in a neo-Venetian Gothic style. The mill itself, opened in 1853 and costing £100,000, was exactly the length of St Paul's Cathedral. Ten years later 805 cottages had been completed, laid out in long, parallel terraces of 200–300ft, but with a variety of styles and decoration which avoided monotony while keeping a density of forty houses to the acre. Salt had, in fact, carried out a survey of his employees' housing needs, and built a variety of units intended to meet the needs of families of different size and social status. The smallest accommodation was contained in the forty-five almshouses, provided rent-free and with a pension of 10s a week for retired workpeople 'of good moral character'. Accommodation for families was in stone cottages lined with brick; water and gas were laid on, and each had a private yard with privy, coalstore and ashpit. 'Nothing should be spared', Salt instructed the architects (Lockwood and Mawson, a Bradford firm), 'to render the dwellings of the operatives a pattern to the country', and the housing and amenities were of a high standard, well ventilated and thoroughly drained. The workmen's cottages consisted of a basement containing cellar and pantry, a ground-floor living-room 14ft by 13ft, a scullery 14ft by 9ft and a large closet, and upstairs three bedrooms. The houses for overlookers, costing £200 compared with £120 for the cottages, contained in addition a basement wash-house, a ground-floor parlour 16ft 6in by 15ft, and from three to six bedrooms. Rents, ranging from 2s 4d to 7s 6d a week, gave a return of 4 per cent, but again the amenities, which included churches and chapels, allotments, reading-rooms, assembly hall, gymnasium, art rooms, public baths (including a Turkish bath) and wash-houses supplied with washing-machines and heated drying cabinets, were provided at Salt's expense. He considered himself well rewarded by the morality and self-respect, the absence of drunkenness and illegitimacy with which his workforce was credited.

After an interval of a quarter of a century or so, employer housing moved in the eighties and nineties into a new and distinct phase with W. H. Lever's Port Sunlight, George Cadbury's Bourneville, and Joseph Rowntree's New Earswick. These represented a new vision of what industrial life might be in a planned, controlled environment combining the advantages of town and country but set in an essentially rural environment. As a total solution to the social problems of an industrialized society their approach, like that of the whole garden city movement which blossomed at the end of the century, was a naïve one, and it is not difficult to poke fun at the 'pantomime vision of bucolic England' where the houses 'tend to look like Anne Hathaway's Cottage with the electricity laid on'.[68] Whatever their mistakes, these were serious and highly influential attempts to offer an alternative to high-density tenement blocks and speculative by-law building in the cities, and to propagate the belief that housing which approached middle-class standards and amenity was, and should be, attainable by wage-earners.

In building Port Sunlight, three miles to the south of Birkenhead, Lever was experimenting in his vision of profit-sharing—the financing of a model community for his employees rather than the annual payment of a lump sum of money. Begun in 1888, the deliberate intention was variety in contrast to urban monotony, curving roads and open-front gardens (maintained by the company) in contrast to the gridiron street system. Houses were either semi-detached or built in groups of four or six separated by open spaces; frontages of 18ft and densities of only eight to the acre compared very favourably with contemporary suburban working-class housing. Two main types of house were built, one with a kitchen–living-room of 182sq ft and three bedrooms (169, 143 and 99sq ft), the other with an

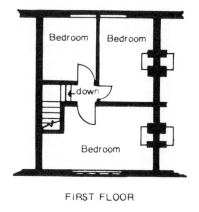

FIRST FLOOR

Feet
0   10   20

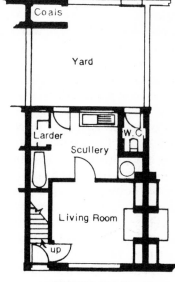

GROUND FLOOR

11   Rear annexe abolished. This advanced design of c 1892 at Port Sunlight has no rear projection but instead a wider frontage. Living room 12ft × 11ft 6in (3·7 × 3·5m), Scullery 10ft × 9ft 6in (3·0 × 2·9m), Bedroom 1 16ft 6in × 9ft (5·0 × 2·7m), Bedroom 2 12ft × 8ft (3·7 × 2·4m), Bedroom 3 9ft × 8ft (2·7 × 2·4m). From J. N. Tarn *Five Per Cent Philanthropy* published by Cambridge University Press 1973

additional parlour (156sq ft) and a fourth bedroom. Both 'kitchen' and 'parlour' types also had a scullery, pantry and bathroom, an important new amenity, and in both the space standards were generous with total areas of 993 and 1,248sq ft respectively. 720 houses were ultimately built, many in modified Dutch and Elizabethan styles, but with barge-boards and half-timbering which were structural, not merely 'applied'. Rents, at about 6s for the smaller houses, were below the commercial value, and the wide range of public amenities was at the expense of Lever Bros.

Although similar in form, Cadbury's Bourneville was different in intent, for it was not devised primarily as a 'company town'. The chocolate factory had been moved from Birmingham in 1879 and a few houses built for employees, but the model village which was begun in 1893 and administered after 1900 by a trust, was intended to be an ideal alternative community. Cadbury employees were always a minority of the residents, and all profits over the 4 per cent return were donated to further development. Nearly a thousand houses had been built by 1912.

At Bourneville, it has been said, 'the straight street of the classical planning tradition had dissolved into trees and gardens, and the terrace had been metamorphosed into a picturesque mansion, which on closer examination turns out to contain five or six cottages'.[69] Houses were built, six to the acre, on the natural contours of the land, unlike Port Sunlight where the site was artificially landscaped, and provided with large gardens planted by the Trust. An important new planning principle was introduced by the requirement that the houses should not cover more than a quarter of the area of the plot, and they were interestingly disposed along winding roads, crescents, closes and culs-de-sac. Again, a variety of styles was consciously adopted, some semi-detached, others in small blocks of three or four with 'tunnel-back' access to the 60 sq yd rear gardens. Houses had either parlour, living-room and kitchen and three bedrooms, or living-room, scullery and three bedrooms. The smaller cottages, which let at 5s a week, had no bathrooms, but had provision for a 'cabinet' bath in the kitchen, off which the WC was situated. Without the urban terrace problem of achieving light at the back of the house, it was possible to adopt a simple, vernacular, square house-plan with no projecting excrescences.[70]

These planning concepts were carried a stage further by Raymond Unwin, the architect of Joseph Rowntree's model village at New Earswick, outside York. As at Bourneville and Port Sunlight, houses were aesthetically grouped rather than regimented; all had utility rooms, and most an upstairs bathroom. But, more than this, Unwin imported and adapted some of the planning concepts of 'middle-class' architects like Voysey and Webb to working-class housing—the belief in a free, organic plan which grew out of the needs of the users and the nature of the site, and, in particular, the conviction that living-rooms should face the sun, whether this meant arranging them at the front or the back of the house. The traditional plan for narrow-fronted terrace houses was therefore abandoned in favour of wider frontages which allowed a better organization of space and took advantage of sun and light. A reverence for rural tradition and craftsmanship was here not degraded into mock-rusticity, but skilfully adapted to modern times and needs. The houses provided a living-room of 180sq ft, a kitchen of 120, bedrooms of 150, 100 and 80sq ft respectively, and a total floor area of 1,002sq ft.

These two possible solutions to the housing of the working classes—multi-storey flats in central areas and garden villages in the suburbs—were both adopted by local-authority housing schemes before 1914, and, in some of the work of the London County Council's Architects Department, began to converge into a third, distinct solution. The history of the legislation under which local councils were empowered to act in housing matters has been admirably documented by Dr Enid Gauldie[71] and need not be repeated here. For building purposes, as opposed to the demolition of insanitary property, the important measure was the Housing of the Working Classes Act of 1890 which followed the Report of the Royal Commission, and which both consolidated and extended the earlier legislation. Its strongest clauses related to the metropolis, where the Royal Commission had considered the housing problem to be most critical. Here, local authorities were empowered to buy as much land as might be necessary for the long-term planning of improvement schemes, and it became an obligation to re-house at least half of those displaced by demolitions. (In provincial towns there was still no obligation, as it was assumed that speculative builders would provide.) House-building by local authorities was allowed by Part 3 of the Act, but hardly encouraged. Where it was carried out, the property was to be sold to private owners within ten years; on the important question of finance, it was assumed that expenditure should be 'defrayed out of the property dealt with', and it was even suggested how 'balances of profits' might be used. Part 3 did, however, also empower local authorities to alter, enlarge, repair and improve existing houses, and to make by-laws for their regulation and management. The important Housing of the Working Classes Act of 1900 extended to provincial boroughs the powers given to London in 1890, and in particular the power to acquire land and to build outside their districts.

More was achieved by the 1890 Act than by the earlier Acts, partly because it could make use of the more efficient system of local administration created in 1888, and partly because the climate of public opinion was much more favourable to housing reform after the disclosures of poverty and physical deterioration at the end of the century. In some towns pressure from citizens' associations and organized labour played an important part in stimulating action. Nevertheless, the total results prior to the outbreak of World War I were small. Of all new houses built between 1890 and 1914 less than 5 per cent were provided by local authorities, the great majority of whom were still very reluctant to enter the field of property-owning when the whole expense had to be borne from the rates. Over the same period loans were sanctioned to urban authorities of only £3,185,000, plus a further £1,318,000 from the Public Works Commissioners. Generally, much more demolition than rehousing was carried out, and many councils, led by Birmingham, deliberately chose to implement a repair and renovation policy rather than rebuilding. J. S. Nettlefold, the influential chairman of Birmingham's Housing Committee, pointed out that under the Act the cost of repair had to be borne by the owner, the authority only having to meet administrative charges, and that the cost of improvement to Birmingham ratepayers had been only 15s a head compared with £56 a head in Liverpool for rebuilding.[72] It is not surprising that many boroughs contented themselves with modernization of unfit property, which included the opening-up of enclosed courts by demolition of the end houses, the provision of sewerage, sinks and WCs to houses, new flooring and plaster, the insertion of bay-windows and thorough repair of roofs and brickwork. By 1913, 2,700 houses in Birmingham had been reconditioned.

(Liverpool was the first provincial city to embark on council building, St Martin's Cottages having been built as early as 1869. This was a tenement block of 124 units, ranging from living-room, scullery and three bedrooms down to a single room and scullery, at rents from 2s 6d to 5s 6d. A larger development of six tenement blocks, designed much on Peabody lines, followed in 1885 at Victoria Square. At first, these dwellings were open to any who applied, and were mainly occupied by the respectable artisan class, but in 1896 the Council decided that only those evicted by improvement schemes should be eligible.[73] An active council had by 1912 provided 2,322 dwellings; 5,500 houses had been demolished and more than 11,000 improved. The net charge to the rates for housing was £37,223 a year, equivalent to 2½d in the pound, and the Council had clearly committed itself to a subsidy, mainly because of its determination to rehouse even the poorest of those displaced.[74]

Most local-authority building programmes fell somewhere between the extremes of Liverpool and Birmingham. Manchester built its first flats in 1896 and a suburban cottage estate at Blackley. Sheffield became involved in a long indecision over whether to build central blocks or suburban cottages, and in the event only 409 houses were built by 1914 although 8,000 people were still living in unfit accommodation, and 17,000 in back-to-backs. But easily the most significant work was that carried out by the London County Council, which energetically and imaginatively accepted the responsibilities given by the Act of 1890. It experimented with both solutions—multi-storey central blocks and suburban estates—and in the end developed a housing layout and type which was distinct from each yet retained some of the merits of both. Tenement blocks were first developed in Beachcroft Buildings, Brook Street, Limehouse, from 1892 onwards, and, more importantly, in the Boundary Street development at Bethnal Green where the first blocks were completed in 1895. This was a large redevelopment on a radial plan covering fifteen acres, involving the displacement of 5,700 people and the rehousing of 5,100. The flats were of one to four rooms, 51 per cent being two-roomed and 37 per cent having three. But there was a new and deliberate attempt to raise the standards of space and amenity compared with those provided by most of the housing trusts, and to plan the layout as an architectural whole, with reference to the road pattern and other buildings. Moreover, there was provision for open space, both in the central raised garden and also between some of the blocks. Care was taken to provide contrasting size and shape, to give residents outlooks and vistas, and to break away from the 'barracky' atmosphere which had for so long been associated with tenements. Professor Tarn has summarized the achievement as 'a new architectural sensitivity' and 'a more humane type of design'.[75]

This successful experiment was developed in a dozen or so further central area schemes before 1914, including the important Bourne Estate off Clerkenwell Road. But in 1898 the LCC decided that in all future schemes it would provide housing equivalent to that displaced, though not necessarily in the same area. This marked the beginning of suburban

development, starting in 1903 with the Totterdown Fields Estate at
Tooting, situated at the terminus of an LCC tramway. Although the
cottages were designed in the vernacular revival style, with sweeping gable
roofs, small-paned sash windows and some rendering to the upper floors, it
was not intended to be a garden suburb and was, in fact, a high-density
development at 227 persons to the acre. Nevertheless, this was achieved
with an open layout of terraces with front and back gardens and slightly
curving roads which disguised the modified gridiron plan. A number of
features were successfully borrowed from the model village movement—variety in elevations and building lines, the avoidance of back projections, the provision of a bathroom in most cottages, and so on. Houses of
four types were built, the largest having parlour, living-room, three
bedrooms, scullery and bathroom, a total area of 994sq ft, and the smallest
a kitchen–living-room, two bedrooms and a scullery, totalling 524sq ft.

Similar developments followed at Norbury, at White Hart Lane,
Tottenham, and, perhaps most successfully of all, at the Old Oak Estate,
Acton, begun in 1911. Here the houses were combined in a variety of groups
around small open spaces to produce a new type of urban landscape which
avoided the monotony of the by-law street and the somewhat artificial
rusticity of the garden suburb. In these estates relatively heavy densities
were achieved without building high and without overspreading expensive
land. New designs were prepared for each site, instead of adopting standard
plans. Great attention was given to the visual effect and amenity of the
estate as well as to sensible internal organization of the individual units.
The Architects Department of the LCC under the direction of W. E. Riley
was not only beginning to evolve another physical 'solution' to the problem
of urban housing, but one which had a concern for non-physical factors
such as the visual effect of the development and the quality of life of the
inhabitants. After a long separation, aesthetic, architectural and personal
considerations were again coming together, and the quality of mass housing
was beginning to take a leap forward when further progress was interrupted
by the outbreak of war.

7

HOUSING THE SUBURBANS

Carefully avoiding the conventional, but thorny, demarcations of 'class', C. F. G. Masterman in his brilliant portrait of English social structure published in 1909 adopted descriptive distinctions—'The Conquerors', 'The Suburbans' and 'The Multitude'. 'The Suburbans', he believed, were 'practically the product of the past half century' and had greatly increased even within the last decade.

> They form a homogeneous civilization—detached, self-centred, unostentatious—covering the hills along the northern and southern boundaries of the city [London], and spreading their conquests over the quiet fields beyond. They are the peculiar product of England and America: of the nations which have pre-eminently added commerce, business and finance to the work of manufacture and agriculture. It is a life of Security; a life of Sedentary occupation; a life of Respectability; and these three qualities give the key to its special characteristics. Its male population is engaged in all its working hours in small, crowded offices, under artificial light, doing immense sums, adding up other men's accounts, writing other men's letters. It is sucked into the City at daybreak and scattered again as darkness falls. It finds itself towards evening in its own territory in the miles and miles of little red houses in little, silent streets, in number defying imagination. Each boasts its pleasant drawing-room, its bow-window, its little front garden, its high-sounding title—'Acacia Villa' or 'Camperdown Lodge'—attesting unconquered human aspiration ... The women, with their single domestic servants ... find time hangs rather heavy on their hands. But there are excursions to shopping centres in the West End, and pious sociabilities, and occasional theatre visits, and the interests of home ...[1]

If the middle classes are hard to define, they are equally difficult to count. Membership was never a matter solely of income or occupation, though both of these mattered. It was, as Masterman clearly saw, more a question of style of life, of habits, tastes, values and aspirations which were quite distinct from those of the classes above and below them. Almost in desperation, one feels, at the impossibility of precision, Seebohm Rowntree in 1901

Evolving the local authority suburb. LCC Totterdown Estate, Tooting, c1903. Road layout was orthodox by-law gridiron, but house forms broke new ground. Terraces were of limited length and strongly modelled with bold gables. House plans were simple, with 15ft 6in (4.7m) frontage and no rear annexe projection. Typical accommodation was parlour, living room and scullery, with two bedrooms and bathroom on first floor (*Greater London Council*)

Nos 2–16 Belsize Park Gardens, Hampstead, London. Built by Daniel Tidey in the 1860s on land belonging to the Dean and Chapter of Westminster, an example of the continuing use of the 'classical' style with regular stuccoed fronts by speculative builders and developers. Residents of Belsize Park were comfortably off, but generally not 'carriage folk' (*Robert Thorne*)

Nos 50–56 Elsworthy Road, Hampstead, London, built by William Willett in the 1890s on the Eton College Estate. By their use of red brick, gables, tile-hanging and white-painted bay windows, the Willetts 'put Norman Shaw on the production line' (F. M. L. Thompson). Small front gardens and neat privet hedges have replaced the area steps leading to the vanished basement kitchens: the regularity of the 'classical' street has dissolved into 'garden city' irregularity (*Robert Thorne*)

An early English 'bungalow', designed for the Bellagio estate in Surrey (now Dormans-land) in the late 1880s. With commuting potential, this development (probably not speculative) of large bungalows and country houses was intended for an upper-middle-class clientele seeking a secluded rural retreat. The Indian verandah has been combined with a thatched roof and a faintly Gothic turret. From Briggs *Bungalows and Country Residences* 1891

The flight to the suburbs. An advertisement of the early 1900s for Golders Green, with 'copy' by William Cowper. The images are rural and romantic – the winding road, the gardens, the cottage-style house with lattice windows, dormer and sham half-timbered gable. The beginning of the great lower-middle-class exodus from the cities, made possible by improved transport (*London Transport*)

The soldier's dream, 1918; the dust jacket of *The Home I Want* by Richard Reiss. In the last year of the war, 41% of conscripts were medically graded C3 and unfit for military service. The poor state of the nation's health was widely associated with bad housing, over-crowding and malnutrition. In the illustration the returning warrior seeks to escape from decaying nineteenth-century industrial housing to the kind of garden city development on which many of the new council estates were modelled

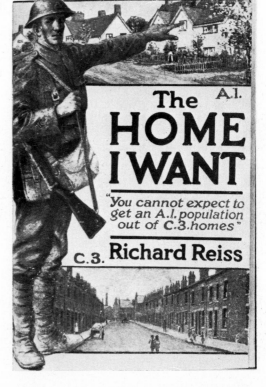

Homes fit for heroes: local authority semi-detached houses of 1919 at Fishponds Estate, Bristol. Housing standards declined soon after this (*City of Bristol Housing Department*)

Inner city high density: six-storey balcony access flats, Ebury Bridge Road, City of Westminster, designed by A. J. Thomas in 1936. Plan shown in text illustration 14 (*Anne-Marie Ehrlich*)

rested his distinction between 'working class' and 'middle class' on the keeping of a domestic servant, since resident help in the house promoted a 'woman' into a 'lady', with all the implications of gentility which that term carried.

In 1851 the professions, using the term broadly to include not only law, medicine and religion, but education, literature, science, art and amusements, numbered 245,000 persons or 2·8 per cent of the occupied population of England and Wales: trade (wholesale and retail), public administration, and commerce (including clerks, accountants and bankers) numbered 644,000 or 7·6 per cent of the occupied population.[2] If we add to these 249,000 farmers and graziers (3 per cent) we have 13·4 per cent of the occupied population, and allowing a margin for minor occupations and for persons of modest independent means, we may assume a total of something over 15 per cent. What is certain is that the class was expanding, both absolutely and relatively to others. Thirty years later, in 1881, the professions had grown to 3·4 per cent, the commercial occupations to 10·4 per cent, while the decline of the farmers to 1·9 per cent did not prevent the total growing to 15·7 per cent and, with 'extras', to over 17 per cent.

By the beginning of the twentieth century a proportion of about 20 per cent is indicated. In 1909, L. C. Money divided the total population, then $44\frac{1}{2}$ million, into three broad income categories: those with more than £700 a year, those with between £160 (the point at which income tax then began) and £700, and those with less than £160 a year—each of which enjoyed the same one-third share of the national income. In terms of numbers, however, the distribution was highly unequal. The wealthiest group, earning more than £700 a year, comprised only 280,000 households which, with dependants, numbered 1,400,000 people. These were the 'upper' middle classes, who in terms of income, at least, merged easily into the ranks of the landed gentry and even the aristocracy. Below them were the much broader sections of the middle and lower middle classes, the men of 'moderate incomes' beloved by Victorian political economists, and to whom L. C. Money gave a range of £160 to £700 a year. In 1909 they numbered, with their dependants, 4,100,000, and covered a range of occupations from senior teachers in elementary schools and nonconformist clergymen at the bottom to solicitors, accountants, managers and senior clerks in the Civil Service at the top. Probably the upper ceiling for very experienced clerks in legal and insurance offices was £500–£600, but the majority rose to no more than £150–£200, and only just scraped into admission: many earned as little as £60 or £80 a year, and though they might dress like a gentleman could scarcely live like one.

Here, then, was not a single social class, but a tier of sub-classes stretching from bare sufficiency to extreme wealth. Yet although there were major differences between top and bottom there were enough things in common to warrant a single label. Some margin of income over necessary expenditure, a strong sense of 'respectability' associated with work, sobriety, polite manners and broadly Christian observance, the ability to keep a wife who did not work outside the home and could employ some help within it, and a central, deeply-rooted belief that the family and the home were the pillars both of a good society and of private happiness, united these disparate elements into a group powerful enough to set the moral tone and the economic pace of Victorian England. Above all, the home, and the house which accommodated that precious institution, were of central interest and importance. To choose it, furnish and decorate it, repair and care for it provided satisfactions which were far more than material—a proper place in which to rear children, to entertain friends, to retreat from the cares of the world and take an honest pride in one's possessions and achievements.

This intense interest and pride in the home held good for all those who had any real choice over their dwelling-place and any real power over the way they used and furnished it. As early as 1847, G. R. Porter, a sharp observer of the social scene, had noted:

> In nothing is the improvement here mentioned more apparent than in the condition of the dwellings of the middle classes. As one instance, it is not necessary to go back much beyond half a century to arrive at the time when prosperous shopkeepers in the leading thoroughfares of London were without that now necessary article of furniture, a carpet, in their ordinary sitting-rooms: luxury in this particular seldom went further with them than a well-scoured floor strewn with sand, and the furniture of the apartments was by no means inconsistent with this primitive, and, as we should now say, comfortless state of things. In the same houses we now see, not carpets merely, but many articles of furniture which were formerly in use only among the nobility and gentry.[3]

Precisely how this increasing concern for comfort and luxury in the home was interpreted and manifested depended partly on taste and partly on economic resources, but the important point is that it extended throughout the class. Somewhere near the bottom of the scale, Mr Pooter took endless delight in 'The Laurels', Brickfield Terrace, Holloway, his six-roomed semi-detached house ('not counting basement') with its ten steps up to the front door, its 'front breakfast-parlour', and its 'nice little back garden which runs down to the railway'. Holloway was convenient for Pooter, a clerk of twenty years' standing, to travel to the City each day, and the landlord took £2 off the rent for any disturbance the trains might cause. There was one servant living in and an occasional charwoman; the drawing-room had green rep upholstery covered in chintz to prevent fading; there was a bathroom (the date is 1892) but no dressing-room, and Mr Pooter buys imitation stags' heads for the hall, made of plaster-of-paris and 'coloured brown'—they 'give it style'.[4]

At the upper end of the spectrum the luxury would be obtrusive and pretentious. Augustus Hare, who visited many of the great country seats in the 1880s, found that the most luxurious were the houses of the new rich: Hutton Hall, home of the Middlesbrough Peases, was 'intensely luxurious', Elveden, the Guinness home, 'almost appallingly luxurious', and Worth Park, home of the Montefiores, worse still—'the ultra-luxurious house . . . where the servants have their own billiard-tables, ballroom, theatre and pianofortes, and are arrogant and presumptuous in proportion'.[5] Such palatial residences of the great industrial and financial magnates take us beyond the range of the middle classes and of this study. Our concern is with houses that were speculatively built rather than commissioned, were not individually architect-designed (though standardized architects' drawings may have been used, or adapted) and which served a very approximate income level of about £150–£700 a year—'The Suburbans' rather than 'The Conquerors'.

Masterman's description of the class over-simplified but typified it accurately enough with respect to its residential location. In one sense the 'flight to the suburbs' was thrust upon the burgeoning middle classes, for by mid-century available sites in or near the centres of large cities had generally been taken up, and the redevelopment which was a continuous process in later Victorian times was almost always for shops, offices and commercial premises rather than houses. In London the great residential developments begun in Georgian and Regency times were now almost complete, the last house in Belgrave Square being built in 1850, and Eaton Square finally completed in 1853; after that, new building had to shift to South Kensington, Bayswater, and further afield.[6] There was no way in which the population of Greater London, which grew from 2,235,000 in 1841 to 6,581,000 in 1901, could be housed except by outward expansion, and what was true of London was true, to a lesser degree, of all the industrial towns. The growth of suburbs was the characteristic and inevitable form of urban development in the later half of the century, and produced what was perhaps the greatest single change in the living habits of the English people since the industrial revolution. In retrospect, it is possible to see that it was a natural consequence, first, of the separation between workplace and home, and second, of improving communications which continually extended the daily travellable distance between the two. Industrialization also divided more sharply than before the use of time, making a clear distinction between 'work' and 'non-work' leisure activities, and in this respect, too, the suburbs with their parks, gardens, tennis and golf clubs were a natural response to the changing economic structure of society. Equally important, the availability of undeveloped land at substantially lower costs than central sites enabled builders to provide a range of house-types—terraced, semi-detached and detached of varying sizes—to suit differing family needs and income levels, so that the relative homogeneity of urban housing became replaced by differentiated and, sometimes, highly individual forms expressive of personal taste.

Suburban living was, therefore, not only inevitable, but positively desired for the opportunities it offered of physical separation from the 'lower orders' and the dirt, noise, disease and crime which accompanied them in the over-crowded town centres. The total separation which the great country house afforded, encapsulated in its own geographical territory and strictly-controlled social environment, was not economically possible for the middle classes, but the suburb gave a high degree of single-class exclusiveness behind frontiers which were clearly distinguishable on the ground even when not openly labelled as 'private'. So strong was this desire for protection, based perhaps on fear that this tender flower of civilization would be contaminated, even destroyed, by contact with 'the multitude', that many suburbs fought hard, and often successfully, to prevent the building of tramways and the extension of cheap workmen's fares on the existing railway routes to their territories. The attitude was well expressed by William Birt, the General Manager of the North Eastern Railway Company, in evidence to the Royal Commission on the Housing of the Working Classes in 1885: 'The selection of the workmen's escape routes to the suburbs should be strictly limited . . . Other districts which are not spoilt should not be thrown open to the working classes, otherwise these districts will become spoilt too.'

The question of 'where to live—town or suburbs', was an irresistible subject for writers on domestic economy throughout the period, and the ways in which they argued the rival merits of the two provide a comment on what were considered to be the important criteria of residence. The question was posed as early as 1844 in *An Encyclopaedia of Domestic Economy*, where it was argued that a town house was superior for 'social intercourse and varied enjoyment by means of public and private parties, theatres, concerts, balls, public libraries, museums, exhibitions of works of art' and the like. It was recommended, however, that care be taken over the width and direction of the street, the aspect and healthiness of the district. The advantages of suburbs were their generally more healthy situation, and 'the pleasure to be derived from a garden and from the cheerful and enlivening effect of trees and vegetation in general, together with quiet and absence of smoke, and innumerable disagreeable objects constantly presented in cities'. Of possible speculative interest was the fact that since land was cheaper, 'a field or two, attached to the house' might be acquired, 'and this additional space may be built upon'.[7] Later writers were generally less reticent about recommending the suburbs. Mrs J. E. Panton, whose book *From Kitchen to Garret* of 1888 was intended for those who were neither very rich nor very poor, wrote:

To young people . . . I would strongly recommend a house some little way out of London. Rents are less; smuts and blacks are conspicuous by their absence;

a small garden, or even a tiny conservatory, are not an impossibility; and if 'Edwin' has to pay for his season-ticket, that is nothing in comparison with his being able to sleep in fresh air, to have a game of tennis in summer, or a friendly evening of music, chess or games in the winter, without expense . . .

Specific suburbs recommended by Mrs Panton included, to the south, the higher parts of Sydenham, Lordship Lane, Forest Hill, Elmer's End ('where there are some extremely pretty and convenient villas'), Penge, Dulwich and the best parts of Bromley, and, 'to those who do not mind the north side', Finchley, Bush Hill Park and Enfield.[8]

On the whole, contemporary opinion was strongly in favour of the suburbs for the fresh air, the lower rents, the roomier houses planned with consideration for the needs of a family, the recreational opportunities and the advantages of a garden for the children. More informed opinion found, for example, in the architectural press, was often critical of the construction and materials which went into the 'pretty villas', while *The Builder* expressed alarm at the speed and results of the 'Building Mania':

East, west, north and south our cities and towns are extending themselves into the country . . . Houses spring up everywhere, as though capital were abundant, as though one-half the world were on the look-out for investments, and the other half continually in search of eligible family residences, desirable villas and aristocratic cottages . . . Streets, squares, crescents, terraces, Albert villas, Victoria villas and things of the same inviting character stand up everywhere against the horizon, and invite us to take them . . . We are disposed to ask in these days, when we contemplate the number of houses in course of erection for the rich, where the poor are to be housed? One would think that there was no increase of population [below] the classes which rejoice in five hundred a year.[9]

But no such warnings could stop the march of the suburbs over the green fields, a march which became almost a charge in the two or three decades before 1914. In 1881 W. S. Clarke could write of 'the fair dwellings and picturesque retreats which form that lovely fringe—the Suburban Homes of London'.[10] He listed and described no less than eighty-nine suburbs, stretching in a wide circle from Croydon in the south to Twickenham, Acton and Ealing in the west, Harrow, Mill Hill and Enfield to the north, Wanstead and the Crays to the east. Not all were middle-class preserves, and some could scarcely have been regarded as 'lovely' even by so enthusiastic an advocate, but the vast area they covered—a distance of about twenty miles from east to west and the same from north to south—was impressive testimony to the advance of bricks and mortar. By the century's end, every sizeable town exhibited the same phenomenon, though on a smaller scale and at shorter distances from the centre. The social distinctions between the suburbs were, however, no less sharp. If London had its Dulwich, Richmond and Edgware, the same single-class exclusiveness was to be found in Bristol's Clifton, Cotham and Redland,

Nottingham's Wollaton, West Bridgeford and Mapperley Park, or Manchester's Alderley Edge and Wilmslow.

What the suburbans expected of their houses can be gathered partly from the treatises of contemporary architects and designers which were written as guides to builders and clients, and partly from what we can infer from the actual shapes on the ground. Fortunately for us, the Victorians were given to analysis and categorization, not least in matters to do with the home. 'Find out what will make you comfortable,' advised John Ruskin, 'build that in the strongest and boldest way, and then set your fancy free in the decoration of it . . . Do what is convenient . . . only be steadily determined that, even if you cannot get the best Gothic, at least you will have no Greek . . .'[11] These precepts—'comfort' and 'convenience'—were accepted without question by subsequent writers as the basic requirements of houses of all kinds and sizes. The important question was how they were to be interpreted and achieved, and in this connection two works which were highly influential—Robert Kerr's *The Gentleman's House* (1864) and J. J. Stevenson's *House Architecture* (1880)—are particularly informative, and deserve some consideration here.

Robert Kerr, a well-known architect and Professor of the Arts of Construction at King's College, London, began by remarking that no book whatsoever had hitherto been published on the subject of domestic plans (though he acknowledged that 'the indefatigable Loudon' had touched indirectly on it). Kerr listed twelve general considerations which should govern the plan of any gentleman's house, however modest.

1   Privacy of the family apartments should be the primary rule. There should be a complete separation of the rooms and offices used by the servants, who should be 'invisible and inaudible', and speculatively-built villas were often to be condemned for not having separate entrances, properly-designed passages and partitions, and windows which did not admit conversation and smells from the kitchen to the drawing-room. In larger houses there should be separate doors, corridors and staircases so that lines of traffic should not cross, while externally terraces and walks should not be overlooked from the servants' quarters.

2   The second requirement should be Comfort which, the author believed, was better understood in England than in any other country, and was 'essentially a Northern idea'. It involved freedom from draughts, smoky chimneys, kitchen smells, damp, vermin, noise, dust, dark corners, blind passages, musty rooms, excessive sultriness and excessive cold, but it also implied that the house and every room in it should be carefully planned for its purpose and the furniture it would contain.

3   This related closely to the criterion of Convenience, which meant that all the functions of the household—which included the 'two communities' of family and servants—should be capable of being carried out in harmony. The plan must therefore accommodate individual habits and

tastes—whether the family was given to entertaining, or to solitude, for example.

4 Spaciousness. If economy demanded, it was preferable to lose a room or two than to have all rooms too small and uncomfortable, for 'the spirits, and even the self-esteem of a man seem to expand and acquire vigour under the simple influence of elbow-room'.

5 But spaciousness must not be allowed to conflict with Compactness. This was often a problem in large country houses, where 'the very completeness of convenience in one form produces inconvenience in another; passages become tortuous and interminable and the family rooms themselves part company. The object of compactness is to maximize ease of communication to all parts of the house.'

6 Light and air. Every room must have adequate natural supplies of these, and 'borrowed' light or ventilation should be avoided.

7 Salubrity requires that close attention be paid to the situation, soil and drainage of the site, and to the disposition of 'offices', stables and outbuildings 'likely to have in any way an unwelcome odour'.

8 Aspect and prospect. The plan should be made to take advantage of natural scenery, and for each room to receive the benefit of the daily course of the sun.

9 Cheerfulness should be a leading characteristic, and will depend much on sunlight and on the comfort and decoration of rooms.

10 Elegance, which 'displays finish, precision, quiet beauty, without ostentation of any kind . . . it is not rich, or elaborate, or sumptuous, or gay; it is the subdued power which corresponds to cultivated, perhaps satiated, taste'.

11 But Importance requires that the home of the gentleman should equally be removed from any meanness. The principle is that all should be displayed to the best advantage, but without trick or affectation.

12 Ornamentation. 'A Gentleman's House ought to be not merely substantial, comfortable, convenient and well-furnished, but fairly adorned . . . clinging to the grace of elegance . . . but avoiding nonetheless that poverty of dress which is not self-denial, but inhospitality'.[12]

Almost twenty years later J. J. Stevenson proposed a list of ten 'characteristics of modern planning' which in many respects followed Kerr closely, but included some new considerations which altered Kerr's emphases significantly. These reflected some changes in attitudes towards what was considered an ideal plan. Stevenson placed as his first requirement what he described as 'multifariousness'. 'Keeping pace with our more complicated ways of living, we have not only increased the number of rooms in ordinary houses, but have assigned to each a special use. Instead of the hall and single chamber of the Middle Ages, with which even kings were content, every ordinary house must have a number of separate bedrooms, at least three public rooms, and a complicated arrangement of servants' offices.' He agreed that the plan must give isolation to the several parts, and separate communication to each principal room from a central hall, not by inter-communicating suites, but differed somewhat from Kerr on the complete separation of 'the two communities', family and servants.

> Should the mistress not have the run of her own house? Should the master not have his own servants when he needs them? The treatment of servants as an inferior class, whom it is shocking to the refined feelings of their superiors to see or to come in contact with; who have no interests in common with the master; who are paid to do their work . . . but no more, helps to produce the want of interest in their work, the love of dress, and the frequent changing of their places, of which mistresses nowadays complain so loudly.

The general principle, Stevenson believed, was that each servant should have his or her own place in which to work, without interference from others. The butler and parlourmaid should have their pantries, the housemaid her closet, the scullery-maid her scullery, and they should have their living-room (the servants' hall) and bedrooms, but they should not be able to shut themselves off from the family in a separate establishment where the mistress finds herself an intruder.

Such recommendations indicate the beginning of a more humane approach to the 'servant problem' which was already dawning by the 1880s, as more attractive opportunities for work began to open up to women and girls. In two other requirements—simplicity and warmth—Stevenson also represents more modern concepts of planning. There should be a minimum of staircases, passages and odd corners, no steps down into rooms, no necessity to carry food across the hall to the dining-room. And waste of heat in the house should be avoided. The front door should open into a lobby; fireplaces should be sited so as to prevent draughts, and not built on outside walls.[13] With practical considerations such as these, planning was beginning to move from its concentration on style towards a greater concern for amenity.

Underlying these declared requirements of a house lay a set of values, largely unarticulated, which had profound influence on the form and plan of middle-class housing. In that it was a new and largely self-created class which needed identity, reassurance and acceptance, it believed that an appropriately impressive residence gave visual expression to its social status and ideals—that the house announced achievement and conferred status better than any other possession could do. Despite their generally critical attitude towards the aristocracy, the middle classes were obliged to recognize that they were still accepted as the arbiters of fashion and taste, and therefore tended to look to their pattern of social and domestic arrangements and produce scaled-down versions for themselves. This in part explains the attraction for the middle classes of suburban life and of 'historic' styles of building which seemed to invoke images of a noble, rural inheritance. There was an infinite gradation of scale and opulence from the mansion with its suites of state apartments and reception rooms to the large town house with double drawing-room, library and boudoir and the modest suburban villa where, as Dickens remarked, every man of any social pretensions had his best parlour and some little back room or other which he called his study. The various 'territories' of the great country house, so minutely organized and stratified because the activities and interrelationships of the occupants were themselves so complicated and subdivided,[14] were reproduced in miniature in the middle-class house, and made to serve the same fundamental objects of privacy and display. For this reason, an article in *The Nineteenth Century* in 1888, advising its readers 'How to Live on £700 a Year', when they had learned extravagant tastes from wealthy parents, believed that 'the most expensive habit which we have acquired is false pride'.[15]

If the Victorian house served, first, as a reassurance of social status, an equally important function was to represent the middle-class ideal of home and family life. As J. A. and O. Banks have shown, this sprang largely from the concept of 'the perfect wife' whose central role was seen as being to create a home providing comfort and emotional stability for her husband and children.[16] What this involved in terms of domestic arrangements and economy was well expressed by Mrs Sarah Ellis:

> Not only must the house be neat and clean, but it must be so ordered as to suit the tastes of all, as far as may be, without annoyance or offence to any. Not only must a constant system of activity be established, but peace must be preserved or happiness will be destroyed. Not only must an appearance of outward order and comfort be kept up, but around every domestic scene there must be a strong wall of confidence, which no internal suspicion can undermine, no external enemy break through.'[17]

This idea that the home was a place of refuge—a 'sanctuary' or a 'walled garden'—in which the husband could recover from the pressures of business life while his wife and children remained inviolate from the temptations of the wicked world, lay at the root of the desire for privacy and separation. 'This is the true nature of home', wrote Ruskin. 'It is the place of Peace; the shelter, not only from all injury, but from all terror, doubt and division.'[18] To love, and to minister unto, her husband and children were the highest virtues and duties of woman, and they required that, on marriage, a wife must, at least in part, withdraw from the world and devote herself to a 'rational seclusion', giving up any thoughts of an active life, and restricting her social intercourse to carefully controlled situations based on the home.

In this respect, the 'Rules of Society' which were developed as a strict code of etiquette by the nineteenth-century aristocracy, and acquired from them by the middle class, had important effects on the plan of the house.

Leonore Davidoff has argued that a society based upon achievement found these rules necessary in order to control and legitimate the new social relationships. The increasing separation between public and private life, between work and leisure, meant the virtual confinement of social life to private houses, where a well-understood code of etiquette would ensure that only acceptable persons were received and that social interaction normally took place only in set places and at set times.[19]

Later in the century other legitimatizing institutions developed, such as the public schools and competitive examinations for the Civil Service, but in the meantime the rules of society were the chief means of placing newcomers in 'the social landscape', and these rules were primarily arbitrated and enforced by women. Since active housekeeping and gainful employment were unacceptable for a 'lady', a life of conspicuous leisure was almost all that was open to her in the intervals between child-bearing. The days could be comfortably filled by a finely-regulated round of 'leaving cards', 'morning calls' (in fact, paid in the afternoon), 'At Homes', dinner-parties, soirées, balls and other events which were most fully developed in upper-middle-class households but were copied on a more modest scale well down into the suburban fringe.[20] The minimum requirements for participation were not too onerous—at least one respectable-looking maid to open the front door and answer bells, and a house of a size and character of which one need not feel ashamed.

But if the game of etiquette was to be played successfully the house needed certain attributes to provide the proper settings for the various social rituals. Callers would be received by a servant at the front door and shown into the hall to wait while the member of the family was sought or while the mistress decided whether or not she was 'at home'; the hall was necessary to 'hold' visitors and to protect the family by space and time from intruders. It was therefore more than a mere passage between different parts of the house, having important functions as a waiting-room and display area which announced to the visitor certain things about the taste and social status of the household. The most important rooms were, however, the reception—that is, receiving-rooms—for guests, which were required to be spacious, impressive and elegant. Respectability demanded at least three—the drawing-room and dining-room which had public functions, and a third room usually described as the 'parlour' (or morning-room or breakfast-parlour) which was primarily the family room but might also be used for entertaining relatives or intimate friends. This reserved the drawing-room for 'calls', 'at homes' and for evening use by the family or by guests before and after dinner. The parlour might also be used for family meals, reserving the dining-room for Sundays and for formal dinner-parties. Larger houses, of course, multiplied these divisions, with ladies' sitting-rooms, boudoirs and dressing-rooms, and 'male territory' which might include study, library, billiard-room, smoking-room and gun-room.

Since the rules of etiquette forbade smoking in the presence of ladies (even in the garden, unless with their consent) one room in the house where it could be enjoyed was desirable.

Finally, the rules of etiquette, as well as the dictates of comfort, required an abundance of personal attendance which relieved the mistress of domestic duties and released her for participation in society. As has been shown elsewhere,[21] the numbers and duties of domestic servants were carefully defined and categorized by the writers on domestic economy in strict accordance with income, so that the size of staff announced within fine limits the economic position of the employer. In the kind of house with which we are concerned here, from two to five servants would be usual, and even five—implying a coach and a coach-house—would often put the house beyond our speculatively built limit. The middle-class villa typically had to accommodate from two to four domestics, which would mean a couple of attic bedrooms, probably shared, besides the working quarters of kitchen, scullery, pantries, larders, and possibly wash-house. By the end of the century house design was often also including a small maids' sitting-room where the kitchen was not sufficiently large to accommodate a table and a few chairs. The needs of 'the other community', though not regarded with the same consideration as those of the family, therefore had important effects on the size and plan of the middle-class house.

So far we have considered mainly social determinants of middle-class housing, but clearly the type and quality of residence which a particular family occupied depended ultimately on what they could afford, or were willing, to pay. Building costs varied widely with size, site and location from a mere £300–£400 for a modest suburban villa to £2,000 or more for a large town or country house, though speculative building usually stopped at around £750–£1,000. Some indication of the relative size and cost of houses is provided by the London Building Act of 1774 which divided houses into seven classes by reference to their size, height, value and number of storeys. First Rate houses were over £850 in value and 900sq ft on the ground floor, or 3,600sq ft for a four-storeyed house; Second Rate were over £300 and 500sq ft per storey, Third Rate over £150 and 350sq ft, usually on three storeys totalling 1,050sq ft. Fourth Rate houses, intended mainly for working-class families, were under 350sq ft on two storeys only, and their total area of under 700sq ft was therefore a mere one-fifth of that of the First Rate.[22] Values had moved upwards since 1774, though not greatly. In 1864 Robert Kerr calculated the current cost at £40 per 100sq ft for family rooms and £28 per 100 for servants' rooms, an average of 34p (in modern terms) per sq ft. For a cost of £1,253 he designed a house with family accommodation of hall, dining-room, drawing-room, four bedrooms, one dressing-room, nursery, bathroom and WC (area 2,230sq ft), plus servants' quarters of kitchen, scullery/wash-house, larder, pantry, store-room, linen-closet, knife-house, ashbin and WC, cellars for wine, beer and coal, and one bedroom (area 1,290sq ft), a total superficial area of 3,520 sq ft.[23]

Few Victorians bought their houses, partly because of the underdeveloped state of building societies and partly because rented accommodation suited a class which was economically and geographically mobile. Contemporary advice often suggested that one should not take a lease longer than three years since by then one would be ready to move into different accommodation better adjusted to changing income and family needs. But the cost of building directly affected the level of rent charged, this usually being set at around one-twentieth of the cost. Prospective tenants had to make a nice calculation of the fraction of their annual income which could safely be set aside for rent, keeping in mind other necessary outgoings. Most mid-Victorian writers on domestic economy accepted that one-eighth, or 12 per cent, of income was the appropriate fraction for rent, taxes and repairs, though towards the end of the century some were suggesting that this might not now be enough to meet increases in the cost of living. W. R. Greg in *Keeping Up Appearances* (1875) argued that the cost of living for the middle classes had risen 25 per cent in the last twenty-five years, citing particularly rent and the wages of servants, and noting that the style of living in matters such as food, drink and dress was now much costlier.[24] For persons with incomes between £100 and £200 a year, only marginally admissible to the middle class, J. H. Walsh suggested a rent of £15–£20 a year which would provide a six-roomed house, 'composed simply of a basement, ground, and first floor, in each of which there are two rooms . . . They are seldom ornamented in any way externally, though in some few cases, in late years, such an attempt has been made by means of stucco and cement, covering very inferior brickwork, and only resulting in premature decay.' With an income of around £500 a year, a much more substantial ten-roomed house was possible, letting at about £55 a year in London and costing £800–£1,000 to build. This could be very comfortable for a small family, though 'the small size of the rooms precludes all large social meetings'. But with an income of around £1,000 a year a man might afford 'a large and roomy house' of sixteen rooms, 'quite sufficient for any ordinary family'. It would have good dining- and drawing-rooms, a library, eight bedrooms, dressing-rooms, and two servants' rooms in the roof; 'the kitchens are underground, which is universally the case in London'. There were WCs on the ground and first floors, but no bathroom.[25]

In 1901 G. S. Layard published a series of Family Budgets which itemized the expenditure of imaginary families of different income levels. As an example of the lower middle class he took a cashier aged forty in a firm of London solicitors, earning £150 a year, and having two children. A London clerk, Layard pointed out, had to decide whether to live near his work in lodgings or in a block of tenement flats such as those in Finsbury,

Lambeth and Southwark, or to go further afield to one of 'the clerks' suburbs' such as Clapham, Forest Gate, Wandsworth, Walthamstow or Kilburn. Here there were thousands of 'snug' six-roomed villas let for 10s to 12s 6d a week, while those living in the centre paid more than this for two or three rooms. The cashier pays 12s 6d, but takes in a relative lodger, and therefore pays £26 rent a year; rates and taxes add £5 3s 5d a year, making £31 3s 5d, —'a terribly large but necessary slice'. In fact, he is paying one-fifth rather than one-eighth of income for rent, and if to this is added a second-class railway season ticket at £7 a year, gas, coal, oil and wood at £9 17s 0d, and house expenses at £5.4s 0d, the total expenditure on the home is one-third of income. There is no living-in domestic servant here.[26]

In the same issue G. Colmore published a model budget for £800 a year. He pointed out that the traditional fraction of 10 per cent of income to rent might be right at £10,000 a year, but that at £800 a rent of £90 or more was probably necessary, which, with rates and taxes, would mean £130. Where to live depended on whether one wished to be within 'the dinner-party radius'—if so, Bayswater, Kensington and Bloomsbury were in, Hammersmith, Shepherd's Bush and Kilburn were not. In view of the increasing costs of domestic service, the wife must be prepared to supervise and interest herself in household affairs, and the man must be his own butler; Colmore suggests only two staff, a cook at £20 a year and a house parlourmaid at £18. If we add these to the rent of the house, and include repairs at £50 a year and coal and gas at £21, we have a total house expenditure of £239, approaching the same fraction of one-third as was paid by the solicitor's clerk.[27] For these 'middle-middle-class' families the cost of domestic service brought housing expenditure to much the same proportion as in the lower-middle class, though, of course, with added comfort and personal attendance.

Clearly, the amount which families were able or willing to devote to housing directly affected the size, quality and location of their accommodation. Builders responded as well as their imperfect knowledge of the market allowed them to do with a variety of housing types—urban and suburban, terraced, semi-detached and detached—which experience suggested would be acceptable to the pockets and tastes of different sorts of tenants. It is unlikely that the building trade itself was a major, positive influence on house form. Large-scale builders like Thomas Cubitt who could design and execute a single house, a London square or a royal palace with equal skill and felicity[28] were quite exceptional, even at the close of the period. As H. J. Dyos has shown, the vast majority of speculative houses continued to be built by very small firms, even in London where there was scope for larger-scale activity than in the provinces. In the 1840s half of all London firms built only one or two houses a year, and thirty years later there was no change in the situation.[29]

It is also unlikely that such little men would have taken much initiative in design or methods of construction. The necessity to build an easily saleable or lettable house almost demanded that builders should not be innovatory—that they should be a step behind the latest fashion rather than in front of it. A conservative industry catered for a largely conservative market by following and modifying the designs in technical trade guides, or by using the standardized architects' plans which were specially produced for speculative builders. In any case, experienced builders were quite capable of executing their own drawings and calculating their quantities without benefit of professional assistance. The customer generally had little or no opportunity of influencing the design, since he did not usually appear until the house was at the decorating stage, though speculators catering for a somewhat higher end of the market would sometimes only complete the shell and give the client a considerable choice over the internal divisions, fittings and embellishments. Already in 1888 Mrs Panton was urging that 'female architects *for domestic architecture solely* [my italics] would be a great help to all who have to live in houses planned and executed by men'.

What the tenant of a speculatively built house got, therefore, was usually a simplified, scaled-down version in the general style which architects were using for custom-built houses. Often it adopted only the superficial trappings of the current idiom—the style of doorways, window openings, decorative features and so on—while making little or no change in the basic construction or internal plan. At the lower end of the suburban market, the speculators produced dreary, if respectable, monotony, in long streets of terraced or identical semi-detached houses, a far cry from the individuality to which the better-off aspired. It was against this depressing stereotype 'villa' that Ruskin and others inveighed:

> ... thousands of houses, built within the last ten years, of rotten brick, with various iron devices to hold it together ... They are fastened in a Siamese-twin manner together by their sides, and each couple has a Greek or Gothic portico shared between them, with magnificent steps, and highly-ornamented capitals. Attached to every double block are exactly similar double parallelograms of garden, laid out in new gravel and scanty turf ... [30]

Professor Dyos has suggested that there was very little contemporary criticism of the standards of work of speculative builders before the 1880s. Complaints were certainly frequent by that decade, now that building was in theory subject to inspection by surveyors of the local boards, though there was strong suspicion that in new suburban areas officials were sometimes in league with jerry-builders not to enforce the by-laws. The most common complaints at this time were of rising damp due to inadequate or non-existent damp courses, uneven floors, sagging roofs caused by insufficient scantlings, defective tiles or slates admitting rain to the roof-space and bedrooms, scamped plumbing and fittings in bathrooms and WCs, and bulging garden walls caused by cracked piers. But precisely similar complaints had been common since at least the middle of the century, and lead one to believe that cheaper-quality middle-class housing was almost as subject to jerry-building as working-class housing. In 1865 the *Daily Telegraph* published a series of letters which suggests that a well-built house in the London suburbs was difficult to find for those in the middle-income range. The correspondence began with a letter from 'W.H.W.' who claimed that he had searched for a house from Erith in the east to Chertsey in the west: he wanted to pay not more than £40 a year, and needed two reception-rooms, kitchen and four bedrooms. He eventually took the best he could find, with a kitchen three-parts underground and a double reception room with communicating doors which continually admitted a draught as they were so ill-fitting. The green wood used in doors and windows had so twisted and shrunk that there were gaps of up to an inch in the window-frames, and in frosty weather he crouched over the fire while a thermometer at his back registered 38 °F. The bedrooms were damp, and plaster was already falling from the walls. Was not some different kind of building possible, he asked, plain and solid? This was merely vulgar and camouflage for all its marble mantelpieces, 'not a house in the true sense of the word'.

'Master of Arts' replied to say that he rented a detached, substantially-built 'Elizabethan' villa in Kensington, where he could swing a cat in the drawing-room and a kitten in the dining-room. It costs £120 a year, but he was willing to pay so much for his 'absurd finials and grotesque gargoyles' as a refuge from 'the hateful rows of plastered tenements with toy-box pilasters and pediments'. The London villa at £50 a year, he believed, was the most uncomfortable abode in the world: there was no honest work in it, and the trade was in the hands of 'a sordid and ignorant class'.

This attack prompted replies by 'Fair Play' and 'E.T.E.', who, if not builders themselves, certainly came to their defence. The trouble was, they argued, that people with £300–£400 a year wanted to pay a rent of £40 for a 'showy' house. For this they should not expect drawing-rooms, dining-rooms and breakfast-parlours, but one good living-room: for the price of a cottage they demanded a villa. E.T.E. calculated that such houses occupied about 24,000cu ft which, at 6d a cubic foot, cost £600, land adding at least another £100. £40 a year was not a fair return on outlay when repairs, insurance and vacancies were deducted. Solid, plain houses could be built, but not for £40 a year.[31]

How far clients wanted a 'showy' house, and how far builders forced them to do so by offering little alternative, is impossible to know; probably it was something of each. No doubt most customers wanted a house that was roughly in keeping with the fashionable architectural style. Speculative builders were intelligent enough to know this, or they did not survive, and they competed with each other to produce the most easily disposable property at the lowest possible price. A cottage with a single living-room was unlikely to compete with a villa with three reception-rooms, which, Mrs Panton assured her readers, were now to be expected even in small houses. The Victorian middle classes wanted space in their houses for the reasons previously given, and they wanted individuality which would express their independence and originality. It was this characteristic which most struck foreign visitors to England like Dr Carus, physician to the King of Saxony:

> Up to the present moment, the Englishman still perseveres in striving after a certain individuality and personal independence, a certain separation of himself from others, which constitutes the very foundation of his freedom . . . it is that that gives the Englishman that proud feeling of personal independence which is stereotyped in the phrase 'Every man's house is his castle'. This is a feeling which cannot be entertained, and an expression which cannot be used, in Germany or France, where ten or fifteen families often live together in the same large house . . . The English divide their edifices perpendicularly into houses—whereas we Germans divide them horizontally into floors . . .[32]

Individuality was also expressed by the architectural style of the house—an assertion of individual difference in contrast to the anonymity of the Georgian terrace. The eclecticism of the latter half of the century offered a bewildering variety from which to choose, Robert Kerr in 1871 describing no fewer than eleven styles from which the client could select. In fact, all stemmed from one or other of the two principal sources over which 'the Battle of the Styles' raged throughout the period—the Classical, with Italian, French or English Renaissance decoration, and the Gothic or Picturesque with its irregular exterior and plan.

Neither style completely conquered the other at any point, but in the middle decades of the century the advantage generally lay with the Gothic. In the 1860s a few speculative builders still had regard for order and symmetry in street elevations and continued to build plain, well-proportioned terraces in an essentially classical style, but in the following decades the terrace often degenerated into a mass of projecting porches, bay-windows, and heavy ornamental details such as keystones, cappings, coloured brickwork and ornamental tiling. The availability of cheap glass in large sheets further encouraged builders to exaggerate window-openings, especially on the ground floor, and to destroy the nice proportions of wall and windows which had formerly been well understood.[33] The degenerated terrace of the seventies and eighties showed the façade broken up by tiers of large, angular bay-windows, steeply pitched, ornamental roofs, often with attic dormer windows, and heavy stucco trimmings in Renaissance or Gothic style. The general effect of gloomy clutter was enhanced by the large areas of plate-glass, which in many lights showed up as empty black or grey spaces.

In the detached and semi-detached suburban villa speculative builders had more scope to follow Ruskin's advice to 'introduce your Gothic line by line and stone by stone; never mind mixing it with your present architecture; your existing houses will be none the worse for having little bits of better work fitted to them . . .' With such authority behind them, builders felt almost a moral obligation to add some Gothic features to what was often a basically unchanged box—a medieval-style porch, pointed heads to doors and windows, projecting 'bow'-windows supported on carved brackets, turrets and castellations—which might be mingled with equally characteristic Renaissance features and with quite inappropriate large plate-glass windows. On the small plots of suburban streets the effects of such idiosyncrasies were often grotesque. Where, at a higher level of taste and income, the whole house was professionally designed in a vernacular style, so that the exterior reflected the internal plan in a natural, organic way, the result could be attractive and harmonious. The prototype of this development is usually taken to be the 'Red House' at Bexleyheath, Kent, designed for William Morris by Philip Webb in 1859. It was a two-storied house of L-shaped plan, built of red brick with a high-pitched, red-tiled roof, and containing a number of romantic, though not dominating, features such as oriel windows, gables and a turret. With its principal rooms facing north, and without benefit of a bathroom, it may not have been an entirely comfortable house, but in its return to the vernacular tradition of building it became, as John Gloag says, 'the progenitor of a new school of domestic architecture'.[34] Morris fondly believed that the Red House was 'in the style of the thirteenth century', but in this and his later work Webb combined so many materials, features, forms and details that there was no single guiding principle except the reverence for traditional, indigenous building technology; he was, in fact, developing an 'astylar' vernacular architecture.[35] Popularized, modified and miniaturized (and often satirized), it was to become a dominant influence on the forms of middle-class housing for the next hundred years, inspiring agreeable 'country houses' in southern commuter villages like Gerrards Cross and Clandon, and less pleasing 'Tudor semis' along the arterial roads of most large towns.

The Red House was one reaction to the ugly artificiality of much mid-Victorian housing: another, quite different, was a return to more classical symmetry which goes, rather inappropriately, under the name of 'Queen Anne'. It is usually associated with the architecture of Norman Shaw, and with work at Bedford Park, Chiswick, and Cadogan Square, but the real originators of the style were probably W. Eden Nesfield and J. J. Stevenson in the late 1860s. Its characteristics were a return towards more symmetrical composition, the use of English and Dutch Renaissance details and a quality of lightness and delicacy achieved through proportion and balance. Externally it was typified by the use of red brick, white-painted woodwork and sliding sash windows. This 'free Classic' architecture, wrote Stevenson in 1874, 'has neither the exquisite grace of refinement of Greek, nor the romance and high aspirations of Gothic, but it is perhaps not, therefore, the less suited for the common daily wants of English life'. One is tempted to think that it also represented a rejection of the gloomy moral seriousness of the Gothic.

Norman Shaw was undoubtedly the chief popularizer of the style, and his work at Bedford Park between 1875 and 1881 has often been hailed as the first creation of a garden suburb. Deliberately located at Chiswick to be within thirty minutes' commuting distance of the City, the layout and street pattern were largely determined by the carefully-preserved existing trees. The width of streets and the spaces between buildings were also strictly controlled so that new vistas were constantly opened up against the backcloth of light filtering through the foliage. The Park was planned to be a community, with its Club House, Tabard Inn, church, shops and, characteristically, its Art School, and from the first it enjoyed the reputation of an aesthetes' colony. Walter Creese has argued that its 'garden suburb' reputation cannot be justified because of the block system of land division which produced a fairly regular pattern of long, narrow plots,[36] but the disposition of clumps of houses in winding, tree-lined roads produced a predominantly rural atmosphere which was almost unique in suburban housing of the period.[37]

The Bedford Park houses were individually designed, detached and semi-detached, but linked into a coherent composition by the common 'Queen Anne' style. The extreme cost was £700 for a detached house, £1,100 for a pair. They incorporated a number of important technical developments intended to give the suburb sanitary as well as aesthetic advantages. External plumbing was introduced by Shaw after the Prince of Wales's typhoid attack in 1871, soil and waste-pipes being placed on the outside walls of the houses, with free ventilation and intercepting traps. This also allowed water-closets to be brought out of the garden into the house, and hot and cold water supplies were fitted to all houses. Shaw was also responsible, with Webb and Devey, for bringing the kitchen out of the basement on to the ground floor, an innovation which was unusual so near to London. Externally, the houses had interesting and varied elevations, with sash windows, semi-elliptical pediments and scrolls, and often balconies to the first floor; rooms were spacious and light, comfortable but unpompous. Although the plans and sizes varied, there were usually three reception rooms (typically, two about 18ft square and one smaller), kitchen and pantries, four double bedrooms, a dressing-room, bathroom and WC on the first floor and two or three further servants' bedrooms on the second floor. Some had a studio at the top of the house as befitted the vision of an artistic colony.

In the hands of the speculative builders Shaw's work became vulgarized into mere ornamental features—porches, verandahs, 'Dutch' gables and small panes to the upper sashes of windows—added on to a basically unchanged semi-detached plan, and such houses became a common building type towards the end of the century, especially in the London suburbs. Lasting and important effects, however, were the incorporation of lavatory and bathroom to the house, and the elevation of the kitchen to the ground floor, made possible by the wider frontages which suburban sites allowed (typically 50ft for a pair of semi-detached houses in Bedford Park) and encouraged by an increasing concern for convenience as domestic servants became dearer, scarcer and more selective.

These new planning concepts were further developed by later vernacular architects such as C. F. A. Voysey and Edwin Lutyens who worked in the tradition of Webb rather than Shaw. To Voysey, 'good design must grow out of requirements and conditions—fitness is the basis of beauty'. This shattering principle was, by the 1890s, beginning to produce a 'new architecture' which drew on both Gothic and Classical pasts, but united them in an individual style characterized by simplicity, respect for materials, craftsmanship and proportions. Voysey houses were usually recognizable by their roofs of green slate and walls of cement roughcast applied to 9-inch brick (rather than 11-inch cavity) for economy, warmth and aesthetic texture: his preference was for long, low-ceilinged rooms well-lighted by wide windows. Voysey's houses were not so much 'astylar' as 'non-stylar' or even 'anti-stylar'—the deliberate replacement of style and precedent by the abstract visual stimulus of 'Nature' and the overriding conviction that form should grow organically out of requirements. His lead was followed by many lesser architects such as Ernest Gimson and Sydney Barnsley, who turning their backs completely on the urban problem as a creation of alien, industrial forces, concentrated on small country houses, especially in the Cotswold idiom. Edwin Lutyens and others adapted the 'free rustic' into a more romantic, picturesque style with both Tudor and Renaissance echoes. Like Shaw, Lutyens introduced a number of new planning concepts. His rooms were particularly well lighted from windows on two or three sides, made possible by a free, irregular plan which even included some 'open-plan' features. Houses were sited carefully in relation to natural contours and to their gardens, which became important features of this school of building.

The detached country house of Edwardian times, often with 'Tudor' half-timbering, gables and other picturesque details and standing in its carefully-tended acre or half-acre garden, was the commercial outcome of this trend. Usually intended for management by one, or at most two, domestic servants, its three reception rooms and five or six bedrooms (still, often, two in the attic) were on a more modest scale than the architect-designed country house, though the individuality of each was carefully ensured by distinctive features. For larger-scale housing developments the 'free rustic' was obviously less suitable than neo-classical forms, and for the most famous of the Edwardian estates, Hampstead Garden Suburb, the architects Parker and Unwin worked in a style reminiscent of Shaw's

Bedford Park. The intention of the suburb, which was conceived by Henrietta Barnett in 1905, was that it should reintegrate the social classes which suburbanization had hitherto divided. Hampstead was therefore to provide houses on the edge of the Heath for working people within a 2d tube fare of London as well as for middle-class and professional people. In practice, villa prices which ranged from £425 to £3,500 attracted a wide social and economic representation, but scarcely reached the working classes who were 'zoned' in a 70-acre development of workers' cottages to the north. Built of silver-grey brick with red dressings, with white window sashes and often balustrades and balconies to bring their occupants close to nature, they were disposed irregularly in wide roads, culs-de-sac, closes, courts and quadrangles built around greens, The low average density of eight to the acre permitted some layouts which would otherwise have contravened by-law regulations.

By the later nineteenth century the trend was towards a reduction of the spatial divisions and separations which had characterized mid-Victorian design towards a more open, fluid organization of space. The increased horizontal spread of both detached and semi-detached houses compared with the former narrow-fronted urban plan encouraged this change, while the elevation of the kitchen quarters to the ground floor, which was common by the eighties and nineties made a larger ground plan inevitable. With this greater floor area, bedrooms could now be concentrated on the first floor, together with the bathroom and lavatory, either dispensing with a second storey altogether or reserving it for one or two servants' rooms.

On the ground floor three reception rooms continued to be regarded as the minimum, with the third, variously described as 'morning-room' and 'breakfast-parlour', sometimes reserved for the mistress's use. Mrs Panton in 1888 ordained that it should be decorated in sage-green ('taking care there is no arsenic in it') and the doors painted with pale pink flowers; it should contain a sofa, desk, revolving bookcase, little tables, basket-chairs and foot-stools, together with the equipment for her painting or other recreations.[38] The dark and dusty dining-room of twenty-five years ago with its immovable furniture, heavy curtains and carpets was now out of favour: rooms, it was now thought, should be light and cheerful, and used with reference to comfort and sunshine rather than by their description. By the end of the century the importance of the dining-room as the principal room of the house was beginning to suffer some decline. Formerly it had often also served as the family living-room, with the drawing-room preserved from the children and reserved for evening use and entertaining. Such dining-rooms were usually as large as, and sometimes larger than, the drawing-room, J. J. Stevenson in 1880 recommending a width of 15–20ft and a length of 18–30ft, and suggesting 18ft by 25ft as 'a very convenient size for all family purposes'.[39] By the turn of the century the function of the dining-room was often becoming limited to the serving of meals and, with the addition of a desk or bureau, for use as a writing-room where the house did not contain a study, while family life increasingly centred round the morning-room during the day and the drawing-room in the evening. In middle-income Edwardian houses the drawing-room was almost always the largest room in the house, at 20ft by 14ft and more compared with a dining-room which was shrinking towards 16ft by 13ft. On the other hand, the entrance hall had often grown in area and importance from the mid-Victorian passage which was often no wider than 5ft or so. Like many writers of the day, Mrs Panton believed that nothing added so much to the appearance of a house as the hall. Hats and coats were not to be hung there, but taken to other rooms or to the kitchen passage, and it was to be furnished with an old oak settle, bamboo chairs or a settee, an umbrella-stand, an aspidistra in a brass pot, and velveteen curtains draped across all doors.

The wider and more irregular plan of Edwardian houses, especially country houses of the vernacular idiom, favoured such use of space, and in some houses areas were deliberately made more flexible by the use of folding or double doors which could in effect throw one room into another. Thus, the hall might be used as an extension to a reception room, not merely as a place to 'hold' callers, the drawing-room might open by glazed doors into a conservatory (used for displaying blooms, not for growing plants), the dining-room might have seats built round the curve of the bay-window, while an irregularly-shaped drawing-room might have a 'library corner', a 'cosy corner' or an 'inglenook' with seats round the fire. In these and other ways the strict categorization of Victorian rooms was beginning to yield to a more open and flexible use of space, and to more irregular planning which took greater account of natural light and outlook. The bedroom floors naturally offered less scope for such innovations than the ground floor. Children, and even servants, could be tolerated on the same floor by Edwardian times, and the single bathroom, not yet 'en suite' in the moderate-sized house, might serve for the whole household, though a servants' lavatory was usual, either upstairs or in the kitchen regions. It was considered more important that the principal bedroom should have a communicating dressing-room for the head of the family, so that his wife could dress and be attended by a servant in the bedroom rather than for reasons of conjugal modesty.

No house-type other than the villa commanded any significant middle-class following until late in the century. Flats, however suitable they might be thought for the working classes, were not favoured as family accommodation at any time in the period, and for long continued to be associated with 'bachelor chambers' such as those in The Albany and those built by Decimus Burton in Regent Street. Family flats were almost unthinkable before the 1850s, despite the increasing scarcity and cost of central sites, especially in London, and *The Builder* seems to have been alone in advocating them as a solution to the problem of urban sprawl. An article in 1849 castigated the 'higgledy-piggledy style of middle-class dwelling' and argued that 'the time has now arrived when the expansion and growth of this city must be upward in place of outward—when "houses" must be reared above each other . . . instead of straggling miles farther and farther away from the centre'.[40] The first outcome of this new interest was a block of upper-middle-class apartments built in the new Victoria Street to the design of Henry Ashton between 1852 and 1854. Reminiscent of Berlin models, they had a ground floor of shops, and four storeys of flats, typically containing a hall, drawing-room 21ft by 15ft, dining-room 15ft by 15ft, kitchen 15ft by $13\frac{1}{2}$ft, scullery, four bedrooms, a servants' bedroom and two WCs. There were principal staircases in the grand manner, and a separate servants' stair, but only tiny interior courts which admitted little light. Rents were high, at £80–£200 per annum according to size and position, and probably because of this, and their uncertain social rating, they were not regarded as commercially successful.

The immediate progress of the middle-class flat was slow, confined largely to established fashionable areas of London and to use by childless families. It was often regarded as providing a base for professional or social activities for those who also possessed a house in the country, T. H. S. Escott in 1879 claiming that flats were now in considerable favour and that rents had doubled in the last five years.[41] The most ambitious development of what *The Builder* described as 'residential towers' was at Queen Anne's Mansions, St James's Park, where the first tall flats in London were begun in 1873; these were of 10 to 14 storeys, the highest over 150ft above ground, but made accessible by lifts.[42] With rents at £60 per annum for two rooms and £300 for six, they were much in demand, and building of further blocks continued until 1889. They were intended as 'service flats' which could be run with a minimum of domestic help, and therefore provided a restaurant and 'public saloons' as well as room service. But fully 'federalized' or 'associated' apartments, which made progress in the United States towards the end of the century, were not popular in the strongly individualistic English climate, where flat-dwellers still expected personal, residential service. Domestic quarters in flats were often badly designed, extremely cramped and lacking in light and ventilation, even to the point of providing a bedroom for two maids so small that there was only space between the bunk-beds for one to dress at a time. *The Lancet* in 1905 discovered servants' rooms which never enjoyed direct sunlight and only admitted diffused light for a few hours a day in summer: it considered that such conditions warranted the attention of medical officers of health.[43]

Two other housing types made some impact on middle-class living towards the end of the century, both of them associated with the cult of nature and the increasing popularity of outdoor recreation. To live in a country cottage, it was pointed out in 1906, was no longer confined to a single class of people or a humble way of life: a cottage, smaller in area than a tradesman's house, was the home of one of our royal princesses, and made up for its lack of space by its elegant simplicity and frugality.[44] The drift to the countryside was, in part, a natural extension of the same forces which had already drawn the middle classes to the suburbs—an escape from the dirt, noise and smell of the towns, a 'search for environment' amidst gardens, trees and low densities. By the century's end some of its former advocates were beginning to see the suburb as an artificial creation, a mere apology for nature in which urban values and attitudes were still dominant. Fast communication by rail and, by now, the motor-car, made a home in the real countryside a possibility—for the man who wanted a quiet retreat from his work in town (either for daily or weekend use), for the scholar and artist, the invalid or convalescent, and for the growing numbers of retired people. Above all, it was 'the symptom of a revolt on the part of many men and more women against the tyranny of the town house, with its standing problem of servants and its inevitable problems of cleaning and maintenance, entertaining on a scale which is "expected", and being more or less permanently "at home"'.

Middle-class cottages, it was assumed, would cost between £200 and £1,000, at the latter well above the price of a substantial suburban villa. They should be designed for running by one resident servant, with daily help from the village, and should have a few, sunny rooms rather than many small, dark ones. They should preferably be built on low, spreading lines, sited to take advantage of the natural contours of the land, and, where possible, using local materials. The preferred styles were the vernacular of such architects as Webb, Lutyens, Detmar Blow and Guy Dawber, care being taken to avoid the deliberately 'quaint' or 'picturesque'. Interiors were to be plain, comfortable and convenient. 'The formal drawing-room has been abolished'; much more appropriate for a cottage is the 'main living-room' for family use, which might have a quiet corner if L-shaped, or a small 'lounge' or smoking-room leading off it. Another way of securing some privacy in a small house was to fit up a bedroom as a 'bed-sitting-room', and where there are children in the house a play-room 'for game or drill' was an admirable idea. 'And when the cult of the body is fully believed in—when physical exercise is regarded as a part of education and citizenship—perhaps the household will assemble for exercise as regularly as once upon a time it assembled for prayers.'[45]

In such statements there is discernible the beginning of a radical change in the concept of the house as a place not primarily for the display and ritual observances of its adult occupants, but for the rational use and recreation of all its members. Ruskin's 'temple' was beginning to dissolve into a 'machine for living'. It was carried still further in the development of the bungalow, which, as A. D. King has shown, was at first associated exclusively with the bathing resort and regarded as a second or alternative home for summer and weekend use. Like the country cottage, the bungalow represented a set of ideological values—the quest for nature, solitude and isolation in a health-giving environment—though it was more closely associated with particular forms of recreation, especially sea-bathing, golf, tennis, walking and bicycling.[46]

As a building-type there was nothing new about the single-storey house, numerous examples being given by J. C. Loudon in his copybook of designs published in 1833 as suitable for lodges, gardeners' cottages and so on. But the modern bungalow (the 'bangla' of Bengal) was first developed as an Anglo-Indian house-type and, because of its ease of construction and suitability for hot climates, spread to become the predominant colonial building form in the nineteenth century. In England the first bungalow to be so named was built in 1869 at Birchington, near Westgate-on-Sea, Kent, for occupation by an architect. (The station at Westgate was opened in 1870.) Built of prefabricated blocks in the short space of two months, it was described as a 'portable dwelling', though it consisted of eight rooms, two verandahs and a basement containing wine, beer and coal cellars. The next year some larger versions were built at Birchington which contained nine bedrooms (two for servants), a dining-room, study and a 33ft 'saloon . . . arranged to admit a billiard table capable of forming a buffet when required'; croquet lawns sloped down to the bathing-sands, where private dressing-rooms were provided. The houses were centrally heated, and sold complete with furnishings, linen and even plate at prices from 1,000 guineas to 1,800 guineas for the largest.

These early bungalows were described as combining 'real comfort' with 'pleasing rusticity'; they were 'cosy', 'rural-looking', 'quaint' and 'perfect as to sanitary qualities'. At this time their use seems to have been confined to the upper classes and wealthy professional people. By the late eighties the bungalow began to move inland, with the first development at East Grinstead by R. A. Briggs in 1887: 'Bellagio' was to be 'a delightful rural retreat for tired Londoners', with social intercourse provided by a club-house and recreations including hunting, shooting, fishing, tennis, cricket and football. By the end of the century the bungalow was spreading both geographically and socially—to hillside and countryside as well as to seaside (though still concentrated in the south-east of England) and to a wider middle class looking for a permanent home within commuting distance of town, or for a retirement home. Builders like P. H. Harrison popularized and democratized the bungalow in the first decade of the twentieth century, typically providing living-room, kitchen, four bedrooms and bicycle store at the modest cost of about £300; no fewer than two hundred were built by him between Lancing and Worthing at what became known as 'Bungalow Town'.

Bungalows, cottages and flats, important as they were later to become as middle-class housing types, made only slight inroads on the supremacy of the villa in the period before 1914. Convenience and ease of running were not yet important determinants when domestic servants were still relatively cheap and plentiful, and this explains, too, why domestic technology made only slow progress in an age remarkable for scientific invention. Thus, while there was abundant labour to light, replenish and clear away fires in living-rooms and bedrooms, the Victorian and Edwardian house continued to be heated by coal long after central heating was a proven and economical alternative. J. C. Loudon described a system of heating by warm air flues invented by Strutt of Belper about 1810,[47] though heating by hot-water pipes was generally preferred and was in fairly common use for public buildings and very large houses by mid-century. But for ordinary houses neither central heating nor 'closed stoves' which were popular in America were at all common before Edwardian times, and English people of all social classes continued to have a deep-seated sentimental attachment to open coal fires. By the 1880s, however, a number of gas stoves were on the market, and made some headway in the next decade when it became possible to hire them from gas companies and to pay for the gas on the 'penny-in-the-slot' system. In her edition of 1888 Mrs Beeton particularly recommended them for use in bedrooms where 'the expense and great trouble of coal fires renders their use practically prohibitory, whereas a good hot gas-fire can be obtained for half an hour, night and morning, at a cost of 6d per week or less'.

By contrast, the development of new forms of domestic lighting was impeded more by technological difficulties than by human resistance. The labour and inconvenience of lighting, replenishing and extinguishing candles, and of re-filling, trimming and cleaning oil-lamps can scarcely have commended them, quite apart from the inadequate illumination which they gave, yet until mid-century—and much later in many homes—there was no alternative to their use. Although lighting by gas was being developed experimentally by Murdoch as early as 1802 and was used for street-lighting in St Margaret's, Westminster, in 1814, it was quite unsuitable for the rooms of ordinary houses owing to inadequate ventilation. For domestic use the major improvements came with the invention of the atmospheric burner about 1840 and, more importantly, the incandescent gas mantle in 1885 which for the first time produced a steady and diffused light. Even so, gas-lighting had serious disadvantages of smell and of damage to decorations. By the 1880s an alternative was becoming available in electricity. Peterhouse College, Cambridge, was so lighted in 1882, while at Hatfield House Lord Salisbury for a time obliged his guests to dine by arc-light. For domestic use the 'Ediswan' carbon-filament lamp was preferred and remained unchallenged until tungsten filament and gas-filled lamps were invented just before World War I.[48] Electric lighting, even in wealthy households, was still new in 1898 when Dorothy Peel's book on household management, *The New Home*, strongly recommended it on grounds of cleanliness, economy and 'the extreme facility with which the switches can be turned off and on'. The 'Electrical Fair' held at the Crystal Palace in 1891 demonstrated a variety of electric cooking appliances, though the first Belling electric fire was not marketed until 1912. In fact, the domestic use of electricity made no rapid advance in England, partly because only about 2 per cent of homes were connected to the mains in 1910 and partly because the cost remained high; a number of progressive power undertakings (the 'point fivers') were just beginning to cut charges from 8d to $\frac{1}{2}$d a unit in 1914 when war intervened.[49]

The Victorian middle classes are traditionally supposed to have esteemed cleanliness next to godliness, though in this respect, too, there was often a long gap between invention and adoption. For the disposal of human refuse the early Victorians relied on the privy or 'necessary', usually not integral with the house but sited separately at the rear or at the end of the garden. More often than not, it was a simple cesspool which required regular empty-ing by the 'night-soil' men, though sometimes it was connected to the exist-ing inadequate sewers which had been designed only for the removal of surface rainwater, and emptied into rivers which generally became heavily polluted. The water-closet, which could trace its origins to Tudor times, was developed into something like its modern form, with overhead cistern, S-shaped soil pipe and valves, by Alexander Cumming and Joseph Bramah in the 1770s, but only when towns began to acquire proper sewerage systems from the 1850s onwards when non-porous clay pipes became cheaply avail-able did water sanitation make much progress. The integral water-closet came to be built into new middle-class houses in the seventies and eighties, usually on the main bedroom floor, and, in larger houses, on the servants' floor also, though this was sometimes replaced by a 'housemaids' closet' with a sink for the discharge of upstairs slops. A ground-floor 'cloakroom' opening off the hall and intended mainly for the use of male visitors, was often, though by no means universally, included by the end of the century.

Frequent bathing can hardly have been a characteristic of the middle classes before the 1860s or thereabouts. Until then, runnning water was rarely piped beyond the kitchen—and even then only a cold supply—and to bathe in a tin bath or round tub before the kitchen fire, with the chill taken off by a few cans of hot water, must have been a frequently-shirked duty. More attractive hip, slipper and lounge baths for use in the bedroom were popularized by the Great Exhibition in 1851, though they still required to be emptied by hand, as did the early fixed baths which began to be fitted in bedroom recesses in the houses of the rich from the 1840s. In the ordinary house, the fixed bath made little progress until plumbing brought piped water to the upper floors and provided drains for the removal of the used water. In advanced architect-designed houses a bathroom was coming to be provided by the 1870s, but in speculatively-built houses not until the 1880s or even later.[50] Even then, baths were often fitted with a cold water supply only. The problem of supplying hot water was the subject of numerous experiments—the bath set in a metal case around which flowed water heated by a small furnace, the tank or cistern separately heated by the hot-water geyser and so on—until a piped supply heated from the kitchen range or boiler began to be installed late in the century. By 1902 the opinion was expressed that 'there is a room which no self-respecting householder can do without, and that is the bath room. One can only marvel at the astonishing fact that, prior to twenty or thirty years back, the majority of small and medium-sized houses, and perhaps fifty per cent of the larger ones, were built without bath rooms'.[51]

The kitchen quarters of Victorian houses underwent little fundamental change until the closing years of the century, when the growing cost and scarcity of domestic servants awakened mistresses to the possibilities of technology. J. J. Stevenson in 1880 advised several modern appliances such as a scullery with two sinks and hot and cold water, and a larder with space enough to accommodate a refrigerator, but in the matter of cooking conservatism still prevailed, the author recommending the old open fire for roasting meat with 'a few gas jets for boiling pans [as] a useful addition'. The alternative, which began to be developed from the 1820s and 1830s onwards, apparently first in the Leamington area, was the closed range, which, as the name implies, was more like a stove with the front of the fire filled by an iron door and the top by a plate with apertures for fitted pans. Still regarded as experimental by Webster's *Encyclopaedia of Domestic Economy* (1844), great economy was claimed for the closed range by its use of only one and a half tons of coal a month. Numerous types of what came to be known as the 'Kitchener' were shown in 1851, ranging from a small version with single oven and water-boiler to a monster 18ft range with two roasters, two steam-boilers, one water-boiler and no less than six ovens. Made of cast iron, ranges had to be built in and flued and were regarded as landlords' fixtures, a fact which helps to explain their slow progress in working-class homes. In mid-century they cost from £7 15s 0d to about £25, with another £3 or £4 for installation.[52]

Cooking by gas, which had been employed by the great chef Alexis Soyer at the Reform Club in the 1830s, made slow progress in the home, though it, too, received much publicity at the Great Exhibition. Mrs Beeton in 1861 did not regard the gas cooker as a serious possibility, and it seems to have been first used in the 1870s and 1880s as a supplement to the coal range for particular cooking operations such as slow stewing, and for use in summer. Its popularity spread in the 1890s when gas companies began to rent out cookers and made gas available on the penny-in-the-slot system. The outstanding disadvantage of gas cookers, as of the electric cookers which began to appear at the end of the century, was that they only cooked, whereas the range also provided hot water and space heating for the kitchen: while coal remained cheap and servants continued to be available its supremacy was not seriously challenged.

Although, as we have seen, the kitchen often became raised from basement to ground-floor level in the late Victorian and Edwardian house, little change in its layout or basic equipment is observable. Mrs Beeton's edition of 1888 still recommended a kitchen table which should be 'massive, firm and strongly made', a large dresser with drawers below and four or five tiers of open shelves above, and cupboards built into the recess formed by the piers which flanked the range. The only concession to modern ideas of hygiene was the suggestion that walls should be covered with a washable paper and all fittings and furniture varnished so that they might be wiped with a damp cloth. Almost no thought had yet been given to the planning of the kitchen with a view to lightening the labours of cooks, kitchen-maids and scullery-maids. In America, where 'the servant problem' was experienced earlier, and more middle-class women actually worked in their kitchens, serious consideration was given to the organization of the work process as early as 1869 by Catherine E. Beecher. Her ideas, based on the cook's galley in ships, divided the kitchen into 'units' for different functions, provided continuous work-surfaces, and removed the iron range into an adjoining 'stove room'. By 1912 the beginnings of scientific management in kitchen planning can be discerned in the work of Christine Frederick, who carried out time-and-motion studies of household tasks and found, for instance, that she made '80 wrong motions in dishwashing alone, not counting others in the sorting, wiping and laying away'.[53] In the United States such discoveries quickly began to have effects on the design of domestic equipment, the height and dimensions of working surfaces and the overall planning of the kitchen in order to minimize fatigue and unnecessary drudgery. Among the English middle classes, for whom the 'servantless house' was still almost an indecency, such revolutionary ideas as yet found no following.

PART 3: 1918–1970

8

COUNCIL HOUSING, 1918–1939

While the housing of the working classes has always been a question of the greatest social importance, never has it been so important as now. It is not too much to say that an adequate solution of the housing question is the foundation of all social progress ... The first point at which the attack must be delivered is the unhealthy, ugly, overcrowded house in the mean street, which all of us know too well. If a healthy race is to be reared, it can be reared only in healthy homes; if drink and crime are to be successfully combated, decent, sanitary houses must be provided; if 'unrest' is to be converted into contentment, the provision of good houses may prove one of the most potent agents in that conversion.

Extract from the King's Speech to Representatives of the Local Authorities and Societies at Buckingham Palace; *The Times*, 12 April 1919.

THE HOUSING PROBLEM IN 1918

The influence of war, especially of total wars of which that of 1914–18 was the first, in precipitating changes in society and in social policy is now well established.[1] In particular, Professor R. M. Titmuss has argued that as the scale and intensity of conflict grew to involve the whole population and as the resources necessary to wage total war demanded ever greater sacrifices from the people, a commitment on the part of government to major social reforms came to constitute the other side of an unwritten social contract. In short, modern war was only acceptable if it held out the prospect of a better world and a better life for its survivors.[2]

While it explicitly raised expectations about women's emancipation, educational reform, the expansion of national insurance and many other matters, the wartime coalition government of Lloyd George bent its greatest efforts to the planning of a post-war housing policy, enshrined in the phrase which became both a rallying cry and an election promise. As Walter Long, the President of the Local Government Board, put it 'To let them [our heroes] come home from horrible, water-logged trenches to something little better than a pigsty here would, indeed, be criminal . . . and a negation of all we have said during the war, that we can never repay those men for what they have done for us'.[3] From the time of the appointment of the Second Reconstruction Committee in February 1917 a national housing programme came to be regarded as the pivot of post-war social policy, and from the first the problem was seen as both a quantitative and a qualitative one—it was not to be just a matter of providing enough houses but of building enough good homes for the men who had suffered and for their children who would restore the depleted strength of the nation.

The crucial change was the reluctant recognition that private enterprise would not be able to supply houses of the quantity and quality now demanded at rents which many of the working classes could afford. As earlier chapters have shown, this had long been recognized in the exceptional circumstances of rural housing and, by the time of the Royal Commission on Housing of 1884–5, in the case of workers' housing in central London. But up to World War I the belief persisted that the private builder would continue to meet all normal housing needs and that the housing function of local authorities would be a minor one, restricted mainly to the accommodation of families displaced by sanitary improvement schemes. As late as 1913, the *Annual Report* of the Local Government Board, while noting that inspection and collection of data by local authorities had brought to light a 'hitherto unsuspected need' for more and better housing, concluded that 'private enterprise has always been, and, so far as can be foreseen, will continue to be, the main source of the provision of houses for the working classes'.[4]

The idea that central government finance should be used to subsidize local-authority building gradually became acceptable to the wartime planners of reconstruction. By 1917, an Advisory Housing Panel under the chairmanship of Lord Salisbury had already concluded that existing forecasts of post-war needs were 'far too low', and that 'private enterprise cannot be expected to supply' the deficit. As a member of the Panel, B. Seebohm Rowntree submitted a Memorandum which crystallized the new thinking and, as P. B. Johnson has written, 'raised the whole level of the housing debate'.[5] He proposed, and the Panel accepted, a target of 300,000 houses in the first year of peace, to be achieved by a 'partnership of responsibility' in which the state would aid and the local authorities would own. The precise form and details of the state aid, however, remained a matter of dispute until the end of 1918. What was ultimately decided was that the 'partnership' between state and local authorities included a partnership in financial responsibility also, and that the local authority's contribution should, in effect, be limited to the product of a specific rate increase.

The housing 'emergency' of 1918 was, in fact, made up of a number of distinct causes, by no means all of which were attributable to the war. In the

Privately-built bungalow: this three-bedroom example in Nottingham cost £450 when new in 1932. Plan in text illustration 17 (*Cecil Howitt & Partners*)

Semi-detached speculation: Elmer Gardens, Isleworth. Typical plan of such houses is shown in text illustration 16 (*Radio Times Hulton Picture Library*)

Keeping ourselves to ourselves: private detached house of 1938. Traditional pitched roof rests uneasily with modern horizontally-proportioned windows. From Prizeman *Your Home, The Outside View (Blue Circle Group)*

Influence of Dudley Report: local authority houses at Knowle, Bristol, built in 1949. Porches are characteristically post-war in appearance (*City of Bristol Housing Department*)

New town interpretation of
Parker Morris: The Brow,
Runcorn New Town.
Compact brick-built three-
bedroom, five-person, houses
by Development Corporation
architects, 1969. Plan
measures 20ft 6in frontage ×
19ft 9in (6.2 × 6.0m) (*John
Mills Photography Ltd*)

High rise and fall: the
notorious Ronan Point flats,
Newham. In 1968 a gas
explosion caused collapse in
this 23-storey prefabricated
concrete tower block. The
building was similar to many
others, and the costs of
modifying this type of
structure exceeded £100m.
(*Popperfoto*)

1960s revivalist styles in speculative building, Hurstpierpoint, Sussex. *Upper left:* contemporary Regency semi-detached with slender balconies and decorated entrances. *Upper right:* chalet bungalow with eyebrow dormer, weather boarding and leaded lights. *Lower left:* 'Spanish style' detached, with integral garage. *Lower right:* smaller detached with mixed Georgian and interwar ancestry. From Prizeman *Your Home, The Outside View (Blue Circle Group)*

Terraced town houses by Eric Lyons for Span at Blackheath, late 1950s. This approach influenced much subsequent local authority and some private schemes. In this example accommodation consisted of combined living/dining room, kitchen, study, three bedrooms and bathroom. Particular attention was paid to landscaping (*Eric Lyons and Partners*)

years immediately before 1914 there had been a serious slackening in the rate of house-building which was already threatening to produce a critical shortage of accommodation in relation to the level of new family formation. Up to 1910 about 85,000 new houses had been built each year; after the introduction of the Land Values Duties in that year output fell rapidly, and in some towns scarcely balanced losses due to demolitions—in London between 1911 and 1915 more rooms were actually destroyed than built. There followed four years of war in which a mere 50,000 houses were added to the total stock, including those built for war workers, often in areas not appropriate to peacetime needs. The 1919 shortage was, therefore, the 1914 shortage accentuated. Despite the death of nearly three-quarters of a million men in the forces there had been no slackening in the rate of family formation and, therefore, in demand for accommodation.[6] Dr Marian Bowley has calculated that the shortage of houses in England and Wales at the time of the Armistice was 600,000 and by 1921 no less than 805,000.[7] The result was that many of the heroes of the trenches returned to housing conditions worse than those which they had left and were forced to share accommodation with relatives, to occupy one or two rooms in tenemented houses or inhabit a variety of 'temporary dwellings' which included wooden shacks, caravans and railway carriages often totally without sanitary arrangements. In 1921, 30 per cent of all households were living in dwellings having not more than three occupied rooms, 20 per cent were sharing dwellings with at least one other family (compared with 15·7 per cent in 1911) and 9·6 per cent of the population were living at a density of more than two adults to a room.[8]

A second, immediate, cause of the post-war housing crisis was the Rent and Mortgage Restriction Act of 1915. Passed at a time when sharply rising rents were causing widespread discontent in areas of war industry, and especially in Glasgow where a rent strike threatened to take on revolutionary overtones, the Act in effect fixed rents at the levels existing at the outbreak of war (or at the rent at which first let during the war, if not previously let). Intended only as a wartime emergency measure, the Act became politically impossible to repeal in the post-war circumstances of rapid inflation and acute housing shortage. On the other hand, the fact that rents were now artificially pegged to the levels of a vanished age meant that few, if any, speculative builders would come forward to build low-cost houses at uneconomic rents, especially at a time of rocketing costs of labour and building materials. This meant that the post-war housing shortage, though a national one, was concentrated among the lower-paid workers, and it was assumed that about two-thirds of the 'need' was for 'Class C' houses rated at not more than £13 per annum, or £20 in London. These were precisely the kinds of house which private enterprise could not now be expected to supply.

These facts in themselves constituted a quantitative problem sufficiently serious to necessitate a major change in housing policy, but, as we have seen, the war had also stimulated a social conscience about the quality of working-class life which now regarded much pre-war housing as unacceptable. The general expectation in 1918 was not only of many more houses but of greatly improved houses with standards of design, comfort and convenience previously available only to a minority. It is just conceivable that speculative builders could have provided minimum-standard accommodation at an economic rent in the post-war years, but the acceptance of the separate dwelling with ample accommodation and services made inevitable a massive contribution by local authorities which was unparalleled elsewhere in the world. 'The comfortless and badly planned house with no garden must be a thing of the past', wrote the author of *The Home I Want* in 1918, summing up the hopes of a generation: it should be of pleasing appearance, in healthy surroundings, and should provide for 'cheerfulness, breadth and quiet restfulness'.

THE TUDOR WALTERS REPORT

Against the background of a predominantly Victorian inheritance the recommendations in 1918 of the Tudor Walters Committee on the standards of post-war local-authority housing were revolutionary, constituting a major innovation in social policy and in the future character of working-class life. The Report drew upon the earlier experience of model towns and the garden city movement, on the concepts of planning developed by Ebenezer Howard, Raymond Unwin and others, and, in part, on pre-war proposals emanating from the Local Government Board itself. That much-maligned body had in 1912 recommended that cottages for the working classes should be built with wider frontages and grouped round open spaces which would form recreation grounds, that they should have three bedrooms, a large living-room, a scullery fitted with a bath and a separate WC to each house with access under cover. Five model plans were suggested, two with parlours in addition to the living-room and one of semi-detached type, with superficial areas ranging from 820sq ft to 1,230sq ft.[9] A further influence during the war itself was housing erected by government bodies, such as the Well Hall Estate at Eltham, built by the Office of Works for Woolwich Arsenal workers. These were important testing grounds for ideas in house design, and were widely reported.[10]

Nevertheless, the Tudor Walters recommendations were qualitatively different from anything which had gone before, and were to remain a standard throughout the inter-war years and, arguably, for much longer.[11] In July 1917 the Local Government Board set up, as part of the wider strategy of post-war planning, a committee to 'consider questions of building construction . . . of dwellings for the working classes'. Its chairman was Sir John Tudor Walters, MP, and, significantly, the members included

Raymond Unwin, one of the principal architects and exponents of the garden city movement. The Report,[12] published in 1918, explicitly stated that its objects were to 'profoundly influence the general standard of housing in this country', and to encourage the building of houses of such quality that they would remain above the acceptable minimum standards for at least sixty years. The Committee had listened to much expert opinion and, interestingly, had taken note of recommendations from the Women's Housing Sub-Committee of the Advisory Council to the Ministry of Reconstruction which was independently investigating the design of working-class houses, the desirable number and size of rooms, and the importance of privacy, aspect and other environmental factors. 'We regard it as essential that each house should contain as a minimum three rooms on the ground floor (living-room, parlour and scullery) and three bedrooms above—two of these being capable of containing two beds. A larder and a bathroom are essential.'[13]

On the siting and layout of working-class houses Tudor Walters recommended a maximum of twelve to the acre in towns (eight in the country) and the desirability of not covering large areas with houses all of one kind accommodating tenants all of the same social class. The advantages of culs-de-sac for cheapness and for deterring through traffic were noted, but a minimum of 70ft between opposing houses was thought necessary to allow proper penetration of sunlight in winter. A particular target of attack was the monotony of long, parallel terraces having rear access by back streets and alleys. Instead, the Report recommended secondary access at the side of semi-detached houses and by ground-floor passages through larger blocks. It was assumed that the maximum length of terrace would be eight houses, though in fact four or six were much more common.

Of the houses themselves, Tudor Walters recommended that there should be a variety of types to suit different needs and localities, but the deep, narrow-fronted 'by-law house' should be avoided for its inevitable rear projections which reduced air and light to the back of the house. Wider frontages were greatly to be preferred (the average in Tudor Walters plans was 22·6ft) as providing more air, light and garden space, and ideally the living-room should be a 'through' room from front to back of the house; in any event, it must be a large, bright room sited with reference to sunlight rather than convention. The key to internal planning was rightly located in the division between living-room and scullery, and this in turn depended largely on where cooking was to be done. Three basic plan types were therefore suggested in order of ascending cost: the simplest having a living-room with a range where most of the cooking would be done and a scullery with gas cooker for occasional use, sink, copper and bath; the second having a grate in the living-room suitable only for limited cooking, but with the bath removed from the scullery to a separate bathroom; the third having no provision for cooking in the living-room, but possessing the luxury of an upstairs bathroom. The assumption was that as living standards rose there was increasing desire for the separation of functions—that cooking would increasingly be done in the scullery although meals would be eaten in the living-room, that bathing in the scullery, still less in front of the living-room fire, was a poor alternative to the privacy of a separated bathroom. Again, each of the three basic types was planned with a superior version having a parlour and a separate bathroom. The Report made it clear that a third living-room was a reasonable and proper expectation, and that a house with a parlour was 'undoubtedly the type . . . desired by the majority of the artisan class. It contains only what is regarded by them as necessary accommodation for the proper carrying on of family life'. In fact, about 40 per cent of local-authority houses based on the Report contained parlours.

The recommendations as to space were generous by previous standards—855sq ft for the three-bedroomed non-parlour house and 1,055sq ft for the parlour type, both exclusive of fuel and other stores. With the urgent need for family accommodation, only about 15 per cent of houses were not three-bedroomed, by contrast with the estimate that of all pre-war houses some 60 per cent were only two-bedroomed. A first bedroom of about 150sq ft, a second of 100 and a third not less than 65sq ft were recommended as giving adequate separation of the sexes in the normal five-person family. The large bedroom was matched by an even larger living-room of 180sq ft, though where a parlour was also provided it might be somewhat reduced. A parlour size of about 120sq ft was thought to be adequate for the purposes envisaged—a quiet room for reading and writing, for an elderly or invalid relative, for receiving visitors not of the family and for occasional formal entertaining.

In total, the Report was thorough, imaginative and innovatory, ranging, as Christopher Powell has said, 'from the provision of door latches and rust proofing to the quality of labour and the siting of places of worship'. Yet it was by no means unrealistic or utopian. Much thought was given to the soaring costs of building and the likely shortage of skilled labour; economies of scale in the building industry were advocated and large-scale standardization of materials and fittings 'on the lines adopted for the manufacture of a motor car'. The forward-looking character of the Report is seen in recommendations such as those for district heating of houses by the use of waste heat from power-stations, the development of interchangeable building components, the need to phase public transport with the building of new estates and the advantages of more flexible by-laws which would encourage new ideas in planning and construction. In these and many other ways the Tudor Walters proposals were remarkably far-sighted and progressive, yet the external design of the houses themselves—'cottages' as they were described throughout—was firmly rooted in a vernacular, rural idiom which pictured groups of buildings of traditional appearance dotted about a landscape of winding lanes, trees and gardens. The Report was to give a particular stamp to the character of local-authority housing, almost always in new, low-density suburban estates, which at the time was accepted unquestioningly as the best and natural way of housing the urban working classes.

The translation of the Tudor Walters images into actual shapes on the ground was through the Local Government Board, the central department responsible for housing before the creation of the Ministry of Health. In 1919 the Board issued a *Housing Manual* containing advice and instructions to local authorities as to the terms on which government grants would be available. Interestingly, while adopting all the broad principles of Tudor Walters, the *Manual* was even more generous in its space recommendations—900sq ft for three-bedroomed, non-parlour houses and 1,080sq ft for parlour types, the minimum size for the living-room 180sq ft and for the scullery 80sq ft, for the larder 12–16sq ft and for the coal store 15sq ft. Every house was to have an internal WC, usually sited off a back lobby, and a bath either in a bathroom or in the scullery.[14] Like the Report, the *Manual* stressed that the new housing should 'mark an advance on the building and development which has ordinarily been regarded as sufficient in the past', and gave much attention to the planning and layout of estates for both practical and aesthetic considerations. It is still with a sense almost of surprise that one reads in the *Manual*:

> By so planning the lines of the roads and disposing the spaces and the buildings as to develop the beauty of vista, arrangement and proportion, attractiveness may be added to the dwellings at little or no extra cost. Good exterior design in harmony with the surroundings and adapted to the site should be secured . . . By the choice of suitable local materials, and the adoption of simple lines and good proportion and grouping of buildings, with well-considered variation in design and in the treatment of prominent parts, good appearance may be secured within the limits required by due economy.

HOUSING UNDER THE ADDISON ACTS

The new policy of state-aided housing was initiated by two Acts passed in 1919 by the coalition government and under the immediate supervision of Dr Christopher Addison, President of the Local Government Board and, later, the first Minister of Health. The Housing and Town Planning Act required local authorities to survey the needs of their areas for houses within three months, and then to make and carry out plans for the provision of the houses needed, with the approval of the Ministry of Health. What had been permissive powers in the Housing Act of 1890 now became mandatory. All losses in excess of a penny rate incurred by local authorities would be borne by the Treasury, provided the schemes were approved by the Ministry. In effect, the state had taken responsibility for the provision of working-class houses, since the local contribution was little more than a token and the whole intention was that ratepayers would not be subjected to an uncertain obligation. It was further provided that up to 1927 (by which time it was expected that the housing crisis would be over) rents of the new council houses should be fixed independently of costs and, in general, in line with the controlled rents of existing working-class houses. The improved amenities of the new houses might be taken into account, but so also should the capacity to pay of particular tenants for whom the houses were intended. In this way it was made quite clear that economic rents were not to be expected until the shortage was solved and normal market forces could again operate.[15] The immediate post-war housing policy was completed by the Housing (Additional Powers) Act which was designed to stimulate private builders into greater activity. A lump sum subsidy of £150–£160 was offered to any builder who built a house not exceeding a certain size either for sale or for rent; there was no restriction as to price or as to who should occupy them.[16]

For a variety of reasons which lie outside the scope of this account, the Addison Acts failed to produce working-class houses in the numbers that had been looked for. The immediate need in 1919 had been put at 500,000: by 1921, when all new approvals were stopped, 214,000 houses had been sanctioned, and in 1922 the new Minister of Health expressed the hope 'that future State intervention in any form will not be required, and that the building industry will return to its pre-war economic basis'. In reply to questions about the housing problems of newly-married couples he suggested that 'they should be so happy that they can enjoy living even in one room ... Isn't the demand of the newly-married for a separate house a comparatively modern development? In China and the East generally, I understand, they continue to live under the parental roof quite contentedly'.[17] What had particularly alarmed the government, now that the brief post-war boom had turned into depression, was the unexpectedly high cost of building under the Act—on average, about four times that of pre-war compared with a mere doubling of the general price level. In Manchester, for example, houses which had cost £250 to build in 1914 cost £1,250 in 1920, and their economic rent would have been 30s a week instead of the 12s 6d which was charged.[18] The average cost of all Addison houses was just about £1,000.

Of the quality, as opposed to the quantity, of Addison houses there was little if any complaint. Indeed, in terms of space standards at least they were the best of all inter-war local-authority houses. For the first time mass housing had the benefit of professional designing, since Dr Addison appointed a number of architects to the Housing Department of the Ministry of Health to draw up model plans for the guidance of local authorities. Most of the cottage plans were the work of S. B. Russell, FRIBA, who summarized the 'cardinal principles' of good design as 'the proper disposition of streets and buildings, a sunny aspect for the living-rooms and for as many bedrooms as possible, a cool position for the larder, easy access to the coal store both from outside and in the house, the avoidance of projections in the rear which cut off light and air, and waste in passages, staircases and landings'.[19] The plans had no binding force, and local authorities were free to modify or change them provided they kept within the spirit of the recommendations and space requirements. In fact, most authorities drew up their own plans, using their own Architects Department if they had one (more often, the Engineers Department) or employing a leading local architect for important schemes. In any event, the Ministry plans were highly influential in promulgating the expected standards and helping to shape opinion.

It is clear that in respect of space the Tudor Walters and the LGB *Manual* recommendations were interpreted very liberally and often exceeded, the first Ministry of Health Report showing that subsidies were being granted for three-bedroomed houses of not less than 950sq ft and up to as much as 1,400sq ft,[20] a size comparable with many 'middle-class' detached houses and considerably larger than most speculative semi-detached. The Ministry had issued five principal plan types which fell into two broad categories—'A' (non-parlour) and 'B' (parlour) types. The most widely-built were A3 (living-room, scullery and three bedrooms) followed by B3 (living-room, parlour, scullery and three bedrooms); a small proportion of B4s were allowed on most estates and a still smaller proportion of A2s on some. A4 was similar to A3, but with a fourth attic bedroom above the rest. As time went on, the Ministry's policy became less favourable towards variations from the A3 and B3 types, the strongest encouragement being given to A3 which in November 1920 cost about £100 less than the parlour version. Further economies were made by generally placing the bathroom downstairs, so saving piping and plumbing, and by not providing a hot-water supply to the bath; this had then to be obtained from the copper, sited either in the bathroom or in the adjacent scullery.[21]

In fact, the differing interpretations and varying degrees of skill and imagination which local authorities applied to these basic models produced a wide variety of housing types in different parts of the country. Possibly some of the best 'Addison' houses were those built in 1921 at Short Heath, near Wolverhampton, where the A3 had a through living-room 16ft by 12ft 6in with good casement windows at each end, a cooking-range and a large cupboard to one side of the fireplace. The scullery contained a glazed sink fitted with hot and cold water, a draining-board and a 'portable' gas-copper (not too popular in the colliery districts where many householders had free coal and preferred a built-in brick furnace) and provision for a gas cooker if the tenant wished to provide; there was a well-ventilated larder, and the WC and coal-store were sited in a rear lobby. Upstairs were three bedrooms 14ft by 11ft, 11ft by 10ft and 8ft 8in by 8ft and a bathroom 7ft by 5ft. The B3 houses were similar, but with the addition of a small parlour, a hot

CLASS B. PAIR, Southerly Aspect.

Ministry of Health, Plan No. 164.

Front Elevation.

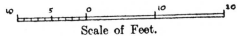

Scale of Feet.

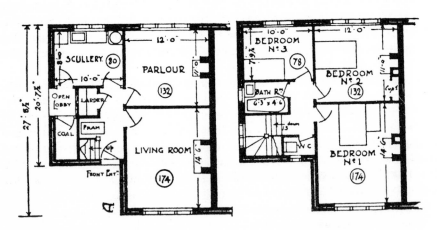

Ground Floor Plan.   First Floor Plan.

(Reproduced by permission of the Controller of H.M. Stationery Office.)

12 Tudor Walters influence. Parlour type three-bedroom semi-detached houses, designed by Ministry of Health c 1920 for local authorities. Living room 14ft 6in × 12ft (4·4 × 3·7m), Parlour 12ft × 11ft (3·7 × 3·4m), Scullery 10ft × 8ft (3·0 × 2·4m), Bedrooms also correspond to these sizes. From *The Houses of the Workers* by A. Sayle, published by Fisher, Unwin in 1928

airing-cupboard and the WC placed upstairs. In some, the standard of fittings was considerably higher, with a fitted dresser in the living-room, a fixed basin with hot and cold taps in the bathroom and large hanging cupboards in the two main bedrooms. All houses had a small front lobby, a well-lighted staircase and landing and separate access to all bedrooms. The density of twelve to the acre allowed a small front garden and a good-sized rear plot.

In London the LCC scheme drawn up in 1919 was to build 29,000 dwellings in five years to accommodate 145,000 people: in the event, 8,799 were erected under the Addison Act before its early termination. The Council's architects drew up a series of standard plans which were used on all LCC cottage estates in differing proportions and often with an admixture of three- and five-storey flats which helped to prevent monotony. The commonest cottage type was the S3 which provided a living-room 13ft 4in by 11ft 9in, a 'kitchenette' 11ft 9in by 6ft 3in, bathroom, larder and coal-store and, above, three bedrooms 17ft 11in by 9ft 2in, 10ft 10in by 9ft 3in and 8ft 6in by 7ft 8in, the larger bedrooms having built-in cupboards. Type S1 (the parlour version) had a parlour 12ft 9in by 9ft 3in with folding double doors to the living-room which thus gave a very large area 22ft 6in by 12ft 9in; in this version the bathroom was upstairs. All the Addison houses had 'secondary means of access' to the rear without passing through the house, provided by passage-ways between each pair of intermediate houses, though in post-1924 schemes this was dropped for reasons of economy. Blocks of four or six cottages were most common, the elevations being usually of a 'garden suburb vernacular' character and the general appearance was enhanced by the preservation of existing trees and the planting of greens and shrubberies.[22]

The size, organization and experience of the LCC's Architects Department, which went back to the beginning of the century, generally ensured good standards of layout and design, but not all provincial towns were so fortunate. In his survey of York in 1936 Seebohm Rowntree was strongly critical of that city's schemes which by then had built 3,297 houses on seven estates, accommodating 24·9 per cent of the working-class population. The planning had been carried out by the city surveyor all too often on the old, gridiron system of streets.

> Unfortunately . . . little or no attention was paid to aspect, the same type of plan being used whether the houses faced north, south, east or west . . . Sometimes, where an attempt has been made to introduce variety, the designs definitely drop into a lower grade. A few are quite frankly ugly. A serious blot on the whole of the estates is that adjoining most of the houses are little sheds built of brick and with flat, cemented roofs. They are intended for garden tools, bicycles and so forth, but they look like privies . . .[23]

Nevertheless, Rowntree was obliged to admit that the houses were 'immensely in advance' of what had preceded them. Instead of being built fifty per acre, there were only 10–13; many had grass verges 9ft wide and gardens of 200–300sq yd; all had baths, internal WCs, larders and coal-stores under cover—things unknown in working-class houses before 1920. The largest were the parlour houses, which made up about one in six of the council stock. These typically had front lobby 6ft by 4ft, parlour 12ft by 10ft 6in with a bow window, living-room ('kitchen' in this part of the world) of the same dimensions fitted with a range, built-in dresser, sink and gas or electric cooker for summer use, and three bedrooms 10ft 6in square, 10ft 6in by 9ft and 9ft square. The upstairs bathroom also contained a WC and a wash-basin. Modest as these were, they cost £1,137 in 1923.

In general it seems that consumer satisfaction with Addison houses was very high. Comparing the B3 with the best type of pre-war parlour house, the advantages most often cited were the convenience of planning of the rooms, the lightness, and the great value of the bathroom, now generally used for washing which had formerly been done at the kitchen sink or in basins. Comparison of the A3 with a smaller, pre-war terraced house of 'two up and two down' yielded the even greater advantage of a third bedroom, a bathroom and an internal WC. In both cases housewives almost invariably found the new houses 'easier to run' and preferred the larger living-room. Criticisms tended to centre around the parlour and, more often, the scullery. The Ministry's view of the parlour was that 12ft by 10ft, or even 10ft by 10ft, was large enough for a room mainly used only once a week, but tenants often found it difficult to fit into it the prized possessions which had formerly gone into a room typically 14ft 6in by 12ft—the piano, couch, centre table and chairs, cabinets and so on. In this and other respects tradition and sentiment died hard. More importantly, the new sculleries were often less than the 10ft by 8ft of the old, and sometimes lost some of their space to larders or bathrooms. An enquiry into the new houses carried out in 1923 by the Women's Committee of the Garden Cities and Town Planning Association noted a growing tendency to use the living-room/kitchen purely as a sitting and dining-room and to banish all work to the scullery—'the modern workshop'. It argued that this trend should be taken into account in planning larger and better-fitted sculleries with more storage accommodation and better provision for heating and ventilating. For the same reason, it was felt that cupboards and dressers in the living-room were unwanted, and that the combination range was now an expensive anachronism.[24] It was in the provision of some services that the new houses had changed least. Space heating was still by solid fuel fires in the living-room, often in the two main bedrooms, and sometimes in the scullery copper, and the inconvenience of not having a hot-water supply to the bath was considerable. Again, gas-lighting was still installed on some urban estates, though electricity was now making rapid progress. These were, perhaps, minor faults in what were generally well-designed, convenient, and often attractive houses.

HOUSING UNDER THE CHAMBERLAIN AND WHEATLEY ACTS

In 1923 another Housing Act was introduced by Neville Chamberlain, Minister of Health in the new Conservative Government. The intention was primarily to encourage private enterprise building. A Treasury subsidy of £6 a house for a maximum of twenty years would be paid either to private builders or to local authorities provided the houses were up to a required minimum but did not exceed a stated maximum size: they could then be either let or sold at any price. No subsidy from the rates was required, but Section 6 of the Act stated that local authorities would only be allowed to build if they could convince the Minister that it would be better if they did so than if they left it to private enterprise. The Act therefore constituted a complete reversal of the policy, begun in 1919, of encouraging the local authorities to become major providers of working-class housing, and even the role of State aid was strictly limited by fixing a low maximum contribution and by making it available only until October 1925. After that, it was confidently assumed, houses would be built by the unaided efforts of private enterprise.

In fact, the unreality of this optimism was soon apparent, and the subsidy was extended until 1929, though at a lower rate of £4 a house after 1927. In total, the Chamberlain Act yielded 438,000 houses over its six years of life, 363,000 by private enterprise and only 75,000 by local authorities.[25] Private house-building was undoubtedly stimulated to some extent by the subsidy, which local authorities were permitted to pay as a lump sum, varying from £75 to £100, but probably to a greater extent by falling building costs after 1920 and an expansion of home-ownership made possible by easier mortgages. The cost of the average non-parlour, three-bedroomed house fell from £930 in August 1920, to £436 in March 1922, and to £397 by 1927,[26] but these changes had little direct effect on the availability of houses for working-class renting, though they marked the beginning of an important expansion in owner-occupation for the lower middle classes.

The standards for grant eligibility were now made less generous than formerly. It was believed in government circles that housing enthusiasts had pitched their expectations too high, and that now the need was for more basic non-parlour houses which would be cheaper to build and could be let at lower rents. The Housing Act of 1923 therefore defined the superficial areas of houses qualifying for subsidy as a minimum of 620sq ft and a maximum of 950sq ft for two-storey cottages, and 550sq ft to 880sq ft for single-storey cottages, bungalows and flats. The Minister was also empowered to reduce these minima by a further 50sq ft where a local authority satisfied him that because of special circumstances in its area there was a need for smaller accommodation. The great majority of three-bedroomed local-authority houses built after 1923 had superficial areas between 750 and 850sq ft instead of the average of 900sq ft proposed in the

1919 Manual, and which had, in fact, often been exceeded.

What these changes meant in practice was not a major departure from Tudor Walters layouts and plans, but generally smaller, cheaper houses which cut down on what were regarded as inessentials. Probably one of the most serious economies was in the matter of separate rear access, which had always been provided in the early schemes. In 1924 the Ministry agreed that this could be dispensed with in houses smaller than 830sq ft, provided an internal passage-way through the house could be planned which avoided passing through the living-room or the parlour, if there were one. The inconvenience of negotiating bicycles and perambulators from the front door, through the lobby and scullery to the back of the house must sometimes have been considerable, and the undesirability of carrying dust-bins from back to front even worse. One advance introduced by the 1923 Act was the requirement of a fixed bath which, in the next year, had to be placed 'in a bathroom', but the earlier provision of boilers for water-heating now generally gave way to the use of the scullery copper, with connection to the bath by a semi-rotary pump or a syphonic apparatus. There were some economies in construction by the use of cheaper drainage systems, reduced joinery specifications, reductions in roof-pitch and smaller structural timber sizes, while externally garden walls came to be replaced by posts and wire and footpaths were reduced and simplified.[27] Some of this was merely trimming, and some desirable economy: the main losses under the Chamberlain Act were the smaller average size of houses and the preference given to non-parlour types at the very time when the standards of space in working-class housing had been making a major advance.

In 1924, only a year after the passing of the Chamberlain Act, the Labour Party came to office for the first time and another Housing Act was introduced by Wheatley, the new Minister of Health. Its primary purpose was to restore the local authorities to their position as house-providers, and to encourage them to greater activity by higher subsidies and the promise of a long-term housing programme. The new Act was a recognition that the shortage of working-class houses in 1924 was greater than it had been in 1919: that local authorities, building workers and manufacturers needed to be assured of a fifteen-year programme which would gradually raise output from the present 60,000 houses a year to between 150,000 and 225,000. A Treasury subsidy of £9 a house for forty years (£12 10s 0d in rural areas) would be granted for houses built by local authorities provided they met the same standards as those laid down in the Chamberlain Act, but only if the houses were let. Rents were to be fixed in relation to the prevailing controlled rents of pre-war houses, so the contribution of the local authorities was fixed at a maximum of £4 10s 0d a house for forty years. In practice this meant, therefore, that average rents could be fixed at a level which would prevent any loss greater than £13 10s 0d a year.[28]

The Wheatley Act, which remained in operation until 1933 (though with a reduction of the Exchequer subsidy to £7 10s 0d in 1926), is generally regarded as the most successful of the inter-war housing measures. It produced a total of 508,000 houses, all but 15,000 provided by local authorities. However, this figure needs to be seen in the perspective of the total of 2,459,000 houses built in England and Wales between 1919 and 1934, equivalent to one-third of all the houses available at the end of the war. The significant point is that out of these 2½ million new houses, only 31 per cent were built by local authorities, and of the 69 per cent built by private enterprise only one quarter had the assistance of a subsidy. The need which had been identified in 1919 for a great increase in working-class houses for renting had not, therefore, been met. Between 1919 and 1934 there was an increase of ordinary working-class houses with rateable values up to £13 of only 19 per cent, while more typically 'middle-class' houses rated at £14-26, the majority of which were built for sale, increased by 60 per cent, and houses rated at £27-£78 increased by 48 per cent.

The actual houses produced under the Wheatley Act were much the same in area and plan as under Chamberlain, though in the continuing climate of economy former minima now often became maxima. Thus, the 1927 *Housing Manual* still recommended 180sq ft as the desirable area for living-rooms, though many were now being built smaller than this, and where a parlour was also provided it was suggested that this need be 'little more . . . than a recess opening from the living-room'. The LCC, as well as developing many new cottage estates, now resumed its pre-war policy of building multi-storey dwellings, especially for the rehousing of unhealthy areas. True, the pre-war 'tenement' was now the 'flat', lighter, airier and more spacious than its predecessor. Former densities of 250-300 rooms to the acre now gave way to a maximum of 175. Every flat had its own WC and bath, a scullery which was growing into a kitchen, a larder and a coal-store, and a dust-shoot was provided on each floor. The average floor area was 20 per cent greater than in flats built before the war, and in the 1920s the Council did not normally build higher than five storeys. Two principal flat types were produced—the 'normal' and the 'simplified'. The former offered a living-room of 160sq ft, a first bedroom of 120sq ft and others of 100sq ft, units of from one to four bedrooms being provided. Each flat extended from front to back, giving through ventilation, and had balcony access with the kitchen and domestic offices at the front to minimize internal noise. Kitchens were particularly well fitted, the bath with table-top being a considerable space-saver, though the coal-fired copper was something of an anachronism. Cooking was by gas-stove, no range being provided in the living-room. The 'simplified' version had only a small scullery and WC besides the living-room and one or two bedrooms, a wash-house containing bath and copper being shared by two or three flats which opened from a common lobby.[29]

COUNCIL ESTATES AND COUNCIL TENANTS

The involvement of the local authorities in the provision of accommodation, which began importantly in 1919, constituted a minor revolution in the standards of working-class housing and living. By generally adopting the principle of cottage estates in garden suburbs it involved the dispersal of hundreds of thousands of people from crowded inner-city areas to new residential districts on the outskirts and, in some cases, to totally new planned communities far from people's former homes. The local authorities' housing policies therefore institutionalized for the working classes the process of suburbanization which the middle classes had followed since at least the middle of the nineteenth century, but developed what had been a largely unconscious process for the few into a planned policy for the many. The most spectacular developments of the 'mass

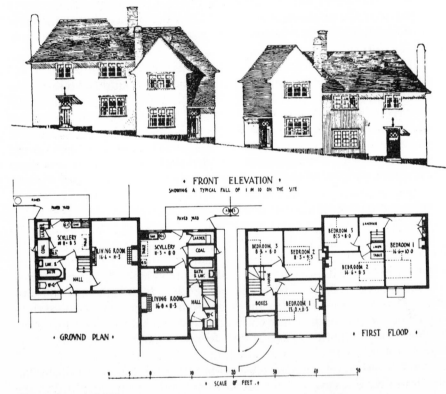

DESIGN TYPES A18, A18 1.

13   Non-parlour type three-bedroom semi-detached houses, designed by T. Cecil Howitt for City of Nottingham in 1920s. Typical living room 16ft × 11ft 3in (4·8 × 3·4m), Scullery 11ft 3in × 8ft (3·4 × 2·4m), Bedroom 1 13ft × 11ft 3in (4·0 × 3·4m), Bedroom 2 11ft 3in × 9ft 3in (3·4 × 2·8m), Bedroom 3 8ft 6in × 8ft (2·6 × 2·4m) (*Cecil Howitt & Partners, Nottingham*)

suburb' were those undertaken by the London County Council, which obtained sites outside the then boundaries of London, particularly to the east into Essex, and planted huge estates on what had been farmland and marsh. The outstanding example was Becontree, begun in 1921 and completed in 1934, by which time it accommodated 90,000 residents and was the largest planned residential suburb in the world. But what the LCC did on so massive a scale was followed more modestly by Manchester, Liverpool and Birmingham, by Nottingham, Leeds and Bristol, and by almost every town, large and small, throughout the country.

A new pattern of life was thereby created for millions of people. It almost inevitably meant a geographical separation of home from work—at Becontree, for example, there was very little industry until Ford's came to nearby Dagenham in 1931, and at that time two-thirds of the men were commuting daily to London. For housewives and children the adaptation to a new environment and a changed lifestyle were probably even more difficult, and the sociological and psychological problems of adjustment to life on large council estates which almost always lacked a familiar community structure excited much contemporary discussion and some criticism.[30] Our concern is primarily with the houses themselves, which necessarily tended towards a standardization of size and design. Two-thirds of all inter-war council houses had three bedrooms, only 4.3 per cent had one bedroom and only 3.7 per cent four bedrooms. There were fewer than 100,000 flats, making up 8.5 per cent of total dwellings, and these were in any case concentrated in London and a few other cities. Again, elevations were usually kept to a common pattern throughout an estate and often throughout all a local authority's housing schemes—usually some broadly 'vernacular' cottage style, though distinctively 'Tudor' in Nottingham's schemes and predominantly 'Georgian' at Wythenshawe, Manchester Corporation's vast satellite garden town. The more enlightened Architects Departments were aware of the dangers of mass uniformity and did much to vary layouts, the grouping of houses and elevations, yet although over ninety different types of housing were built at Becontree the development as a whole still presented a monotonous, mechanical appearance. Aesthetically, council housing was most successful on smaller estates which had natural advantages of trees and contouring, and where groups of houses could announce an individual identity, not submerged in a landscape of uniformity.

There is little doubt that the great majority of council tenants approved of what was offered to them and took a new pride in their homes, gardens and possessions. 'The thing that pleased us most when we first moved here', said one tenant, 'was to have a house of our own, with electric light and a bathroom and a scullery with running water. We'd been in two rooms in Bethnal Green, with a tap and WC three flights down and shared with two other families ... I thought [the new house] was just like a palace.'[31] Sometimes the standard of accommodation was in advance of the experience of the occupants, especially when they were removals from slum areas, and the persistent stories of 'coal in the bath' which were current from the 1920s onwards doubtless had some basis in fact. In his social survey of York, Seebohm Rowntree noted the great contrast between council houses kept by careful housewives and those of slovenly tenants, and argued that there was a case for requiring a period of training in houses set apart for the purpose before new accommodation was offered. Some families who had been used to living in overcrowded conditions found a five-roomed house expensive to furnish and heat, and instances were recorded of whole families continuing to sleep in one bedroom in order to keep warm.

Just before the outbreak of World War II, Mass Observation carried out a large-scale 'Enquiry Into People's Homes' which was particularly concerned to test satisfaction and to identify causes of complaint. It was significant that of many types of working-class housing examined, satisfaction was highest (80 per cent of the sample) on housing estates and lowest (62 per cent) in privately-rented old houses. A majority of all respondents identified their 'ideal house' as a small house in a garden. Only one in ten wanted a bungalow, and only one in twenty a flat. In general, satisfaction with homes centred around 'convenience', especially in kitchens and in facilities for children. The preferred size of house was two living-rooms in addition to the scullery/kitchen, with three bedrooms on a separate floor, and a growing preference not to eat in the room where cooking was done was noted. People increasingly wanted a 'sitting-room' away from the living/eating room, and this, together with possession of a bathroom, was the major social dividing-line. All who could afford it wanted a modern house with a bathroom—not downstairs and certainly not in the scullery. The combined bathroom/lavatory was also unpopular, and there was strong demand for a wash-basin in bathrooms. Satisfaction was lowest with kitchens, which many believed should be larger, better fitted and better ventilated. Externally, the desire for gardens and for 'privacy' (interpreted as not sharing accommodation or facilities and not being overlooked) came out as overwhelmingly important. Clearly, the 'fit' between people's preferences and what the better council houses provided was a close one, and even at Becontree/Dagenham, which the authors of the report described as a one-class suburb 'devoid of imagination' where 'a hundred thousand people have been dumped down', 85 per cent of tenants liked their houses, 63 per cent liked the neighbourhood and 14 per cent wanted to own their houses.[32]

Such reactions naturally raise questions about the tenants themselves, and especially about their economic and social status. Throughout the 1920s the policy behind local-authority housing was that it should 'bridge the gap' between what private enterprise could provide and the housing requirements of the area—that is to say, it should be for 'general needs', not only for the poor, and certainly not only for the poorest. In practice, council houses went largely to a limited range of income groups—small clerks and tradesmen, artisans and the better-off semi-skilled workers with average-sized families and safe jobs. A survey of the occupations of tenants on five of the principal LCC cottage estates showed that 22·6 per cent were skilled workers, 31·3 per cent semi-skilled, 17·1 per cent transport workers, 10 per cent black-coated workers, 5 per cent retail traders, 3·6 per cent Post Office workers and 2 per cent policemen or servicemen. Only 2·5 per cent were pensioners.[33] Similar results came from a study of the applicants for council houses in Liverpool. Their incomes were, on average, higher than those of the working classes in Liverpool generally; 20 per cent of them were non-manual workers and fewer than 7 per cent were casually employed. The average family size of the successful applicants was 4·25 persons, and normal-sized families had substantially better chances of acceptance than the unusually large or small. In the great majority of cases Liverpool council tenants paid higher rents than they had paid before moving—an average of 14s a week compared with 9s 11d in private tenures—but in return for this they now occupied an average of four rooms instead of two, and so had doubled their amount of accommodation in return for a 40 per cent increase in rent.[34]

Typically, then, the council tenant was a man in a 'sheltered' manual job which had not been seriously endangered by the depression, who earned slightly more than the average wage and had a family of two young children. Naturally there were variations in this pattern, some councils favouring families of above-average size, some aiming particular estates at income groups slightly above or below the average, but not until the slum-clearance programmes of the 1930s were housing policies specifically directed towards the poorer working-classes. Even so, there is evidence that many council tenants found the economic burdens of occupation unexpectedly and uncomfortably high. The extra costs of travel to work, the expenses of furnishing a larger house—frequently met by hire-purchase commitments—and of heating, lighting and gardening, and the higher prices which had to be paid in suburban shops which often enjoyed almost a monopoly position, were conservatively estimated at around 10s a week, quite apart from increases in rent, which often made the standard of life of men earning 50s or 60s a week precarious. On Liverpool estates in 1931/2, 29 per cent of all tenants were in arrears with rent by an average of 30s. On the LCC's Watling estate, whose tenants were described as approaching 'the élite of working-class families', there were 10 per cent of removals each year and 47 per cent stayed less than five years, the great majority of these returning to private tenancies. On the Becontree estate the 9.30 am bus to Barking on Monday mornings, known locally as 'the pawnshop bus' from the bundles which the passengers carried, was an established phenomenon. Again, a much-quoted study of rehousing in Stockton-on-Tees showed that in a sample of families removed from a slum area to a council estate the general mortality rate actually rose from 22·9 per thousand to 33·5 per thousand, the authors arguing that malnutrition had increased because of reduced expenditure on food. After increased rent and other expenses had been met, there now remained only 2s 11d per week per man equivalent for food compared with 4s 0d formerly.[35]

The housing problem continued to be unsolved in the twenties because private enterprise built very few houses for letting, because local authorities did not build sufficient houses, and because those that were built were let at rents too high for lower-paid workers, for those for whom employment was insecure, and for the unemployed whose numbers grew to reach 3,000,000 by 1931. The fundamental problem was the level of rents in relation to earnings. Although the heavy Wheatley subsidies had been specifically designed to reduce the level of rents, they could not bring council houses within the reach of the mass of poorer workers who everywhere continued to live in old, rent-restricted property, much of it turning into slums. Examples might be multiplied from many parts of the country. In Sheffield average council rents in 1932 for three-roomed houses were 10s 9d a week and for four-roomed houses 12s 11d compared with an average of 7s 6d in the old central areas of the city; 7·3 per cent of householders paid over a third of their income in rent, another 20·5 per cent more than a fifth.[36] In Manchester average council-house rents were between 13s and 15s a week, almost twice the 7s to 9s paid by slum tenants;[37] in York, the average rent of slum houses was 6s 6d.[38] Surveys repeatedly showed that the lower the income, the higher the proportion devoted to rent, and that immediately before the outbreak of World War II the poorest groups, with incomes under 40s a week, were spending 33·5 per cent on accommodation. The problem which continued to elude housing reformers was how to bring a house of acceptable standards within the means of such people.

THE ATTACK ON THE SLUMS

By the late twenties the growing belief was that council house building had now all but met the demand of those who could afford the normal, subsidized rents, and attention increasingly turned to those millions of families still occupying old, decaying and slum property who had not so far shared in the upgrading of standards of many working people. Emphasis in housing policy therefore began to swing away from 'general needs' towards 'special needs' of particular categories, and in this sense the thirties were to mark something of a return to the 'sanitary' considerations which had characterized policy in the later nineteenth century. Before a major commitment of the state to slum clearance and rehousing became acceptable, however, two less radical lines of approach were widely canvassed.

As many saw it, the problem was to bring a new house, with acceptable standards of space and convenience, within the reach of that sector of the working classes whose limit of rent was around 9s a week, including rates, rather than the 13s or more of most existing council houses.[39] The reconditioning of older property had made considerable progress in some cities, but was not thought to be the solution: no amount of 'improvement' could re-site houses from crowded city centres or basically change the problems of density, traffic, noise and the lack of social amenities. More new accommodation in an improved environment was still required, many believed, but it need not necessarily be of the same high, almost lavish, standards produced by the Housing Acts. A powerful report by the Industries Group of Political and Economic Planning argued that a reorganized building industry, taking full advantage of cost-reduction techniques, could provide 'minimum standard' working-class houses on an economic basis. At that time (1934) the smallest A3 houses were costing on average £320, which implied a rent of 11s 8d, but this might be brought down to £260 and a rent of 10s or less by setting up a large building corporation which would be able to take advantage of the economies of scale, by bulk purchase of building materials, standardization and economies in labour. The 'minimum standard' house would be built at a density of sixteen to the acre instead of twelve, and with a floor area of 700sq ft rather than 760 or more for the three-bedroomed house. The Report also noted that there was an increasing need for more two-bedroomed houses in view of smaller family size: it was suggested that probably 50 per cent of families needing separate accommodation were now in this category.[40]

The alternative line of argument was the more optimistic one that the housing problem was in process of solving itself anyway. Local-authority building was already going far to meet the needs of tenants at around 13s a week. For a higher wage-earning group—the skilled workers, foremen, clerks, small shopkeepers and junior public servants—the private housing market was now making rapid progress with new houses for owner-occupation. The chief beneficiaries of the mass provision of speculatively-built houses for sale were the expanding lower middle classes, who seized this opportunity to up-grade their housing standards by exchanging an inconvenient Victorian house in a congested part of town for a new 'labour-saving' semi-detached villa in the suburbs. But, the optimists argued, this thereby released thousands of serviceable older houses for rented occupation by the working classes, who could up-grade their own standards from terraced cottages, back-to-backs or tenements. Thus was born the convenient concept of 'filtering up', by which it was assumed that as more new houses, from whatever source, came on to the market, national standards of housing would inevitably improve as groups of people occupied the accommodation vacated by those immediately above them in the economic hierarchy. Ultimately, the slums themselves would wither away, or at least be confined to small proportions which could be dealt with by the existing processes of council activity.

'Filtering up' did not, in fact, affect the housing standards of the poorer working classes in any significant way. The argument assumed that people were mobile—physically and economically—and in the circumstances of the great depression this was not so. The unemployed, under-employed, casually employed and precariously employed were unable to move out of slums and tenements where, at least, they had some sort of roof over their heads, because they could devote no more money to rent and in many cases were in arrears to their present landlord; a new landlord would want to see some rent in advance. Moreover, the operation of the Rent Restriction Acts had the effect of deterring tenants from moving, since an empty house to which they might have moved must normally be a decontrolled house. Thus, if a tenant moved, he would lose his security of tenure, and would normally have to pay a substantially higher rent. But, quite apart from this, filtering up did not work on the expected scale because, although the total number of houses increased rapidly between the wars, it did not increase as rapidly as the rate of new family formation. Crude calculations which demonstrated that houses had grown more rapidly than population—and that therefore there ought to be more per head—ignored the fact that most people live in families, and that although families were smaller than they had been in the Victorian age, they still needed to be separately accommodated. Between 1923 and 1934 an additional 1,225,000 families were formed. When the existing housing shortage of 1923 is added to this, and the wastage of older houses by demolition is subtracted, there remained in 1934 an absolute shortage of 127,000 houses, making no allowance for what needed to be done to improve existing conditions.

By the late twenties the realisation that a decade of housing policies and programmes had had almost no effect on the conditions of the poor was beginning to lead to a demand for an effective anti-slum campaign. The development of the movement was inhibited by political divisions and by the view, widely held in some circles, that slums (like poverty) were not so much due to an unsatisfactory environment as to individual failings of personality. The opinions of Dr Hanschel, who described slum-dwellers as a 'sub-species of *Homo sapiens*' found some support. 'There exists evidence for the probability that some, at least, of this sub-species' young are like the parent, hopeless and helpless by reason of stamped-in mental defect . . .'[41] Many who did not go so far as this could still believe that slum-dwellers constituted a special problem and a special order of society principally because they were undisciplined, thriftless, shiftless and intemperate. The true nature and size of the problem was only slowly forced on to the public conscience by the accumulation of unpalatable facts and statistics which made it clear that any real solution was beyond the powers of individuals and even of local authorities.

But no amount of statistics could describe the realities of overcrowding and slum-life as it was experienced locally throughout the country—in London's 30,000 'basement' dwellings, in the chaotic jungle of narrow streets and courts in the Thames-side boroughs between Wandsworth and Deptford, in the 75,000 back-to-backs of Leeds, of which 33,000 were estimated to be unfit for human habitation, in the old, industrial hearts of the Black Country, South-East Lancashire, the West Riding, Durham, Tees and Tyneside. 'No other civilized country has such vast tracts of slumdom', wrote one observer in 1935. 'For size and density, foul air and wretchedness, the slums of Britain are in a class apart.'[42] Only 37 per cent of London families had a house or flat of their own, and one-third of London's population lived at a density of more than three people to two rooms: the Census of 1931 showed fifty-four families in the City of London living at seven or more to one room. According to her medical officer of health, Manchester had 70,000 unfit dwellings; there were still 60,000 back-to-backs in Sheffield, 38,000 in Birmingham, 30,000 in Bradford. And worse still were the hundreds of thousands of tenemented houses in the poorest parts of almost every town where families lived in one or two rooms of decayed houses, sharing one lavatory and one water-tap among thirty, forty or fifty people.

The 'anti-slum campaign', although it lacked a central organization, became one of the first social issues to evoke widespread national concern and to use modern methods of mass publicity, ranging from newspaper special reports and broadcast talks to appeals by the Church of England and speeches by the Prince of Wales. At one level, a Special Committee of the National Housing and Town Planning Council in 1928 showed that the slum problem had not improved since 1918, and that there were at least 1,000,000 unfit and 2,000,000 overcrowded houses.[43] At the other extreme, emotional and outraged accounts of slum life and its associated problems of poverty, crime and prostitution were published by Joan Conquest ('an ex-nursing sister') who described a consumptive family of seven inhabiting a 'black hole' of a damp basement at a rent of 15s a week, and a family of twelve occupying two rooms at 25s a week in a house which contained nine families, two lavatories almost always out of order, and no bath.[44]

The foundations of modern slum clearance were laid by the Greenwood Act, passed by the Labour Government in 1930 as the economic depression moved into crisis. The Act for the first time introduced an Exchequer subsidy specifically for slum clearance and, importantly, related the subsidy to the numbers of people displaced and rehoused: the intention was to prevent the pre-war practice of demolition by local authorities without replacement. Also, by basing the subsidy on people rather than houses, it would make it easier for councils to deal with the problem of large, poor families, since the subsidy would increase with the size of the family rehoused. For urban areas, the subsidy would be £2 5s 0d per person for forty years and an additional £1 5s 0d per person for forty years when the cost of acquiring sites was unusually high and rehousing would have to be provided in flats. The local authorities' rate contribution was fixed at £3 15s 0d per house or flat for forty years, and the level of rents charged was to be at their discretion. Authorities were to be free to adopt any scheme of rebates or differential renting they chose, provided that the rents were what tenants 'could reasonably be expected to pay'. Finally, local authorities were required to submit programmes of their slum-clearance plans with a view to solving the problem, if possible, within five years.

Owing to the economic crisis of 1931 and government changes, the scheme did not properly begin until 1933, when it was adopted by the Housing Act of that year. This made it clear that the government's policy would be 'to concentrate public effort and money on the clearance and improvement of slum conditions', and that private enterprise would mainly be relied on to provide further supplies of ordinary working-class houses. Official policy had implicitly abandoned any general responsibility for housing, thus overturning the policy of the Wheatley Act, in exchange for the promise of a strong commitment to slum clearance. The great loophole of the 1933 Act was, however, the absence of clear guidelines to local authorities as to what constituted a slum requiring demolition and rehousing. The programmes which were produced and accepted by the Ministry of Health totalled a mere quarter of a million out of the 9·4 million houses in England and Wales: the LCC condemned only 33,000 out of 749,000 houses, Manchester 15,000 out of 180,000, Newcastle only just over 1,000 out of 61,000.

By 1939 the official calculation of the number of slum houses requiring demolition had been almost doubled to 472,000; 245,000 had been demolished or closed, and 255,000 new houses or flats had been built in replacement, plus another 24,000 built specifically for the relief of over-crowding. At the outbreak of World War II, therefore, about half the officially admitted slums had been cleared, though it is fair to point out that more had been achieved in the five-year programme than under all the earlier schemes since 1890, and that the Ministry had accepted that 'slum clearance is a continuing process'. It could also take comfort in the fact that a further 439,000 houses had been repaired and made fit for habitation.[45]

The publicly-provided accommodation of the 1930s was affected in two principal ways by the new emphasis on slum clearance. First, although cottages continued to be the main form of provision, further economies in space and standards were an almost inevitable consequence of the drive to rehouse large numbers of former slum-dwellers on the new 'cost-per-head' basis. Standards probably reached their lowest point around 1936, and it was not without difficulty that the fundamental principles of Tudor Walters were maintained in face of pressure for the 'minimum standard house'. On cottage estates the now well-established practices of layout and density were, however, continued at twelve to the acre, not least because of sanitary considerations. Economies tended to be concentrated in the dwelling itself in favour of simpler elevations and plans, reduced floor areas and greater emphasis on three- and two-bedroomed, non-parlour types. Officially, room sizes were not changed, but what had changed in practice was the former generosity of interpretation and an increasing tendency to regard the minimum as the maximum. On some large estates where there had been continuous development over the whole inter-war period, three distinct zones of housing, representing Addison, Wheatley and slum-clearance policies, were clearly visible on the ground.

The second change brought by the thirties was an increasing emphasis on

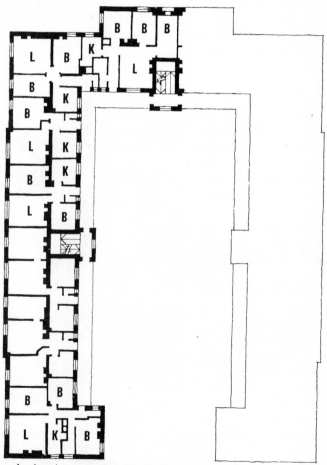

14 Local authority six-storey flats in Ebury Bridge Road, City of Westminster, 1936. Access to the fourteen flats on this typical floor is by stairs and balcony on the courtyard side of block. Key: L Living room, K Kitchen, B Bedroom. Drawing by C. G. Powell based on *Flats* published by Ascot, London in 1938

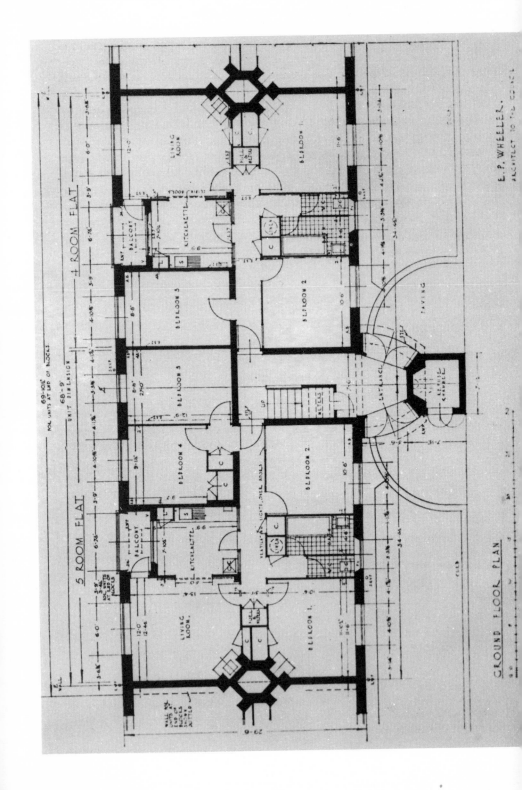

GROUND FLOOR PLAN

E. P. WHEELER.
ARCHITECT TO THE COUNCIL

the flat as an alternative to the two-storey cottage in a garden suburb. The scale of change should not be exaggerated—flats contributed only 5 per cent of total subsidized building between the wars, though 40 per cent of that in London and 20 per cent in Liverpool—but the important point was that in the thirties multi-storey living began to acquire a less grudging acceptance as a normal means of accommodation in cities. In the immediate post-war years a reaction against urbanism had held up the individual house in its own garden as the ideal, flats being castigated by leading housing authorities as 'vertical slums' and 'opposed to the habits and traditions of our people'.[46] But by the late twenties the flat movement was beginning to gain strong support from architects of the 'Modern Movement' who extolled the virtues of the Viennese workmen's flats and the scope which large structures offered for imaginative design. Environmentalists welcomed the idea of inner city development as a means of preserving the vanishing countryside, while social idealists and churchmen argued that former slum-dwellers could best be regenerated by housing them in a way which did not involve the destruction of their existing communities.[47] The practical impetus was provided, however, by the special subsidy for flats offered by the Greenwood Act, and the termination of the general Wheatley subsidy in 1933. In London, flat-building exceeded cottage-building for the first time in 1936, and by the outbreak of World War II several provincial cities had embarked on sizeable programmes—9,000 in Manchester, 5,000 in Liverpool and 1,000 in Leeds.

Whether financial or ideological considerations were uppermost is difficult to know. It is certainly not the case that flat-building was preferred because of cheapness—it soon became known that five-storey flats were between one-third and two-thirds dearer than non-parlour houses, and for the equivalent floor area almost double—though the additional subsidy must have gone some way towards equalizing costs. In terms of standards, public-authority flats of the thirties were considerably better designed and fitted than those of the previous decade, though still smaller in area than council houses. A new set of plan-types introduced by the LCC in 1934 provided for living-rooms of 150–160sq ft and main bedrooms of 110–120sq ft; two-roomed flats had a floor area of about 420sq ft, three-roomed of 530–550sq ft and four-roomed of 660sq ft. Each flat now had a separate bathroom, besides kitchen and WC, and a trend towards the use of gas and electricity for space- and water-heating is noticeable, although living-rooms continued to be built with open coal fires.[48] However, versions which were either inferior or superior to these standard types were also

---

15 LCC 'new flats', 1937. These three- and four-bedroom flats had stair instead of balcony access, larger floor areas and other improvements compared with earlier plans. Living room of four-bedroom type 13ft 4in × 12ft (4·7 × 3·7m), Bedroom 1 11ft 6in × 10ft 6in (3·5 × 3·2m) (*Greater London Council*)

built, the former going under various names such as 'simplified', 'reduced standard of finish' and 'modified', the last having reduced ceiling heights and floor areas. Some had only a recess in the living-room for a kitchenette and some, as on the Coventry Cross Estate, Poplar, a shared bathroom and washhouse for every three flats. At the other end of the scale, some highly-rented types were introduced in 1937 having internal staircase instead of balcony access, small private balconies, floor areas increased by up to 100sq ft, WCs separated from bathrooms and improved gas and electric services.[49]

Generally regarded as the most lavish of the inter-war flat developments was that at Quarry Hill, Leeds, where the Labour Council, returned in 1933, planned a massive slum-clearance and rehousing scheme within a mile of the city centre. In the words of Dr Ravetz, 'Nothing was to be spared to make it the most advanced, magnificent and luxurious estate the world had yet seen, a fitting compensation to slum dwellers for years of neglect and an architectural embellishment to the centre of Leeds'. In addition to very high standards of fittings and services, including an advanced system of refuse disposal, a radio relay system and lifts to the eight-storey blocks, particular attention was paid to communal amenities such as gardens and playgrounds, tennis courts, shops, crèches, a community hall, communal laundries and drying rooms. Although Quarry Hill was the exceptional show-place, other local authorities including the LCC, Manchester and Liverpool were also developing blocks of 'new flats' in the later thirties which did something to change the image of flat-dwelling by their standards of comfort, privacy and amenity. It is, however, significant that none of these were 'high-rise' in the modern sense, having normally only five storeys and, exceptionally at Quarry Hill, eight. Nor should the popularity of flats among tenants be exaggerated, a study of London's most modern flats in 1938 by Mass Observation showing that while 80 per cent of tenants could think of no improvement, 90 per cent liked their fitted kitchens and 78 per cent liked the neighbourhood, 60 per cent would still have preferred a small house or bungalow.

CONCLUSION

The housing history of the inter-war years shows both success and failure. The success lay in the great output of new houses, built at a faster rate than in any previous period, the greatly improved physical standards of these houses, both internally and externally, compared with the Victorian provision for the working classes, and the powerful attack which had been mounted on the slums in many parts of the country. In the twenty years before 1939, 3,998,000 new houses were built, 1,112,000 by local authorities and 2,886,000 by private enterprise of which 430,000 were subsidized. In round numbers, therefore, state-aided housing contributed $1\frac{1}{2}$

million of the 4 million new homes. This meant that in 1939 approximately one-third of all houses were new, representing a major change in the age composition, and in the standards of amenity, of the housing stock. This upgrading was especially rapid during the great building boom of 1933–8, when an average of 334,000 houses a year were produced. Reformers could optimistically believe in 1939 that the housing 'shortage' was all but over, and that if such rates were continued the future problem would be qualitative, not quantitative.

One reason for the false optimism was, quite simply, ignorance, for until the results of the 1931 Census were published it was not known how rapid had been the rate of new family formation. All previous calculations based on projected population growth—which was correctly assumed to be declining—instead of on the growth of families, now proved to be hopelessly wrong. But the other outstanding reason was that a clear and consistent housing policy had not been pursued between the wars. In terms both of numbers and of standards, housing had been a political football kicked backwards and forwards between the opposing parties. One had put its faith in private enterprise and accepted state aid only as an emergency measure; the other had attempted to make public housing part of the normal social responsibility of government, but had lacked the political power and the economic resources to do so. In summarizing the housing conditions of the working classes on the eve of World War II, one could follow the same fractions which John Boyd Orr used in describing their nutritional status: about one-third well housed in new, healthy accommodation, a second third inhabiting older, 'by-law' houses, sanitary but lacking in modern amenities and comforts, and a remaining third in very sub-standard property, much of it slum or rapidly becoming so. Housing problems and housing issues were, therefore, far from resolved in 1939, when they had to be thrust into the background for the next six years.

9

SPECULATIVE HOUSING, 1918–1939

Between the two world wars new shapes on the ground began to appear all over England on the edges of the towns and cities, in the suburbs, along the arterial roads, in the coastal resorts and even in the remote villages, which by their number and external similarity might seem to suggest to an outside observer that some new race or class had suddenly appeared, clamorous for accommodation. In the development of English housing types, middle-class housing of the inter-war period, most typically represented by the semi-detached villa situated in a newly-developed suburban area, seems to mark a disjunction with the past, and an entry into a new era of mass housing still today the most characteristic expression of English domestic architecture.

Such housing was, in fact, the response of the building industry to the needs of a middle class which had greatly swollen in size but was poorer than its Edwardian predecessor. In some respects it was, indeed, a new class, for its composition had burst out of the rigid confines of the nineteenth-century social structure to admit new occupations which were neither 'professional' nor 'gentlemanly'. World War I brought a large increase in the number of non-manual workers, benefiting from the profits of industry and commerce, the expansion of administrative and executive posts and the demand for more civil servants, scientists and specialized technicians. Subsequently, in the twenties and thirties the economy continued to demand more personnel in service and 'tertiary' occupations such as management, teaching, administrative and clerical work, retailing, distribution and entertainment, and fewer at the level of primary production in factories, shipyards, coal-mines and on the land. If the 'white-collar worker' was not strictly born between the wars, he grew to manhood then. Most significant was the growth of the professional classes, from 744,000 in 1911 to 1,493,000 forty years later, but also striking was an almost threefold increase of clerical workers and a doubling of foremen, inspectors and supervisors. On the basis of non-manual occupations, the middle class increased from 20·3 per cent of the total population in 1911 to 30·4 in 1951.

Here was a great army of new recruits to the class, keenly anxious to demonstrate their arrival by the adoption of a life-style which separated them from the respectable poverty from which many had risen. To live in a new suburb rather than an old, overcrowded town, in a detached or semi-detached villa rather than a terraced or back-to-back house, above all, to be able to buy a house instead of merely renting it, and to luxuriate in the sense of security and achievement which property-owning brought, were their predominant ambitions. The new arrivals shared with the older members of the class the belief that family and home were the central life interests, and that the house, which enshrined these institutions, had an importance far beyond other material objects. But the new recruits almost always entered the class at the bottom, and the growth of numbers was therefore mainly downwards into categories of occupation and income which only just qualified for admission. The Victorian middle class grew mainly by accepting a larger 'lower middle class' whose aspirations, though similar, were necessarily more modest. At the same time, many members of the traditional middle class were experiencing reductions in wealth, with consequent effects on their standards of life. Wartime and post-war inflation hit hard at those living on fixed incomes and lagging salaries, while greatly increased income tax cut earned incomes and profits substantially. On the eve of World War I the standard rate of income tax stood at 1s 2d in the pound. By 1918 it had reached 5s, and it remained at 4s–5s between the wars until raised to even higher levels in 1939.

The sharp bite of taxation on the 'older' middle classes, coupled in some cases with the effects of economic depression, resulted in some significant changes in patterns of expenditure. Many middle-class families were forced to economize on their large houses, their domestic staffs and the public-school education for their sons which had formerly been the most recognizable characteristics of the class. The sharply mounting costs of private education could be met in part by smaller family size, the long-term decline of which reduced the average number of children per family from 5·8 in 1871 to 2·2 in the 1930s. Increasing taxes, local rates and the wages of domestic servants could only be met by smaller houses which could be run by one or two staff rather than three or four, or even, if need be, by none at all. The result was, therefore, a growing convergence of standards between the established members and the new entrants to the class, reflected, among other things, by an increasingly standardized type of house appropriate for a small family with little domestic help.

THE PROVISION OF HOUSES

Between the wars private building made a remarkable effort to meet the housing demands of this group, extending the possibility of home-ownership well down into the lower middle classes and even into the upper levels of the working classes. By the 1930s a regular salary or wage of £200 a year was widely regarded as adequate security for a mortgage which might involve repayments of as little as 9s a week, well within the reach of engineers, fitters, printers, engine-drivers and other skilled workers. New houses have probably never been so cheap or so widely available as in the mid-thirties, when, it has been calculated, the length of time that a man earning the average industrial wage would have to work in order to buy one was 2·5 years.[1] In total, between 1919 and 1939, 3,998,000 new houses were built, 2,886,000 by private builders and 1,112,000 by local authorities. Starting practically from standstill in 1919 after five years' dislocation by war, the building industry delivered no fewer than 1,617,000 houses in the boom period 1935–9, with private-enterprise housing reaching particular peaks of 287,500 houses in 1935 and 275,200 in 1937. Thus some 72 per cent of all houses built between the wars were built by private enterprise, and of these the vast majority were built for sale rather than rent. The consequence was an important shift in the tenure of property towards house-ownership. In 1947 (when the position had changed little since 1939), 27 per cent of houses in England and Wales were owner-occupied, the highest proportions being in the Midlands (32 per cent) and the South and East (29 per cent), and the lowest in London (23 per cent).

Our concern here is with the products of the speculative builder who catered, very broadly, for an income level of around £200–£600 a year with houses costing about £400–£1,000 in the Greater London area and about £300–£800 elsewhere. At around £1,000 a purchaser would generally expect an individual, architect-designed house, probably detached and standing in a quarter- or half-acre plot, though in some sought-after London suburbs speculative builders occasionally asked up to £1,250 or more for large semi-detached houses. The lower limit was also variable, with small houses and bungalows in cheap parts of the country sometimes offered for as little as £250. It must also be remembered that property values changed sharply over the twenty-year period in line with general movements in costs and prices. In the immediate post-war years a pent-up demand combined with scarcities of materials and general inflation to force up house prices to unprecedented levels, especially in the London area, where at Mill Hill in 1920 cottages with only two bedrooms, one living-room and a tiny kitchen 8ft 3in by 6ft 9in cost £1,100 without land, and at Sanderstead three-bedroomed semis cost £1,200.

Prices began to fall from the summer of 1920, reducing building costs per square foot from over £1 in early 1920 to 9s 4d by 1922, and the price of a small, three-bedroom, non-parlour house from £930 to £436. From 1923 onwards the rate of building climbed steadily, apart from temporary setbacks in 1927–8, and prices continued their downward drift; by 1932 three-bedroom, two-reception-room semis were being offered by Blackwell and Meyer of Bexleyheath for as little as £395 freehold and £295 leasehold.[2] At the top end of the market A. W. Curton in 1935 offered large semis in Edgware with six bedrooms, three reception rooms and a breakfast-room at £1,785, while a few luxury speculative semis were offered at Osterley for as much as £2,500. By the later twenties the range for the 'standard' two-reception and three-bedroom semi in Greater London was around £600–£850, but in the boom after 1932 most builders concentrated on the lower end of the market, opened up by the easier availability of mortgages to better-paid manual workers. Much depended on the social status of the suburb, the plot size—especially the frontage—and the number and size of rooms, but in the years immediately before the outbreak of World War II many semi-detached houses were available in Greater London in the range £400–£600, and in provincial towns at up to £100 less. On the outskirts of Loughborough a small semi-detached bungalow could be had for as little as £250.

Low interest rates, low material costs and low wages were combining to bring about a housing revolution which profoundly affected the lives of millions of people. The creation of a mass market for home-ownership depended on the expansion of building societies which, although well-known since the Act of 1836, had generally been small-scale, local and little developed.[3] In 1910, 1,723 societies advanced £9,292,000 on mortgage during the year, the total balance due on all mortgages being £59,696,000.[4] By contrast, in 1938, £137,000,000 was advanced (and in 1966, £1,244,750,000). For the borrower the critical questions were the amount of deposit and the monthly repayments required, which naturally varied with the cost of the house and the state of the credit market. The societies did not work so closely together in these matters as they were to do subsequently, but it may be said that in general up to about 1930 most societies required a 25 per cent deposit but that after this easier credit facilities reduced the requirement to only 5 per cent or 10 per cent of the society's valuation. Societies worked on the general principle that outgoings, including local rates, should not exceed one-quarter of net income, which, at the prices prevailing in the twenties, meant a minimum salary or wage of about £4 a week allowing repayments of 15s a week upwards on a modest house. More common were repayments in the range £1–£1 10s 0d a week, and in any case societies needed to be assured of a regular income, especially in a period of mass unemployment.

With cheaper house prices and lower interest rates in the thirties the possibility of a mortgage spread from white-collar occupations to ieast some higher-paid manual workers. £500 'Arcadia' houses were advertised in 1936 with repayments of 13s a week as available to those earning the 'normal workers' wage of £3 15s 0d', while the New Ideal Homesteads £395 house was available for 9s a week plus rates. These were, however, untypically cheap, and not many houses were built at such prices. Generally in the thirties around £1 a week bought the standard three-bedroomed

£650 house, while earnings of £300–£500 a year (teachers, bank officials, Executive Class civil servants and lower-paid professionals generally) would comfortably buy substantial semis or even detached houses of £1,000 or more. The major difficulty for the lower-income groups was the deposit rather than the repayments. In a period of embarrassingly swollen assets after 1931 the societies offered mortgages at 5 per cent and 4½ per cent interest, extended the repayment period from 15–20 years to 25–30 years, and developed various devices to reduce the amount of the deposit and the legal and survey charges. Especially important in developing the lower end of the market was the Builders' Pool system, under which the builder himself advanced cash to the society to make up most of the difference between the mortgage and the valuation, so limiting the purchaser's deposit to 5 per cent or even less. With life assurance policies or occupational pension schemes as security the deposit could sometimes be remitted altogether, and even the legal charges covered by slightly increased repayments. By the later thirties the speculative housing market was glutted, and builders in fierce competition with each other were anxious to make house-purchase as painless as possible by negotiating the most advantageous terms for their clients. By 1938, 1,300,000 borrowers were taking advantage of the buyer's market to move into home-ownership and a growing proportion of them—37 per cent in the case of the Abbey Road Society—were wage-earners.[5]

LOCATION

Three major influences affected the provision of middle-class housing in the period—location, transport and the building industry. Almost inevitably by now, a new house meant one outside the existing city centres and urbanized areas, and to that extent the question of 'where to live' was an easier one than it had been for the Victorians. In practice it usually meant a choice between a speculator's suburban development lying 10–15 miles from the centre of London and up to 5 miles from the middle of Birmingham or Nottingham, or a more remote commuter village in process of transformation into a higher-income dormitory. The long-established movement outwards to the periphery was now strongly reinforced by improved means of communication, both public and private, by shorter working hours and by the desire of the socially mobile to escape from the undesirable associations of city life. Inevitability therefore combined with preference to produce the suburb as the most characteristic form of housing development of the period. The prerogative of the wealthier in Victorian times was now within the reach of a much broader class who did not need to be at the office until 9 o'clock, had a day and a half or two days' break at the weekend, and enjoyed holidays with pay and the prospect of a superannuated retirement, but the intentions of the new suburbans were probably much the same as those of their predecessors had been. 'It is not clear what is the precise motive in this exodus', wrote Martin S. Briggs in 1937,

> whether it is a love of gardening, whether it is considered good for such children as are still occasionally born, or whether the sight of trees and fields is the chief attraction. Probably this obscure process is a form of nostalgia, because many suburban people are country-born, and it may account for the love of 'half-timber' gables, leaded lights, inglenooks, and all the supposed concomitants of the rustic cottage which make many cheap villas look so ridiculous, but it is certainly strong enough to compel the family breadwinners to travel long distances to work, strap-hanging in crowded trains . . . Two hours so spent every day is a terrible waste of time and nervous energy![6]

This assumption that every Englishman was, or felt that he was, a disinherited country gentleman accorded reasonably well with the image of some inter-war suburbs where houses exhibiting rural rather than urban characteristics were disposed at low densities (usually not more than twelve to the acre) in general pursuance of garden city principles. A carefully-designed development would be marked by a variety of house-styles, winding roads, closes and crescents, generous gardens, tree-plantings and grassed verges. But often the speculative suburb lacked any overall plan, being developed road by road by numerous builders until the land ran out. Again, it was very common for new suburbs to develop along and behind existing main roads because services (water, gas, electrical and sewage conduits) were easily accessible, and a much smaller charge for road-making could be set against each house than when new roads were constructed at right angles to the existing. The result of such activity was sometimes a long sprawl of monotonously similar semi-detached houses, along a busy arterial road, backed by a waste of derelict agricultural land and remote from amenities such as shops, schools and stations.[7]

There were, of course, sharp social differences between this kind of anonymous development and that of more fashionable suburbs such as Edgware, Mill Hill or Northwood. Such social differentiation was made explicit by the Town Planning Act of 1932 which introduced the concept of 'zoning' by which districts were scheduled for development at differing densities from twelve houses to the acre down to only one to the acre. Yet whatever their particular place in the hierarchy of snobbery, all suburbs shared the same characteristic of one-family houses in gardens and in an environment more or less removed from the dirt, noise and congestion of the city. The alternatives—a modern 'flat' close in to the centre or a cottage or bungalow deep in the disappearing countryside—were, as we shall see, attractive or possible only for a tiny minority.

To its critics the spreading suburb was an endless target for sarcastic humour directed at its derivative architecture, bourgeois attitudes and petty snobberies. Builders played upon the sensitivities of their customers by stressing the selectivity of their developments, Novean Homes addressing their advertisements to 'families of good breeding who wish to acquire a house to be proud of at a cost of less than £1 a week'. The naming of roads as Drives, Avenues, Lanes and Way(e)s to evoke rural images was also important. Much was also made of the healthiness of suburban life, a theme which chimed in well with the open-air cult of the thirties: estates were described as being in 'clear, brilliant air', 'high above the fog belt and the probability of floods', and 'amid the fairyland of Surrey' (Tattenham Corner), while one enthusiastic builder claimed that 'a summer at Feltham has the health value of a trip round the world'. Diminutive semis were described as 'Cosy Palaces' with 'Baronial Halls', and 'Every One Different' was applied to basically identical houses; 'The Monk's House' and 'The Sunshine House' were obvious subjects for the satire of Osbert Lancaster, who identified for the intelligentsia the new architectural styles of 'Stockbrokers' Tudor', 'Wimbledon Transitional' and 'By-Pass Variegated'.[8]

Many inter-war suburbs were, indeed, the very opposite of Ebenezer Howard's vision of the garden city which would combine the advantages of town and country, for they had the advantages of neither. The nineteenth-century upper-middle-class suburb could be admired—or, at least, understood—as an expression of romantic idealism, but what, asked Lewis Mumford, could possibly justify the formless, tasteless, mass suburb, 'a multitude of uniform, unidentifiable houses, lined up inflexibly, at uniform distances, on uniform roads, in a treeless communal waste, inhabited by people of the same class, the same income, the same age-group . . . The ultimate effect of the suburban escape in our time is, ironically, a low grade uniform environment from which escape is impossible'.[9] Yet the new suburbans were impelled by the same kinds of drive and probably achieved the same kinds of satisfaction as their predecessors. Old or new, the suburb represented, as Mumford rightly observed, 'the collective attempt to lead a private life', and in particular it provided the ideal environment in which to locate and operate the domestic ethic. For the lower-income groups who increasingly composed the suburban residents, work was not the 'central life interest' so much as a means to an end, and satisfaction was found in family and house-based activities centred around the children, gardening, home-improvement and home-bound leisure activities. The social anonymity and lack of intellectual or cultural amenities of suburban life both encouraged and obliged such preoccupations, while the interest and pride which the new home-owners lavished on their property provided an important outlet for demonstrating individual abilities and individual social and economic gradations. It may be, too, that the suburban concentration on the small nuclear family accommodated in a single-family dwelling was a compensation for the reduced area of kinship and social contacts involved by the removal from more densely populated urban areas. The fact was that, for all its limitations and failings, the suburb represented

16 Selling the semi-detached: an advertisement for speculative houses c 1937. This typical plan has drawing room 12ft × 15ft into bay (3·7 × 4·6m), Dining room 14ft × 6in 10ft 9in (4·4 × 3·3m), Kitchen 11ft × 7ft (3·4 × 2·1m), Bedroom 1 11ft × 15ft into bay (3·4 × 4·6m), Bedroom 2 14ft 3in × 11ft (4·3 × 3·4m), Bedroom 3 7ft 2in × 6ft 9in (2·2 × 2·1m) (S. E. Rasmussen, *London: The Unique City*, Cape, 1938)

a kind of utopian ideal, an arena for a new and better life for family and children, based on a house with substantially improved space and amenity standards. As J. M. Richards observed, these modest semis were the 'castles on the ground' for a first generation of proud house-owners, and because such houses represented the ambition of the great majority of English people they were the true contemporary vernacular style whose origins lay in the English Picturesque tradition and the English school of landscape gardening.[10]

TRANSPORT

The mass suburb could not have occurred without greatly improved travelling facilities, private and public, and many suburbs, especially in the Greater London area, were virtually created by underground and rail extensions. For the middle and upper middle classes the motor-car became increasingly important between the wars as the vehicle for the journey to work or, in remoter districts, the journey to the local railway station. Car-ownership, which had totalled only 32,000 in 1907 and 109,000 in 1919, increased dramatically to 2,000,000 in 1939.[11] Urban road improvements and the construction of new arterial roads and 'by-passes' such as the North Circular and the Kingston By-Pass improved access to the cities and provided scope for speculative building along their routes. But a motor-car at a minimum cost of £100 remained something of a luxury for most white-collar workers in the period, and for them the important changes lay in the development of public transport. For provincial towns and cities, where the new suburbs still often lay no more than three or four miles from the centre, electric tram and trolley-bus extensions and, even more important, the inception of motor-bus routes, were the crucial changes. The flexibility of the motor-bus, which could reach into hinterlands and beyond the built-up areas independently of rails or overhead wires, eventually gave it the victory over other forms of urban transport. Bus services were especially convenient for new suburban areas lying off existing main roads, and in some of these 'builders' buses' were offered as an initial inducement to purchasers until a local authority or private contractor should supply a service.

The vast expansion of London suburbia between the wars was much more due to rail and underground extensions which brought new areas up to distances of twenty miles or more within the attractive influence of the capital.[12] The boom period of Greater London house-building, almost all of it suburban, developed from 1926 onwards when the annual output rose from 25,200 to a peak of 72,700 in 1934. In total, between 1921 and 1937, 1,400,000 people moved to outer London, the population of the central area falling by 400,000. By about 1928 bus services had reached to every London suburb of any size, linking them to the new stations along the extensions of the Underground and Metropolitan lines: in 1924 the Northern line was extended to Edgware, in 1933 the Piccadilly line to Cockfosters, while sections of the Southern Railway were electrified in the twenties to bring a faster service to the developing commuter villages around Guildford. Direct advertisement by the railways, naïve as it now seems, probably played an important part in enticing residents to the new districts. Thus the Underground advertised:

> Stake your Claim at Edgware. Omar Khay-yam's recipe for turning the wilderness into paradise hardly fits an English climate, but provision has been made at Edgware of an alternative recipe which at least will convert pleasant, undulating fields into happy homes. The loaf of bread, the jug of wine and the book of verse may be got there cheaply and easily, and, apart from what is said by the illustration, a shelter which comprises all the latest labour-saving and sanitary conveniences. We moderns ask much more before we are content than the ancients, and Edgware is designed to give us that much more.[13]

Perhaps the best-known advertising guide was the Metropolitan's *Metroland*, the name being first coined in 1914 for a booklet which was issued annually from 1919 onwards with increasing amounts of space given to housing developments. In close association with the railway company, new estates were developed at Neasden, Wembley Park, Pinner, Rickmansworth, Chorley Wood and along the Uxbridge branch at Rayners Lane, Eastcote, Ruislip and Hillingdon. 'My Little Metro-land Home', a vocal one-step, was published in 1920.

THE BUILDING INDUSTRY

The vast majority of the new houses were designed by the builders themselves, without benefit of architects, and consisted largely of variations on a standard plan dictated by plot size and, ultimately, by cost.[14] Most purchasers, with little or no experience of planning procedures or building construction, were probably only too glad to be able to choose from a variety of completed houses or from the 'show houses' by which speculative builders advertised their developments. 'House-hunting' became a popular weekend activity between the wars. In any case, the individual, architect-designed house, not part of an estate development and therefore unable to take advantage of the economies of scale, would normally have to be placed in a much higher price-bracket. In 1925 it was said that 'to employ one's own architect and to build to special specifications' was not normally possible for houses costing less than £1,000[15] and in H. Myles Wright's collection of architects' plans for 'small houses £500–£2,500' published in 1937 very few indeed were less than £1,000 despite the fall in costs. Architects' fees on a £1,000 house were there given as £80, and on a £2,000 house as £120.[16] A noticeable change was beginning to occur, however, in some of the larger and more reputable firms engaged in large estate developments in Greater London and other areas. John Laing and Sons, the civil engineering firm which entered the speculative housing market in 1930, set a new trend by employing a panel of architects to design their three- and four-bedroomed detached houses, and at Strawberry Hill, Twickenham, no less a figure than Sir Henry Banister Fletcher, the famous architectural historian, was engaged to design an estate of houses 'all different'. Crouch, Wimpey, Berg and other large building firms came to use professional architects in the thirties with generally good results in their designs and site layouts, though in the provinces the small firms who typically built only half a dozen houses or so a year rarely found it necessary or worthwhile.

Much criticism was directed, at the time, at the quality of speculative building, the term 'jerry-built' often being applied indiscriminately to almost all lower-priced housing. The most common complaint of the architects was that intense price competition as builders vied with each other to reach the lower end of the market had forced down the quality of work and materials, and obliged builders to concentrate on external appearance and 'gimmicks' which would sell the product. The client was offered mock Tudor beams, imitation leaded lights, pebble-dashed brickwork and, internally, tiled bathrooms or carved staircases instead of cavity walls and solid workmanship. The gains and losses are not easy to weigh. The inter-war purchaser almost certainly got more for his money, both in terms of size and amenity, but he probably sacrificed lasting quality and, if he stayed long enough, had to meet heavier repair costs. A Danish observer has argued that English housing of the period was flimsier in construction than on the Continent because of the persistence of 'the cottage ideal' and the determination to have a separate house with as many rooms as possible. The Englishman on the Continent or in America 'will long for his lightly-constructed house, where the damp winter air whistles through the rooms accompanied by the rattle of the doors and the windows'.[17]

In fact, many higher-priced speculative houses were extremely well built, both by previous and subsequent standards, using traditional methods and materials such as hand-made bricks and tiles, stone and hardwoods which now place them in the luxury class. Even low-priced houses built by a conscientious firm could make confortable, efficient houses, as a leading architect confirmed:

> Let it be admitted ... that he [the speculative builder] is very often a benefactor. How many of us older people can recall the occasion when we first saw the small house that solved all our problems! In my own case, it was not only very small and very attractive, but also incredibly cheap. We lived in it for many years, yet in all that time no glaring defects revealed themselves, and nothing went wrong. The planning was extraordinarily compact, the various fittings and appliances functioned satisfactorily, and the fireplaces and the simple mouldings were in good taste. It was, in fact, a house that a young architect was not ashamed to occupy ...[18]

Competition for the unwary customer too often led to concentration on the superficial and showy, but it also speeded up improvements in standards in both space and equipment, and in the use of new materials and methods of organization. The 11in cavity wall, the bituminous sheeted flat roof, glazed panels for use in bathrooms and kitchens, rubber and lead-sheathed flexible electric cables and the use of plywood and similar materials in large areas were all examples of thoroughly satisfactory products which first appeared, or were finally proved, during the housing boom. Again, the larger firms tended to set the pace, Costains using cavity walls from 1924 onwards when they were still uncommon in modestly-priced houses, the Berg brothers in south London pioneering the hall-to-hall semi and the integrated garage. Reputable builders often set very high standards for their speculative estates, John Laing in the thirties requiring cavity walls, oversize timbers in roofwork, tiles laid over roofing felt, concrete foundations under partition walls, copper hot water cylinders and pipes, steel joists above window bays, all hidden woodwork primed before being placed in position, and so on. The concern of the larger builders both to raise standards generally and to receive credit for their own rectitude led, in 1937, to the formation of the National Housebuilders' Registration Council under the chairmanship of Sir Raymond Unwin, a voluntary body which extended membership to firms prepared to build to standard specifications and to give purchasers a two-year warranty to repair defects. More than a thousand firms registered during the first year, including most of the large London builders who used the guarantee in their advertisements.[19]

A notable feature of house-building at this time was the increasing importance of the services or fittings demanded by the purchaser, which had the effect of reducing the proportion of total cost which could be given to the basic fabric. In the past, houses had not been much more than shells containing windows and fireplaces, but having almost no other equipment for heating, lighting, washing or cooking. Lewis Mumford has calculated that in 1800 the structure alone represented almost nine-tenths of the value of the house and land. Throughout the nineteenth century there was a slow but regular increase in the amount necessary for land and apparatus, until about 1900 the curve began to take a sharp turn upwards as the house systems such as heating, lighting and plumbing became more sophisticated and costly. By the 1930s these were accounting for approximately one-third of the whole cost, and, with land, as much as half of the total cost.[20] The house was increasingly becoming a shell to contain a range of complicated services—water, drains, gas, electricity, heating and lighting systems and so on—which, some architects hoped and believed, would ultimately transform it into 'a machine for living in'.

Prospective purchasers not only expected their houses to be brighter, cleaner, more comfortable and easily-run than their parents' had been, but that amenity should go with appearance. A bathroom with a fixed bath and hot and cold water supplies was, no doubt, a good thing in itself, but infinitely preferable if the bath were enclosed, the walls half-tiled, the taps and shower-attachments chromium-plated. Particular importance was attached to the fitting and convenience of the kitchen now that many middle-class housewives were having to venture for the first time into the former domain of the cook, or, at best, were seeking to entice that vanishing race to stay. The result of the combined pressure for amenity and display was that even low-priced speculative houses were expected to include services and fittings which would have been found only in much more expensive, architect-designed houses before 1914. Thus, the New Ideal Homesteads Type K house, costing £595 in 1934, included such things as two-way light switches in the hall and landing, gas and electric power points at the fireplaces, tiled surrounds and solid mahogany or oak mantels, a back-boiler to the dining-room fireplace to supply hot water, French casement doors to the garden, a kitchen tiled to dado height and fitted with sink, draining-board, kitchen cabinet, larder and two gas points, tiled fireplaces in the two main bedrooms, a heated linen cupboard and a wardrobe cupboard. Berg houses of the period, selling at just over £1,000, had 11in cavity walls of facing brick or stucco to choice, an integral garage 14ft 8in by 8ft, Crittall steel-framed windows with leaded lights, front doors in oak or pine, narrow strip British Columbian pine floors, curtain rails and boxes, pedestal wash-basin and shower fitting with mixer, copper piping throughout and loft pipes lagged, while A. W. Curton's £1,200 detached house of 1935 had a solid oak handrail and newel posts with pedestal lamp to the staircase, oak-panelled walls to the dining-room, a gas washing-machine in the kitchen, a marble dado in the bathroom, an Ideal coke boiler or gas circulator for water heating, and a separate lavatory with 'low-down' suite.

These improvements in fittings and amenities in the home were, perhaps, more important than any changes in design or spatial standards. The increased comfort and convenience of heating, lighting and cooking by electricity were especially significant. Whereas in 1910 only 2 per cent of houses were wired for electricity, by 1939 some 75 per cent were; of these, 30 per cent had a vacuum-cleaner, and 80 per cent an electric iron. In 1939 nine million wireless licences were issued.[21] Such amenities were rapidly becoming the desired criteria of a modern house and, particularly by the thirties, builders had to pay increasing attention to these relatively expensive 'service' aspects of their houses. In order to be able to offer so much, builders had to make very fine calculations as to the cost of land, labour and materials, and, as in the past, they were critically dependent on the movement of interest rates for the advances they had to borrow. After their high levels in the immediate post-war years, building costs began to fall after 1926 to reach their lowest level in 1934; similarly, high interest rates in the twenties were reduced drastically after the economic crisis of 1931, with the National Government deliberately stimulating a 'cheap money' policy.

Between 1929 and 1938 investment in residential construction absorbed not less than half the total of domestic investment, and builders now found little difficulty in raising loans from banks, building societies and private individuals at rates around 4 per cent. They were also helped by generally low land prices, though these varied considerably between the nearer and farther suburbs, and between fashionable and less fashionable districts. Since frontage to the road was the dearest aspect, and the normal basis of cost, this determined the typical shape of plots as narrow and long, utilizing every foot of frontage as economically as possible. For the cheapest semis plots were often only 20–25ft wide, for those with a garage or, more commonly, garage space, 30–35ft. A detached house would typically require 40–50ft, while beyond this would take one into fractions of acres and beyond the limits of speculative building. Some larger developers took pains to preserve trees and other natural features, and to landscape their estates with winding roads and closes, grass verges and even communal greens and gardens, but all too often the cheaper houses were set in parallel rows, on identical-sized plots, facing each other across the regulation building-line and distinguishable mainly by their decoration and subsequently–added garage excrescence. To quote typical land costs could be misleading where variations were so great. One contemporary authority suggests that £5 a foot frontage was the average for London suburbs,[22] but plenty of outer suburban and provincial land was bought at £100 an acre or less, which could imply plot costs of as little as £10.

By the general standards of industry and commerce, speculative builders operated on small margins of profit. Building costs in the thirties generally ranged between 10d and 1s 4d a cubic foot, with 1s as an average, implying about £400–£500 as the basic cost of a house of 1,000sq ft. A net profit of

10 per cent represents a fair average for this period, with a range between 7 per cent and 14 per cent. A builder at Feltham, Middlesex, who made £79 profit on houses selling at £425 and £550 seems to have done unusually well. Keen competition usually kept the margins low, and builders had to devote increasing amounts to advertising and sales promotion which sometimes included floodlighting and firework displays on their estates. Free season tickets for up to a year, turfed and planted gardens, furniture, extra kitchen equipment and, in one case, a free motor-car with a £1,000 house were extra temptations for the newly-married couple at whom much of the publicity was aimed.

SOCIAL INFLUENCES ON DESIGN

The factors so far considered—location, transport and the building industry—were the most important general considerations affecting housing for the middle classes in the period. What determined the actual form of that housing was a range of broadly social factors which directly influenced need and choice. Chief among these were important demographic changes in the English population and family structure. The very rapid growth of population which had characterized the nineteenth century had now markedly slowed down, mainly as a result of a sharp decline in the birth rate to the point where experts in the thirties were confidently predicting an actual fall in total numbers in the not-too-distant future. As a result of the adoption of deliberate family limitation, the birth rate steadily declined from 28 per 1,000 in 1901–5 to 15 in 1931–5, and with this reduction the average number of children per family fell from 3·5 to 2·2 over the same years. Social class continued to have marked effects on fertility between the wars, considerably smaller families being found among non-manual than among manual workers (1·93 compared with 2·49 children in 1925–9). The important point is that all families were, on average, considerably smaller than they had been at the beginning of the century, and, in particular, professional and 'middle-class' families were smaller than the average, consisting in many cases of only one or two children. The housing requirements of such families were obviously very different from those of Victorian times when five or six children had been usual, and almost one in every five marriages had produced ten or more children. Yet, although families of the inter-war years were individually much smaller, there were many more of them to be accommodated as an increasing proportion of the population married, and married at an earlier age than previously. In 1931, 42·8 per cent of the population was married, compared with 34·8 per cent in 1901, and the figure was to grow to 50·5 per cent in 1951. In spite of the slow growth of total population, therefore, the number of separate households requiring accommodation continued to increase rapidly, from 8½ million in 1911 to 15 million in 1961. One further demographic factor also affected the housing stock importantly. As the increasing conquest of disease in the twentieth century constantly extended the expectation of life, more people were surviving to old age and continuing to need separate housing long after their children had married and established new households: in 1906 the proportion of over-sixties in the population was only 7·6 per cent, but in 1936 it was 12·9 per cent and by 1951, 15·7 per cent. For all these reasons, the increasing need in the inter-war years was for many more, but smaller, units of accommodation, particularly suited to the newly-married, to small families, retired couples and one- or two-person households.[23]

A second social change which had important effects on the middle-class house was the increasing scarcity of domestic servants after World War I. The war reduced the number of domestic servants by approximately a quarter, and in the succeeding years the growth of shop work, light factory trades, minor professions and, most spectacular of all, clerical work, continued the process. By the thirties living-in maids were increasingly hard to find and considerably more demanding as to wages, free time and conditions of work. Servant-keeping was never again available to the middle classes as a whole, and increasingly became a privilege of upper income-levels. Whereas in the commuter areas of London the number of servants per 100 households had been 24·1 in 1911, by 1921 it was already 12·4 and continuing to fall. One important result of this on house design was that few speculatively-built houses now made provision for resident staff, and in higher-priced architect-designed houses only one or, at most, two maids were assumed where in Victorian times families of comparable means would have employed from three to five staff, often including one male servant.[24] With smaller family size and a greatly reduced number of servants, the 'two households' which the Victorian middle-class house had had to contain had, in effect, shrunk to one.

Changes in social attitudes and values which were, in turn, partly the result of demographic, economic and occupational changes, also had important effects on the design and plan of middle-class housing. As home-ownership expanded and family size diminished, the importance attached to the home constantly increased, and in this respect the inter-war generation was perhaps the most family-minded and home-centred one in history. What had formerly been the interest of a narrow group of society—in selecting their house, furnishing and decorating it, maintaining its fabric and cultivating its garden—was becoming diffused over a much broader stratum whose cultural and intellectual horizons were often more limited than those of their predecessors. The home therefore tended to become a more dominating interest and influence than ever before, the representation of material and emotional ambitions to which ever more people aspired as it became more attainable. The number of books and articles in the periodical and daily press dealing with such matters as acquiring a house, furnishing, decorating and maintaining it, far greater than in the previous century, is testimony to the central importance which the subject had achieved. 'The home is by far the most important institution in the lives of the British people', readers of a *Daily Express* publication were told.

> Never before has there been such a demand for well-built, scientifically-planned houses. A new consciousness of home-making has been born. Men and women are equally enthusiastic. Together they study house plans and schemes of decoration: together they devise ways and means of owning homes of their own, and their interest is fostered and encouraged by manufacturers and designers of home equipment and household utilities. For indeed, a modern, well-equipped home is a worthwhile possession, whether it consists of three rooms or thirty. It gives a sense of security and comfort and intimacy essential to real family life.[25]

Yet there was an important gap between the way in which the design and planning of the house was described and analysed by contemporary writers and the actual shapes which multiplied on the ground. Contemporary 'enlightened' opinion, typically expressed by architects and designers of the Modern Movement was strongly functionalist, regarding the house, in the famous phrase of Le Corbusier, as 'a machine for living in', no more and no less. Anthony Bertram, the leading exponent of design in the thirties, argued that historically the evolution of the house had been from amalgamation (in the medieval hall) to disintegration and, now, re-amalgamation in the contemporary house plan. We were now more honest and more logical. We can no longer endure the rambling, expensive houses of the past, he thought, so our living-room has again become the 'great hall', once more used for eating, entertaining, recreation, even sleeping. Today we want spaciousness, but cannot afford large houses, so we must have fewer, larger rooms: we are slowly escaping from the vulgarity of the last century, which confused form with decoration and relied on deception and misuse.

> The Victorian drawing-room was sentimental-romantic. The world is concerned today with planning. Such a living-room [ie the functional, all-purpose room] is an expression of man's present economic and social efforts: it is in sympathy with Communism, the Fascist corporate state, the Milk Marketing Board, the London Passenger Transport Board, the planned capitalism of P.E.P., the railway timetable.[26]

The fact was, however, that the vast majority of English people of all social classes obstinately refused to accept functionalism any more than they would embrace Communism or Fascism. The functionalists' case rested upon the false assumption that people were basically logical about their houses, and on a misreading of social trends which, they believed, were reducing the importance of the home in favour of travel, outdoor recreation and the 'open air life'. We have argued the contrary of this—that the home and the domestic ethic were taking on ever larger roles as central life interests—though this is not to deny that important social changes were occurring which did affect the plan of the house and the use of space. One, the decline of domestic servants and the increasing amount of housework which middle-class wives were obliged to take on, contributed to a smaller house size, to a re-designing of the kitchen quarters and to a greater emphasis on convenience and labour-saving devices generally. The pattern of middle-class domestic life, formerly spread over drawing-room, dining-room, morning-room and study, began to contract towards a more flexible use of two or three reception rooms with, sometimes, a kitchen used for the consumption as well as the preparation of meals. A decline in the formality of social relationships after World War I also had important effects on room use, especially in the matter of reception of visitors. The middle-class drawing-room and the lower-middle-class parlour had been primarily reserved for entertaining, therefore requiring additional, variously-named living-rooms for family use. Between the wars it became much more accept-able for guests to be entertained in the family rooms, so helping to break down the former separation between public and private space in the house. The formality of relationships in the Victorian home had been partly, perhaps largely, determined by the need to demonstrate social differences to inferiors. Now that the servants had fled, or could only be induced to stay by more sympathetic treatment, that need had disappeared.

Generally freer and more open relationships between the sexes, and between adults and children, also contributed to the decline in formality and the former separation of different types of accommodation which it had demanded. Children, once confined to the care of nannies in day- and night-nurseries, were now acceptable from a much earlier age in family dining-rooms and sitting-rooms, and from being the almost unrecognized appendages of family life were rapidly taking a place at the centre of it. Similarly, the separate male and female 'territories' which had characterized larger Victorian houses gave way before the advance of women's equality and the general democratization of domestic life. Wives and unmarried daughters who spent their days at home had almost inevitably taken over areas of the house for their own use, particularly the drawing-room and the morning-room, relegating the men to their study or library, but now that daughters worked, and both sexes smoked, talked about the same things and listened to the same gramophone or wireless set, sexual separation and privacy in the home were increasingly regarded as outmoded and eccentric.

Yet, despite these trends towards a more egalitarian society, the home continued to be, as it had in the past, the most important mark of social differentiation and the most significant symbol of social status. As house size moved towards a more standard pattern, greater emphasis came to be placed on services, on equipment and furnishing which had important display functions in announcing subtle distinctions of wealth, taste and refinement. Women's magazines, the daily press and architectural journals played a major part in encouraging conspicuous consumption in such things as elaborate kitchen and cleaning equipment, light fittings, new types of furniture, wall and floor coverings which only a minority could achieve; and as technology continued to develop improved refrigerators, heating systems, washing-machines and the like, the home continued to provide the ideal setting for the exercise of snobbery and social pretension.[27] In these respects, too, the functionalists misread the times. People did not want 'a machine for living in' so much as a vehicle for living out a fantasy.

ARCHITECTURAL INFLUENCES

Architectural style had relatively little influence on speculatively-built housing of the period, partly because professional architects were themselves engaged in a new 'Battle of the Styles' and partly because very few were engaged in the provision of speculative housing. Since no one style dominated the period, builders were free to adopt and adapt whatever best fitted the constraints of cost, land and materials within which they worked, being careful to avoid fashions likely to be too extreme or ephemeral for their basically conservative clientele. If one broad style could be said to characterize the period it was the 'vernacular revival'—the return to traditional English rural forms which had been pioneered by Webb and popularized by Voysey, Lutyens and others around the beginning of the century. It was not so much a style as an idiom, for it borrowed from many previous centuries to produce the general effect of a country cottage or, on a larger scale, of a farmhouse or small manor-house. R. W. Brunskill has pointed out that more 'vernacular' details were used in building in the fifty years after 1900 than in all the centuries before, and that 'the housing estates of the 1930s display more half-timbered gables than will ever be recorded in Worcestershire or Kent'.[28]

Houses of this type, usually detached and sited on half-acre or larger plots, continued to be built in the more affluent suburbs from before World War I up to the outbreak of World War II. They were typically long, low, sprawling houses set beneath wide, spreading roofs broken by gables and with deep eaves. On the ground floor they often had long bands of mullioned windows and on the first floor dormer windows, in both cases having diamond-paned leaded lights. Walls were usually in red brick, sometimes plain rendered relieved by exposed beams (structural or artificial) and herring-bone brickwork. An appearance of age was often given by incorporating details from several periods and by the use of premature repair-work. Also characteristic was the conscious use of local materials such as flint, thatch, and natural oak doors and window-frames. Although such houses were essentially astylar, adaptations of an idiom rather than copies of the past, it may be said that until the 1920s the dominant influences were Elizabethan and Jacobean, and that subsequently neo-Georgian influences were more marked, with a more regular façade, sash windows rather than mullions and less prominent roofs and chimneys. Either style in the hands of a sensitive builder could produce comfortable houses which fitted happily into a lightly built-up landscape. Degenerated as it became at the hands of the speculator into the semi-detached stereotype with applied 'Jacobethan' ornamentation, it no doubt deserved the scorn which critics of taste enjoyed pouring on it. The fact probably was, as J. M. Richards has argued, that people demanded very much what they were given, and that 'there is no popular demand for what superior people call "good taste"'.[29]

Something like this ideal type, scaled down as resources required, remained the model of the vast majority of the English middle classes between the wars. It was challenged, though not very seriously or for very long, by the appearance of 'the Modern Movement', a European reaction to traditional styles which was symbolized and stimulated by the publication of Le Corbusier's *Vers Une Architecture* in 1923. In this, all historical styles were derided, and the case vehemently argued that a house should be designed as functionally as a ship, an aeroplane or a motorcar: the architect, beginning with a definition of needs like the engineer, should work outwards from this, so that his plan would possess the logic and simple beauty of the machine. The implementation of such ideas depended crucially on the use of new building materials, particularly reinforced concrete, which allowed walls to be constructed merely as containing shells for large areas of glass, the load being carried by a steel or reinforced frame rather than by load-bearing walls. In fact, no new principle of construction was involved here, as the Tudor timber-framed house had been closely similar, but the possibilities of casting large amounts of concrete in prefabricated sheets or blocks, of first floors cantilevered out over the ground floor, of flat roofs and walls of glass, opened up fascinating prospects to a group of enthusiastic young architects.

The Modern Movement was experimented with, rather than adopted, in England. From 1925, when 'New Ways', the first cubist, rectilinear house was built in Wellingborough Road, Northampton (appropriately, for an engineering industrialist), a scattered number of houses in the modern idiom began to appear in the newer suburbs and, perhaps less incongruously, in more isolated rural sites. One vaguely cubist village was laid out (by Crittalls) at Silver End in Essex for disabled ex-servicemen from 1926 onwards,[30] and some impetus was added to the movement after the closing of the Bauhaus by Hitler in 1932 and the flight of Professor Gropius, Erich Mendelsohn and other apostles of modernism to England. But despite great publicity in the architectural journals, and its undoubted influence on the design of blocks of flats, offices, factories and Underground stations, the Modern Movement never found acceptance in the English house. For its full effect, the style required large scale, and most people found it impersonal, even inhuman, serving the needs of masses rather than individuals. Large areas of staring white concrete, frequently stained after a few winters, did not fit easily into the suburban or rural landscape; walls of glass, unless accompanied by expensive heating and ventilating systems, were often either too cold or too hot for the English climate; flat roofs had only limited use for sunbathing and quite often allowed the penetration of rain. The results, especially in the hands of less adventurous architects and speculative builders, were greatly modified versions of the 'sun house', usually characterized merely by flat wall surfaces—often of cement rendering over traditional brick—wide windows which sometimes extended round corners, and a general absence of decoration. To some small extent, therefore, the new style became absorbed into the suburban milieu in the form of semi-detached, flat-roofed concrete houses of familiar size and plan, and only very few houses, usually built for architects, artists or educationists, reflected the uncompromising radicalism of Le Corbusier.[31]

The basic fault of much 'functional' architecture was, quite simply, that it was not functional for English social habits or the English climate—that sun-roofs and first-floor living-rooms cantilevered out into the garden might look appealing as photographs in architectural journals but lacked conviction as the setting for suburban domestic life. 'This apparent failure of the reformers in the realm of domestic architecture is, one fancies, one of psychology', wrote Osbert Lancaster in 1939. 'The open plan, the mass-produced steel and plywood furniture, the uncompromising display of the structural elements, are all in theory perfectly logical, but in the home logic has always been at a discount.'[32] Externally, this was certainly true. In so far as functionalism made any progress in the English home it was in kitchens, bathrooms and WCs where sentiment usually gave way to cleanliness and modernity.

HOUSING TYPES

The sort of house which the great majority of inter-war suburbans wanted, escaping as most were from the monotony of terraces in central or inner-suburban areas, was something like a country cottage of some historical style, preferably individually sited and individual in character. Ideally, it might be a Tudor cottage in a country lane, but equipped with modern conveniences and supplied with nearby shops, schools and transport. The impossibility of providing these on a mass scale resulted in the compromise of detached or, more often, semi-detached houses of basically similar plan though with some distinguishing external features, situated in a newly laid out estate with all the rawness of concrete roads and unmatured gardens.

The builders' problem was to try to create uniqueness and individuality in houses which, given the price limits, were necessarily very similar in size, shape and plan, especially when joined together in pairs with a common gable. Some sort of 'character' could cheaply be provided by mock half-timbering, lattice windows, stained glass, 'Gothic' front doors, crazy paving footpaths and similar decorative features having a vaguely rural, old world atmosphere. Anthony Bertram explained the popular love of the 'Tudoresque' as being based on fear and a wish to escape from the present; the threat of war and the fear of economic depression engendered a romantic hunger for an imaginary ideal of the past when life was simple and secure. While he was giving a series of radio talks on modern design which strongly criticized sham architecture, many listeners wrote in protest to say 'the suggestion of those quiet old days gives us the restful atmosphere we seek in our homes'.[33]

As well as seeming to supply an anchorage in the past, the use of decorative features from historical styles provided a sense of individuality or, at least, of distinctiveness from working-class housing. The bay-window to the front living-room, usually carried up to the front bedroom, was the most obvious way of pointing the difference between a privately-owned house and a local-authority house. But, ideally, individuality went well beyond this—to uniqueness, irregularity of outline, some uncertainty or even mystery about the disposition of rooms. Something like this was possible in larger, detached houses, and had been deliberately incorporated by the 'vernacular' architects at the turn of the century, but the challenge of making scores of identically-designed semi-detached houses 'all different' often only produced absurd and ineffectual suggestions of irregularity in projecting bays, framework gables, ornamental porches, oriel or 'cathedral windows' to staircases, and so on. 'Every house different' and 'No pair of houses alike in road' were favourite advertisement slogans, often achieved by spurious decorative devices though, in more select developments, by considerable ingenuity in the use of old timber, old bricks mixed with new, hand-made tiles and the like. Many developers offered a variety of styles on their estates, mixed bungalows with houses, sprinkled a few detached among the semi-detached or inserted an occasional concrete 'Sunshine House' to break the monotony of brick gables and pitched roofs.

The semi-detached house was by far the most common building type, particularly in the Greater London region, though rivalled by the small detached house in provincial suburbs where land and labour costs were lower. Bungalows also sprang into popularity between the wars, and with their variants of 'semi-bungalow' (one bedroom in the roof space) and 'chalet' (two bedrooms in the roof) were especially common in cheap-land areas such as outer suburbs and semi-rural sites, and in coastal towns and retirement districts. Although semi-detacheds were not unknown, the bungalow was essentially a detached type of dwelling, giving optimum physical isolation on four sides and, therefore, maximum individual identity. Anthony King has shown how the bungalow became democratized between the wars, changing from a holiday or weekend home for the wealthy to become a permanent residence for all social levels. It fitted in particularly well with the demographic trends which were producing a higher proportion of older people in the population, with expansion in public transport and private car-ownership, and with the increasing cost

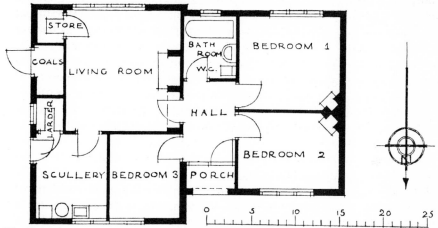

17   Economy and convenience: a private bungalow in Nottingham, 1932 designed by T. Cecil Howitt. Living room 13ft 6in × 13ft (4·1 × 4·0m), Scullery 9ft × 8ft (2·7 × 2·4m), Bedroom 1 11ft 6in × 10ft 3in (3·5 × 3·1m), Bedroom 2 11ft 6in × 8ft 3in (3·5 × 2·5m), Bedroom 3 9ft × 7ft 9in (2·7 × 2·4m) (*Cecil Howitt & Partners, Nottingham*)

and scarcity of domestic servants. In *The Book of Bungalows* published in 1920, P. Randall Phillips extolled its principal virtues as 'not over-costly to build, less expensive to furnish, and easy to run'—significantly, he was also the author of *The Servantless House*. It was the labour-saving aspects of a small, compact house on one floor which were most stressed in *The Daily Mail Bungalow Book* and many similar publications in the twenties and thirties, and the fact that the advantages of modernity chimed in so happily with a rural-romantic 'cottage' image made it especially attractive at this time. Some developments, mushrooming along unmade tracks by the coast or on the edges of villages, were unplanned and unlovely, consisting at their worst of prefabricated wooden shacks delivered, ready to erect, to the nearest goods station for £200 or so, and given the loose control which some rural district councils exercised, it was impossible to prevent 'holiday' or 'weekend' retreats from becoming permanent homes. There was no lack of critics of the 'bungaloid' phenomenon, which, according to the author of *England and the Octopus* (1928), 'constitutes England's most disfiguring disease, having, from sporadic beginnings, now become our premier epidemic'.[34]

No other housing type between the wars seriously challenged the overwhelming popularity of individual houses and bungalows. The alternative, strongly urged by modernist architects and planners in the thirties on grounds of both private convenience and public conscience, was the flat, situated in a purpose-built block of apartments close to a city centre. It was, wrote two enthusiasts in 1937, 'a housing type peculiar to our own era, a solution to the problem of housing by the provision of homes in multi-storey buildings'. In towns of any size, it was argued, houses were being crowded out into suburban areas, with consequent spoliation of the countryside, and long and inconvenient journeys to work for their residents. Flats had been unpopular in the past mainly because they were unscientifically planned, resulting in dark rooms where the sun never entered, overlooking depressing, unhygienic courts. But these disadvantages could now be overcome by proper planning and the use of modern constructional techniques, the concrete frame building being particularly suitable for multi-storey blocks.[35] Much thought was given to the problems of access and lighting, and most of the solutions subsequently adopted in high-rise dwellings—corridor, gallery, direct and direct grouped access (generally involving the cruciform plan)—were all in use in the decade.

Despite much publicity, and some imaginative designs by leading contemporary architects such as Frederick Gibberd, E. Owen Williams and Lubetkin and Tecton, the flat as a middle-class dwelling-type did not spread significantly outside central London and a few coastal resorts, and even here it was usually designed as minimum accommodation for bachelors or childless couples rather than for families. Even so, rents in speculatively-built blocks compared unfavourably with mortgage repayment on a house. In Pullman Court, Streatham, a modest development for office workers, £68 per annum was charged for one-room flats and £105–£130 for three rooms, while at Embassy Court, Brighton, two-roomed 'luxury flats for professional and business classes' cost from £120 per annum and four-roomed flats up to £500. Such developments, which often included the provision of garages, restaurant, sporting and social amenities, were important in helping to dispel the commonly-accepted image of blocks of flats as barrack-like tenements for the working classes, but there is little evidence of their acceptability for family living.

INTERNAL PLANNING

In the actual planning and use of rooms in the inter-war house there was a similar gap between theory and practice—between what architects of the contemporary school advocated and what speculative builders actually provided. The major difference in internal planning was that the functionalists argued for a breakdown of strict divisions in rooms and room use and a more flexible use of internal space. Some recommended a completely 'open plan' living area—hall-living-eating area with the stairs rising out of it—which, according to M. W. Barley, was only a return home of an export to America in the seventeenth century.[36] At the least, the living-room should be the largest, sunniest room for mixed use, with, if necessary, areas screened off for dining, sitting or studying, but capable of being opened up when necessary. This all-purpose room should be the hub and centre of the house, carefully sited with relation to the garden and to views, and since central heating had made the open fireplace a thing of the past, furniture could now be disposed freely to make the maximum use of space and outlook. Where privacy was needed, bedrooms should be used as sitting-rooms or studies, with built-in furniture and beds which could be folded away or used as seats in the daytime.[37] They might open on to a sleeping-terrace for summer use, and many modernists, following Le Corbusier's dictum, 'Never undress in your bedroom', recommended a dressing-room 'en suite'. The kitchen quarters should be the best-planned part of the house, freed from the snobbish desire to hide all working parts, while the need for service rooms such as sculleries, larders and pantries had all but disappeared with the use of built-in equipment, refrigerators, kitchen cabinets and working surfaces.

As previously suggested, the full effects of such ideas were realized only in a small number of architect-designed houses built for special clients who dared to risk the scorn of neighbours and the rigours of the English climate. Most inter-war houses, whether speculatively-built or customer-built, followed a more or less traditional internal plan, modified in some respects from Victorian times by the social changes and trends in fashion already described. A fairly clear break occurs between detached and semi-detached houses, usually at a price level of around £1,000, although instances of both types were to be found above and below this figure, depending on size and location. The detached house obviously allowed for greater irregularity and variety in planning, which makes generalization hazardous, though some widely-observed characteristics can be noticed. In such houses, the entrance hall remained an important feature for the reception of guests and for display purposes. Quite commonly it was described as a 'lounge hall' and intended to be furnished with easy chairs and occasional tables, though how far a circulation area could be satisfactorily used is doubtful. But with parquet floor, panelled walls, a fireplace and a large stained-glass staircase window, perhaps including an imitation coat-of-arms, it evoked a sense of importance and harmonized well with a 'Jacobethan' façade. A 'dining-hall' was occasionally adopted, but was generally not approved. A small lobby between hall and front door was, however, recommended, as also a cloakroom with hand-basin and WC. From the hall, doors gave separate access to two or three reception rooms and to the kitchen quarters, the latter sometimes screened by an inner hall or lobby. The modernists' suggestion of combining dining-room and drawing-room (now increasingly known as 'sitting-room' or 'lounge') was only rarely adopted, and even the

Edwardian practice of intercommunication by folding doors was not common. A change is noticeable, however, in that the sitting-room was now almost always the largest room, often running through the depth of the house, and the dining-room was reduced to a small, squarish room reserved only for that purpose. The sitting-room, deprived of its past formality, was now usually the family living-room, taking the place of the middle-class Victorian parlour: typical sizes for the sitting-room were up to 20ft by 14ft, with the dining-room around 15ft by 12ft. Larger detached houses usually had a third reception room, which might be a morning-room or a study, depending on the habits of the family, of around 10ft or 12ft square: if the former, it would be used as the family day-room, reserving the largest room as a more formal drawing-room.

All architectural writers in the period agreed that the large Victorian kitchen, with its great iron cooking-range, open-shelved dresser and complex of adjoining service rooms was now a thing of the past. The kitchen should be the best-planned room in the house, convenient and compact, fitted with dust-free cupboards and with scientifically-placed cooker, sink and work-tops to minimize movement and effort. With the spread of electricity in the late twenties, the 'all-electric kitchen' became popular, with numerous power points for cooker, refrigerator, washing-machine, electric iron and so on, though hot water was more often supplied by an anthracite boiler than by gas or oil. The accent was upon lightness, cleanliness and convenience, whether for mistress or maid, and in households wealthy enough to employ one or two servants the strong recommendation was for a small maid's sitting-room off the kitchen where she could rest and take her meals. Everything possible must be done to make her life 'happy and contented', and she should have a 'pretty, well-equipped bedroom' which 'should be regarded by all the household as the maid's private sanctum'.

Upstairs, it was assumed that there would be fewer, and smaller, bedrooms than formerly, four being generally regarded as the minimum in a medium-sized house. The provision of built-in wardrobe cupboards, and of hand-basins with hot and cold water eliminated the need for cumbersome bedroom 'suites', and twin beds or divans were increasingly in favour. Larger houses often had a second bathroom, sometimes 'en suite' with the principal bedroom, though dressing-rooms were less common than formerly. Single bedrooms could be as small as about 9ft 6in by 6ft, double bedrooms about 12ft by 12ft or the equivalent, but despite the increasing accent on comfort and convenience, bedrooms often continued to be equipped with a small fireplace, sometimes with an inset electric bar, since 'popular opinion in England is against the provision of radiators in bedrooms'.[38]

The semi-detached house offered much less opportunity for variety in room-use and the assertion of individuality, which had to be restricted mainly to decoration and furnishings. The plan of the typical semi was almost inescapable—a porch sheltering the front door, a hall/passage about 6ft wide from which the stairs rose to the first floor, a front room (usually the 'parlour' or 'drawing-room') with bay-window to give additional light and space, a smaller rear room (usually the dining-room) and a kitchen with larder behind the hall and to the side of the dining-room. Above were two double bedrooms corresponding to the living-rooms, a small third bedroom over the hall and a bathroom and WC over the kitchen. Occasionally, the living-rooms would be reversed, with a smaller dining-room at the front and a larger lounge at the rear, having French doors to the garden. In small houses, approached by a side entrance, there might be only one living-room, a rear kitchen and downstairs bathroom. Room sizes varied directly with price, but in the 'typical' five-roomed semi were of the order: sitting-room 15ft by 12ft, dining-room 14ft by 11ft, kitchen 10ft by 7ft, bedrooms 15ft by 11ft, 14ft by 11ft and 8ft by 7ft, though there were many variations on this standard pattern. Characteristics of such houses were the very small kitchens, bathrooms and third bedrooms, often described as 'box-rooms', which would just admit a single bed or, sometimes, only a child's cot. At prices over £1,000 a larger main reception-room up to 200–250sq ft and a further small bedroom could be expected, and at this level, too, an integral garage and consequentially larger bedroom areas were common.

The extent to which such houses represented an improvement on previous standards depends, of course, upon what they replaced, and it is important to remember that, despite the unprecedented level of building activity between the wars, nearly half of all houses in 1939 were still more than sixty years old. For those who moved from an older terraced or semi-detached house in a Victorian middle-class suburb the advantages were mainly of amenity rather than space. Their former house, often with more living-rooms and bedrooms to accommodate a larger family and a domestic staff, may well have been larger than the 1,000sq ft of the typical new semi or the 1,500sq ft or so of the new detached house. The advantages lay in such things as a convenient, modern kitchen, a bathroom with hot water supply, electricity for lighting, heating and cooking, lighter, sunnier rooms and, almost certainly, a substantially larger garden. A detached house commonly enjoyed a plot of from one-eighth to half an acre, while even a narrow-fronted semi might have a garden of 100–300ft in depth. But the greatest beneficiaries of the new housing were the families of lower-paid professionals and better-paid manual workers who were able to qualify for a mortgage and to move from a small, rented terrace house or, in London, from two or three rooms to a bright, new suburban house which would some day be their own. For such families the convenient kitchen, the bathroom, the internal WC, the third bedroom and the garden where flowers and vegetables could be grown and children could play, were not merely novelties, but luxuries. They opened up possibilities of a new and decent life away from the noise and dirt of Victorian cities, of healthier children and of parents who, through the ownership of property, could elevate themselves in the estimation of the world. Physically, the minimal five-roomed semi made civilized life, in middle-class terms, possible for a small family. It allowed for a proper separation of eating and living, for a proper separation of ages and sexes for sleeping, for cleanliness, order, ventilation and recreation. Emotionally, it satisfied the deeply felt needs of ownership, of security and of control of one's environment. House-ownership defined status better than anything else, conferred respectability and responsibility and made a man a fully participant member of society. The values of the new suburbans were, no doubt, often petty and uncultivated, snobbish and competitive, dominated by a narrow concern for home and family which blunted their awareness of the alarming economic and political problems of the day. 'The English house', wrote John Gloag, 'still shows the Englishman's mastery of the art of living a private life.'[39] That ideal of privacy, which the Victorian middle classes had made the corner-stone of their domestic life and which had now been spread to a much broader band of society, was, by 1939, about to be rudely invaded.

10

PUBLIC AND PRIVATE HOUSING, 1945–1970

DEMOGRAPHIC TRENDS

The housing history of the years since 1945 is complex and controversial. On the one hand, the period achieved significant improvements in output and standards and major advances in the space, design and layout of houses, their amenities and fittings, which brought appreciably higher standards within the reach of a greatly enlarged section of society. On the other hand, the period closed with the housing problem still unsolved, with increasing numbers of homeless people, the perpetuation of slum and sub-standard dwellings, and widespread public concern about the social and environmental effects of some new types of building. No detailed chronology of a crowded twenty-five years, which witnessed no fewer than eleven major Housing Acts, is attempted here. We are concerned, as before, to identify trends, measure changes and, especially, to evaluate the quality of accommodation which became available to the English people in the post-war period.

The fundamental issues in housing are demographic, or, more specifically, the relationship between the number of houses and the number of people or families to be housed. Although since the last war the English population has not exploded as it did in the nineteenth century, the birth rate has remained higher than many expected, and higher than it was in the 1930s. Between 1931 and 1951 (there was no Census in 1941) 3,806,000 people were added to the population of England and Wales; between 1951 and 1961, 2,347,000; and between 1961 and 1971, 2,658,000. But houses are occupied, on the whole, by households rather than by individuals, and the even more significant fact in post-war demographic history is that household formation has been much more rapid than the growth in the number of individuals. A complex series of changes—an increase in the proportion of people married, earlier marriages, smaller family size (from an average of 3·4 children to women marrying in 1900–9 to 2 for those marrying in 1940) and greater expectation of life—has meant that the population now contains a far greater number of separate, though smaller, households than in the past. Thus, while in round figures the population of England and Wales grew from 38 million in 1921 to 48 million in 1966, the number of private households almost doubled from 8·7 million to 15·7 million.[1]

The implications of this change for housing needs are immense. Separate households in general require separate accommodation, and the fact that households are smaller than in the past means that they require separate, but different, accommodation. In 1901, average household size was 4·6 persons, in 1931 it was 3·7 and 1966, 3·0: between the wars the commonest household size was three people, now it is two. It is the spectacular increase in the small households of one and two persons, which increased from 21·5 per cent of all households in 1911 to 45·9 per cent in 1966, which is mainly responsible for the change. In the past, houses had to accommodate parents with young children and adult sons and daughters for many years: now, family formation has been compressed into a much shorter period of the family cycle. A century ago the 'average' mother would be aged fifty-six before her last child was fifteen, and would have only another ten years to live, whereas women marrying in 1950 had reared their last child to the age of fifteen by forty-five and could then expect another thirty years of life.[2]

At both ends of the age-scale, therefore, small households greatly increased. Many unmarried sons and daughters set up independent households who formerly lived on at home. Marriage takes place, on average, five years earlier than it did at the beginning of the century, and fewer married couples wish to share accommodation in the parental home. Family-building ends earlier in life, but the demand of couples, and later of widows or widowers, for accommodation stretches further forward into the future, to a time when, in old age, they may have special housing needs. The housing market has been especially slow to respond to the fact that almost half of all households in the country now consist of only one or two persons, and that 13 per cent of the population are aged over sixty-five compared with 5·2 per cent in 1911. The result is that the housing stock, most typically represented by the three-bedroomed, five-person house, is increasingly out of line with household needs. Houses have become larger and more homogeneous in size as family groupings have become smaller and more disintegrated, so that while in 1891 dwellings of one or two rooms constituted 16 per cent of occupied housing, in 1961 they represented only 4·6 per cent.[3]

Two further demographic trends are important in relation to housing needs and use. The first is the flight of domestic servants and their virtual disappearance from middle-class homes, which has had significant effects on the size and planning of more expensive privately-built houses. In 1861, 12 per cent of all households had resident domestic staff. Between the two world wars the numbers of servants fell by half, though they were still found, and planned for, in the more affluent homes. By 1951 a mere 1·2 per cent of households had resident servants, and separate provision for them in the ordinary house had ceased. On the other hand, housewives who formerly confined their energies to the drawing-room and dining-room now found themselves cooking, washing, cleaning and generally maintaining houses which had not been designed with a primary view to convenience, and spending much of their time in kitchens which were 'fit' only for servants. One of the important consequences of the servantless house has been the elevation of the kitchen from the cheerless, Victorian scullery to the centre of household activity, skilfully planned, equipped with labour-saving devices, and often furnished as a room where at least some family meals are normally eaten.

The increasing concern with convenience has also been furthered by another recent demographic trend—the employment of married women outside the home. Before the last war this was unusual in working-class families, and almost unknown in the middle class. Today, more than 40 per cent of all married women are gainfully employed, and more than half of all employed women are married. The effect of this revolutionary change has been twofold. Wives who spend all or part of the working day outside the home have tended to rationalize household duties, to put a high priority on appliances, automatic central heating, easily-cleaned surfaces and so on; at the same time, their increased economic resources have made possible a larger expenditure on home aids and on consumer durables generally. Precisely how the financial equation between increased earnings and increased expenditure works out is impossible to say, and it may be that some wives work principally in order to buy the sort of home and equipment they wanted anyway, but the evidence seems to be clear that working wives do reduce the time spent on household tasks—in a recent French study by as much as twenty-eight hours a week.[4] Demographic trends are, therefore, of major importance both quantitatively and qualitatively—in determining both the degree of 'fit' between houses and people, and the nature of accommodation that is required by a rapidly changing society.

ECONOMIC AND SOCIAL CHANGES

Closely related to these demographic trends, though distinct from them, are a set of economic and social changes which have profoundly altered patterns of living since the last war. There can be little doubt that in the quarter-century between 1945 and 1970 the English people as a whole were more prosperous than at any comparable period in the past, were able to achieve higher living standards, better housing, clothing and diet, more leisure and more material possessions than they had enjoyed before. These improvements in living standards were most marked in the working classes who, by contrast with their position before the war, benefited from practically full employment, a well-developed system of social security, and wages which moved ahead of the relatively low rates of inflation. Those who gained most in economic terms were the clerical occupations, semi-skilled and unskilled workers, all of whom increased their real earnings more than the average, and considerably more than professional and some other 'middle-class' groups. A general narrowing of differentials—between professional workers and manual workers, between skilled and unskilled, between adult and juvenile, and between male and female—has been a significant characteristic of post-war wages history.[5] Over the whole century from 1860 to 1960 it is likely that real income per head increased approximately three times with particularly rapid increases in the 1870s, the 1930s and the 1950s.

One important result of increased real earnings and greater regularity of employment has been a major change in housing tenure and, especially, a great increase in home-ownership. In 1945 only 26 per cent of all houses in England and Wales were owner-occupied; by 1966 the proportion was 47 per cent and by 1973, 53 per cent. House-purchase, financed mainly by the building societies, which in 1966 alone advanced 444,000 new mortgages totalling £1,245 million, had come within the reach of a much broader section of society than in pre-war days and was now widespread among better-paid manual workers. People transferred from rented to owned accommodation for a variety of reasons, voluntary and involuntary—for greater independence and security, to obtain an investment which increased in value more than almost anything else, and sometimes because purchase was the only way of obtaining a house in certain areas. It should also be remembered that with rising earnings and lower tax thresholds, the income tax relief on mortgage interest, estimated at around £300 million in 1971, was also a considerable inducement, amounting to a subsidy of about £60 a year on each mortgaged house.[6] The proportion of houses rented from local authorities or new town corporations also more than doubled since the war, though from a lower base, from 12 per cent in 1947 to 30 per cent in 1970. By contrast, houses let by private landlords, which in 1947 constituted 58 per cent of the housing stock, had already shrunk by half by 1961, and in 1973 accounted for only 14 per cent of houses. To describe such a massive change in tenure within twenty-five years as revolutionary is not inappropriate.

'Revolutionary' was also the word used by the Parker Morris Report of 1961, *Homes for Today and Tomorrow*, to describe the social changes since 1945.[7] The Report drew particular attention to the growth of household appliances, already evident in 1961, and rapidly increasing as a phenomenon of the 'affluent society'. By 1963 a television set was to be found in 82 per cent of all private households, a vacuum cleaner in 72 per cent, a washing machine in 45 per cent and a refrigerator in 30 per cent. What was equally striking was that ownership of such things had spread down the social scale and the gap between professional and manual workers had greatly narrowed. A recent study of a slum area in Leeds, scheduled for demolition, indicated that an equally high priority was placed on such possessions even here, 74 per cent of households having a television, 41 per cent a vacuum cleaner and 38 per cent a washing machine. In another slum area, St Mary's, Oldham, where few had fixed baths or a hot water supply and half shared outside WCs, 67 per cent of the houses were rated as comfortably furnished and a further 24 per cent furnished luxuriously, with deep pile carpeting, smart modern furniture and decorations.[8] Standards of furnishing, fittings and decoration, though difficult to quantify statistically, undoubtedly rose for almost all social groups in the fifties and sixties, and it is likely that the primacy of the bedroom, which Dennis Chapman in 1955 found took the highest proportion of furnishing expenditure,[9] gradually shifted in favour of the living-room and the kitchen. For planning purposes, the important point is that as a measure of prosperity reached more and more families, the instinct to accumulate more material objects also spread down the social scale, and houses which were formerly required merely to provide minimum shelter took on new roles for the storage and display of possessions.

The desire for increased space also followed as a result of the greater time spent in the home and the greater interest taken in it. Average working hours fell from fifty-three a week at the beginning of the century to forty-two in the 1960s, and much of this increased leisure time has been spent in the home and in family-based activities. In his study of prosperous manual workers in 1961, Ferdynand Zweig concluded that improvements in housing conditions in the last decade had been one of the most potent factors in the transformation of the working man's way of life. The change was typified by a shop steward, now living in his own house, who observed:

> In the previous house the front door was never meant to be used: we had a settee across it. Everyone, including the postman, called at the back door. Now it is different. We've moved to the front.[10]

'Moving to the front', believed Zweig, was a symbolic gesture, representing a shedding of a sense of inferiority and a replacement of the 'kitchen mentality' by the 'living-room mentality' (a decade later, the word might have been 'lounge'). Life on suburban estates encouraged home-centredness and pride in possessions, an environment where status was measured in terms of trim front gardens, window displays and kitchen gadgets. 'I have many things which would be unthinkable to my father', said one worker, and another, 'I never saw my father handling a [paint] brush: now it seems I have a use for my brush the whole year round'. In many respects the attitudes and values of these affluent manual workers mirrored those of the Victorian middle classes—security-mindedness, rising expectations of comfort and convenience, for which hard work was justified, a belief in the home as the centre of relaxation and happiness, pride in and ambition for children and family. 'I am a fairly domesticated animal', commented one worker; another, 'My house is my hobby'.

Again, the 'public' aspects of life in formerly poor communities, living in the streets, courts and public houses, have given way in the suburban estates and new towns to increasing privatization and more controlled social relationships. The sociability which is supposed to have characterized life in the slums has declined with affluence, and the attempts by some idealist architects to recreate 'mateyness' in neighbourhood units and blocks of flats have not met with the universal approval of residents. Former slum-dwellers may not care to be forcibly reminded of the past by the deliberate use of brick detailing of cotton mills in their new homes[11] when they are busy developing bourgeois tastes and attitudes.

In these respects, then, the post-war years saw a 'levelling up' in housing standards and expectations for significant numbers of the working classes. Similarly, changes within the middle classes, resented by some as a 'levelling down', had the effect of narrowing the formerly wide gap between the two groups. With the departure of domestic servants and the development of more democratic relationships between husbands and wives and parents and children, a decline in formality brought middle-class social and domestic patterns more into line with the rest. For economic reasons, too, the spatial requirements had to be contracted. In many cases, existing larger houses have been divided, while higher-priced houses built since the war have generally shrunk by at least one reception room and one or two bedrooms.

Although home life is constructed around a framework of customary ways which are difficult to change in fundamentals, the middle-class pattern has had to adjust to the greatly increased costs of maintaining large houses. Thus, kitchens are now used for eating some meals by all social classes, a practice unthinkable before the war in houses where servants were employed. Again, in pre-war houses with three living-rooms it is not uncommon to find that now it is the smallest (usually known as the 'morning-room') which is the most-used family room, often because it is warm and conveniently placed close to the kitchen.[12] Few families now seem able to use three living-rooms effectively unless the third has some specialized use such as a study or children's playroom. Both in the size of houses and in the use of space, middle-class and working-class patterns have converged, and the proportion of households with standards markedly above or below the norm has continued to fall.

HOUSING POLICY

Detailed analyses of post-war housing policies have been made elsewhere[13] and are not attempted here, but it is necessary to recall the principal benchmarks in a history which, in many respects, closely resembled that of the years 1918–39.

In at least two respects, however, the housing situation in 1945 was very different. First, the problem itself was vastly larger after six years of war in which there had been very little civilian building and, on the contrary, extensive destruction of property by enemy air attacks. A total of 475,000 houses were either destroyed or made permanently uninhabitable[14] and a much greater number damaged. On the other hand, two million marriages had taken place, and the birth rate began to move up from 1941 to reach a peak of 20·7 in 1947. But second, in 1945 there was no longer any hesitation by the State in involving itself in a housing policy. The Labour Government elected in 1945 needed no persuading that it would have to play the major part in promoting new homes at a time of urgent national need: the Government's dilemma was not the will, but the means, to do so when faced with the competing claims of industrial reconstruction, nationalization and the welfare state programmes, and with problems caused by the balance of payments and shortages of materials.

Despite the formidable obstacles, housing policies began in 1946 in a spirit of optimism reminiscent of 1919. For the first ten years or so house-building was to be for 'general needs' and would be carried out mainly by the local authorities. By 1957 the impressive total of $2\frac{1}{2}$ million new houses and flats had been built, three-quarters of them by local authorities. The Housing (Financial and Miscellaneous Provisions) Act of 1946 granted a Treasury subsidy of £16 10s 0d per house for sixty years, provided there was a local authority subsidy of £5 10s 0d; as in the past, additional grants were available for high-cost land, for rural areas and for the building of flats.

The Labour Government's achievement—approximately 900,000 houses by 1951—fell short of the target of 240,000 a year, and was one of the reasons for its electoral defeat. The promise of '300,000 houses a year' by the new Conservative Government was in fact redeemed by 1953 when 319,000 were built, and exceeded in the following year with a record 348,000, though the figure shrank subsequently. Harold Macmillan's success was due to a combination of more generous subsidies, raised to £26 14s 0d a year by the Housing Act of 1952, and a stimulus to private builders as licences became more easily available and were removed altogether in 1954. Council tenants began to be encouraged to buy their houses and improvement grants to private landlords became available.

Again, the resemblance to inter-war policies is noticeable. By 1954 the Government had convinced itself that the general housing shortage was on the way to being solved, and that the emphasis should again be turned to the problem of the slums. The Housing Repairs and Rents Act of 1954 reduced subsidies for general needs while retaining them for the clearance of slums, of which the local authorities had estimated there were 850,000. Two years later subsidies for general needs were totally abolished, and were kept only for slum clearance and the building of one-bedroomed dwellings. Through the rest of the fifties the Government pinned its faith on private enterprise, on encouraging owner-occupation by making loans available on older property, and on the Rent Act of 1957 which, it was hoped, would introduce greater mobility into the housing market by the partial removal of rent control.

By the end of the decade, however, it was clear that a new housing crisis was looming. In particular, much publicity was given to the growing problem of homelessness, the increasing scarcity of rented accommodation and the insecurity of tenants in London and other large cities. Behind the 'affluent society' still lay much private squalor in the housing conditions of lower-paid workers, immigrant groups, old people and others who had not been in a position to press their claims on national prosperity. In 1961 the Conservative Government brought back a general needs subsidy on a complicated formula intended to relate the amount to the financial needs of different areas, and in 1964, as the general election drew near, passed a comprehensive Act which set up the Housing Corporation with the duty of encouraging housing societies, and with power to borrow up to £100 million from the Treasury to encourage the building of houses for letting at cost rents. In the event, the Conservative Government fell from office in 1964 in a year of record housing output—374,000, of which 218,000 were built by private enterprise and 156,000 by public authorities.

The new Labour Government set itself an ambitious target of 500,000 houses a year by 1970, but as the economic climate worsened and devaluation came in 1967, the figure was quietly dropped. In 1967 a new Housing Subsidies Act altered the basis of Exchequer grant, which until now had been a flat sum per house for so many years, to a low-interest loan which, in effect, enabled local authorities to borrow at a maximum of 4 per cent. As interest rates rose so also did the amount of subsidy, and by 1969 emphasis was switched towards the rehabilitation of existing, older property with more generous grants in Improvement Areas. Nevertheless, the rate of new building under the Labour Government continued at a high level, the years 1965–9 inclusive producing approximately 1·8 million houses with a peak in 1968, almost equally divided between the public and private sectors.

Once some of the immediate post-war housing shortage had been met, an increasingly important place was given to slum clearance and the improvement of unfit dwellings. In 1951, one-third of the housing stock was more than eighty years old, and many houses lacked the sort of amenities which had been normal in council houses since 1919: 37 per cent of all households lacked a fixed bath, 8 per cent a WC (another 13 per cent were required to share), 6 per cent piped water (another 14 per cent sharing) and 6 per cent a kitchen sink. Smaller dwellings, often accommodating old people, were considerably worse supplied with amenities than the average, 64 per cent of two-roomed dwellings being without a fixed bath.[15] On the outbreak of war in 1939 the officially-designated slums had numbered 472,000: in 1954, when the local authorities were required to survey their needs, and, for the first time, national criteria of 'unfitness' were laid down, they totalled 847,000. The rate of demolition in the later fifties, at 20–35,000 a year, was not impressive, though the Conservative Government optimistically believed that the problem was diminishing and in 1963 Sir Keith Joseph forecast the end of the slums within ten years. A new local authority survey in 1965, however, showed 824,000, almost exactly the same as a decade earlier, while a Ministry survey of 1967, carried out by public health inspectors working to a common standard, arrived at a depressing 1·8 million slum houses, much more widely spread over the country than had previously been assumed.[16] Through the sixties demolition was at the rate of 60–70,000 houses a year, and at this level the solution of the problem constantly receded. In all, some 900,000 slum dwellings were demolished in England and Wales between 1945 and 1968 and more than 2½ million people removed, but a huge problem of decayed, unfit houses still persisted in the older industrial towns like Liverpool (92,000 unfit dwellings in 1965), Manchester (55,000) and Birmingham (42,000).

NEW PLANNING CONCEPTS

The location of post-war local-authority housing was planned to a much greater extent than in the past and, in particular, opinion generally ran strongly against the further development of amorphous suburban council estates. In 1948 a Committee on the Appearance of Housing Estates pointed out that although some pre-war developments had been attractively laid out and provided 'a pleasant and neighbourly background for real community life', there were many others 'where all individuality and homeliness have been lost in endless rows of identical semi-detached houses. The depressing appearance of these estates is very largely due to monotony in design and layout, and to the repetition of the same architectural unit in dull, straight rows or in severe, geometrical road patterns which bear no relation to the underlying landscape features . . .'

Much of the thinking which was to dominate public-authority housing policy in the future was already evident here—the concern for environment and community, the desire to encourage variety while preserving harmony and beauty in the whole, above all, perhaps, the anxiety to prevent the spread of further suburban dormitories which had neither the advantages of town or country nor real identity of their own. Caught up in the spirit of socialist euphoria, many architects and planners saw themselves as social engineers whose principal, and complementary, tasks were to create community and beauty, to reunite the social classes which the nineteenth century had divided by restoring the town as a natural and desirable organ of civilized life.

These new philosophies found expression in several different directions—the rehabilitation of decayed city centres: the creation of 'neighbourhood units' and 'mixed development' schemes where a variety of house sizes and types would, it was hoped, mix the social classes; high density, multi-storey building which would lift the streets into the sky; and traffic-free 'pedestrian precincts' to protect those who remained on the ground. The revival of urbanism was also characteristically expressed in the New Town movement, designed both to prevent the continued growth of existing cities and conurbations by a policy of dispersal and at the same time to create new urban communities which would enjoy the benefits of planning, social admixture and a range of industries providing employment for a substantial proportion of the inhabitants. In many respects the new town concept was a return to the original garden city ideas of Ebenezer Howard which had subsequently been misapplied in the creation of suburban housing estates.

The first stirrings of the new idea had been heard just before the outbreak of World War II in the Barlow Report (Report of the Royal Commission on the Distribution of the Industrial Population) which had recommended the enlargement of some small towns and the creation of some new ones in order to provide industrial dispersal. In 1944 the Abercrombie Plan had further suggested the creation of ten new satellite towns to relieve pressure in Greater London. These ideas came together in the New Towns Act of 1946, and in a rush of enthusiasm fourteen new towns were designated by 1950, mainly, though not exclusively, in the south-east. After an interval of eleven years, eight more were named between 1961 and 1967, predominantly in the north of England. A third, and distinct, phase is noticeable thereafter of towns planned to grow to a much larger size than the earlier ones but from existing bases: of these, Milton Keynes, scheduled to reach a quarter of a million, was the outstanding example.

In all, twenty-two new towns were approved in England and Wales between 1946 and 1972. In many, the standards of layout and design of individual houses and groups have been very high, often better than those in local-authority schemes. Judged in terms of user satisfaction many have been successful as social experiments, though some suffered from an inadequate phasing of house-building with the provision of shops, schools and other amenities. But although the new town movement has rightly attracted much attention and admiration, its contribution to housing provision has so far been small. By 1972 the new towns had built 155,000 dwellings, while local authorities and private enterprise had added another 59,000 within their areas; their total population was 611,000, equivalent to 1·2 per cent of the population of the country. No brave new world had emerged from the new towns, no radical shift in the established pattern of cities and suburbs.

HOUSING TYPES AND STANDARDS—PUBLIC AUTHORITY

As World War II drew towards its close a determination to do both more and better than had been achieved after 1918 is evident in many aspects of social policy. New and improved standards of public housing for the people (not merely for the 'working class') were to take their place beside the Education Act, the National Insurance scheme and the National Health Service as part of the grand concept of a Welfare State which would both protect individuals and, in time, transform society.

As we have seen, the contribution of public authorities to the total housing programme after 1945 was much greater than after 1918, though subject to deceleration and acceleration, and to some changes in direction, mainly at the dictates of economic policy. In terms of standards of layout, design, accommodation and services the record was generally a good one, though here too there were advances and retreats which broadly reflected the state of economic health of the nation. In general, the quality of local authority housing was considerably higher than that of pre-war building, either council or speculative. Better layouts, better architectural designs, more intelligent planning and use of space and markedly improved technical equipment followed from the increased use of architects by local authorities and the positive lead given by the Ministry through its official Design Manuals.

The determination to avoid some earlier mistakes was particularly evident in the matter of estate layout. The pre-war suburban council estate had come to be a subject for attack on the grounds of its aesthetic and social monotony, and a strong preference for what came to be known as 'mixed development' was characteristic of many post-war schemes. The idea that estates should contain a mixture of building types—houses of different sizes, flats and maisonettes grouped as an architectural whole—owed much to the view of some sociologists that single-class housing estates were responsible for developing 'suburban neurosis' and for keeping the classes apart, and that it should be within the architect's brief to create 'neighbourhood spirit' and 'social integration'. This 'neighbourhood unit' concept of planning, which apparently originated in the New York Regional Plan of 1928, was explicitly referred to in Abercrombie's Greater London Plan of 1944.

The major government report on the design of post-war houses, the Dudley Report,[17] was also published in 1944, and its main recommendations were embodied in the Housing Manual of the same year. It was intended to do for post-war housing what the Tudor Walters Report of 1918 had done for inter-war housing, but to up-grade former standards in line

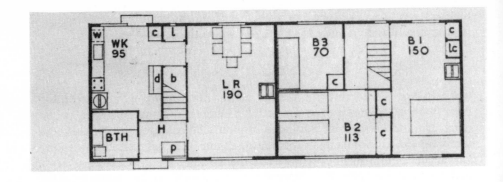

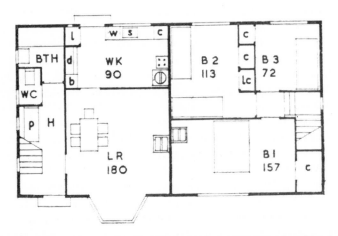

18 Post-war standards: an example of working-kitchen plan from the official *Housing Manual 1944*. Five people were accommodated in this wide-frontage design of 800sq ft floor area. Key: B bedroom, BTH bathroom, H hall, LR living room, WK working kitchen. Room areas shown on plan in square feet (*HMSO*)

with new needs, social trends and expectations. It began by identifying two major defects in pre-war council housing—lack of variety in the dwelling type, and the living-space too cramped and sometimes not adapted to modern needs. Three-bedroomed, non-parlour houses built under the 1923 and subsequent Acts had averaged 750–850sq ft overall, exclusive of stores; the Dudley Report recommended for these a minimum of 900sq ft, exclusive of stores, which was adopted in Ministry Circular 200 in 1945 and the *Housing Manual* of 1949. This allowed for a living-room of 160–200sq ft, a first bedroom of 135–150sq ft, a second of 110–120sq ft, and a third of 70–80sq ft. The Committee had heard much evidence, including that from women's organizations (which perhaps tended to represent 'middle-class'

rather than 'working-class' views), on the question of kitchen arrangements, which it recognized largely determined the plan of the house. It was
observed that in the pre-war house cooking had gradually been moving
from the living-room (still often provided with a range) to the
scullery/kitchen, where meals were increasingly being eaten, although this
had not been intended by the planners. Three planning possibilities
existed—first, to retain the traditional large living-room/kitchen where
meals would be cooked and eaten, with a small scullery containing the sink
and wash-boiler; second, to have a large living-room where meals would be
eaten, but a good-sized 'working kitchen' for cooking, particularly by gas
and electricity: and third, to have a smaller living-room and a large dining-
kitchen where meals would be cooked and eaten (in which case, a separate
wash-house would be necessary). The sizes of the two rooms would be
varied according to the plan type, *Circular 200* of 1945 recommending
living-room sizes of 160–220sq ft, a working-kitchen of 90–110sq ft, and a
dining-kitchen of 110–130sq ft.[18]

In this respect, planning ideas had taken an important step forward since
1918. It was recognized that gas and electricity had largely replaced
cooking by solid fuel in many parts of the country, and that as a matter of
convenience families wished to take at least some meals in the place where
the cooking was done, and also increasingly wanted a comfortable
living/sitting-room separated from kitchen smells and washing. Whether
there should be a second living-room—a 'parlour'—was still a vexed question in 1944. Families of above average size, it was felt, might need a small,
quiet room—now described as a 'sitting-room' rather than a
'parlour'—which could be as small as 110sq ft, and in this case the living-
room could be reduced to 170sq ft; it was clearly intended that there would
be a much reduced proportion of 'parlour houses'.

The other outstanding improvement which followed from the Dudley
Report was a general raising of the level of services and equipment. This
was especially evident in respect of kitchens and bathrooms. Kitchen
fittings now included sink and draining-boards, working surfaces, a
ventilated larder and cupboards for dry goods and crockery which were
generally carried up to ceiling height; early post-war kitchens also included
a small refrigerator, though this was omitted as costs rose. Probably their
greatest weaknesses were still size and an inadequate number of power
outlets for the growing number of electrical appliances which came to be
housed. Bathrooms, which before the war had often been placed in a bleak
space off the scullery without a hot water system, were now generally
moved to the bedroom floor. For families of five or more persons the 1945
Circular required two WCs (one in the bathroom and the other separate,
generally on the ground floor), another advance which was sacrificed to
economy in 1951. Other design improvements introduced in 1945 included
better lighted staircases and landings, an outside store of 50sq ft, increased

cupboard space and wardrobe cupboards in at least some bedrooms (at a recommended 2ft run per person).

It was still assumed in 1944 that the most common building type would be the semi-detached house with three bedrooms to meet the needs of the normal four- or five-person family. Although there was some experimentation with non-traditional materials such as steel frames clad in concrete or expanded clay, brick remained the usual form, and the 1944 *Manual* directed that outside walls should be 11in cavity; unrendered 9in walls would be regarded as sub-standard.[19] In this and other ways the best of pre-war practices were now being accepted as normal for local-authority housing. But in respect of housing types attitudes were still conservative. Flats received only one page of text in the 1944 *Manual*. It was thought that some might be necessary, 'even for families', in areas where high densities were unavoidable, but they should avoid the unpopular courtyard layouts and include a sunny balcony wherever possible. Some thought was given to the housing needs of old people, who could be accommodated in specially designed cottages or the lower floors of blocks of flats; they should not be segregated from other sections of the population, and should be positioned to give 'an interesting outlook from the living-room window'. In one of the rare mentions of central heating in the *Manual* it was suggested that in old people's houses there might be 'a small amount . . . to give "background" warmth'.

In the euphoria of 1945 hopes ran high that the recommendations of the Dudley Committee would open a new chapter in the history of housing standards. In terms of total floor area, amenities and services they represented a considerable advance on Tudor Walters twenty-five years earlier, and even more on the reduced standards which had been imposed in the thirties. But the pattern of events was shortly to follow that of the years after 1918 with depressing similarity. For a few years the official Housing Manuals accepted and even exceeded the Dudley recommendations. They were naturally interpreted differently by different local authorities, as had been the intention, some councils like the LCC favouring the 'working-kitchen' plan, others the kitchen/dining-room. There was noticeably more variety in housing density than in the pre-war estates, where 'twelve houses to the acre' had often been followed unquestioningly; the 1944 *Manual* recommended, in effect, a zoning of densities according to nearness to the town centre from 120 persons to the acre down to thirty persons to the acre in the outlying suburbs. This greater freedom of site planning produced two important related results—more 'mixed development' and a greater variety of house types and sizes.

'Mixed development' implied that there should be a greater variety of house sizes, both larger and smaller than the standard three-bedroomed, five-person house, in order to ensure a better 'fit' between house size and family size and a better 'mix' of the social classes. It was argued that there was need for more single-storey cottages for old people, more three-storey terraced houses for above-average families and higher income groups, and a proportion of flats, both low-rise and high-rise, for the needs mainly of childless families and for the sake of architectural balance. Mixed development began to be adopted in the late forties, particularly by the LCC in such schemes as the Somerford Estate, Hackney (1949), and in some new town developments such as Harlow where the first tall point-block was used in a scheme of 1950. Probably the most influential and widely-acclaimed mixed development scheme of this period was the LCC's Alton Estate at Roehampton (begun 1951) where a balanced group of eleven-storey point-blocks, four-storey maisonettes and two-storey houses was built on twenty-five acres, formerly the terraced gardens of large Victorian houses, where trees and landscaping were carefully preserved to give exciting views.

By the end of the decade, however, the post-war advance in standards was beginning to turn into an ordered retreat in the face of growing economic pressure. In 1951 the requirement of two WCs for a five-person household was reduced to one. More importantly, the minimum space standard of 900sq ft was relaxed, provided that 'aggregate living areas' were not reduced, an economy usually met by lowering circulation space in lobbies, passages and landings. Former minimum room sizes now became the maximum, and in the following years many three-bedroomed houses were built within the pre-war range of 750–850sq ft. Greater priority was also given to four-person houses having one double and two single bedrooms and total areas down to 740sq ft, exclusive of stores.

One important result of the economy measures of the early fifties was, therefore, increased variety of house-types and a marked breakaway from the traditional semi-detached. A revival of terraced housing was encouraged, maisonettes in four-storey blocks were increasingly employed, and flats in a variety of shapes—T-blocks, Y-blocks and cruciform-blocks—became a common feature of the sky-lines of many cities. These new forms chimed in with the growing emphasis on slum clearance and redevelopment in urban areas where land costs were an important factor, as also with the concept of 'neighbourhood units' which many planners believed would restore urbanism as an enviable way of life. Schemes like the LCC's Brandon Estate (1960), which incorporated modernized Victorian houses, high-rise flats, old people's homes and a square of four-storey maisonettes, were widely acclaimed as recreating the character and variety of Georgian town life.[20] Meanwhile, the average floor area of the three-bedroomed house continued to fall from the peak of 1,055sq ft in 1949 to 897 ten years later.[21]

The fifties saw two further developments which were also in line with the revival of urbanism. The first—a new type of housing layout which abandoned the orthodox street frontage—was a direct response to the growing volume of traffic in towns resulting mainly from increased car-ownership. If the pleasures of town life were to be restored, houses needed to be segregated from the noise and dirt of traffic by a new system of layout which would relegate the motor-car to its proper place as servant rather than master. What became known as 'Radburn' layouts (after a pioneer New York estate of the 1920s) began in a number of towns in 1950–2, all based on the idea of a traffic-free estate enclosed by a perimeter road. From this, culs-de-sac gave access to the vehicular side of houses but prevented 'through' traffic, while footpaths provided access to the pedestrian fronts of houses. At the centre of the unit would be sited the shops and public buildings, forming a pedestrian precinct. Numerous modifications and simplifications of the original Radburn principles were officially recommended in the manual *Houses* (1953) and were adopted slowly by some local authorities and new town corportions. They represented a major departure from traditional street planning and architecture, and their unfamiliarity was not always welcomed, but they inserted an important principle into planning, that man needed protection from his own technology.

The other significant change of the decade was the marked increase in the proportion of flats built by local authorities, and a decline in the traditional semi-detached house. Flats of all storey heights and maisonettes accounted for 55 per cent of all tenders approved by 1964; the growth of tall (five or more storeys) blocks was slower, accounting for 9 per cent of local authority building between 1953 and 1959, but reaching a peak of 26 per cent in 1966. Thereafter there was a rapid decline to 10 per cent by 1970. In retrospect, the high-rise flat was clearly an episode which did not fulfil the expectations of its proponents and never commanded the widespread affection, or even approval, of users. Dr E. W. Cooney has argued convincingly that the high flat represented an architectural ideal, the initiative for which lay with architects and planners who had come under the influence of the Modern Movement and pioneers such as Le Corbusier and Gropius in the 1930s. The vertical garden city was to replace the horizontal, wasteful of land and materials and ecologically unjustifiable. Moreover, it was believed that tall blocks would be able to take advantage of industrialized building methods which would give them distinct economic advantages over conventional structures.[22]

Tall blocks, as we have seen, first impinged on the urban landscape in the early fifties as part of 'mixed development' schemes. Their subsequent progress was encouraged by the demographic need for a greater proportion of one- and two-bedroom accommodation units, and by the increasing emphasis on inner-city slum clearance and redevelopment. It may also be that reasons of municipal prestige played a part, as they had sometimes done in the rivalry over the construction of town halls in the nineteenth century. By the middle of the decade government policy to extend green belts to cities other than London, and a new subsidy arrangement by which for the first time grants increased with the height of blocks over six storeys,

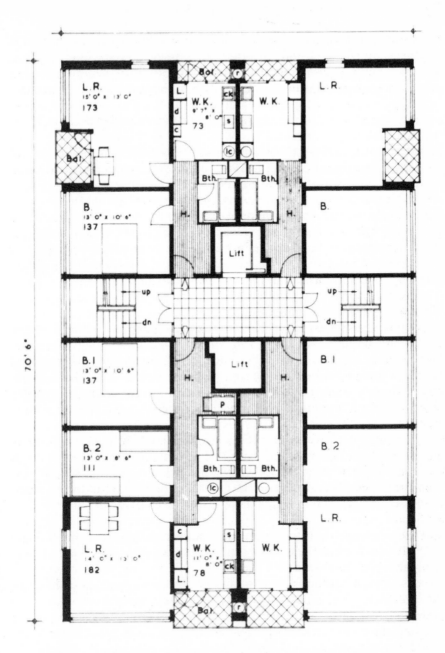

19   Tower flats. Typical floor plan published by Ministry of Housing and Local Government in 1958. Each floor contained a pair of four-person flats (684sq ft each) and a pair of two-person flats (498sq ft each). Vertical circulation was by two stairs and two lifts. Internal, mechanically ventilated bathrooms were a novelty of the time. Estimated average cost £2,110 per flat (*HMSO*)

led to the adoption of tall point blocks of up to twenty-two storeys in Sheffield and Salford, though other cities such as Manchester resolved against them. But, however opinions might divide as to their aesthetic and sociological merits or demerits, many local authorities came to accept that high-rise was an inescapable consequence of the need for much higher densities (of at least 140 persons/acre) in the inner cities if 'decanting' and 'overspill' were to be avoided.

The reaction against the current forms of high-rise is usually associated with the Ronan Point disaster in 1968. In fact, tall blocks had come under increasing criticism on social grounds since the early sixties, especially when, contrary to original intentions, they were used for the accommodation of families with young children. The architectural profession, which had been among the strongest advocates of high-rise, now increasingly spoke out against it. In an article entitled 'The Failure of "Housing"' in the *Architectural Review* in 1967 Nicholas Taylor complained that 'More slums are likely to be built in the next five years than in the past twenty'. The growing disillusionment of the architectural profession with the ways in which high-rise was being used, or abused, by local authorities coincided with growing doubt as to whether there were significant savings either in land or in building costs, and in 1967 official policy committed a *volte face* by abolishing the additional subsidy for storeys above six. The structural failure at the Ronan Point block next year only served to confirm opinions already largely formed that in future towers in the sky should be regarded as an abnormal building type reserved for special needs and under strict controls.

The abandonment of high-rise flats as a major housing type seems to have been broadly in accord with the weight of public opinion. The attitudes of users towards flat-dwelling depended largely on the composition of their families, surveys in the late fifties indicating that while many single persons and childless couples positively liked living in flats, the overwhelming majority of families with children disliked them on the grounds that they were too noisy, too small, and 'not the right place to bring children up'.[23] It may be that the initial hostility declined with increasing use and familiarity, for in an extensive enquiry in 1972 into residents' reactions to various types of housing, only two-fifths of housewives with children under the age of five expressed unhappiness at living off the ground. What apparently emerged as the main criterion of satisfaction was not density or building form as such, but the general appearance and character of the estate and the way it was looked after.[24]

In fact, much thought had been given to standards of space and amenities in flats in an effort to raise them well above pre-war levels. In the Dudley Report and the succeeding Manuals, room sizes in flats were to be the same as those for houses; a move away from balcony access to the costlier but more comfortable staircase access was noticeable, and there was considerable inventiveness in the design and equipment of kitchens. The problem of clothes drying in flats, for example, was largely overcome by the provision of drying cabinets, either private or communal, while for refuse disposal the advanced French water-borne system (the Garchey system) was occasionally installed at a cost of £70 per flat. Other advances were made in the heating and ventilating of high blocks, while freer planning of living space was made possible by the mechanical ventilation of bathrooms and WCs, which no longer had to be sited on external walls in order to provide windows. Again, since solid-fuel heating was not suitable for high flats, space and water heating by gas and electricity were encouraged, and, later, forms of district heating by hot water from a central boiler. Space standards suffered some reduction in the fifties, however, in line with the prevailing economy, and, unlike houses, minimum space standards applied only to living-rooms and bedrooms, not to the total area. High-rise dwellings built by the LCC were smaller than houses having the same number of bedspaces by an average of about 80sq ft.[25] In 1956 the LCC adopted a scheme which gave a range of floor areas from 510sq ft for flats with two bedspaces up to 794sq ft for maisonettes with five; through the sixties, however, there was a significant trend towards smaller units of accommodation so that in 1969 40 per cent of all flats constructed had only one bedroom and a further 45 per cent two.

The Tudor Walters Report of 1918 and the Dudley Report of 1944 had represented two landmarks in the design of public authority houses. The third, the Parker Morris Report, *Homes for Today and Tomorrow*, published in 1961, was potentially even more important in that it recommended standards for all new houses, whether public or private, and was intended to relate housing needs to the new social and economic trends which had developed since the war—the so-called 'revolution in expectations'. Significantly, the first section of the Report was devoted to an examination of 'New Patterns of Living', referring to the fact that 1,000 families moved into a newly-finished house every working day, that one household in three now possessed a car, and two in every three a television set.

All these changes are beginning to mean an easier, more varied and more enjoyable home life. Housewives now increasingly look to machinery to lighten their household tasks, and the family, and husbands in particular, now expect to help with much of the work that previously the housewife was left to do . . . These changes in the way in which people want to live, the things which they own and use, and in their general level of prosperity, and perhaps also the greater informality of home life, make it timely to re-examine the kinds of homes that we ought to be building . . .[26]

The recommendations of the Report were dominated by two overriding considerations—more space and better heating. Increased space was needed for activities demanding privacy and quiet, for larger storage and circulation areas, for the housing of the greater amount of equipment now in use, and to increase the sizes of kitchens. All social classes, it was agreed, now took some meals in the kitchen, which should therefore be large enough for a table and chairs as well as being conveniently arranged for easy housework. Previous Reports had determined the sizes of rooms with specific labels which assumed that their use would follow conventional patterns: this had imposed a uniformity on house-plans based on Dudley and the subsequent space reductions of the fifties. Parker Morris preferred to concentrate on the activities for which households of different types would use their homes, and the best ways of accommodating these within a total area. The whole approach of the Report was, therefore, a fundamental, radical one which questioned existing assumptions such as the number of storeys a house should have, whether the same space should be given to sleeping and sanitary functions as to all other uses, and the functions that furniture was expected to perform.

In effect, the Report recommended that houses for families should have two day-rooms—one to cater for activities needing privacy and freedom from disturbance, the other a dining area which might be either a meals space in a working kitchen, a differentiated meals area still within the kitchen, or, in larger houses, a separate room used for family meals and entertaining. No other 'reception room' was mentioned, and the Report therefore marked the public demise of the 'parlour'. Additional privacy for adolescent and older children could be provided by the use of bedrooms as bed-sitting-rooms for study or hobbies. Houses for five or more persons should always have two WCs, one separate and the other combined with the bathroom.

Special attention was devoted to the kitchen in a final effort to elevate it from the dreary scullery to the heart of the house. It should be large enough to accommodate the increasing quantity of household equipment, and properly planned, with, for example, space for a washing-machine near the sink. Extensive study of working operations in the kitchen had led to the establishment of a 'work sequence standard' of work surface/cooker/work surface/sink/work surface, unbroken by doors or other traffic ways, which should be provided in all kitchens, preferably in a U-shape to minimize movement. Only about 5 per cent of existing kitchens conformed to this pattern. It was also particularly important that kitchens should be amply

---

20   Parker Morris five-person house published by Ministry of Housing and Local Government, 1963. Subsequent houses of Parker Morris standards were usually of a simpler, cheaper form. Key—Ground floor plan: 1 lobby, 2 WC, 3 dining hall, 175sq ft, 4 bedroom 4, 57sq ft, 5 kitchen, 82sq ft, 6 living room, 151sq ft, 7 refuse, 8 garage/store, 9 garden store, 10 garden, 11 parking area, 12 access, 13 access common open space. First floor plan: 14 bedroom 2, 94sq ft, 15 bedroom 1, 128sq ft, 16 bedroom 3, 73sq ft, 17 bathroom/WC. Total area including stores 1,092sq ft (HMSO)

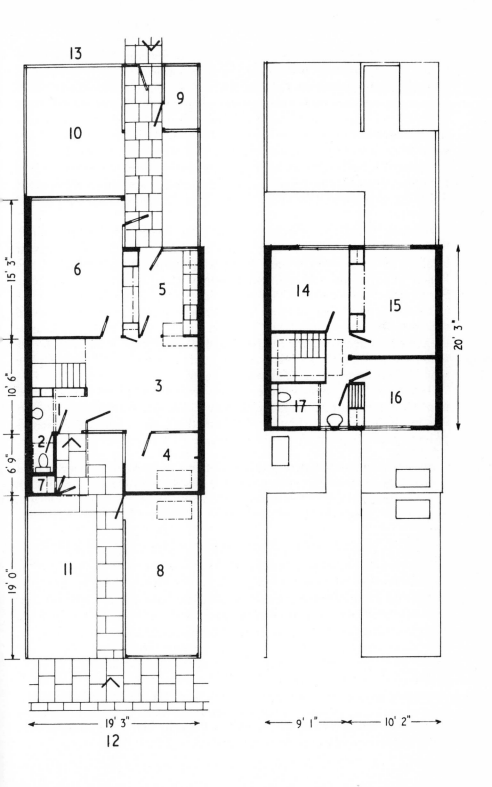

supplied with electric sockets, the Report recommending 15–20 per house instead of the average of six found in new houses.

Considerable increases in storage space were needed to accommodate the growing possessions of families. It was suggested that storage space in or adjacent to kitchens should be at least 80cu ft (instead of the 40cu ft commonly supplied); on the other hand, the larder was of declining importance with the growing use of refrigerators and packaged foods, and might now be replaced by a cool cupboard. A long-term trend towards the use of built-in furniture, especially in bedrooms, was also noted, and wherever possible wardrobe cupboards should be provided at the rate of 2ft of rail per occupier.

In total, these requirements implied both larger and better-planned houses than were currently being built. For a five-person family the current local authority house averaged 900sq ft including the general store: the Parker Morris house required a minimum of 910sq ft plus 50sq ft of store. For flats and maisonettes the intention was that space standards should be raised to the equivalent of those in houses so that a four-person flat would require an increase from 670 to 750sq ft, plus storage in both. In all cases, the recommended areas were to be regarded as minima: 'floor areas larger than these will often be called for, and should be encouraged'. The complete space specifications were as shown in Table 5.

Taken by themselves, the space recommendations represented important, but not revolutionary, advances. The new feature of the Report was its recognition that houses were something more than mere shelters providing an adequate separation of functions in a sanitary environment.

> An increasing proportion of people are coming to expect their home to do more than fulfil the basic requirements. It must be something of which they can be proud, and in which they must be able to express the fullness of their lives. There is, therefore, an increasingly prevalent atmosphere in which improvements in housing standards will be welcomed and indeed demanded, and in which stress will be laid upon quality rather than mere adequacy.

This growing interest in quality was evidenced, as we have seen, by the Report's concern with such things as brighter and better-fitted kitchens, the second WC, improved electrical installations and more cupboard and wardrobe provision. But, after more space, pride of place was given in the Report to better heating. 'Family life is both communal and individual . . . This dual tendency has always been handicapped during the winter months, except amongst the well-off, because of the inability of most people to afford heating in more than one or perhaps two living rooms.' The result was that in most houses half the rooms were used for sleeping purposes only. In local authority houses the most common provision was still an open fire with a back boiler for hot water, while a few only had a high-output back boiler capable of heating one or two radiators. In tall flats in recent years

TABLE 5   Recommended Standards Relating to Floor Space

A home to be built in the future for occupation by:

	6 people	5 people	4 people	3 people	2 people	1 person

should be designed with a net floor area of at least:

square feet

	6 people	5 people	4 people	3 people	2 people	1 person
3-storey house*	1050	1010	—	—	—	—
2-story centre terrace		910	800	—	—	—
2-storey semi or end	990	880	770	—	—	—
Maisonette				—	—	—
Flat	930	850	750†	610	480	320
Single storey house	900	810	720	610	480	320

*These figures will require modification if a garage is built in
†720 if balcony access

and general storage as follows:

square feet

	6 people	5 people	4 people	3 people	2 people	1 person
Houses‡	50	50	50	45	40	30
Flats and Maisonettes						
Inside the dwelling	15	15	15	12	10	8
Outside the dwelling	20	20	20	20	20	20

‡Some of this may be on an upper floor; but at least 25 square feet should be at ground level.
(Homes For Today and Tomorrow, *HMSO*, 1961.)

electric floor warming or gas warm air systems had sometimes been installed. The Parker Morris recommendation was that in future all houses should be equipped to heat the kitchen and circulation areas to a minimum of 55°F, and living areas to 65°, when the outside temperature was 30°, while in the future installations capable of also heating bedrooms to 65° might be required. It was important that the occupier should be able to control the degree of heating and, hence, the expenditure.

It had been intended that the Parker Morris recommendations would not immediately be made mandatory, but should gradually be adopted by both public and private builders. The Report itself acknowledged that the additional costs of building to the new standards would add from $8\frac{1}{2}$ per cent to 15 per cent to a five-person house, even without central heating. In fact, the average cost of local authority three-bedroomed houses rose from £1,611 in 1961 to £2,951 in 1967, and this background of inflation acted as a serious disincentive to the adoption of costlier standards. By 1965 only 20 per cent of new council houses had fully incorporated Parker Morris recommendations[27] and an uncertain, though probably smaller, proportion of private houses, and it was this slow progress of voluntary adoption which moved the Labour Government to make Parker Morris recommendations mandatory for public sector housing in new towns in 1967 and for local authorities in 1969—although interpreted as maximum standards and not, as originally intended, as recommended minima. They have not yet been made mandatory in the private sector.

The intention was that Parker Morris houses would be able to utilize their larger areas for freer, more flexible planning which would break away from conventional allocations of space. On the other hand, the needs of economy and the increased use of industrialized building techniques tended to militate against individuality and to produce their own kind of standardization. Probably the 'typical' Parker Morris house of the sixties was terraced rather than semi-detached, with a large through living-room, a kitchen large enough for meals, and three bedrooms. Circulation areas were noticeably larger than formerly, while larger 'picture' windows gave lightness to interiors. The Report had offered some encouragement to 'open planning' of interiors, but the enthusiasm for this was waning by the sixties and its most noticeable effect was in the kitchen/dining area where forms of unit 'room dividers' became common. Although the decade was marked by considerable fertility of architectural ideas for the 'adaptable house' and even the 'expendable house', the fact was that within the cost and space limits of the two-storey house the scope for innovative planning was extremely limited. More could be done with the three-storey house, built for larger families and higher income levels: here, a garage and store could be provided on the ground floor, a large living area on the first floor and bedrooms on the second. More radical plan types included L-shaped and 'patio' houses which gave a high degree of privacy in the rear gardens, but both were relatively expensive and were not widely adopted.

Some of the best interpretations of Parker Morris, as of earlier standards, came from the new towns, whose development corporations were usually keenly aware of the opportunities and responsibilities of planning communities for the future. Here there were often attempts to build in styles which would harmonize with the local vernacular, and new-town houses were often a successful compromise between the stark prefabricated styles of the post-war era and more traditional forms. Thus, at Hatfield (1955) individuality was given to terraced houses by separate gables, while at

Basildon New Town (1956) many of the terraces were designed with a deliberately 'cottagey' appearance.[28] The increasing use of prefabricated materials led to the revival of a conflict among architects as to whether they should accept the simplicity and uniformity of unrelieved surfaces or seek to disguise them with applied 'cladding' in familiar materials. Generally, disguise won the day, and in the sixties the simple lines of many new-town and local-authority houses became masked by claddings of brick, tile, clapboard and plastic. As roof-pitches were lowered and chimney-stacks virtually disappeared, these devices may be seen as despairing attempts to preserve some identifiable 'character' in the house in the face of increasing standardization of external appearance.

HOUSING TYPES AND STANDARDS—PRIVATE

The most striking single fact in the history of post-war housing is the revolution in tenures which has made property-owning, if not fully democratic, at least no longer elitist. Before 1914 less than 10 per cent of all houses in England and Wales were owner-occupied, in 1950, 29 per cent and in 1970, 49 per cent. Owner-occupied houses were of varied type, size and age, from Victorian villas to between-the-wars semis and post-war 'town houses'; they did not represent one particular type of house or one class of occupier. By the sixties, for instance, there were marked trends towards the purchase of former council houses, and towards the 'gentrification' and sale of Victorian cottage property, both formerly rented. Our main concern here, however, is with the three million or so new houses, privately built between 1945 and 1970 and which by the latter date accounted for nearly one in five of all private family dwellings.

With this rapid growth of owner-occupation, the pride of possession and the home-centredness of social life became more pronounced and more widely diffused than formerly. The house continued to have a major function as a status symbol and 'a symbol of the self' which announced to the world information about its owner's character, tastes, interests, wealth, plans and aspirations.[29] Indeed, as economic differences within and between the social classes narrowed, and the form of the house became increasingly standardized, minor differences had to be exploited to convey identity and individuality. In the past, the size of the house and garden, its environment, condition and general character had immediately proclaimed the social position of its occupier, but in the post-war world housing standards increasingly converged, partly because the quality of local authority housing was deliberately raised and partly because that of private housing was tailored to a mass market which, at the lower end, was scarcely distinguishable from that for council housing. As the size and structure of the two types of dwelling came closer together, it became ever more important to accentuate the identity of the private house by such symbols as a distinctive façade and front garden. The occupier himself could further 'personalize' the external appearance of the house in ways not open to the council tenant, and could also demonstrate social status by more advanced and expensive equipment within the home—for example, lighting, cleaning and cooking appliances of a type made fashionable in women's magazines.[30]

Certain characteristics of the privately-built post-war house therefore emerge. First is the increasing convergence of what in earlier chapters we described as the 'middle-class' and the 'working-class' house, and the increasing conformity between the two in terms of space and amenity standards. The proportion of larger houses in the total housing stock markedly declined between 1911, when 16 per cent of houses in England and Wales had seven rooms, and 1961 when only 7 per cent had this number; similarly, small dwellings with only one, two or three rooms, which in 1911 accounted for 25 per cent of the total, fell to 15 per cent in 1961.[31] This trend towards the medium-sized house of four, five or six rooms accorded with changes in family size and with the decline of resident domestic servants and their need for accommodation. By the late sixties only 4 per cent of new private houses were being built with four or more bedrooms—twice the proportion of council houses, but still very much less than before the war.

A second characteristic, which followed from the decline in number of rooms, was a decline in total area, and an increasing concentration of privately-built houses in the range of 750–1,000sq ft—the size associated with local-authority building since the Tudor Walters Report. Evidence of this has been collected by the Building Research Station from the records of mortgages granted by the Co-operative Permanent Building Society in 1962. These show that of the houses built before 1920 on which mortgages were granted 41 per cent fell into the 750–999sq ft range, 24 per cent into 1,000–1,249, 9 per cent 1,250–1,499 and 11 per cent over 1,500sq ft—a total of 44 per cent in the 'larger' category of over 1,000sq ft. Of the houses built in 1962, 65 per cent were in the 750–999sq ft range, 19 per cent between 1,000 and 1,249, only 5 per cent 1,250–1,499 and 3 per cent over 1,500—a total of only 27 per cent in the 'larger' bracket.[32] At the top end of the private market, of course, some 'luxury' houses continued to be built at 1,500sq ft or more, and a few at 2,000sq ft, but these now represented an almost insignificant proportion of the output.

Some further characteristics of the privately-built house emerge from a study by the Building Research Station of the plans of eighty houses offered for sale in 1966 by four large building firms, and a comparison of these with plans of local-authority houses designed in accordance with Parker Morris standards. The privately-built houses ranged in price from £2,500 to £22,500, with overall floor areas of 500–2,000sq ft. Nearly a quarter of the eighty houses, mostly those in the cheaper price range, fell short of Parker

Morris space standards. The number of day-rooms ranged from one to three in the most expensive, one being the most common, but it was noticeable that proportionately more space was given to the living area than in local-authority houses, presumably because a large 'entertaining room' had important status symbolism. On the other hand, kitchens were generally smaller than in local-authority houses, commonly 75sq ft rather than 90–100sq ft, and although fittings were often more expensive, they did not satisfy the recommended work sequence pattern in half the plans. Provision for storage was usually well below Parker Morris standards except in the most expensive houses. In the plans designed for a five-person family, the space per person was 185sq ft compared with 192sq ft recommended by Parker Morris.

The interesting question is whether such differences—the larger living-area, the more expensively fitted kitchen often too small to allow space for dining—reflected preferred differences in the living patterns of the two sets of users, or whether they represented builders' 'selling points' directed more towards social differentiation, real or imagined. What, in fact, did the buyer look for in a new house? The answer would probably lie in a complicated equation of convenience, utility, comfort, environment and social status, with, in many cases, a lower priority given to functional than to symbolic factors. It remained important in the fifties and sixties, as it had in the inter-war period, that the private house should be readily distinguishable from the council house, both externally and internally. It should reflect membership of a distinct group, the possession of distinct tastes and values and the ownership of a distinctive level of material possessions. As the size and design of private and public housing converged ever more closely, it became increasingly important to accentuate remaining differences.

Externally, the appearance of the private house tended to reflect current fashions more quickly and completely than the more conservative public-authority house. There was, however, no dominant architectural idiom, and no single stylistic message filtered through to the speculative builder from the pages of the architectural 'glossies'. Where the building firm was large enough to employ or commission architects of repute—and a growth in size of operations was a marked characteristic of the post-war building trade—some simple, effective designs resulted which made use of architectural blocks of terraces set in careful landscaping. Some of the most acclaimed work of this kind came from the collaboration of the architect Eric Lyons with the contracting firm of Span. Houses built by such large companies as Taylor Woodrow, Laing and Wimpey also had the benefit of architectural design, and brought high standards of construction and simple outlines into mass housing. Departures from the orthodox pre-war semi-detached plan were early introduced by such firms, including integrated and linked garages filling the unsightly 'gap', terraced houses, three-storey town houses and four-storey maisonettes, many of which were later adopted in local-authority schemes. If there was any one stylistic influence in the façades it was probably the 'functional' characterized by flat wall surfaces, large square or oblong 'picture' windows, low-pitched roofs, and the use of coloured panels or timber for decorative effect.

In the hands of less skilled and sensitive builders the smaller speculative house was often made the subject of much crude ornamentation with the aim of evoking images either of the past or of some fashionable 'contemporary' style. The 'Tudorbethan' style was much less in evidence than before the war, though some sham half-timbering was being reintroduced in a few houses in the late sixties; much more popular were 'Georgian' and 'neo-Georgian' styles, characterized by pedimented porches, small-paned windows (not now generally sash) and non-working louvred shutters. They had the advantage of giving to the small detached house the logical plan of a large through living-room to one side of the narrow hall, with dining-room and kitchen to the other, and could easily be adapted to terraced and courtyard formations. Larger versions, designed for the 'executive' end of the market, were sometimes described as 'Colonial style', and incorporated double garages under a colonnaded façade. Bow-windows, imitation coach-lamps and concrete classical urns were frequent embellishments of all these types. For those with 'contemporary' tastes the dominant influence was the 'Scandinavian', instantly recognizable by its exaggeratedly pitched roof sweeping almost to the ground on some elevations, use of dormer windows and timber fascias: the effect would often be carried through internally by pine-panelled kitchens and timbered ceilings. One of the distinguishing features of private houses was now the almost universal provision of garages, often in a separate block for smaller terraced houses but usually integrated or incorporated into the detached house to give direct access from the kitchen or utility room.

Any of these styles, faithfully executed and detailed, could make convincing and comfortable houses, though there might be doubts about the appropriateness of the 'Scandinavian' in the English suburbs or the 'Colonial' squeezed in between Victorian villas. But too often, as in the thirties, the detailing was merely crude and clumsy, stuck on to a standard design to give a spurious individuality and, perhaps, to make it abundantly clear that no local council could have authorized such idiosyncrasy. It was easy enough to poke fun at the more recent eccentricities of suburbia, as it had been with 'By-Pass Variegated' in the thirties.

The newest, flat-fronted versions of the suburban house often boast a band of white-painted clapboarding, reminiscent of the charming rural architecture of Kent and the coastal districts of Essex, or of cedarwood cladding in the Scandinavian fashion . . . These variations attempt to provide meaningless, mass-produced designs with a reassuring suggestion of individuality. In the names they choose, in the irrational design of their gates, the varieties of hedging they grow, in their sudden indulgence in a splash of mauve or orange paint, in their weakness for crazy paving, concrete gnomes and rabbits crouching on the rims of bird baths or peering from miniature caverns in the rockery ... the occupants themselves make faint, despairing gestures of personality in a world deprived of those attributes of period and locality which once gave precise definition to every house, and thus furnished a firm framework for each individual life.[33]

Internally, also, the 1,000sq ft three-bedroomed speculative house was chiefly distinguished from local-authority housing by details of fitting, finishes and equipment rather than by fundamental design differences. A preference for two 'reception rooms', even though these might be only of the order 12ft by 12ft square, survived through the fifties, or where only one large living-room was provided it was often in an L-shape which allowed for a screening of the dining area. A 'feature' fireplace of brick or stone was often provided, with variations at the purchaser's expense. Much emphasis was placed on the 'luxury kitchen', which usually included half-tiling of the walls, stainless steel sink unit, wall and floor cupboards with plastic laminate working surfaces and serving-hatch to the dining area. A ground-floor 'cloakroom' (WC and hand basin) was becoming more common, though far from universal. A hot-water boiler was usually fitted in the kitchen, capable of warming two or three radiators in the hall and living rooms, though by the sixties full central heating, often by warm air ducts rather than radiators, was increasingly common. This adoption of full or partial central heating, the provision of a garage and of a second WC, of hardwood floors to the hall and, sometimes, the 'lounge', and attractive fittings to the kitchen and bathroom (coloured 'suites', thermoplastic flooring, fluorescent lights, venetian blinds, etc) represented the major differences between the smaller speculative house and that built by public authorities. But the element of choice was also important. Most builders, even of small developments, offered two or three versions of a basic design which gave some variety of rearrangement to the living area or the size and number of bedrooms. Moreover, if he bought at a sufficiently early stage, the client could usually negotiate minor changes such as flooring, fittings, extra power outlets and wardrobe cupboards. Such relatively minor differences might assume major importance as symbolizing the discretionary power of ownership as opposed to the lack of choice of a council tenant.

Some idea of the changing characteristics of low to medium priced speculative houses may be gathered from the records of Taylor Woodrow Houses Ltd who by 1954 were building 1,000 houses a year, predominantly in the South and Midlands, although the firm had originated in Blackpool. In 1953 one of their main developments was the 'Garden City Estate', Kidlington, where semi-detached houses of 910sq ft (21½ft frontages) were being sold at £1,655. These had an 'adequately sized' dining-room 12ft 6in by 11ft 8½in heated by a continuous burning fire with back boiler, a lounge

11ft 8½in by 11ft 3¼in (heated by electric fire) and a kitchen 11ft by 6ft 9in (two electric points, Marley composition tiling, hardwood draining boards, ventilated larder). There were two double bedrooms with 'sufficient space for full-sized bedroom suites', and a small third bedroom in which the often protruding bulkhead was avoided. In 1954 similar semi-detached houses were being built at Old Windsor for £1,950 and detached at £2,750. The plan was still conventional and the elevation strictly utilitarian. In 1955 the firm resumed building in Blackpool after thirty years, offering a three-bedroomed semi at £1,895 which could be acquired for a deposit of £95 and weekly repayments of £2 6s 0d. They were described as having 'kitchens which would do credit to mansions—kitchens complete with electric washing machines, refrigerators, stainless steel sink units with draining boards, electric clocks, batteries of cupboards, the tops of some of which serve as tables too. The interiors are not only luxurious, but gay—the cupboards are in red and ice-blue, with decorative designs on the doors'.

Until now Taylor Woodrow's designs had been traditional, if not old-fashioned, but in 1956 they launched 'The Home of Tomorrow' at Crawley New Town, costing £2,195 and built on the revolutionary 'open plan' system. It was described as 'well within the financial reach of Mr and Mrs Everyman', and 'the house every woman has dreamed about'.

Design is based on the open planning idea—a bold step indeed from the orthodox type of house of the 1930s for the whole ground floor is intercommunicated. Entering the house, with its attractive reeded glass door screen and shelves by the front door, is the lounge hall—a spacious, elegant room, 18½ feet long and 12 feet wide. Along the whole facing wall are built-in shelves, to hold, perhaps, a few cherished books, a choice ornament, treasured knick-knacks, or one of those delicate, trailing indoor plants. These are centred by an electric fitted log fire. The lounge sweeps through to the dining area, nearly 11 feet square, with its low, wide picture frame window. It leads to a dream of a kitchen, which again follows the wide-open look. A feature of this is the bright stainless steel, double-sided sink unit with built-in cupboards above and below. Another wall has more long built-in cupboards, and there are yet others to ceiling height, while still more are built around the most up-to-date of refrigerators, which is set at eye-level. Perhaps the most unique of all is a specially made breakfast table fitment covered with scarlet formica at working top height with a cascade of drawers—one green baize lined for cutlery—and a space for the washing machine. Yes—this, too, is included in the price, and believe it or not, so is the electric clock on the wall.

The design also had central heating by warm air ducts—an unusual innovation in a house at this price.

Thereafter, the open-plan house was built on several Taylor Woodrow developments, usually together with conventional two-living-room types and bungalows. In 1958 the kitchen was redesigned to include an English Electric cooker withan eye-level oven and a hot-plate built in to the worktop, a double sink unit and waste extractor. Another new feature of this period was the increasing provision of garages or, in the cheaper houses, garage space. By the sixties garage and background central heating were nearly always included, and the open plan continued to be built throughout the decade—by 1967 the current version of this, the 'Californian', was selling at £5,075. The most expensive house offered at this time was the 'County D9', a four-bedroomed detached house at £7,450 which included a ground-floor cloakroom with half-tiled walls, a combined lounge and dining-room separated by a sliding screen, mosaic hardwood flooring to the ground floor, a fully fitted kitchen with half-tiling, coloured sanitary ware in the bathroom, built-in cupboards in the principal bedrooms and central heating by a gas-fired warmed air appliance. In the medium-priced houses of the late sixties the separate dining-room had disappeared in favour of a dining area in the large living-room and a breakfast area in the kitchen. The most expensive houses being built in 1970 at High Wycombe were just under £10,000: they had a combined lounge/dining room 22ft by 12ft, four bedrooms and double garage, and either a 'utility room' adjoining the kitchen or a small study. Interestingly, where extra space was available in these larger houses it was given either to a service function (in effect, the old scullery renamed 'utility room' but used primarily for clothes washing) or as a quiet retreat from the single, all-purpose living-room.[34]

Beyond this range designed for the mass market were the 'luxury' houses selling, in the late sixties, at prices from around £10,000 to £20,000. Unlike those just described, which were usually built in developments of a hundred or more houses, the 'luxury' house was typically one of a small development of a dozen or fewer houses—detached if in the suburbs and on a plot of a quarter of an acre or less rather than the half-acre or more of pre-war days; in towns, it was frequently a three-storey terraced house with small 'patio' garden. In these houses the large 'drawing-room' of 200–300sq ft survived, as did a separate dining-room, though, at around 150sq ft considerably smaller than in the past. A third reception room, the 'study', at around 100sq ft was normal, and an indication of the professional occupation of the owner. Kitchens in such houses were 150sq ft upwards, often with a breakfast area or 'breakfast bar'. By 1970 the plastic, clinical kitchen had often given way to a more homely 'farmhouse kitchen' with pine-panelled walls and natural wood finishes. A separate utility or laundry room meant that the kitchen was now often used for all family meals and, in the servantless house, was the real centre of middle-class family life. Too much space, even in a fully centrally-heated house, might be dysfunctional, and the daily living of families rarely spread over more than two rooms; others, the survivors of the former 'receiving' or 'state' rooms, might still be needed for ceremonial occasions where status required a public identity separate from the private.

Bedrooms in the 'luxury' house necessarily changed less. There would be four or five rather than three, with an increasing number of built-in wardrobes and dressing-tables rather than suites of bedroom furniture. The major change here was the provision of the 'en suite' bathroom or shower-room to the principal bedroom. A descendant of the Victorian dressing-room, it gave privacy to the parents and released the second bathroom for use by children or guests; its fittings and decor—the tiling, coloured 'suite', sunken bath and gold-plated taps—became considerable status symbols, vying in importance with the kitchen fittings and the 'Adam style' or natural stone fireplace in the drawing-room.

In the post-war speculatively-built house, therefore, as in the local-authority house, the most significant improvement was in quality rather than in any increase of space. The meaning of 'quality' here also needs to be narrowed to refer not to actual building construction—the standard of which was often very high in pre-war housing—but primarily to amenities, services and fittings. Before the war, the smaller house, whether private or public, was not very much more than a weather-proof box divided into a series of spaces by partition walls. Compared with its Victorian predecessor, it had made important advances such as a proper water supply and waste system, an internal WC and, probably, a bathroom, and more convenient lighting and cooking arrangements by gas or electricity, but beyond this, internal fittings were often quite minimal—a kitchen fitted with a sink, a draining-board and a couple of shelves, no hot-water supply to the bathroom, a single electric point on the upstairs landing to serve the power needs of three bedrooms, and so on. The greatest advances in the post-war house have been in respect of comfort and convenience, represented by improved heating systems, better fitted and equipped kitchens, bathrooms and WCs properly incorporated into the house-plan, adequate electric power outlets and increased storage space, including storage of the car.

These improvements in housing quality ultimately depended on the economic growth of the fifties and sixties and on the rising standards of living of many people whichwere especially reflected in the drive towards home-ownership and home-improvement. As one of the world's affluent societies England was able to command larger houses, giving greater separation of activities, than almost any other country, so that whereas in 1961 only 5 per cent of dwellings consisted of one or two rooms, in Italy 42 per cent did so, in Poland 58 per cent and in Mexico 80 per cent.[35] Amenities, though less quantifiable than rooms, would almost certainly have exhibited the same trend. But by 1970 the expectation of continued advances was in doubt, mainly because of escalating costs of land, labour, materials and finance for new house-building. Neil Wates, the managing director of one of the largest building firms, reported to *The Times* that in some respects standards in private housing were declining. Ten years before, 'middle market' houses had been increasing in size, but were now reducing; standards of fittings and fixtures reached a peak about 1965 but had since fallen except in the upper reaches of the market, and things such as hardwoods, block flooring and superior sanitary ware which had formerly been fitted as 'standard' were now being either reduced or omitted. Improvements which had been maintained—largely, he believed, through the activities of the National House Builders' Registration Council—included better central heating and insulation.[36] It was a timely warning that further progress in housing quality was not inevitable, and that housing, like any other aspect of the standard of living, depended crucially on the state of the nation's economic health.

11

RETROSPECT AND PROSPECT

Certain broad generalizations emerge from this study of changes in housing standards over the last century and a half. Judged by the kinds of criteria which have been used in earlier chapters to measure housing quality—overcrowding, amenities, proportion of sharing households and the like—there can be no doubt that by 1970 a major improvement had taken place in the housing conditions of most English people. But this improvement was mainly a recent one, noticeable in the inter-war period, but particularly concentrated in the decade of the 1950s. Viewed over the whole period of this study, the housing experience of many people showed little major change until, in the years after World War II a period of rapid house-building, both public and private, coincided with full employment and a rising standard of living to produce an effective demand.

From the late nineteenth century overcrowding was used as the principal test of housing quality. In its crudest form it merely counted the number of persons per dwelling, taking no account of variations in their size, but it was useful as a measure of the extent to which different activities in the home could be separated and hence of the degree of privacy which individuals could enjoy. The overall change—from 5·11 persons per dwelling in 1861 to 2·97 in 1966—was dramatic, especially as most of the improvement was concentrated into the last thirty years. In the reduction of the most severe overcrowding the decade of the 1930s appears to mark a turning-point.[1] A measure of persons per room is clearly more meaningful, and began to be used at the end of the nineteenth century as a test of 'overcrowding' on the basis of two adults per room (children under ten counting as half). In more recent surveys the base-line was raised to $1\frac{1}{2}$ adults per room. In 1911, 16·9 per cent of all households in England and Wales were living at a density of more than $1\frac{1}{2}$ persons per room, while in 1961 only 2·8 per cent still remained. It may well be that, against a background of generally rising standards and expectations, a realistic measure of overcrowding ought to be more sophisticated than this, but more elaborate data for the past do not exist. The simple test of persons per room is still the best tool we have for recording changes over time, and indicates a reduction in high room densities to negligible national proportions by 1970.

But although gross overcrowding of Victorian proportions had all but ceased by the end of our period, the improvement was by no means equally shared. While the mean number of persons per room fell consistently from 1·10 in 1911 to 0·66 in 1961, the greatest gains in terms of space went to small households of three persons or less. Households of five persons showed only a marginal gain—1·00 person per room in 1911, 1·03 in 1931 and 1951 and 0·97 in 1961; in the last year, households of eight or nine persons still had a room density of 1·47. To this extent, therefore, there was still a persistence of the long-established pattern of the greatest amount of overcrowding occurring in the largest households, a condition often likely to exist during the family-building stage of the life-cycle. In 1970, people enjoyed their most spacious housing conditions towards the end of their lives, while a significant proportion still experienced overcrowding when their growing families most needed space.

In the nineteenth century, as we have seen, space correlated directly with income, so that middle-class households generally had substantially lower densities than the working classes. Although this has remained broadly true, the gap between the classes has narrowed very considerably. In 1966 self-employed professional workers had a ratio of 0·45 persons per room, employees and managers of large firms 0·53, while unskilled manual workers at 0·65 were not so outstandingly different as in the past. It is now clear that more important as a determinant of housing density than socioeconomic grouping is type of tenure. In terms of space, the owner-occupier at 0·59 persons per room in 1961 had the greatest advantage. Those renting private furnished accommodation were housed considerably less spaciously at 0·81 persons per room, while, surprisingly at first sight, the least favourably accommodated were local-authority and new-town tenants at 0·84. (This is, of course, largely explained by the policy of many councils of giving preferential allocation to larger families.)

It is important to note, too, that regional differences still constituted a major determinant of housing density at the end of the period, and that the pressure of population in the south-east was reflected by markedly higher densities in the metropolis. In 1966 the Greater London region had twice the national average of people living at more than $1\frac{1}{2}$ per room (2·4 per cent compared with 1·2 per cent), while the Eastern region had only 0·5 per cent and the South-Western 0·7 per cent. This concentration of crowding in the metropolis was also illustrated by the statistics of households sharing accommodation in tenemented houses (ie not structurally separate dwellings such as self-contained flats). Although the national figure for households sharing improved from 15·7 per cent in 1911 to 7·3 per cent in 1966, in Greater London in the last year 24·2 per cent of households shared compared with the next highest, Merseyside, at 7·2 per cent and the West Midlands conurbation at 5·3 per cent.[2]

At the extreme end of overcrowding and pressure on accommodation still lay a problem of homelessness. What the true figures of the 'homeless' were in 1970, or at any earlier time, is impossible to know. Victorian England was familiar enough with the tramp, and with the men, women and children who slept out in the parks and under railway arches, but official statistics relate only to recent years and only to the numbers of persons provided for in local-authority temporary accommodation. They therefore demonstrate trends in the amount of that accommodation available rather than the number of people requiring it, such accommodation normally being provided only for families with children, not for single persons. Though of limited use, therefore, the figures show a clear upward trend for London since the war, rising from 3,500 persons in 1951 to 8,600 in the Inner London boroughs in 1970. An estimate of the single homeless in 1966 gave 11,000.[3]

The problem was essentially one of the great cities, and especially of London, where more than a third of the nation's homeless were concentrated. John Greve, the author of a study of the problem in London, believed that its main cause was a serious restriction in the amount of unfurnished accommodation available at a time when the number of households was continuing to rise. Slum clearance, sales of houses to sitting tenants, and 'middle-class colonization' had all reduced the supply of accommodation for letting, and had produced increased overcrowding and sharing in boroughs such as Kensington and Chelsea, Westminster and Islington. In the last, the proportion of people living at more than $1\frac{1}{2}$ per room, at 9·8 per cent in 1966, was four times the average of Greater London, and the proportion of sharing households, at 57 per cent, almost eight times the national average.

Homelessness and sharing were two surviving, though localized, housing problems in 1970. A third, much more widespread in its incidence, was that of obsolete and decaying housing which was now unacceptable in terms of standard and amenity. Despite the active building programmes since the war, in 1967, 38 per cent of all houses in England and Wales dated from before 1919, and, in fact, because of the slow rates of building between 1900 and 1914, many of these were now more than seventy years old. A high proportion of this older housing stock was still seriously deficient in basic amenities, let alone in modern comforts. Evidence from the sixties showed that lack of amenities correlated closely with the age of the dwelling and the type of tenure, the least advantaged groups being the old and the newly-married occupying privately rented accommodation where much of the older property was concentrated.[4] A survey which was carried out in 1962 showed that 53 per cent of private unfurnished tenants were without a fixed bath, 42 per cent without a hot water tap, 44 per cent without a garden and

7 per cent without a flush toilet.

By then, the need for rehabilitation of older property was coming to be seen in a wider context of social policy. Continued demolition, slum clearance and the dispersal of urban populations to suburban fringes and new towns was beginning to drain the life away from the inner cities, to transform once thriving town centres into derelict wastes or into shopping precincts peopled only during business hours. These anxieties coincided with the view of an increasing number of architects and planners that many later Victorian houses were soundly constructed and could, with modernization, continue to provide useful accommodation without social upheaval. As part of their policies of urban renewal, councils in many cities compulsorily purchased areas of older houses for renovation, or incorporated such property into schemes of mixed development. Between 1945 and 1968 almost $4\frac{1}{2}$ million houses (not including war-damaged houses) were made fit either by the owner or by local authorities, and improvement grants were approved for 1,300,000 dwellings. In relation to the total housing stock of approximately sixteen million, the statistics of improvement represent a major, if still incomplete, achievement.

If we turn from the national statistics of housing to the quality of houses themselves, it is clear that the most striking improvement achieved in the last century and a half was in the accommodation of the working classes. The pace of that improvement was quicker in the twentieth century than in the nineteenth, it varied importantly between town and country, and again between town and town. The development of a sanitary house, with adequate standards of construction, water supply and sewerage, was the product of the Public Health Acts and, more especially, of the building by-laws from 1875 onwards, which brought about a major, and largely unrecognized, advance in working-class housing standards. The transformation of the sanitary house into a larger, lighter, better-equipped and more comfortable home was principally the result of the involvement of the State in the subsidization of mass housing from 1919 onwards, and the adoption by local authorities of the successively higher standards set by the Tudor Walters, Dudley and Parker Morris committees. These owed much to the new concepts of house planning and estate layout developed by 'model' employers and the garden city movement at the end of the previous century: in turn, the improved construction and design of local-authority houses between the wars and after 1945 had the effect of generally raising the standards of lower-priced speculative housing. In both types, the entry of the architect into mass housing—first, in the case of local-authority building and, increasingly from the 1930s onwards, in speculative building—must generally be accounted a major gain, though the power which the expansion of public housing brought to planners and local authorities to determine the form of people's homes sometimes produced insensitive results.

The predecessor of the urban industrial worker's house was the rural labourer's cottage, which, despite the scattered attempts at improvement by 'model' landlords, continued to represent the lowest levels of any widespread building form throughout the nineteenth century. The evolution of the urban working-class cottage was from general to more specialized functions as the amount of available space increased. Even the back-to-back house, normally containing three or four rooms, represented an improvement on the rural cottage with its single living-room and attic bedroom. House for house, the back-to-back almost certainly represented the first rung on the ladder of improvement of working-class housing. It was a type deliberately designed for those on low earnings, and because it was cheaply rented, it almost always allowed occupation by a single family.

To this extent, the midland and northern towns like Nottingham and Leeds which had high proportions of back-to-backs were fortunate. In London, Liverpool and Manchester, where there were large populations of casual labour, the great housing evil was multi-occupation, where families could afford to rent only one or two rooms in a larger house and were obliged to share totally inadequate amenities. In such areas the creation of slums was an almost instantaneous process rather than, as elsewhere, a gradual deterioration as better-paid workers migrated to improved housing as it became available. The housing experience of different towns therefore varied importantly with their general level of prosperity and employment structure, 'artisan' towns with high proportions of skilled, well-paid workers generally enjoying superior accommodation to mining, unskilled and 'casual labour' towns. Given the small scale of the building industry and the unsophisticated nature of economic knowledge and forecasting, market forces generally responded remarkably well to demand, occasionally upset by changes in the level of prosperity of a town and rapid movements of population inward or outward.

From the minimal degree of shelter and separation afforded by the back-to-back, the through terrace house of the later nineteenth century was a major advance in space and amenity, usually providing two living-rooms and scullery, three bedrooms, an individual, external WC and a small yard or garden. The previous housing standards of the artisan increasingly became the standards of the regularly-employed, semi-skilled worker, as the former began to move out to suburban cottages and semi-detached villas. But the greatest advance in working-class standards came with the Tudor Walters recommendations for local-authority houses in 1918. In this, the standard formerly achieved by the lower middle classes—the semi-detached house in a low-density development, the 'parlour', the kitchen instead of the scullery, the bathroom and the internal WC—was democratized to a much wider section of the working classes. In such houses, perhaps for the first time in the experience of many working people, the continuum of progress was passing from functionalism to symbolism, from concern for efficient, healthy shelter towards conscious attempts to shape the environment and create beauty.

In physical terms the greatest gains which local-authority housing brought to its tenants were increased space and privacy, sanitation which encouraged modesty as well as cleanliness, and a garden which developed healthy children and sober husbands. What had been typically middle-class characteristics—the privatization of domestic life, cleanliness, sobriety, concern for the special needs of children—thereby became more widely diffused to a class whose rising standards of living and expectations encouraged the adoption of such values.

From the 1920s to the 1960s the advance in space standards and amenities continued, though interrupted by periods of economic restriction and temporary reduction. It is clear that the two world wars both produced major gains, both followed by some losses in periods of economic restraint. Parker Morris in 1961 was the first peacetime Report to emerge from a background of rising living standards. Thus, the average floor area of three-bedroomed houses built under subsidy fell from 860sq ft in 1920 to 720sq ft in 1932, reached a new peak of 1,050sq ft in 1948, fell to 900sq ft in 1960 but then renewed an upward movement under the influence of Parker Morris.[5] There was, therefore, frequently a wide gap between the space standards recommended and those achieved, Dr Hole calculating that in the period from 1920 to 1965 the achieved increase amounted to 1sq ft of floor space per person in every seven years compared with a recommended increase of 1sq ft in every 1·3 years.[6] High rates of building output often produced reductions in area, while periods of low output often coincided with increases in space.

Again, it is significant that increases in the overall size of local-authority houses went primarily towards enlarging 'service', storage and circulation areas rather than 'living' areas. Thus, living-rooms and bedrooms did not benefit greatly from the evolutionary process after 1920, the greatest gains going to such things as the incorporation of a bathroom and WCs into the house, the transformation of the scullery into the kitchen, more generous passages and landings and increased storage space. This has been a continuous trend, confirmed by Parker Morris with its insistence on the need of the modern house to accommodate increasing quantities of possessions and equipment. The 'usable' amount of space per person has expanded little, so that although public housing achieved a high degree of privacy for families, it did not necessarily do so for individuals. The recognition of an increasing range of individual leisure activities by different members of the family has not yet resulted in the general provision of a second living-room.

In reviewing the history of the middle-class house it is at once obvious that no revolutionary change in preferred house type occurred over the last century and a half. The ideal continued to be a detached or semi-detached house in a suburban or semi-rural setting: the flat did not become a generally acceptable form of dwelling except for specialized needs in certain areas, nor, more recently, has the 'segregated' development which separates the car from the house found much favour. One of the few significant developments of the twentieth century was the spread of the bungalow from its original use as recreational accommodation to become a major type of mass housing, though this involved no break in the tradition of a private, self-contained dwelling. The need of the middle classes to personalize and privatize their territory is apparently as deeply-felt by the new Elizabethans as it was by the Victorians.

The outstanding change, which followed from the successive enlargement of the class and its extension into comparatively lower income groups, was the reduction in size and number of rooms of the average middle-class house. The reduction in family size and the virtual disappearance of domestic servants furthered this trend, so that, by contrast with the working-class house which evolved by expansion and differentiation of functions, the middle-class house plan contracted and moved back towards more generalized use of space. Thus, the two house types increasingly converged. In the inter-war period new private housing was still generally larger than public-authority housing, but the increasing concentration of speculative building on the four/five-person house in the range 750–1,000sq ft gradually brought the two closely into line. By the 1960s only 4 per cent of private houses were being built with four or more bedrooms.

This growing convergence in size did not mean, however, that the two types became indistinguishable as shapes on the ground. Externally, the private house continued to be recognizable by its normally wider frontage and larger plot, its garage or garage space and its more mannered façade, often with some suggestion of an architectural style or contemporary idiom. Internally, the plan of the smaller private house gave little scope for distinctiveness, though it is noticeable that two day-rooms survived more often than in the council house, even when this meant smaller rooms and a smaller kitchen. More importance was also given to halls, staircases and fireplaces, to features such as windows, panelling and floor surfaces, and to the fittings of kitchens and bathrooms. More recently, the installation of central heating has been a distinguishing characteristic, and, to some extent, the adoption of forms of 'open' planning. But, although since the last war more attention has been focused on convenience, comfort and ease of maintenance, the middle-class house, despite its reduced size, continued to represent symbolic values to an important degree, even to the exclusion of functional considerations. Thus, in the typical three-bedroomed house, kitchens were frequently smaller, and the work sequence less well arranged, than in the local-authority house in order to give more space to status areas such as the 'lounge' and hall, while the fireplace continued to be an important feature even after the spread of central heating. Despite the narrowing of differentials of space and amenities, the dwelling-house continued to be a prime indicator of social status for a society in which class-consciousness had not greatly receded.

Both middle-class and working-class houses have, therefore, broadly reflected changes in the economic and social structure, modified by a variety of external forces over which the individual had little control. It remains difficult to know how far the kinds of houses provided by private building and, in the twentieth century, by local authorities, produced satisfaction among their occupants—how far, that is, they fulfilled not merely increasing standards of shelter but the symbolic aspirations which we have argued always formed an important part of the concept of a home. This book has been concerned with housing which was not designed by a client but was produced by others for a 'market'. At its most minimal level, as in the back-to-back, the form of the house was determined mainly by economic factors operating within cultural and regional norms which found that form acceptable, but what the choice of residents would have been had there been real alternatives is unknowable. Similarly, when local-authority houses came to be widely built after 1919, their standards, though commendably high, were based on the recommendations of committees such as the Tudor Walters, on which middle-class women's organizations had been a powerful voice. Put crudely, the council house was a scaled-down version of the sort of house the lower middle classes liked: implicit here was the assumption, as it was in the case of high-rise flats, that others knew best.

Since the last war the need for user studies of occupants' preferences and levels of satisfaction has increasingly been recognized, particularly in respect of public housing.[7] That such studies are still relatively undeveloped is due partly to the lack of an adequate sociology of housing, partly to the methodological difficulty that a user's attitude towards his house will depend largely on his own, limited, housing experience. Thus, in a recent Building Research Station survey when local-authority tenants were invited to describe their 'ideal house', half mentioned a house they knew which was generally another council house occupied by a friend or relative. Very few named a private house of a size associated with middle-class standards. Similarly, few were able to list the number and type of rooms they wanted, and 66 per cent responded to the question merely in terms of specific items of furniture and floor covering they would like to own. Yet, despite their limitations, user studies appear to confirm that a major gap still exists between providers and consumers—between architects and planners who concentrate on the functional, manifest aspects of design, and users for whom latent, symbolic aspects may be more important. Thus, in architectural terms, people frequently use their accommodation 'wrongly', eating meals in kitchens not intended for the purpose, using half the space in their houses only for sleeping, obscuring windows with 'displays' intended to be seen from outside, and so on.

However, certain fairly clear conclusions about use and preference emerged from recent surveys. On the whole, levels of satisfaction with post-war houses were considerably higher with respect to interiors than to external aspects. The majority of families preferred two day-rooms, and certainly two eating areas—one in the kitchen and another either in a dining-room or in the living-room. People liked a reasonable balance in the sizes of different rooms—not, for example, a large living-room of 200sq ft and a kitchen of 90sq ft. There was also a preference for square-shaped rooms as most convenient. The fireplace was still regarded as the focal-point of the living-room, and should be so positioned as to allow a proper grouping of furniture. There was still a tendency for the living-room to be treated and furnished as the 'best' room, with echoes of the Victorian parlour not yet extinct. By the sixties the removal of cooking from the living-room was almost complete, though a 1947 survey had shown that some cooking was still done in 59 per cent (in London only 19 per cent). The general opinion was that the kitchen, now the most intensively-used room in the house, should be a minimum of 100sq ft to allow space for a table and chairs. Double bedrooms of 135–140sq ft were thought satisfactory, but single bedrooms of 70sq ft were often found too small, 90sq ft being preferred: nevertheless, 'multiple use' of bedrooms, for example for children's play, was not widely approved, perhaps because it was still associated with over-crowding and old-fashioned living conditions. There was no substantial demand from four-person families for a second WC provided the first was separate from the bathroom. Almost no local-authority tenants wanted a second bathroom.

On this evidence, the standards of space and amenity recommended by Parker Morris in 1961 would go very close towards meeting occupants' declared preferences, and a recent survey of residents in Milton Keynes New Town appears to confirm this. Here, the great majority of those housed in newly built terraced houses would apparently not choose to reduce the amount of space either for a semi-detached house or for full central heating. If extra space were available residents thought it should go to living areas, and especially to kitchens, rather than bedrooms. Privacy and aspect were the principal requirements of the living-room: it should be a large, bright room, and floor-to-ceiling windows were liked, provided the room was not overlooked. None of the houses had a separate dining-room, and the combined kitchen/dining area was preferred by 80 per cent of residents to the lounge/dining area. However, many felt the need of a separated space for quiet activities—either a heated bedroom or some distinct part of the living area. The chief criticism of terraced housing was noise penetration from neighbours. Half of all residents were willing to pay more rent in order to have full central heating. Seventy-five per cent owned cars (twice the national average for council tenants) and preferred on-plot parking in garages or car-ports to parking away from the house. On the five estates surveyed between 83 per cent and 95 per cent of residents expressed general satisfaction with life at Milton Keynes, and only four out of 300 families wanted to return to their former homes.[8]

User research, then, has generally confirmed a high level of satisfaction with the interiors of modern houses, with the ambitions of residents mainly restricted to a little more of the same—somewhat larger kitchens, more central heating, storage space and garaging. If this is so, the continuum of space development which almost doubled the size of much working-class housing over the period of our study may have come to an end. It would, at least, be unrealistic to assume continued expansion in the size of houses while families remain small and the costs of land, building, heating, maintenance and rates continue to rise. But now that the history of the house has reached the stage of defining, and largely realizing, minimum standards, the question for the future is the direction in which optimum standards might lead.

No revolutionary change in the basic form or location of housing seems likely. The possibility that the majority of English people might in future be housed either in city tower blocks or in new towns now seems remote, and it is more likely that urban renewal will continue to locate most people in existing towns and in fairly traditional types of housing. More separation of traffic, an increased use of 'mixed development' incorporating terraced houses, single-storey cottages and low-rise flats, can be expected to bring greater variety to the urban landscape without fundamentally changing the concept of the individual house. The great age of suburban expansion, which began in Victorian times and reached a climax in the inter-war years, has almost come to an end, and the characteristic house-form which accompanied it—the semi-detached house—is no longer commonly employed. But, equally, the architects' experiment with multi-storey dwellings, which some saw not only as a new way of living but as a new way of life, has apparently also receded into an 'incident', unlikely to be repeated. Through momentous social, economic and political changes in the last century and a half the individual house in a garden has survived as the ideal of the majority of English people—more spacious, lighter, warmer, better fitted and equipped than its ancestor, but in essentials unchanged.

What has become increasingly important to householders in recent years is the general character of the environment outside the home. In a recent survey of residents living on six low to high-density local-authority estates in London and Sheffield, the surprising finding to emerge was that satisfaction with the estate was not determined mainly by such factors as density, building form, living on or off the ground, and problems with children's play, but was clearly related to the appearance of the estate and the way it was maintained.[9] Tenants were more satisfied with their dwellings than with the estate outside, and there were high levels of satisfaction with both low and high density. A majority of adult and elderly householders said that they preferred a flat in a central area to a house on the outskirts, though families with children preferred a house with a garden in more spacious surroundings. But also, the visual characteristics of the buildings strongly influenced attitudes towards the appearance of estates. Large slab blocks were often said to be too massive and prison-like; residents liked a variety of building forms, and preferred estates to have an open appearance.

Such conclusions are perhaps not so obvious as they might seem. In stating their reasons for liking particular estates—that they had plenty of trees and grass, a pleasant layout and good views, and were kept clean and tidy—residents were expressing, if somewhat naïvely, a deeply-felt aesthetic concern about the environment in which they lived. 'Beauty' has not often been explicitly discussed in relation to mass housing. Social policy was initially concerned to create the sanitary house; next to provide sufficient, separate space for the different functions of living and for privacy of sleeping; more recently, to bring rising standards of comfort and convenience into increasingly complicated domestic lives. These were necessary and desirable objectives, but sometimes achieved with too little regard for social and aesthetic consequences. An important direction for the future might be an increased concern for the visual quality of houses and layouts based upon a recognition that homes serve social, psychological and aesthetic needs as well as functional ones. In that event it might not be, as a recent critic has argued, that 'the history of the English house as an individual work of art has virtually come to an end',[10] but that it has entered on a new beginning.

NOTES AND REFERENCES

PART I: 1815–1850

1: PEOPLE AND HOUSES

1 For an analysis of the characteristics of pre-industrial and industrial societies applied to Britain in the eighteenth and nineteenth centuries, see Phyllis Deane, *The First Industrial Revolution* (1965), Chapter 1.

2 The lowest of six estimates was 6,040,000 (Finlaison), the highest 6,517,000 (Rickman). Abstract of British Historical Statistics, B. R. Mitchell and Phyllis Deane (1962). Population and Vital Statistics 1. Estimates of Eighteenth-century Population, p 5.

3 Compiled from Mitchell and Deane, ibid. Population and Vital Statistics 2. U.K. Population and Intercensal Increases, 1801–1951, p 6.

4 A useful collection of the important recent articles on the subject has been brought together in M. Drake, *Population in Industrialisation* (1969).

5 Compiled from H. Barnes, *Housing: The Facts and the Future* (1923), Tables 3 and 4, pp 339–40.

6 Frederick Engels, 'The Condition of the Working-Class in England', in *Karl Marx and Frederick Engels on Britain* (Foreign Languages Publishing House, Moscow, 1953), p 177.

7 Peter Laslett, *The World We Have Lost* (1965), p 90.

8 Roger Smith, 'Early Victorian Household Structure', *International Review of Social History*, Vol 15 (1970), Part 1, p 75.

9 C. M. Law, 'The Growth of Urban Population in England and Wales, 1801–1911', *Transactions of the British Institute of Geographers*, XLI (1967), pp 125f.

10 J. L. and Barbara Hammond, *The Bleak Age* (Pelican Books, 1947), p 36.

11 A. Redford, *Labour Migration in England, 1800–1850* (Edited by W. H. Chaloner, 1964), p 190.

12 William Ashworth, *The Genesis of Modern British Town Planning. A Study in Economic and Social History of the Nineteenth and Twentieth Centuries* (1954), pp 8–9. For this section I am much indebted to Professor Ashworth's seminal study.

13 Mitchell and Deane, op cit. Population and Vital Statistics 8, pp 24–6.

14 *Report to Her Majesty's Principal Secretary of State for the Home Department from the Poor Law Commissioners on an Inquiry into the Sanitary Condition of the Labouring Population of Great Britain* (1842), p 41.

15   George Godwin, *Town Swamps and Social Bridges*, introduction by Anthony
     D. King. The Victorian Library reprint of 1859 edition (1972), pp 57–8.
16   See the illuminating study of the development of Camberwell by H. J. Dyos:
     Victorian Suburb (1961).
17   T. C. Barker and M. Robbins, *History of London Transport*, Vol I (1963), pp
     57–8.
18   Compiled from H. Barnes, op cit, Tables 5 and 6, pp 340–1.
19   *Report on the Sanitary Condition of the Labouring Population of Great
     Britain*, 1842 (Ed M. W. Flinn, 1965), p 5.
20   H. Barnes, op cit, Table 20, p 356.
21   H. A. Shannon, 'Bricks—a trade index', *Economica*, New Series, I (1934), pp
     300–18.
22   B. Weber, 'A New Index of Residential Construction, 1838–1950', *Scottish
     Journal of Political Economy*, Vol 2 (1955), pp 104–32.
23   H. Barnes, op cit, Table 35, p 371.
24   A. K. Cairncross and B. Weber, 'Fluctuations in Building in Great Britain,
     1785–1849', *Economic History Review*, 2nd Series, Vol IX (1956–7), pp
     283–97.
25   H. Barnes, op cit, p 43.
26   E. H. Phelps Brown, Review of Migration and Economic Growth by Brinley
     Thomas (1954). *Economic Journal*, Vol 64 (1954), p 256.
27   See, for example, H. J. Habakkuk, 'Fluctuations in House-Building in Britain
     and the U.S. in the Nineteenth Century'. *Journal of Economic History*, Vol
     22 (1962), p 198. S. B. Saul 'House-Building in England, 1890–1914',
     Economic History Review, Vol XV (1962), pp 119–37.
28   The early history of the building industry, up to the seventeenth century, is
     admirably described and documented by D. Knoop and G. P. Jones, *The
     Medieval Mason* (1933), whose title is somewhat misleading.
29   J. H. Clapham, *An Economic History of Modern Britain*, Vol I, *The Early
     Railway Age, 1820–1850* (1939), p 163.
30   E. W. Cooney, 'The Origins of the Victorian Master-Builders', *Economic
     History Review* (1955), pp 167–76, to which I am greatly indebted for this
     section. See also R. K. Middlemas, *The Master Builders* (1963), for an
     account of large-scale contracting, mainly in railways, by Thomas Brassey
     and others.
31   T. S. Ashton, 'The Treatment of Capitalism by Historians', in *Capitalism
     and the Historians*, edited by F. A. Hayek (1954), pp 43f. In *The Welsh
     Builder on Merseyside* (1946), J. R. Jones confirms that the term was first
     used in Liverpool, though he claims that it originated with a firm of builders
     named 'Jerry Brothers' (p 163).
32   *Morning Chronicle*, 16 September 1850.
33   T. S. Ashton, op cit, p 48.
34   R. W. Postgate, *The Builders' History* (1923), Appendix I, p 455.
35   Henry-Russell Hitchcock, *Early Victorian Architecture in Britain* (1954),
     Vol I, p 409.
36   J. D. Chambers, *Modern Nottingham in the Making* (1945), p 16.
37   Enid Gauldie, *Cruel Habitations. A History of Working-Class Housing,
     1780–1918* (1974), p 172.

38 H. J. Dyos, op cit, p 41, to which I am greatly indebted for this section.

39 Ibid, pp 124ff.

40 On the speculative builder's sources of capital, see H. J. Dyos, 'The Speculative Builders and Developers of Victorian London', *Victorian Studies*, Vol XI, Supplement (1968), pp 641ff.

41 J. N. Tarn, *Working-Class Housing in Nineteenth-Century Britain*, Architectural Association Paper No 7 (1971), Chapter 4: 'Housing and the Architectural Profession', pp 17ff.

42 John Ruskin, *The Seven Lamps of Architecture* (Everyman edition, 1907), Chapter 1, Section 1, p 8.

43 J. L. Berbiers, 'Back-to-back Housing, Halifax', in *Official Architecture and Planning* (December 1968), p 1596.

44 S. H. Brooks, *Designs for Cottage and Villa Architecture* (1839). Probably the best-known of such works was Edward Dobson's *Rudiments of the Art of Building* (1849) which went into thirteen editions in forty years.

45 Charles Singer, E. J. Holmyard, A. R. Hall and Trevor I. Williams (eds), *A History of Technology*, Vol IV, *The Industrial Revolution* (1958) Chapter 15, pp 442ff.

46 See Norman Davey, *A History of Building Materials* (1961), and R. W. Brunskill, *Illustrated Handbook of Vernacular Architecture* (1971).

47 Marian Bowley, *Innovations in Building Materials: An Economic Study* (1960), pp 56ff.

48 T. C. Barker, *Pilkington Brothers and the Glass Industry* (1960), pp 55ff.

2: THE COTTAGE HOMES OF ENGLAND

1 Richard Heath, *The English Peasant: studies historical, local and biographic* (1893), p 59.

2 John Burnett, *Plenty and Want: A Social History of Diet in England from 1815 to the Present Day* (1966), Chapters 2 and 7.

3 Felicia Hemans, 'The Cottage Homes of England' (c 1830):

> The cottage homes of England,
> By thousands on her plains,
> They are smiling o'er the silvery brook
> And round the hamlet fanes.
>
> From glowing orchards forth they peep,
> Each from its nook of leaves,
> And fearless there the lowly sleep
> As the birds beneath the eaves . . .

4 William Cobbett, *Rural Rides* (Everyman edition, 1967), Vol I, p 18. His *Journal* was written between 1821 and 1832.

5 Ibid, Vol II, p 266.

6 The inheritance from the sixteenth century to the eighteenth has been fully documented by M. W. Barley, *The English Farmhouse and Cottage* (1961).

7 In this connection it is worth noting that seventeenth- and eighteenth-century country cottages that have survived to the present day have done so

because, in the main, they were especially well built or have been especially well maintained or restored. To this extent they are untypical of their period: the more typical have disappeared.

8 J. H. Clapham, *An Economic History of Modern Britain*, Vol I, *The Early Railway Age, 1820–1850* (1939), p 27.

9 William Cobbett, *Tour in Scotland* (1833), p 84.

10 James Caird, *English Agriculture in 1850–1851* (1852; facsimile edition, 1968), p 389.

11 John Houseman, *Topographical Description of Cumberland* (1800), pp 50–2. See also R. W. Brunskill, *Vernacular Architecture of the Lake Counties* (1974).

12 Thomas Brown, *General View of the Agriculture of Derby* (1794), p 14.

13 John Boys, *General View of the Agriculture of Kent* (1790), pp 30–1. It should be noted that 'mud' was not necessarily a bad building material: much depended on skill in preparation and application. See Clough Williams-Ellis, *Cottage Building in Cob, Pisé, Chalk and Clay: a Renaissance* (1919).

14 Further details of the state of cottage accommodation at the end of the eighteenth century will be found in the writings of G. E. Fussell, especially *The English Rural Labourer: his home, furniture, clothing and food from Tudor to Victorian times* (1949), and his article, with C. Goodman, 'The Housing of the Rural Population in the Eighteenth Century', *Economic Journal*, supplementary volume (1930).

15 Sir Frederic Morton Eden, *The State of the Poor*, 3 vols (1797; facsimile edition, 1966), Vol. I, p 361.

16 *Labourers' Wages: Report from the Select Committee on the Rate of Agricultural Wages, and on the Condition and Morals of Labourers in that Employment* (1824) p 392.

17 Edward Smith, *The Peasant's Home, 1760–1865*, Howard Prize Essay, 1875 (1876), p 5.

18 David Davies, *The Case of Labourers in Husbandry Stated and Considered* (1795), p 56.

19 *Annals of Agriculture*, collected and published by Arthur Young, 46 vols (1784–1815), Vol 36, p 115.

20 *Reports by Special Assistant Poor Law Commissioners on the Employment of Women and Children in Agriculture* (1843). Report by Mr Denison on the counties of Suffolk, Norfolk and Lincoln, p 221.

21 *Report from His Majesty's Commissioners for Inquiring into the Administration and Practical Operation of the Poor Laws* (1834), p 73.

22 *The Autobiography of Joseph Arch*, with a Preface by Frances, Countess of Warwick, edited by John Gerard O'Leary (1966), p 20.

23 *Reports . . . on the Employment of Women and Children in Agriculture* (1843). Op cit. Report by Mr Vaughan on the counties of Kent, Surrey and Sussex, p 148.

24 Ibid. Report by Mr Alfred Austin on the counties of Wilts, Dorset, Devon and Somerset, p 89.

25 Nathaniel Kent, *Hints to Gentlemen of Landed Property* (1775), p 97.

26 Sir Frederic Morton Eden, *The State of the Poor* (1797), Vol I, p 554.

27 Ibid, Vol III, Appendix XII, 'Expenses and Earnings of Agricultural

Labourers in Various Parts of England, collected in January and February 1796'.

28 James Caird, *English Agriculture in 1850 and 1851* (1852; facsimile edition, 1968), p 474.

29 W. Hasbach, *A History of the English Agricultural Labourer*, translated by Ruth Kenyon (1908), p 248.

30 *Labourers' Wages* (1824) *Report* (op cit), p 47.

31 The Speenhamland system, in operation between 1795 and 1834, provided for an 'allowance' in aid of wages, determined by the number of dependants and the prevailing price of bread. Typically, a flat 1s 6d a week was allowed for a wife and each child up to the number of seven. Thus a single man's entitlement might be only 4s 3d a week, and that for a married man with seven children, 20s 3d.

32 *Report into ... the Poor Laws* (1834) (op cit), p 17.

33 *Reports ... on the Employment of Women and Children in Agriculture* (1843) (op cit), pp 62f, 312f.

34 *Report to Her Majesty's Principal Secretary of State for the Home Department from the Poor Law Commissioners on an Inquiry into the Sanitary Condition of the Labouring Population of Great Britain* (1842), pp 5ff.

35 Quoted in L. Marion Springall, *Labouring Life in Norfolk Villages, 1834–1914* (1936), pp 51–2.

36 *Reports ... on the Employment of Women and Children in Agriculture* (1843) (op cit), p 19.

37 *Seventh Report of the Medical Officer of the Committee of Council on the State of the Public Health* (1864), Appendix VI: Report by Dr Hunter on Rural Housing.

38 Edward Smith, op cit, p 10.

39 *Reports ... on the Employment of Women and Children in Agriculture* (1843) (op cit), pp 19ff.

40 Sir A. H. Elton in *The Agricultural Review* (1853), quoted in Edward Smith, op cit, pp 109–10.

41 Sir Frederic Morton Eden, op cit, Vol I, pp 549–50.

42 John Burnett, op cit, Chapters 2 and 7.

43 *Report ... on ... the Sanitary Condition of the Labouring Population* (1842) (op cit), p 161.

44 Edward Smith, op cit, pp 43–4.

45 Ibid, pp 31–2.

46 Further details of the 'Picturesque' and of model cottages generally are given in G. E. Fussell, op cit, pp 44ff.

47 Christopher Holdenby, *The Folk of the Furrow* (1913).

48 *Report ... on ... the Sanitary Condition of the Labouring Population* (1842) (op cit), p 401.

49 *Journal of the Royal Agricultural Society*, Vol X (1849).

50 Model cottages might, of course, become overcrowded unless strict supervision was maintained. Some of the famous model cottages built at Milton Abbas, Dorset, in 1786 were found to contain eighteen people each in 1841. Nicholas Cooper, 'The Myth of Cottage Life', *Country Life*, 25 May 1967, p 1290.

51   Russell M. Garnier, *Annals of the British Peasantry* (1895), p 395.
52   Quoted by Richard Heath, *The English Peasant: studies historical, local and biographic* (1893), p 79.

3: THE HOUSING OF THE URBAN WORKING CLASSES

1   For example, J. N. Tarn, *Working-class Housing in Nineteenth-Century Britain* (1971), which concentrates heavily on 'model' housing.
2   John Gloag, *The Englishman's Castle* (1944), p 132.
3   See, for instance, the results of researches at the Welsh School of Architecture, UWIST, Cardiff, published as Iron Industry Housing Papers from 1972 onwards.
4   James Phillips Kay, *The Moral and Physical Condition of the Working Classes Employed in the Cotton Manufacture in Manchester* (second edition, enlarged, 1832; new impression, (1969), pp 28–9.
5   P. Gaskell, *The Manufacturing Population of England* (1833); reprint, 1972, p 133.
6   Frederick Engels, *The Condition of the Working-Class in England in 1844* (reprinted 1952), p 26.
7   William Cobbett, *Rural Rides* (1830), Vol II, p 383.
8   Royal Commission on Handloom Weavers. Reports of Assistant Commissioners, Part IV (1840), p 301.
9   Ibid, Part III, (1840), p 543.
10   S. G. Checkland, *The Rise of Industrial Society in England, 1815–1885* (1964), p 239.
11   Geoffrey Best, *Mid-Victorian Britain, 1851–1875* (1971), p 11.
12   H. A. Shannon, 'Migration and the Growth of London 1841–91', *Economic History Review*, Vol V (1934–5), pp 79f.
13   H. J. Dyos, *Victorian Suburb: A Study of the growth of Camberwell* (1961), p 58.
14   H. J. Dyos, 'The Making and Unmaking of Slums', in *The Victorian Poor*, Fourth Conference Report of the Victorian Society (1966), p 29.
15   P. Gaskell, op cit, pp 136–7.
16   *Report on the Condition of the Residences of the Labouring Classes in the town of Leeds* (London, 1842), p 18.
17   Frederick Engels, op cit, p 61.
18   *Report on the Sanitary Condition of the Labouring Population of Great Britain* by Edwin Chadwick (1842), edited with an Introduction by M. W. Flinn (1965), p 93.
19   Ibid, p 105.
20   Ibid, p 225.
21   Ibid, p 215, quoting a report by Dr J. Currie, 'Typhus Fever, the vast amount of produced among the poor of Liverpool from want of ventilation and cleanliness' (1797). Iain Taylor has suggested that the use of cellars in Liverpool may have developed from the tradition of merchant houses there having cellars for warehousing. 'The Court and Cellar Dwelling: The Eighteenth Century Origin of the Liverpool Slum', *Transactions of the Historic Society of Lancashire and Cheshire*, Vol 122 (1971), p 73.

22 J. H. Treble, 'Liverpool Working-Class Housing, 1801–1851', in *The History of Working-Class Housing: A Symposium*, edited by Stanley D. Chapman (1971) p 168.

23 W. G. Rimmer, 'Working Men's Cottages in Leeds, 1770–1840', in *The Thoresby Miscellany*, Vol 13 (1963), p 172 (publication of the Thoresby Society, Vol XLVI).

24 J. Aikin, *A Description of the Country from Thirty to Forty Miles round Manchester* (1795), p 193.

25 *Report on the Sanitary Condition of the Labouring Population of Great Britain*, by Edwin Chadwick (1842), edited with an Introduction by M. W. Flinn (1965), op cit, p 91.

26 W. G. Rimmer, op cit, p 181.

27 J. H. Treble, op cit, p 179.

28 J. Ferriar, *Proceedings of the Board of Health in Manchester* (1805), pp 12–13. Quoted in Frances Collier, *The Family Economy of the Working Classes in the Cotton Industry, 1784–1833* (1964), p 21.

29 *Report on the Sanitary Condition of the Labouring Population of Great Britain*, by Edwin Chadwick (1842), edited with an Introduction by M. W. Flinn (1965), op cit, p 206.

30 S. D. Chapman, 'Working-Class Housing in Nottingham during the Industrial Revolution', in *The History of Working-Class Housing: a Symposium*, op cit, p 153.

31 *Journal of the Royal Statistical Society*, Vol III (1840), p 7.

32 P. Gaskell, op cit, p 138.

33 Frederick Engels, op cit, p 66.

34 *Report of the Select Committee on Building Regulations and Improvement of Boroughs* (1842), X, Appendix 1, p 133.

35 *Royal Commission on Handloom Weavers* (1841), X, p 74.

36 James Phillips Kay, op cit, p 33.

37 P. Gaskell, op cit, pp 141–2.

38 *Leeds Intelligencer*, 15 February 1851. Quoted in J. F. C. Harrison, *The Early Victorians, 1832–51* (1971), p 61.

39 Report by J. C. Symons, Children's Employment Commission (Trades and Manufactures (1843), Vol XIV, pp 37–9.

40 *Report on the Sanitary Condition of the Labouring Population of Great Britain*, by Edwin Chadwick (1842), edited with an Introduction by M. W. Flinn (1965), op cit, p 411f.

41 Thomas Beames, *The Rookeries of London* (new impression of 2nd (1852) edition, 1970), pp 170f.

42 James Hole, *The Homes of the Working Classes, with Suggestions for their Improvement* (1866), pp 43–4.

43 *Journal of the Royal Statistical Society*, Vol III (1840), p 24.

44 George Godwin, *Town Swamps and Social Bridges* (1859). New edition, with an Introduction by Anthony D. King (The Victorian Library, 1972), p 98.

45 Robert Rawlinson, *Lectures, Reports, Letters and Papers on Sanitary Questions* (1876), p 104.

46 Thomas Beames, *The Rookeries of London* (new impression of 2nd [1852] edition, 1970).

47   James Phillips Kay, op cit, pp 36–8.

48   *Report of the Select Committee on the Health of Towns* (1840) Minutes of Evidençe, Qs 2795–9.

49   H. J. Dyos and Michael Wolff (eds), *The Victorian City* (1973), Vol I, pp 367–8.

50   E. P. Thompson and Eileen Yeo (eds), *The Unknown Mayhew. Selections from the Morning Chronicle, 1849–50* (1973), pp 406 and 586.

51   *Report of the Children's Employment Commission (Trades and Manufactures)* (1843), Vol XIV, p 39.

52   Henry Mayhew, *London Labour and the London Poor*, Vol I (1851), p 47.

53   *Report of the Select Committee on the Health of Towns* (1840), p 205.

54   James Hole, op cit, p 40.

55   Thomas Beames, op cit pp 173ff.

56   Quoted in G. M. Young (ed), *Early Victorian England, 1830–1865* (1963), Vol I, pp 128ff.

57   Though the surveyor, James Pennethorne, mentioned back-to-backs in Leeds in 1840 where the upper floor was reached by a ladder-staircase. *Report of the Select Committee on the Health of Towns* (1840), Q 2797.

58   The medical officer of health for Leeds stated publicly in 1885 that local people preferred back-to-backs. M. W. Beresford, 'The Back-to-Back House in Leeds, 1787–1937', in S. D. Chapman (ed), *The History of Working-class Housing: A Symposium* (1971), footnote 78, p 126.

59   Lords Sessional Papers (1842), Vol XXVII, p 240.

60   M. W. Barley, *The House and Home* (1963), p 61.

61   I am indebted for this note to Christopher Powell, who has found examples of back-to-earth houses in Mid and South Wales as well as in Yorkshire and Lancashire; apparently they continued to be built at least until the 1875 Public Health Act.

62   *Report of the Select Committee on the Deficiency of Public Walks* (1833), p 5

63   J. D. Chambers, *Modern Nottingham in the Making* (1945), p 7.

64   Report on Back-to-Back Houses, L. W. Darra Moir, 1910. PP. XXXVIII, p 1.

65   M. W. Beresford, op cit, p 119.

66   Sidney Pollard, *A History of Labour in Sheffield* (1959), p 18.

67   *Report of the Royal Commission on the Employment of Children in Factories* (1833), Vol XX, pp 39–40.

68   J. L. and Barbara Hammond, *The Bleak Age* (Pelican edition, 1947), p 207.

69   R. W. Brunskill, *Illustrated Handbook of Vernacular Architecture* (1971), pp 160f.

70   Samuel Bamford, *Walks in South Lancashire* (1844). Quoted in David Rubinstein, *Victorian Homes* (1974), p 211.

71   *Second Report of the Commissioners to enquire into the State of Large Towns and Populous Districts* (1845), XVIII, pp 611–12.

72   *Report on the Handloom Weavers* (1840), XXIV, p 7.

73   *Report of the Children's Employment Commission* (1843), XV, p 75.

74   On this question generally, see the classic study by Ivy Pinchbeck, *Women Workers and the Industrial Revolution* (1930) and Margaret Hewitt, *Wives and Mothers in Victorian Industry* (c 1958).

75   On community and town planning aspects see William Ashworth, *The*

Genesis of Modern British Town Planning (1954), and Colin and Rose Bell, *City Fathers: the early history of town planning in Britain* (Pelican edition, 1972).

76 Enid Gauldie, *Cruel Habitations* (1974), p 65.

77 Frances Collier, op cit, pp 30–3, 50.

78 *Report on the Sanitary Condition of the Labouring Population of Great Britain*, op cit, pp 303–4, Evidence of Henry Ashworth.

79 Rhodes Boyson, *The Ashworth Cotton Enterprise* (1970), pp 118ff.

80 Anon [Sir F. B. Head], *Stokers and Pokers* (new edition, 1861), p 82.

81 Quoted in W. H. Chaloner, *The Social and Economic Development of Crewe, 1780–1923* (1950), p 48.

82 *Illustrated London News*, Vol 7, pp 244ff, which contains a detailed account of the Bagnigge Wells development.

83 The best accounts of the activities of the two societies are contained in Henry-Russell Hitchcock, *Early Victorian Architecture in Britain* (1954), pp 464ff. J. N. Tarn, *Working-Class Housing in Nineteenth Century Britain* (1971), pp 5ff, and the same author's *Five Per Cent Philanthropy* (1973).

84 Hitchcock, op cit, p 459.

85 James Hole, op cit, p 8.

86 George Godwin, *Another Blow for Life* (1864). Quoted in Anthony King, 'Another Blow for Life', *The Architectural Review* (December 1964), p 448.

87 *Report on the Handloom Weavers* (1840), XXIII, Part II, p 239.

88 *Report of the Royal Commission on the State of Large Towns and Populous Districts* (1844), Vol XVII. Evidence of Samuel Holme, builder, p 186.

89 Thompson and Yeo, op cit, pp 423–5.

90 Technical details of working-class housing from Christopher Powell, 'Coketown Considered: Industrial Workers' Housing from 1840 to 1880', London University Extra-Mural Department, Special Essay, 1966 pp 25ff.

91 G. R. Porter, *The Progress of the Nation* (new edition, 1847), p 533.

92 H. J. Dyos and M. Wolff (eds), op cit, Chapter 14, House Upon House, Donald J. Olsen, p 337f.

93 A. S. Wohl, 'The Housing of the Working-Classes in London, 1815–1914', in S. D. Chapman, op cit, p 24.

94 James H. Treble, 'Liverpool Working-Class Housing, 1801–51', in ibid, pp 165–221.

95 J. D. Chambers, op cit, pp 5ff.

96 The section on Nottingham is based largely on S. D. Chapman, 'Working-Class Housing in Nottingham during the Industrial Revolution', in *Transactions of the Thoroton Society of Nottinghamshire*, Vol LXVII (1963), pp 67f, and his article of the same title in *The History of Working-Class Housing*, op cit, pp 133ff.

97 Similarly, the section on Leeds is based on W. G. Rimmer, *Working Men's Cottages in Leeds, 1770–1840*, Publications of the Thoresby Society, Vol XLVI (The Thoresby Miscellany, Vol 13, 1963), pp 165ff, and M. W. Beresford, 'The Back-to-Back House in Leeds, 1787–1937', in S. D. Chapman, op cit, pp 93ff.

4: MIDDLE-CLASS HOUSING

1   G. D. H. Cole, 'The Social Structure of England', Part I, in *History Today* (February 1951), p 60.
2   G. R. Porter, *The Progress of the Nation* (1847 edn), pp 56ff.
3   For a fuller exploration of the Victorian middle-class family pattern see H. L. Beales, 'The Victorian Family', and H. L. Beales and Edward Glover, 'Victorian Ideas of Sex', in H. Grisewood (ed), *Ideas and Beliefs of the Victorians*, (1949); and O. R. McGregor, *Divorce in England* (1957), Chapter III.
4   For an account of middle-class food and dietary habits in the period see John Burnett, *Plenty and Want. A Social History of Diet in England from 1815 to the Present Day* (Penguin, 1968), Chapters 4 and 9.
5   *A New System of Practical Domestic Economy, Founded on Modern Discoveries and the Private Communications of Persons of Experience* (new edition, 1824). 'Practical Estimates of Household Expenses', pp 423f. The third edition, revised and greatly enlarged, was published in 1823; the date of the first edition, though uncertain, was probably c 1820.
6   J. A. Banks, *Prosperity and Parenthood. A Study of Family Planning among the Victorian Middle Classes* (1954), to which I am much indebted in this section.
7   *Economy for the Single and Married, by One Who Makes Ends Meet* (1845), p 26.
8   'Morals and Manners', in the *Guardian*, 27 January 1858. Quoted in J. A. Banks, op cit, pp 43–4.
9   J. H. Walsh, *A Manual of Domestic Economy* (1857), p 606.
10 Mrs Isabella Beeton, *The Book of Household Management* (1861; *The Times* Facsimile Edition, 1968), p 20.
11 Thea Holme, *The Carlyles at Home* (1965).
12 W. A. Armstrong, 'The Interpretation of the Census Enumerators' Books for Victorian Towns', in H. J. Dyos (ed), *The Study of Urban History* (1968), p 73.
13 Roger Smith, 'Early Victorian Household Structure: A Case Study of Nottinghamshire', *International Review of Social History*, Vol XV (1970), Part I, p 69f.
14 W. A. Armstrong, op cit, p 71.
15 A mean in Class III households in York in 1851 of 0·12 domestic servants, and in Classes IV and V of 0·05: in Nottingham in Class III 0·09 and in Classes IV and V 0·02.
16 For details of the size, structure and organization of domestic service in the nineteenth century, see John Burnett, *Useful Toil. Autobiographies of Working People from the 1820's to the 1920's* (1974), Part Two, *Domestic Servants*, Introduction, pp 135–74.
17 W. Farr, *Vital Statistics* (ed N. A. Humphreys) (1885), p 467.
18 'The Building Mania' in *The Builder* (1848). Quoted in H. J. Dyos (ed), *The Study of Urban History*, op cit, p 255.
19 Leonore Davidoff, *The Best Circles: Society, Etiquette and the Season* (1973), p 73.

20 Geoffrey Best, *Mid-Victorian Britain, 1851–1875* (1971), p 18.

21 H. J. Dyos and D. A. Reeder, *Slums and Suburbs in The Victorian City: Images and realities*, ed H. J. Dyos and Michael Wolff, 2 vols (1973), Vol I, p 369.

22 Henry James, 'The Suburbs of London', *Galaxy*, Vol XXIV (1877), p 778.

23 Nicholas Taylor, 'The Awful Sublimity of the Victorian City. Its Aesthetic and Architectural Origins', in *The Victorian City*, op cit, Vol 2, p 433.

24 No precise date can be given to the rejection of the terrace in favour of the detached or semi-detached villa. It varied locally and, no doubt, was determined largely by land availability. Thus, in Islington the Thornhill Estate of terrace housing was begun in the late 1840s and the first villas of Highbury New Park completed in 1852. But elsewhere in London (eg Belsize Park, Cadogan Square) large terraced houses were still being built in the 1870s and 1880s.

25 John Summerson, *Georgian London* (revised ed 1970), pp 65f, to which I am greatly indebted in this section.

26 Louis Simond, *Journal of a Tour and Residence in Great Britain* (1817), Vol I, p 64.

27 Donald J. Olsen, *Town Planning in London: The Eighteenth and Nineteenth Centuries* (1964), pp 102–3.

28 An important study of middle-class housing in the Victorian period in Exeter, Glasgow, Hampstead, Leamington Spa, Nottingham and Sheffield has now been published. See M. A. Simpson and T. H. Lloyd, *Middle-Class Housing in Britain* (1977).

29 J. H. and M. M. Clapham, 'Life in the New Towns', in G. M. Young (ed), *Early Victorian England, 1830–1865* (third impression, 1963), Vol I, pp 227f.

30 J. F. C. Harrison, *The Early Victorians, 1832–1851* (1971), p 58.

31 F. Engels, *The Condition of the Working Class in England in 1844*, translated and edited by W. O. Henderson and W. H. Chaloner (1958), pp 54ff.

32 Leonore Davidoff, op cit, pp 36f.

33 John Summerson, op cit, p 144.

34 Mark Girouard, *The Victorian Country House* (1971), pp 19ff.

35 John Ruskin, *The Seven Lamps of Architecture* (1907 edn), pp 183–4.

36 A. W. N. Pugin, *The Ecclesiologist*, Vol VII, p 61. Quoted Robert Macleod, in *Style and Society: Architectural Ideology in Britain, 1835–1914* (1971), p 12.

37 R. W. Emerson, *English Traits* (1856), p 61.

38 A. E. Richardson, 'Architecture', in *Early Victorian England*, op cit, Vol II, p 239.

39 On the 'philosophy of comfort' and the characteristics of the Victorian home generally, see John Gloag, *Victorian Comfort. A Social History of Design, 1830–1900* (1961), and *Victorian Taste. Some Social Aspects of Architectural and Industrial Design, 1820–1900* (1962).

40 J. Wildeblood and P. Brinson, *The Polite World. A Guide to English Manners and Deportment from the Thirteenth Century to the Nineteenth Century* (1965).

41 G. Laurence Gomme, *London in the Reign of Victoria (1837–1897)* (1898), pp 136–8.

42 On the architecture of the 'Picturesque' see John Summerson, *Architecture in Britain, 1530–1830* (1970), Chapter 28, and H. J. Dyos and Michael Wolff (eds), *The Victorian City* (1973), pp 433ff.

43 On the Gothic Revival, see John Gloag, *Victorian Taste. Some social aspects of Architecture and Industrial Design, 1820–1900* (1962), Chapter 3, and Robert Macleod, *Style and Society. Architectural Ideology in Britain, 1835–1914* (1971), Chapter 1.

44 Gloag, *Victorian Taste*, op cit, Chapter 4.

45 G. M. Young, op cit, Vol I, p 90.

PART II: 1850–1914

5: HOUSING THE LABOURER

1 Francis George Heath, *The English Peasantry* (1874), pp 105ff.

2 George C. T. Bartley, *The Seven Ages of a Village Pauper* (1874), p 44.

3 The best general account of the influences affecting the status of the labourer in the nineteenth century is still that by W. Hasbach, *A History of the English Agricultural Labourer*, translated by Ruth Kenyon (1908), reprinted 1966.

4 Earnings of Agricultural Labourers. Returns of the average rate of weekly earnings of agricultural labourers in the Unions of England and Wales, S.P. 1873, (358), LIII.

5 B. Seebohm Rowntree and May Kendall, *How the Labourer Lives. A Study of the Rural Labour Problem* (1913), pp 299f.

6 *Report of the Royal Commission on Labour: The Agricultural Labourer*, Vol 1 (England), C.6894 (1893), Part II, p 44.

7 Lord Ernle, *English Farming Past and Present* (new, sixth edition, 1961), Appendix VI, 'The Agricultural Population according to Census Returns', p 507. See also John Saville, *Rural Depopulation in England and Wales, 1851–1951* (1957).

8 *The Land: The Report of the Land Enquiry Committee*, Vol I, *Rural* (1913), p 34.

9 B. Seebohm Rowntree and May Kendall, op cit, pp 14ff.

10 Rev Dr Begg, 'The Necessity for Appointing Public Inspectors for Rural Cottages', *Transactions of the National Association for the Promotion of Social Science*, 1863 (1864), p 764.

11 William G. Savage, *Rural Housing* (1915), pp 272f.

12 Richard Heath, *The English Peasant, Studies Historical, Local and Biographic* (1893), p 50.

13 *Seventh Report of the Medical Officer of the Privy Council*, 1865, Vol 26, App 6, Inquiry on the State of the Dwellings of Rural Labourers, by Dr H. J. Hunter.

14 James Caird, *English Agriculture in 1850–51* (1852; facsimile edition, 1968), p 516.

15   L. Marion Springall, *Labouring Life in Norfolk Villages, 1834–1914* (1936), pp 52–3.
16   Royal Commission on the Employment of Children, Young Persons and Women in Agriculture, First Report, 1867–8. General Report, p XI, and Reports of Assistant Commissioners, pp 35f.
17   Ibid. General Report, p XV, and Reports of Assistant Commissioners, pp 65f.
18   Richard Heath, op cit, p 83.
19   Rev John Montgomery, 'On Overcrowded Villages', *Transactions of the National Association for the Promotion of Social Science*, 1860 (1861), pp 787–8.
20   'The Agricultural Labourers of England', *The Edinburgh Review*, Vol CXLL (1875), p 146.
21   J. D. Dent, MP, 'The Condition of the British Agricultural Labourer', *Journal of the Royal Agricultural Society of England* (1871).
22   Royal Commission on the Housing of the Working Classes. First Report, PP 1884–5, pp 24–6.
23   *The Autobiography of Joseph Arch*, with a Preface by Frances, Countess of Warwick (1898; 1966 edition) p 134.
24   Royal Commission on Labour, Vol V, Part I. General Report by Mr William Little, Senior Assistant, Agricultural Commission, 1894.
25   Ibid. PP Vol XXXV, Part V. Reports of Assistant Agricultural Commissioners: Dr John C. Thresh on Chelmsford and Maldon Rural Sanitary Districts, pp 84–5.
26   J. C. Loudon, *An Encyclopaedia of Cottage, Farm and Villa Architecture and Furniture, etc.* A New Edition, edited by Mrs Loudon (1857), pp 23–6.
27   Ibid, pp 237–8.
28   George Arnold, 'Prize Plan of Double Cottages for Labourers', *Journal of the Royal Agricultural Society of England*, Vol XV (1855), p 455.
29   *Health, Husbandry and Handicraft* (1865). Quoted in Edward Smith, *The Peasant's Home, 1760–1875*, Howard Prize Essay, 1875 (1876), p 57.
30   Thomas Holt Bracebridge, 'On Building Cottages', *Transactions of the National Association for the Promotion of Social Science*, 1857 (1858), p 602.
31   Sir Willoughby Jones, 'On the Best Plan of Construction and Arrangement of an Agricultural Labourer's Cottage', *Transactions of the National Association for the Promotion of Social Science*, 1873 (1874), pp 585–7.
32   Charles Gatliff, 'Improved Dwellings and their Beneficial Effects', *Journal of the Statistical Society*, Vol XXXVIII, (1875). Discussion, p 55.
33   Royal Commission on the Employment of Children, Young Persons and Women in Agriculture, First Report, 1867–8, op cit, pp LVIIf.
34   H. Rider Haggard, *Rural England* (2 vols, 1902); Francis George Heath, *British Rural Life and Labour* (1911); F. E. Green, *The Tyranny of the Countryside* (1913); B. Seebohm Rowntree and May Kendall, *How the Labourer Lives* (1913).
35   On the legislation affecting rural housing, see William G. Savage, *Rural Housing* (1915), especially Chapter 2, pp 35ff.
36   *The Land*. The Report of the Land Enquiry Committee (1913), op cit, pp 116 ff.

6: HOUSING THE MULTITUDE

1 Ebenezer Howard, *Garden Cities of Tomorrow* (1965 edn; 1st edn 1902), p 45.

2 C. M. Law, 'The Growth of Urban Population in England and Wales, 1801–1911', in *Transactions of the British Institute of Geographers* (1967), Vol XLI, p 130.

3 Ibid, p 132. For statistics of the first half of the nineteenth century see Chapter 1, p 7f.

4 H. Barnes, *Housing: The Facts and the Future* (1923), Table 5, p 340. The exception to the generally small size of building firms was in London, where H. J. Dyos estimates that at the end of the century, seventeen firms were building over 40 per cent of houses.

5 W. V. Hole and M. J. Pountney, *Trends in Population, Housing and Occupancy Rates, 1861–1961* (HM Stationery Office, 1971: Building Research Station Publication), p 30.

6 B. Weber, 'A New Index of Residential Construction and Long Cycles in House-Building in Great Britain, 1838–1950', in *Scottish Journal of Political Economy*, Vol 2 (1955), pp 104ff.

7 S. B. Saul, 'House Building in England, 1890–1914', in *Economic History Review*, Vol XV (1962), Pt I, pp 120–1.

8 Ibid, p 128.

9 H. J. Dyos and Michael Wolff (eds), *The Victorian City* (1973), Vol II, p 612.

10 E. W. Cooney, 'Capital Exports and Investment in Building in Britain and the U.S.A., 1856–1914', in *Economica*, New Series, Vol 16 (1949), pp 347ff; 'Long Waves in Building in the British Economy of the Nineteenth Century', in *Economic History Review*, 2nd Series, Vol 13 (2) (1960), pp 257ff.

11 See, for example, A. K. Cairncross and B. Weber, 'Fluctuations in Building in Great Britain, 1785–1849', in *Economic History Review*, 2nd Series, Vol 9 (2) (1956), pp 283ff; H. J. Habakkuk, 'Fluctuations in House-Building in Britain and the United States in the Nineteenth Century', in *Journal of Economic History*, Vol 22 (2) (1962), pp 198ff; J. P. Lewis, *Building Cycles and Britain's Growth* (1965); J. Blackman and E. M. Sigsworth, 'The Home Boom of the 1890's', in *Yorkshire Bulletin*, Vol 17(1) (1965), pp 75ff.

12 *The Times*, 12 and 23 March 1861. Quoted in H. J. Dyos, 'Railways and Housing in Victorian London', II, 'Rustic Townsmen', p 97, in the *Journal of Transport History*, Vol 2 (2), 1955. Kellett suggests that 120,000 people were displaced by London railways. *The Impact of Railways on Victorian Cities* (c 1969), pp 327–8.

13 B. Seebohm Rowntree, *Poverty: A Study of Town Life* (1901), p 166.

14 Report of the 51st Meeting of the British Association for the Advancement of Science (1881): Report of the Committee . . . on the Present Appropriation of Wages, etc. pp 274ff.

15 Memoranda, Statistical Tables and Charts prepared in the Board of Trade. Cd 1761 (1903), p 220.

16 James Hole, *The Homes of the Working Classes* (1866), pp 40–1.

17 Royal Commission on the Housing of the Working Classes. First Report, 1885. Memorandum by Mr Jesse Collings, MP, pp 77–8.

18   Leone Levi, *Wages and Earnings of the Working Classes*, Report to Sir Arthur Bass, MP (1885), p 31.

19   Royal Commission on the Housing of the Working Classes, op cit, p 17.

20   Lady Bell (Mrs Hugh Bell), *At the Works: A Study of a Manufacturing Town* (1907), pp 67–8.

21   H. J. Dyos, 'The Making and Unmaking of Slums', in *The Victorian Poor*, Fourth Conference Report of the Victorian Society (1966), p 31.

22   Mrs Pember Reeves, *Round About a Pound a Week* (1913), pp 30ff.

23   H. W. Singer, 'An Index of Urban Land Rents and House Rents in England and Wales, 1845–1913', in *Econometrica*, Vol 9 (1941), Table 5, p 230.

24   A. S. Wohl, 'The Housing of the Working Classes in London, 1815–1914', in S. D. Chapman (ed), *The History of Working-Class Housing* (1971), pp 26ff.

25   Gareth Stedman Jones, *Outcast London: A Study in the relationship between classes in Victorian Society* (1971), p 216.

26   Sidney Pollard, *A History of Labour in Sheffield* (1959), pp 20, 102, 189.

27   M. W. Beresford, 'The Back-to-Back House in Leeds, 1787–1937', in S. D. Chapman, op cit, pp 115–16.

28   Royal Commission on the Housing of the Working Classes, op cit, First Report, pp 18–21.

29   Enid Gauldie, *Cruel Habitations: A History of Working-Class Housing, 1780–1918* (1974), p 159.

30   A. S. Wohl, op cit, p 41.

31   J. S. Nettlefold, *Practical Housing* (1908), pp 28–32.

32   Sidney Pollard, op cit, p 186.

33   Mrs Pember Reeves, op cit, pp 42 and 76.

34   W. V. Hole and M. T. Pountney, op cit, p 15.

35   *Cost of Living of the Working Classes. Report of an Enquiry by the Board of Trade into Working Class Rents, Housing and Retail Prices, etc.* Cd 3861 (1908), pp 592–3.

36   A. L. Bowley and A. R. Burnett-Hurst, *Livelihood and Poverty: A study in the economic conditions of working-class households in Northampton, Warrington, Stanley and Reading* (1915), pp 18ff.

37   J. W. Papworth, 'On Houses as they were, as they are, and as they ought to be', in *Journal of the Society of Arts*, Vol V (1857), p 317.

38   Frederick Engels, *The Condition of the Working Class in England in 1844* (1845, English edition 1892), pp 57–8.

39   *Lancet*, 21 November 1874, p 739. Quoted in A. S. Wohl, op cit, p 34.

40   For full details of the London building regulations see J. N. Tarn, *Five Per Cent Philanthropy. An account of housing in urban areas between 1840 and 1914* (1973), pp 124ff.

41   James Hole, op cit, p 129.

42   M. W. Beresford, op cit, pp 109ff.

43   J. N. Tarn, op cit, pp 75ff.

44   A. S. Wohl, op cit, pp 30–3.

45   Sidney Pollard, op cit, pp 185–6.

46   Roy A. Church, *Economic and Social Change in a Midland Town, Victorian Nottingham, 1815–1900* (1966), pp 237–8, 349–50.

47   John Burnett, *Plenty and Want. A Social History of Diet in England from 1815 to the Present Day* (1966), Chapter 8.

48   Paul de Rousiers, *The Labour Question in England* (1895; English translation, 1896). Quoted in David Rubinstein, *Victorian Homes* (1974), p 213.

49   S. D. Chapman and J. N. Bartlett, 'The Contribution of Building Clubs and Freehold Land Society to Working-class Housing in Birmingham', in S. D. Chapman, op cit, pp 221ff.

50   *Report of an Enquiry by the Board of Trade into Working Class Rents, Housing and Retail Prices* (1908), pp 84–6.

51   *Second Report of Commissioners for Inquiry into the State of Large Towns and Populous Districts* (1845), XVII, p 613.

52   J. D. Chambers, *Modern Nottingham in the Making* (1945), p 40.

53   Edward Smeaton, *The Sanitary Condition of the Borough of Nottingham* (1873), pp 47–8.

54   Board of Trade Inquiry, 1908, op cit, pp 352–3.

55   Roy A. Church, op cit, pp 344–5.

56   B. Seebohm Rowntree, *Poverty: A Study of Town Life* (1901), p 161.

57   Allen Clarke, *The Effects of the Factory System* (1899), p 134.

58   W. A. Abram, 'Social Condition and Political Prospects of the Lancashire Workman', in *Fortnightly Review* (October 1868), p 429.

59   Francis M. Jones, 'The Aesthetic of the Nineteenth Century Industrial Town', in H. J. Dyos (ed), *The Study of Urban History* (1968), pp 176ff.

60   Robert Roberts, *The Classic Slum: Salford Life in the First Quarter of the Century* (1971), p 20.

61   Frank Atkinson, 'Yorkshire Miners' Cottages', in *Folk Life*, Vol 3 (1965), pp 92ff. (Based on recollections of a West Yorkshire miner and his wife at the end of the century.)

62   'Nunquam' (Robert Blatchford), 'Modern Athens. A City of Slums', in *Sunday Chronicle* (Manchester, 5 May 1889). Quoted in David Rubinstein, op cit, pp 139–142.

63   The best recent accounts of slum living at this period are in Robert Roberts, *The Classic Slum, Salford Life in the First Quarter of the Century* (1971), and Gareth Stedman Jones, *Outcast London. A Study in the Relationship between Classes in Victorian Society* (1971).

64   See, for example, W. Ashworth, *The Genesis of Modern British Town Planning* (1954); J. N. Tarn, *Working-class Housing in Nineteenth Century Britain* (Architectural Association, Paper No 7, 1971) and *Five Per Cent Philanthropy. An Account of Housing in Urban Areas between 1840 and 1914* (1973); Colin and Rose Bell, *City Fathers, The Early History of Town Planning in Britain* (Pelican Books, 1972); and W. V. Hole, 'The Housing of the Working Classes in Britain, 1850–1914. A Study of the Development of Standards and Methods of Provision', unpublished University of London Ph D thesis (1965), which anticipated much of the subsequent writing on improved dwellings.

65   James Hole, op cit, p 60.

66   W. V. Hole, thesis, op cit, p 243, to whom I am particularly indebted for the valuable section on standards of accommodation in model dwellings.

67   E. Akroyd, *On Improved Dwellings for the Working Classes* (1861), p 8.

68 Colin and Rose Bell, op cit, p 267.
69 Vanessa Parker, *The English House in the Nineteenth Century* (Historical Association, 1970), p 39.
70 J. N. Tarn, *Five Per Cent Philanthropy*, p 160.
71 Enid Gauldie, *Cruel Habitations, A History of Working-Class Housing, 1780–1918* (1974), especially Chapters 23–25.
72 J. S. Nettlefold, *Practical Housing* (1908), p 33.
73 A. T. McCabe, 'The Standard of Living in Liverpool & Merseyside, 1850–1875', unpublished Lancaster University MA Thesis (1974), p 62.
74 W. V. Hole, thesis, op cit, p 345.
75 J. N. Tarn, *Five Per Cent Philanthropy*, p 134.

7: HOUSING THE SUBURBANS

1 C. F. G. Masterman, *The Condition of England* (1st edn, 1909; reset edn, 1960), pp 57–8.
2 Geoffrey Best, *Mid-Victorian Britain, 1851–75* (1971), p 85.
3 G. R. Porter, *The Progress of the Nation in its various Social and Economical Relations* (1847), p 532.
4 George and Weedon Grossmith, *The Diary of a Nobody* (1st edn, 1892).
5 Augustus Hare, *The Story of My Life* (2nd series, 1890), III, pp 227, 280, 400. Quoted in Mark Girouard, *The Victorian Country House* (1971), p 19.
6 Henry-Russell Hitchcock, *Early Victorian Architecture in Britain* (1954), Vol I, p 484.
7 Thomas Webster and Frances Parker, *An Encyclopaedia of Domestic Economy* (1844), p 2.
8 J. E. Panton, *From Kitchen to Garret: Hints for Young Householders* (1888), pp 2–3. In a later work, *Suburban Residences and How to Circumvent Them* (1896), some of the disadvantages of suburban life were admitted, but overcome.
9 'The Building Mania', in *The Builder* (14 October 1848), pp 500–1. Quoted in David Rubinstein, *Victorian Homes* (1974), pp 21–2.
10 W. S. Clarke, *The Suburban Homes of London: A Residential Guide.* (1881), p v.
11 John Ruskin, *Lectures on Architecture and Painting* (1854). Quoted in John Gloag, *Victorian Taste: Some Social Aspects of Architecture and Industrial Design 1820–1900* (1962), p 78.
12 Robert Kerr, *The Gentleman's House; or How to Plan English Residences from the Parsonage to the Palace* (1864), pp 73–100.
13 J. J. Stevenson, *House Architecture*, 2 vols (1880), Vol II, House-Planning, pp 47–80.
14 Mark Girouard, *The Victorian Country House* (1971), pp 19ff.
15 George Somes Layard, 'How to Live on £700 a Year', in *The Nineteenth Century*, Vol XXIII (January–June 1888), p 240.
16 J. A. and Olive Banks, *Feminism and Family Planning in Victorian England* (1964), pp 58ff.

17   Mrs Sarah Ellis, *The Women of England; Their Social Duties and Domestic Habits* (1838), p 26.

18   J. Ruskin, *Sesame and Lilies* (1865), II 'Of Queens' Gardens', para 68.

19   Leonore Davidoff, *The Best Circles: Society, Etiquette and the Season* (1973), pp 17ff.

20   Joan Wildeblood and Peter Brinson, *The Polite World: A Guide to English Manners and Deportment from the Thirteenth to the Nineteenth Century* (1965), pp 255f.

21   John Burnett, *Useful Toil: Autobiographies of Working People from the 1820s to the 1920s* (1974), Part 2, Introduction, pp 135–74.

22   W. Vere Hole, 'The Housing of the Working Classes in Britain, 1850–1914: a Study of the Development of Standards and Methods of Provision', unpublished University of London PhD thesis (1965), p 54. Dr Hole's calculation suggests a Fourth Rate house as one quarter the area of a First Rate, but she assumes only three storeys for these, which was uncommon.

23   Robert Kerr, op cit, pp 413ff.

24   W. R. Greg, 'Life at High Pressure', in *The Contemporary Review* (March 1875), p 633. Quoted in J. A. Banks, *Prosperity and Parenthood* (1954), pp 66ff.

25   J. H. Walsh, *A Manual of Domestic Economy Suited to Families Spending from £100 to £1,000 a Year* (1856), pp 96f.

26   G. S. Layard, 'Family Budgets II', in *The Cornhill Magazine*, New Series, Vol X, (January–June 1901), pp 656ff.

27   G. Colmore, 'Family Budgets III. Eight Hundred a Year', Ibid, pp 790ff.

28   See Hermione Hobhouse, *Thomas Cubitt, Master Builder* (1971).

29   H. J. Dyos, 'The Speculative Builders and Developers of Victorian London', in *Victorian Studies*, Vol XI, Supplement (1968), pp 650ff.

30   John Ruskin, *Fors Clavigera*, Letter 29, 'La Douce Amie' (1873). Quoted in David Rubinstein, op cit, pp 23–4.

31   'Modern Houses', correspondence in the *Daily Telegraph*, 16, 18, 21 and 24 October 1865. This revealing exchange was kindly brought to my notice by Robert Thorne, who identifies 'W.H.W.' as William Hale White (Mark Rutherford).

32   Report of the Registrar-General on the Census of 1851, PP. 1852–3, Vol 85, pp xxxv—xxxvi. Quoted in E. Royston Pike (ed), *Human Documents of the Victorian Golden Age, 1850–1875* (1967), p 235.

33   John Gloag, *Victorian Comfort: A Social History of Design 1830–1900* (1961), p 22f.

34   John Gloag, *Victorian Taste*, op cit, pp 94–100.

35   Robert Macleod, *Style and Society: Architectural Ideology in Britain, 1835–1914* (1971), Chapter 3 'William Morris and Philip Webb', pp 40ff.

36   Walter L. Creese, *The Search for Environment. The Garden City: Before and After* (1966), p 89.

37   There were, in fact, numerous smaller suburban developments of similar intention from about 1850 onwards, such as the St Margaret's Estate, Twickenham, where the houses were disposed round several acres of communal ornamental garden preserved from an eighteenth-century estate (see Alan C. B. Urwin, *Twickenham Park* (1965), pp 119–20). Developments

closer to the Bedford Park pattern, in that they did not inherit large open spaces, took place at Cressington and Grassendale Parks in Liverpool from the 1840s.

38 J. E. Panton, op cit, pp 69f.

39 J. J. Stevenson, op cit, p 55.

40 Quoted in Henry-Russell Hitchcock, op cit, Vol I, p 475.

41 T. H. S. Escott, *England: Its People, Polity and Pursuits*, 2 vols (1879), Vol 2, pp 3f.

42 Subsequent legislation limited the height of London buildings, other than churches, to 90ft in 1890 and 80ft in 1894.

43 Quoted in E. S. Turner, *What the Butler Saw: Two Hundred and Fifty Years of the Servant Problem* (1962), p 251.

44 G. L. Morris and Esther Wood, *The Country Cottage* (1906), pp 2–5.

45 Ibid, p 83.

46 Anthony King, 'The Bungalow, Part 2', *Architectural Association Quarterly*, Vol 5, No 4 (1973), to which I am much indebted for this section.

47 J. C. Loudon, *The Suburban Gardener and Villa Companion* (1838), pp 58–9.

48 J. H. Clapham, *An Economic History of Modern Britain* (1951), Vol 3, p 313.

49 Lawrence Wright, *Home Fires Burning: The History of Domestic Heating and Cooking* (1964), pp 164–7.

50 The first house recorded in the architectural press as having hot and cold water piped to all floors was apparently Didsbury Towers, Manchester, built in 1873. (Jil Franklin, *Victorian Studies*, Vol XIX (December 1975), p 229).

51 H. J. Jennings, *Our Homes and How to Beautify Them* (1902), p 236.

52 Alison Ravetz, 'The Victorian Coal Kitchen and its Reformers', in *Victorian Studies*, Vol XI (1968), pp 435–60.

53 Siegfried Giedion, *Mechanization Takes Command, A Contribution to Anonymous History* (1948), pp 516–22.

PART III: 1918–1970

8: COUNCIL HOUSING, 1918–1939

1 See, for example, Arthur Marwick, *War and Social Change in the Twentieth Century* (1974).

2 R. M. Titmuss, *Essays on the Welfare State. War and Social Policy* (1958).

3 Quoted in Richard Reiss, *The Home I Want* (1918), p 3.

4 42nd Annual Report of the Local Government Board, 1912–1913. Part II, Housing and Town Planning (1913), p xxxiv.

5 Paul Barton Johnson, *Land Fit For Heroes: The Planning of British Reconstruction, 1916–1919* (1968), p 66.

6 The total number of additional families requiring accommodation between 1911 and 1921 was 1,093,000 compared with 994,000 between 1901 and 1911.

7 Marian Bowley, *Housing and the State, 1919–1944* (1945), p 12.

8   A. H. Halsey (ed), *Trends in British Society since 1900: A Guide to the Changing Social Structure of Britain* (1972), Chapter 10, 'Housing', pp 300ff.

9   42nd Annual Report of the Local Government Board, 1912–1913, op cit. Appendix No 13, Housing of the Working Classes Acts, 1890 to 1909. Memorandum as to provision and arrangement of houses, pp 46–51.

10 For example, Gordon Allen, *The Cheap Cottage and Small House* (1919).

11 For an excellent assessment of the Tudor Walters Report in the light of subsequent building standards, see Christopher Powell, 'Fifty Years of Progress. The influence of the Tudor Walters Report on British public authority housing examined and compared with present day standards', *Built Environment* (October 1974), pp 532–5.

12 Local Government Board. *Report of the Committee appointed ... to consider questions of building construction in connection with the provision of dwellings for the working classes, etc,* Cd 9191 (1918).

13 Quoted in H. Barnes, *The Slum: Its Story and Solution* (1934), p 337. The Women's Housing Sub-Committee issued an Interim Report in 1918 and a Final Report in 1919.

14 Local Government Board. *Manual on the Preparation of State-Aided Housing Schemes* (1919).

15 Marian Bowley, *Housing and the State, 1919–1944* (1945), pp 16f.

16 F. Berry, *Housing: The Great British Failure* (1974), p 35.

17 Rt Hon Christopher Addison, *The Betrayal of the Slums* (1922), pp 15–16.

18 E. D. Simon, *The Anti-Slum Campaign* (1933), p 11.

19 In B. S. Townroe, *A Handbook of Housing: How to Meet the Problem* (1924), p 83.

20 A. W. Cleeve Barr, *Public Authority Housing* (1958), p 53.

21 A. Sayle, *The Houses of the Workers* (1924), pp 142ff.

22 London County Council, *Housing: with particular reference to Post-War Housing Schemes* (1928), pp 46ff.

23 B. Seebohm Rowntree, *Poverty and Progress: A Second Social Survey of York,* (1941), pp 231ff.

24 B. S. Townroe, op cit, pp 89–91.

25 *A National Housing Policy,* Report of the National Housing Committee (1934), p 47.

26 M. J. Elsas, *Housing Before the War and After* (1942), p 17.

27 Christopher Powell, 'An Analysis of Urban Public Authority Dwelling Types in England and Wales Since 1918', unpublished Brunel University M Tech thesis (1972), p 59.

28 Marian Bowley, op cit, p 43.

29 London County Council, *Housing: with particular reference to Post-War Housing Schemes* (1928), pp 56–65.

30 See, for example, Terence Young, *Becontree and Dagenham: A Report made for the Pilgrim Trust* (1934); Ruth Durant, *Watling: A Survey of Social Life on a New Housing Estate* (1939).

31 P. Willmott, *The Evolution of a Community* (1963), p 7.

32 Mass Observation, *An Enquiry into People's Homes* (1943).

33 Ruth Durant, op cit, Table VII, p 124.

34 D. Caradog Jones (ed), *The Social Survey of Merseyside* (1934), Vol I, pp 271ff.
35 G. McGonigle and J. Kirby, *Poverty and Public Health* (1936).
36 S. Pollard, *A History of Labour in Sheffield* (1959), p 257, note 1.
37 Sir E. D. Simon, *The Rebuilding of Manchester* (1935), p 26.
38 B. Seebohm Rowntree, op cit, pp 239, 255.
39 The rents of 'A3' council houses, including rates, in eight towns in 1928 were as follows: Birmingham 9s 9d–12s 0d, Bradford 10s 11d, Bristol 9s 0d–15s 1d, Liverpool 13s 6d, Leeds 14s 3d–15s 0d, Manchester 14s 4d–16s 1d, Newcastle 12s 7d–15s 11d, Sheffield 13s 10d. The average for 'A3' was 13s 2d, and for 'B3' 15s 8d. E. D. Simon, *How to Abolish the Slums* (1929), Appendix C, Tables II and III, pp 118–9.
40 *Housing England* PEP (Political and Economic Planning) Industries Group (1934).
41 Quoted in B. S. Townroe, *The Slum Problem* (1928).
42 C. R. A. Martin, *Slums and Slummers: A Sociological Treatise on the Housing Problem* (1935), p 29.
43 *A Policy for the Slums.* Report of the Special Committee of the National Housing and Town Planning Council (1929).
44 An Ex-Nursing Sister (Joan Conquest), *The Naked Truth: Shocking Revelations about the slums* (1933), pp 56–7.
45 Marian Bowley, op cit, p 152.
46 B. S. Townroe, op cit, p 61.
47 The contemporary arguments for and against flats are admirably documented by Alison Ravetz 'From Working Class Tenement to Modern Flat', in Anthony Sutcliffe (ed), *Multi-Storey Living, the British Working Class Experience* (1974), pp 122ff.
48 *L.C.C. Housing* (1937), pp 39ff.
49 Christopher Powell, 'An Analysis of Urban Public Authority Dwelling Types', thesis, op cit, p 97.

9: SPECULATIVE HOUSING, 1918–1939

1 J. C. Weston, 'International Comparisons of the cost of Housebuilding', *Journal of Industrial Economics*, Vol XII, No 1 (1963).
2 Alan A. Jackson, *Semi-Detached London: Suburban Development, Life and Transport, 1900–1939* (1973), p 108.
3 On the history of building societies generally see E. J. Cleary, *The Building Society Movement* (1965) and H. Bellman, *The Building Society Movement* (1927).
4 Albert Mansbridge, *Brick Upon Brick, Fifty Years of the Co-operative Permanent Building Society* (1934), Appendix IV, p 176.
5 David C. Thorns, *Suburbia* (1972), p 43.
6 Martin S. Briggs, *How to Plan Your House* (1937), p 6.
7 The Restriction of Ribbon Development Act, 1935, was too late and too feeble to have very significant effect.
8 Osbert Lancaster, *Pillar to Post* (1938).
9 Lewis Mumford, *The City in History* (1961), p 486.

10 J. M. Richards, *The Castles on the Ground: The Anatomy of Suburbia* (1st edition, 1946; 2nd, 1973).

11 J. A. Patmore, *Land and Leisure* (1972), p 12.

12 These developments have been admirably documented by Alan A. Jackson, op cit, to which reference should be made for the details.

13 Robert Graves and Alan Hodge, *The Long Weekend: A Social History of Great Britain, 1918–1939* (2nd impression, 1950), p 172.

14 S. C. Ramsey, FRIBA, in a paper to the RIBA in 1938, estimated that 20 per cent of plans for small houses submitted to building societies that year were architect-designed; ten years earlier, he believed, the proportion would have been only 5–10 per cent.

15 R. A. Bateman, *How to Own and Equip a House* (c 1925), p 93.

16 H. Myles Wright, *Small Houses £500–£2,500* (1937), p 15.

17 Steen Eiler Rasmussen, *London: The Unique City* (English revised edition, 1937), p 306.

18 Martin S. Briggs, op cit, p 30.

19 Alan A. Jackson, op cit, p 153.

20 Raymond McGrath, *Twentieth Century Houses* (1934), p 66.

21 *The Electric Home*. Unit 20 Open University Course 'British Design'.

22 George Cross, *Suffolk Punch* (1939).

23 A. H. Halsey (ed), *Trends in British Society since 1900*, Chapter 2, 'Population and Family', pp 31f.

24 John Burnett, *Useful Toil: Autobiographies of Working People from the 1820s to the 1920s* (1974), Part 2, 'Domestic Servants', pp 135ff.

25 Daily Express Publications, *The Home of Today—Its Choice, Planning, Equipment and Organisation* (nd, c 1935), Introduction, p 8.

26 Anthony Bertram, *The House, A Machine for Living In: A Summary of the Art and Science of Homemaking Considered Functionally* (1935), p 93.

27 Dennis Chapman, *The Home and Social Status* (1955), pp 20–3.

28 R. W. Brunskill, *Illustrated Handbook of Vernacular Architecture* (1971), p 190.

29 J. M. Richards, *The Castles on the Ground* (1st edition, 1946; 2nd, 1973), p 60.

30 Olive Cook, *The English House Through Seven Centuries* (1968), p 311.

31 Paul Thompson, *William Butterfield* (1971) p 378.

32 Osbert Lancaster, *Homes Sweet Homes* (1939), p 76.

33 Anthony Bertram, *Design* (1938), p 58.

34 Anthony King, 'The Bungalow, Part 2', *Architectural Association Quarterly*, Vol 5, No 4 (1973), p 18.

35 F. R. S. Yorke and Frederick Gibberd, *The Modern Flat* (1937), Foreword.

36 M. W. Barley, *The House and Home* (1965), p 69.

37 Raymond McGrath, *Twentieth Century Houses* (1934), pp 39f.

38 Data on interior planning from Martin S. Briggs, *How to Plan Your House* (1937); R. A. Bateman, *How to Own and Equip a House* (c 1925); Daily Express, *The Home of Today* (c 1935); H. Myles Wright, *Small Houses £500–£2,500* (1937); Martin S. Briggs, *Building Today* (1944).

39 John Gloag, *The Englishman's Castle* (1944), p 163.

10: PUBLIC AND PRIVATE HOUSING, 1945–1970

1 A. H. Halsey (ed), *Trends in British Society since 1900* (1972), Housing Table, 10·1, p 299.
2 Calculated from W. V. Hole and M. T. Pountney, *Trends in Population, Housing and Occupancy Rates, 1861–1961* (Department of the Environment, Building Research Station, 1971), Fig 4, p 15.
3 Ibid, p 31.
4 W. V. Hole and J. J. Attenburrow, *Houses and People: A Review of User Studies at the Building Research Station* (Ministry of Technology, Building Research Station, 1966), p 56.
5 On wages, prices and the standard of living generally, see John Burnett, *A History of the Cost of Living* (1969), Chapter 5, 'The Last Fifty Years'.
6 F. Berry, *Housing: The Great British Failure* (1974), pp 130–1.
7 *Homes for Today and Tomorrow* (Department of the Environment, 1961), pp 1–2.
8 *Living in a Slum: A Study of St Mary's, Oldham* (Ministry of Housing and Local Government, 1970), p 9.
9 Dennis Chapman, *The Home and Social Status* (1955), p 42.
10 Ferdynand Zweig, *The Worker in an Affluent Society: Family Life and Industry* (1961), p 5.
11 As in the slum clearance and redevelopment programme for the central area of Preston. See Stanley Alderson, *Britain in the Sixties: Housing* (1962), p 57.
12 Dennis Chapman, op cit, p 67.
13 See, for example, J. Cullingworth, *English Housing Trends* (1965) and *Housing in Transition* (1963); D. Donnison, *Housing Policy since the War* (1960); F. Berry, *Housing: The Great British Failure* (1974).
14 A. W. Cleeve Barr, *Public Authority Housing* (1958), p 22.
15 A. M. Carr-Saunders, D. Caradog Jones and C. A. Moser, *A Survey of Social Conditions in England and Wales* (1958), pp 44–5.
16 *Old Houses Into New Homes*, Cd 3602 (HMSO, 1967).
17 *The Design of Dwellings*. Report of the Design of Dwellings Sub-Committee of the Ministry of Health Central Housing Advisory Committee. Chairman, the Earl of Dudley (1944).
18 A. W. Cleeve Barr, *Public Authority Housing* (1958), p 54.
19 *Housing Manual*, 1944. Ministry of Health, Ministry of Works, p 96.
20 M. and A. Potter, *Houses* (3rd edition, 1973), p 46.
21 D. V. Donnison, *The Government of Housing* (1967), p 167.
22 I am particularly indebted in this section to E. W. Cooney's important essay 'High Flats in Local Authority Housing in England and Wales since 1945' in Anthony Sutcliffe (ed), *Multi-Storey Living, The British Working-Class Experience* (1974), pp 151–81.
23 J. B. Cullingworth, *Housing Needs and Planning Policy* (1960), pp 160–1.
24 *The Estate Outside the Dwelling*. Department of the Environment (1972), p 2.
25 Christopher Powell, 'An Analysis of Urban Public Authority Dwelling Types

in England and Wales since 1918', unpublished Brunel University M Tech thesis (1972), p 190.

26 *Homes for Today and Tomorrow.* Department of the Environment (1961), p 2. (Originally published by Ministry of Housing and Local Government.)

27 D. V. Donnison, op cit, p 278.

28 R. Furneaux Jordan, *The English House* (1959), pp 153–4.

29 J. Prizeman, *Your House: The Outside View* (1975).

30 Dennis Chapman, *The Home and Social Status* (1955), pp 20ff.

31 W. V. Hole, *User Needs and the Design of Houses*, Building Research Station Current Papers 51/68 (June 1968), p 4.

32 W. V. Hole and J. J. Attenburrow, *Houses and People: A review of user studies at the Building Research Station.* Ministry of Technology, Building Research Station (1966), Fig 9.4, p 50.

33 Olive Cook, *The English House Through Seven Centuries* (1968), pp 308–10.

34 Information from *Taywood News*, 1953–1970, kindly supplied by Taylor Woodrow Services Ltd, Southall.

35 W. V. Hole, *User Needs and the Design of Houses*, op cit, Table, p 4.

36 Neil E. Wates, 'Town Planning Policies Producing Smaller, Costlier Houses', *The Times*, 19 October 1970.

11: RETROSPECT AND PROSPECT

1 W. V. Hole and M. T. Pountney, *Trends in Population, Housing and Occupancy Rates, 1861–1961* (1971), pp 3–8.

2 A. H. Halsey (ed), *Trends in British Society Since 1900* (1972), Tables 10.6, 10.7, 10.8, pp 301–2.

3 John Greve, Dilys Page and Stella Greve, *Homelessness in London* (1971), pp 58–9.

4 D. V. Donnison, *The Government of Housing* (1967), pp 215ff.

5 Vera Hole, 'Housing Standards and Social Trends', in *Urban Studies* (November 1965).

6 W. V. Hole and J. J. Attenburrow, *Houses and People, a review of user studies at the Building Research Station.* Ministry of Technology, Building Research Station (1966), p 50.

7 On these generally see W. V. Hole, *User Needs and the Design of Houses*, Building Research Station Current Papers 51/68 (1968).

8 *Architectural Design*, Vol XLV (December 1975), p 165.

9 *The Estate Outside the Dwelling. Reactions of residents to aspects of housing layout*, Department of the Environment (1972), p 2.

10 Olive Cook, *The English House Through Seven Centuries* (1968), p 311.

INDEX

In some cases, sub-entries are listed in page order to give chronological sequence.